In the Course of Performance

In the Course of Performance

STUDIES IN THE WORLD OF MUSICAL IMPROVISATION

Edited by Bruno Nettl
with Melinda Russell

THE UNIVERSITY OF CHICAGO PRESS

CHICAGO AND LONDON

BRUNO NETTL is professor emeritus of music and anthropology at the University of Illinois at Urbana-Champaign. His books include *The Study of Ethnomusicology, Blackfoot Musical Thought,* and *Heartland Excursions.* MELINDA RUSSELL is instructor in music at Carleton College. She is the coeditor of *Community of Music: An Ethnographic Seminar in Champaign-Urbana.*

The University of Chicago Press, Chicago 60637
The University of Chicago Press, Ltd., London
© 1998 by The University of Chicago
All rights reserved. Published 1998
Printed in the United States of America
07 06 05 04 03 02 01 00 99 98   1 2 3 4 5
ISBN 0-226-57410-5 (cloth)
ISBN 0-226-57411-3 (paper)

A publishing subvention from Carleton College is gratefully acknowledged.

Library of Congress Cataloging-in-Publication Data

In the course of performance : studies in the world of musical improvisation / edited by Bruno Nettl with Melinda Russell.
    p.   cm. — (Chicago studies in ethnomusicology)
    Discography : p.
    Includes bibliographical references and index.
    ISBN 0-226-57410-5 (cloth : alk. paper). — ISBN 0-226-57411-3 (paperback : alk. paper)
    1. Improvisation (Music)   I. Nettl, Bruno, 1930– .
II. Russell, Melinda.   III. Series.
ML430.7.I47   1998
781.3'6—DC21   98-3640
                                                                                    CIP
                                                                                    MN

DEDICATED TO THE MEMORY OF

Ernst T. Ferand
(1887–1972)
PIONEER IN THE STUDY OF IMPROVISATION

Contents

ACKNOWLEDGMENTS

The origins of this volume are obscure, going back at least to the 1960s, when Bruno Nettl, stimulated by his study of Persian music, first began giving occasional seminars on improvisation and marveling at the diversity of the world's improvisatory systems and practices. Serious planning began in 1994. Melinda Russell joined the project in 1995 as research assistant at the University of Illinois and remained as associate editor after joining the faculty of Carleton College in 1996.

We are grateful for the support of the Research Board of the University of Illinois at Urbana-Champaign, which provided funds for editorial help from 1995 to 1997, and to the School of Music for a variety of kinds of support. We thank Joanna Bosse, research assistant during 1996–97, who was helpful in a variety of areas but particularly in the preparation of musical examples. We are grateful, as well, to the administration of Carleton College for providing a grant to support the preparation of the index.

We also thank the editorial and production staffs of the University of Chicago Press for their professional expertise and their humane patience in dealing with an unusually complicated and heterogeneous manuscript; and the readers who provided helpful criticisms and suggestions. We wish to express our appreciation to Curtis Black for his excellent copyediting of a complex manuscript.

Last, and most, we wish to express our appreciation to the authors of the studies in this collection. We thank them for permitting us to include their work, and we want particularly to acknowledge their patience and good humor in the face of our frequent and sometimes seemingly inconsistent demands, and the inevitable but unforeseen delays, in what has sometimes been a slow but hopefully rewarding process.

B.N.
M.R.

An Art Neglected in Scholarship

BRUNO NETTL

In the history of musicology, improvisation—sometimes defined as the creation of music in the course of performance—has played a minor role. Musicologists have been concerned in the first instance with composition, and less with the process than with the completed piece of music as set down by its creator. Affected by the research traditions of visual art and literature, they have concentrated on the finished work, analyzed the interrelationships of its components, and looked at its history, but rarely have they been concerned with the varying orders of creativity that may have led to the final product. Although it would be foolish to ignore the occasional reference to improvisation, there are few studies that go into the subject itself in detail, and thus it is reasonable to consider this form of music making as relatively neglected.

With the aim of helping to remedy this situation, this volume presents several studies of musical improvisation in a number of cultures and repertories using a variety of approaches. The purpose of this introductory essay is to provide a common context for these studies by offering some observations on the history of research on musical improvisation, the present state of scholarship, and some of the major issues.

In Musical Scholarship

About twenty years ago, it would have been appropriate to say that only one scholar had devoted himself substantially to the study of improvised music and improvisation. Ernst Ferand (1887–1972) stood out as the quintessential specialist. His book, *Die Improvisation in der Musik* (1938), devoted largely (but not exclusively) to Western music, was then the only substantial work. And Ferand was also the author of by far the largest encyclopedia article on improvisation (Ferand 1957) and other works on improvised European music, and he was generally the person upon whom editors called when the subject needed to be circumscribed. Ferand took a broad view of improvisation, providing historical, ethnographic, and systematic depth, showing that it was many things to many peoples, periods, and groups of scholars.

It is surprising (but may not be to those who know Ferand's book) that no one since Ferand has tried to write a general book on the subject. To be sure, since then, especially since about 1960, scholarship on improvisation has increased greatly, with the expansion of jazz studies and ethnomusicological studies of South, West, and Southeast Asian cultures, and with the growth of improvisatory techniques in experimental music and music education. And yet, even now, the synthetic literature on improvisation—in contrast to studies of individual musics—remains modest.

But progress has been made, as a brief survey of landmark publications of the last three decades readily shows. Two books by authors technically outside musicology have had some impact. David Sudnow's *Ways of the Hand* (1978) analyzes the process of learning jazz improvisation in the author's own experience, relating position and posture of the body, the physical possibilities and tendencies deriving from the structure and physiology of the hand, psychological insight, and approaches of cultural studies, such as ethnomethodology, and of philosophical phenomenology. But essentially it is a case study showing the relationship between conscious intention and behavior in music. Derek Bailey's *Improvisation* (1992) described a number of improvisational systems from the viewpoint of a composer, with emphasis on the relationship of contemporary group improvisation to jazz, baroque, and Indian musics. Here the orientation is practical and principally directed to those concerned with contemporary Western culture but is informed by comparative insight from music history and ethnomusicology. The area conveniently termed "systematic musicology" has also produced contributions. Of particular interest is the work of Jeff Pressing (e.g., 1984, 1988), which deals with physiology and neuropsychology, with motor control, and with concepts of intuition, creativity, and artificial intelligence, proposing a model of improvisation for understanding the processes of learning and performance. Pressing uses cross-cultural data but focuses on the concept of improvisation as something that can be analyzed outside the context of specific cultures.

The art of improvisation, as the concept is ordinarily used in Western discourse about music, appears to be quite different from the improvisatory processes that are necessary in ordinary speech, or from improvisation as a way of dealing with emergencies. Nevertheless, scholars dealing with the concept of improvisation as a universal cutting across cultural domains have used musical improvisation as a model and musicological research as an exemplar (e.g., Tambiah 1985; Tarasti 1993; and the synthesis by Sawyer 1996). The increased attention given to improvisation as an aspect of North American and European music education, some of it reviving ideas of early educators such as Emile Jaques-Dalcroze and Zoltan Kodaly, has produced important research, some of it drawing on the findings of ethnomusicologists (e.g., Campbell 1991).

Ethnomusicologists have dealt with improvised music for over a century, but the study of improvisation as a specific process is a later development. The word does not appear in the indices of major classics by Kunst (1959) and Merriam (1964). One of the earliest studies devoted to improvised performances as such was published by Rycroft (1962). But in the course of the late

1960s and 1970s, as my reference list reveals, a major cluster of publications appeared.

One of the most influential works affecting the study of improvisation was Albert Lord's classic, *The Singer of Tales* (1965). Although the term "improvisation" does not appear, Lord provides models for the understanding of South Slavic oral epic poetry, its structure and methods of performance. A close relationship between oral transmission and improvisation is postulated, and Lord's approach has sometimes led later scholars to the questionable view that all orally transmitted material is not only at some point improvised (which is arguable), but equally improvisatory (which I would deny).

Several conferences and the resulting publications have helped us to make strides. In 1968, a conference on improvisation in a number of cultures was held at the University of Chicago. The resulting papers were not assembled, but some were published individually. Each speaker was asked to address a group of common questions, for example, "How would you define the limits of improvisation in this music?" or "How does the performer learn the archetypal patterns?" and "How has improvisation affected the music that is non-improvised, or vice versa?" (Malm 1975, 44, 64). These kinds of questions suggest that the conference attempted to find a method for comparative analysis. Participants wished to determine what there is by way of improvisation in a variety of cultures, not focusing on cultures and repertories that have, as it were, made a specialty of improvising. Thus William Malm's study of Japanese *Shoden* (cited above) discusses the relationship of variation and improvisation in a music in which improvisation plays a restricted role.

A second coherent group of papers resulted from the Symposium on Improvisation in the Performing Arts in Honolulu, 1983, published together in volume 19 of the *Yearbook for Traditional Music* (e.g., Kaeppler 1987; Kassebaum 1987; Susilo 1987; Sutton 1987; and Trimillos 1987). A conference organized by Bernard Lortat-Jacob and John Blacking in Strassbourg in 1982 produced a volume of papers by European scholars focusing on fundamental issues such as definition (Lortat-Jacob 1987). It is devoted exclusively to cultures of oral tradition, and it attempts to provide a textbook-like survey, area by area, of types of improvisation in various parts of the world, thus becoming one of the fundamental publications on our subject. A group of papers on improvisation was published as a special issue of *World of Music,* examining central issues in the study of improvisation as exhibited in Gregorian chant (Treitler 1991), children's musical behavior (Kartomi 1991), jazz (Smith 1991), and Arabic music (Racy 1991).

Case studies of improvisation, a central core of research, have come largely from three areas: South Asia, Iran, and jazz studies. Illustrations of the literature include a series of dissertations and associated publications on Indian music (Kassebaum 1987; Viswanathan 1977; Slawek 1987; and Kippen 1988), publications on Persian music (Zonis 1973; Gerson-Kiwi 1963; Farhat 1990;

Massoudieh 1968; Wilkens 1967; and Nettl 1992), and a group of studies on jazz (Smith 1983; Owens 1974; Gushee 1981; Porter 1985; Stewart 1979). For each culture area, something approaching a paradigmatic approach may have been established as scholars have concentrated on a particular central problem. Thus, Indian music scholarship has been devoted importantly to the structure and individuality of the various improvisation types. Studies of Persian music have emphasized the nature and structure of the *radif* and its relationship to the performance which derives from it (a relationship sometimes described with statistical data), ascertaining norms, boundaries, and distributions of practices (During 1984; Nettl 1992). The studies of jazz, on the other hand, have concentrated on understanding techniques of individual musicians and analyzing the details of individual performances. The most important publication on improvisation from the 1990s is Paul Berliner's large work *Thinking in Jazz* (1994), which contributes most significantly to the issue of learning improvisation and of preparing both the improvising musician and the individual improvised performance, and as such provides an approach for studies in other musics.

A Neglected Art?
Progress since the 1950s is in part due to the establishment of ethnomusicology and the increasing respectability of research in non-Western cultures. The improvement of technology for sound and visual recording has doubtless played a role. Even so, it must be repeated that among the activities and processes studied by music historians and ethnomusicologists, improvisation plays a small part.

Various factors involving the techniques of music research and the available arsenal of methods could account for this neglect. One factor is the difficulty of discovering processes of musical creativity, and particularly the question of intention. Analyzing a Brahms symphony, one has at hand a score presumably approved by Brahms himself, and one may be justified in assuming that everything in it was explicitly intended to be just as it is. The study of the components and relationships involve one in interpretation of their significance, but all of them are equally parts of the symphony. The study of an improvised performance, however, may require (following preparation of a notation) drawing distinctions between what the artist explicitly meant to play and be perceived by the listener as against what is somehow less essential and predictable. But we can overcome this problem, as music scholars are anything but lazy and are sometimes willing to deal with issues of this kind in the abstract.

It may be more rewarding to look to the status of improvisation in the world of Western art music for insight into its relative absence in music scholarship. The concept of improvisation is actually broader and encompasses more types of creative activity than the concept of composition, defined as an individual writing a score. Nevertheless, musicologists have tended to dismiss it as a single process which is not easily described.

Pointing out that "improvisation enjoys the curious distinction of being both the most widely practised of all musical activities and the least acknowledged and understood," Bailey (1992, ix) argues that improvisation is central to music as a whole, and that the understanding of music at large hinges on understanding something of improvisation. Bailey's statement suggests the conclusion that an adequate paradigm of music making would have improvisation (with a different name? "composition"?—but after all it's performance too) as the centerpiece, with a subdivision of composition (renamed "precomposition"?), under which we place the unimprovised performance of the precomposed (if it can ever exist without *some* elements of improvisation).

Brief consideration of the relationship to composition in cultures without notation or articulated music theory is relevant here. Native American musics provide insight into the concept of improvisation as tantamount to unprepared and sudden composition. Peoples of the North American plains (and others) traditionally sought visions in order to learn songs, and these appeared, usually sung only once by an animal or other vision being, during periods of ecstasy or dreams sometimes brought on by fasting and self-torture. This suddenness of song creation is related to statements by Plains singers to the effect that songs can be and normally are learned in a single hearing, a claim not unreasonable in view of the fact that the forms of these songs are highly consistent, and that the musical content of songs is often virtually predictable from the initial motif (Nettl 1989, 153–54).

In Western rationalist terminology, these songs are improvised when first sung (or perhaps, stated more properly, when first thought, in the course of the vision). But we have also been told that the visionary, upon dreaming the song, sang it to himself and, as it were, worked it out and perhaps practiced it before singing it to his community. Once the song exists it normally takes on the trappings of an established composition. The composer (visionary) is known and remembered, and the circumstances of composition may be recounted before singing. Repeated recordings show that the songs may remain reasonably stable as they are transmitted orally or re-dreamed by other singers. In what sense can the word "improvisation" be applied to this form of composition?

For the Pima people of the southwestern United States, on the other hand, songs not yet composed existed in the supernatural world but had to be "unraveled" by humans in order to be realized or made part of human culture (Herzog 1936, 333). The concept of "unraveling," suggesting calculation, may be related to certain ideas about composition in Western art music, but of course there is no notation, and as a matter of fact, Pima songs are generally not very different in style from those of the Plains. The kind of process which composition is conceived to be may or may not have an effect on style and structure.

A third Native American example comes from the Inuit, who recognize two ways of making songs, a conventional and an improvised one (Cavanagh 1986, 495). The latter involves a type of song represented by the famous song-duels wherein men settle disputes by competitive mocking. The use of a standard repertory of formulas is suspected, but such vocabularies are found as well in societies in which improvisation is explicitly recognized. On the other hand, improvised Inuit songs show no basic stylistic dissimilarity to "composed" and traditionally created songs.

So there are Native American societies in which all composition is improvised in ways that go beyond the simple assertion that improvisation is always present in aural tradition; and others in which the concept of composition as time-consuming labor is recognized; and yet others in which aural composition is distinguished from a more improvisatory, extemporizing activity.

There is, clearly, in the world at large and even in the culture of certain small societies, a wide spectrum of improvisation—a continuum of everything from oral composition without notation and the improvisation of cadenzas whose structures explicitly contradict the formal principles of the rest of the piece, to the ability to improvise works whose forms follow the explicit requirements of highly specialized genres such as fugues, and to pieces whose structure is predicated on choices made by the composer at the beginning of a musical statement. We can hardly imagine types of music and music making as different as the parts of paraphrasing instruments in gamelan, the *swaras* following a South Indian *kriti,* the singing of a Serbo-Croatian epic, and the group improvisation of organizations such as Joseph Holbrooke and the Music Improvisation Company (Bailey 1992, 86–97). Ferand (1957, 1094) provides an outline distinguishing medium (vocal or instrumental), personnel (solo or ensemble), texture (monophonic or multivoiced), technique (e.g., ornamentation, or addition of independent voices), degree (total or partial, absolute or relative improvisation), and form (a large category, contrasting free and bound structures, for example Indian *raga alapana* contrasted with a fugue or with variations over an ostinato). Nevertheless, in the literature of general musicology, improvisation appears as a smaller, less variegated field than (pre)composition.

Changing the values as fundamentally as these paragraphs suggest may indeed require a reinvention of musicology, and even those scholars who might desire such a world turned upside down have little in the way of the needed tools.

In Societies and among Musics

Musicological neglect of improvisation may also stem from attitudes of Western middle-class culture towards the societies in which improvisation is significant—non-Western, perhaps folk, and certainly (in North America) minorities—cultures whose arts may be appreciated but are not to be taken very seriously, belonging to the purview of folkloristics and social sciences. There are those who regard improvisation as the music of the improvident.

The musical establishment to which the profession of musicology belongs—it is an establishment of academics, in departments whose purpose is the study and advocacy of Western art music, and closely associated with the performing world of art music—connects improvisation as a musical practice, but even more as a concept, with a kind of third world of music. Jazz, the music of non-Western cultures, folk music, and all music in oral tradition are somehow included here. Even within the sphere of Western art music, music history texts say little about improvisation per se but are more likely to discuss works in "improvisatory style" (e.g., Stolba 1990, 277), whose characteristic is absence of clearcut structure; and some scholars feel it necessary to "protest too much," as when Wiora (1983, 11) insists that improvised fugues or fantasies in sonata form are not distant from the concept of the musical masterwork.

In the conception of the art music world, improvisation embodies the absence of precise planning and discipline. The most common contrast in the American public conception—it is far from descriptive of actual practice—is between composed art music and improvised jazz, in which art music is correlated with discipline, art for art's sake, reliability, and predictability, while the opposites of these characterizations apply in the case of jazz. There is further correlation between classical musicians as middle class and conventionally moral, as against the old stereotype of jazz musicians as unreliable, with unconventional dress and sexual mores, excessive use of alcohol and drugs, and more (Merriam and Mack 1960; Merriam 1964, 241–44).

Improvisation as the music of people who don't plan ahead and don't have elementary musical technology: can this be the white musical world's way of expressing a racist ideology? But on the other hand, within some white societies, musicians also partake of the stereotypes—they are unconventional and unreliable people—that are more closely associated with black musicians; this may suggest that to white society, African-American people (and by extension other people of color) represent a kind of quintessence of musicianship, and mutatis mutandis, improvisation and orally transmitted music is therefore the most "real" music. The notion that there are musicians who, as it were, can do anything they want on the spur of the moment is strange to the classical musician, who is scandalized by such lack of discipline but also attracted by its presumed liberty (for discussion see Treitler 1991, 66–68; Levy 1990).

If the concept of improvisation in the world of Western art music and in the scholarship derived from it is of a minor art or craft associated mainly with cultural outsiders, the values are reversed in the distinction between precomposition and improvisation found in South and West Asia (Nettl 1994, 58, 62, 64; al-Faruqi 1985, 8). In Iran, the area of my experience, the most desirable and acceptable music is improvised, and within the improvised genres, those lacking metric structure and thus rhythmic predictability are the most prestigious. By contrast, precomposed pieces are less respected, and pieces which have the highest degree of rhythmic predictability—those for example with a rhythmic ostinato—are most to be avoided. There are several reasons for this continuum of musical acceptability. The music most like the singing of the Qur'an—nonmetric vocal improvisation—is most esteemed. Music with edifying words is valued more than instrumental music with strictly entertainment value, and music performed in sacred, academic, or ceremonial contexts more than music performed in informal and even lascivious surroundings.

While disciplined musical professionalism has the highest value in the Western establishment, it is low in the Middle East as compared with expert amateurism. The learned amateur musician avoids designation as a professional because of the low esteem of musicians and music, particularly in its predictable form: The professional must perform when commanded, and play what is requested, and usually performs precomposed pieces—so goes the conventional wisdom—while the learned amateur has freedom to make all of these decisions. Thus in the Middle East, improvisation has the high prestige associated with freedom and unpredictability, while in the West, precomposition has the prestige associated with discipline and predictability. One can make a case for the dominance of these values in the social life of these cultures as well; but music, we all know, may also be used to express opposition to societal trends (a function which improvisation may fill, as shown in the classic study of Katz 1968). In any event, it is no surprise that musicology, a field developed in Germany, emphasizes those values—discipline and predictability—widely respected in German culture, and has privileged the music associated with these concepts (Treitler 1991, 66–68; Wiora 1983, 20–21 and passim).

Elsewhere I have tried to make a case for the suggestions that members of a society tend to see the domains of their culture somewhat as they structure and interpret their society; that we see our repertory as if it were, so to speak, a society of music (Nettl 1995, 121–35). Considering only the classical music world of contemporary America, I proposed that the ruling class was headed by concertos and operas on account of the high degree of hierarchy in their musical structure along with their association with upper social classes. Fugues and string quartets, with structures much more suggestive of equality, have the function of a conscience.

Using a similar perspective would require us to place improvisations and works associated with or reminiscent of improvisation low in the society of musics. The conception of improvisation as lack of planning contrasts with the notion that precision of planning, complexity of relationships, and interrelationships so abstruse as to be discernible only with sophisticated analytical techniques characterize the greatest masterworks, such as Bach's *Art of Fugue* and Beethoven's late quartets. The concept of control characterizing the great classic masters is one of the major criteria of the masterwork, and relates readily to the notion of control of complexity that suggests the musical counterpart of a ruling class. The works most esteemed in the art music world are large, intricately organized works—symphonies, operas, concertos, and perhaps major chamber works and piano sonatas; but rarely would the list include short works that suggest creation on the spur of the moment, such as "impromptus," fantasias, *moments musicaux,* and rhapsodies. So within the realm of art music, improvisation is on a low rung, just as musics outside the realm of art music are often associated with the inferior practice of improvisation. (For the importance of planning and strategy in the creation of true works of art, see Wiora 1983, 9–12; and Nattiez 1990, 69–70.)

In the conception of the art music world, there is a set of parallel contrastive relationships: between composition and improvisation, between crafted and inspired composition, between nature and culture, and also between "feminine" and "masculine" character. But can we tell from the outcome which is which? Compare the nineteenth- and twentieth-century views of the painstaking and often protracted method of Beethoven as against Schubert's quick, spontaneous style of creation (Einstein 1951, 92). Of course these views may not accord entirely with historical reality. Beethoven's habit of sketching motivates us to see his works as the result of hard labor, and the legend of Schubert's composing a lied on the back of a restaurant menu while waiting for his dinner suggests a method of composing quite opposite to Beethoven's. But Beethoven was a famous improviser, and Schubert has his great complexities. Analysis of the two composers' works does not suggest such a great difference, but to some degree it is there.

It is interesting to observe the distinction between the two composers sometimes associated with symbols of gender relationship: Beethoven the masculine, Schubert the feminine (Gramit 1993; Kramer 1993); or Beethoven the cultural technician, Schubert the natural and spontaneous. And it is significant for an understanding of contemporary ideas about art music that this distinction was associated with the possibility that Schubert was homosexual. Here, too, the concept of something improvised—sounding improvised, or known to have been created quickly, or otherwise lacking in obvious preparation—symbolizes the (sexually, culturally, biologically?) inferior.

Now, this view doesn't pertain to improvisation per se. We're talking about Schubert not as an improviser, but as a composer whose creative processes may bear some similarity to the concept of improvisation. What of the great improvisations of Bach, Beethoven, and Mozart, which seem not to be associated with anything feminine? It would seem that in some quarters of twentieth-century Western musical thought, improvisation, a "weaker" form of music making than composition, though not in itself feminine, becomes a weakening or "feminizing" factor when it affects true composition, that quintessentially male form of music making. And it's not beside the point to remind ourselves that throughout the world, improvising is carried out more frequently by males than by female musicians. (But see Koskoff 1987 for various examples of female improvisation.)

In traditional Western art music, there seems to be a dichotomy between improvisatory practices and improvisation as a concept. As practices go, one finds musics in many styles and with various kinds of regulation and degrees of prescription, from the improvisation of strict fugues on themes given on the spur of the moment, on to fantasias performed as cadenzas of concertos, and all the way to the unrestricted creation of "preludes." But the conception of improvisation involves freedom, lack of planning, and unclear relationships among parts and sections. In Western music one may find improvisation in a strict, compositorial style, but also composition, carefully notated, in an "improvisatory" style, and everything in between.

Well, this may be the musical public's evaluation of improvisation and its role in art music, and in other musics. In fact, of course, discipline, intricacy, and control of complexities all play major roles in various kinds of improvisation, as in Indian music with its detailed rules for proceeding, or in organists' practice of improvising fugues on given themes, to mention only two. And yet Western classical musicians are more inclined to see the quality of improvisation as emotional rather than intellectual, as free rather than controlled.

Definitions and Values

To understand further the role of improvisation in music scholarship, it is helpful to look at definitions. A sampler:

For lexicographical purposes, the concept and status of improvisation among the denizens of the art music world and among musicologists importantly involves its relationship to and contrast with composition or precomposition. *The New Grove Dictionary* looks at improvisation from the viewpoint of its end product, using the concept of the musical work as its point of departure: "The creation of a musical work, or the final form of a musical work, as it is being performed" (Horsley et al. 1980, 9:31).

The twelfth edition of the *Riemann Musiklexikon* (Gurlitt and Eggebrecht 1967, 390) draws sharp distinctions between precomposition and improvisation, and also between improvisation and the simple variation of a work that results from the character of individual performance practices: "Improvisation . . . besteht musikalisch im Erfinden und gleichzeitigen klanglichen Realisieren von Musik; sie schliesst die schriftliche Fixierung (Komposition) ebenso aus wie das Realisieren eines Werkes (Aufführung, Wiedergabe, Interpretation)" [Improvisation . . . consists of the simultaneous invention and sonic realization of music; it excludes work fixed in writing as well as the realization of an extant work, i.e., performance, reproduction, interpretation.]

Other reference works try to be extremely general: *The New Harvard Dictionary of Music* (Nettl 1986, 392) simply says, "the creation of music in the course of performance," virtually translating Ferand (1957, 1093). Italian and French music encyclopedias (Sartori 1964; Fédorov 1957), earlier editions of *Grove's* (Taylor 1896a; Colles 1935; Colles 1954) and Willi Apel's *Harvard Dictionary of Music* (1969) all provide definitions resembling Ferand's.

The question of definition is an issue in Lortat-Jacob (1987, 67–69), which contains a short chapter giving definitions of various lengths by the fourteen participants in that volume and in the conference that led to it. As this volume consists of a number of studies that deal with improvisation from a considerable number of viewpoints, it seems essential to provide a definition, and perhaps democratic to allow each author to provide his or her own. Here are some examples:

John Baily: "Improvisation is the intention to create unique musical utterances in the act of performance." Veit Erlmann: "Création d'un énoncé musical, ou forme finale d'un énoncé musical déja composé, au moment de sa réalisation en performance" [Creation of a musical utterance, or final form of a musical utterance already composed, at the moment of its realization in performance]. Micheál O'Suilleabhain: "The process of creative interaction (in private or in public; consciously or unconsciously) between the performing musician and a musical model which may be more or less fixed." Simha Arom: "Au sens strict, interprétation d'une musique au moment même de sa conception" [In the strict sense, the performance of music at the very moment of its conception].

These definitions (and the other ten) do not conflict substantially. In contrast to the gathering of folklorists referred to earlier (Malm 1975), whose participants would have argued whether a particular performance or artifact is truly part of folklore, it seems that the scholars represented in Lortat-Jacob's collection have little difficulty deciding whether something is improvised or not. The issue was, rather, to find an elegant way of saying what is essential or central or required. All together, writing a definition of improvisation seems to have been more a matter of lexicographic niceties than of conceptualization.

If the European musicological world agrees generally on the basic definition of improvisation, there is less agreement among standard reference works on its value, and on what it is that the reader must in the first instance be informed about, and which of its aspects are worthy of discussion. Eggebrecht (Gurlitt and Eggebrecht 1967, 390) locates improvisation squarely in the framework of Western musical concepts, maintaining that it is found only in relatively recent Western music, as musics in oral tradition do not make the distinction between composition and performance which the concept of improvisation implies.

Earlier on, Hans Joachim Moser distinguished between "improvisation" as the spontaneous creation of a musical work in the true sense, using prescribed forms and established principles, and *phantasieren* (musical fantasizing), which he considers less involved with the interrelationships essential to proper music. He argues that the greatest improvisors, such as Bach and Handel, typically produced improvisations which, though based on themes given to them on the spot, resulted in finished, highly disciplined works (Moser 1955, 1:537).

In the second edition of the *Harvard Dictionary* (Apel 1969), after defining improvisation as "the art of performing music spontaneously, without the aid of manuscript, sketches, or memory," Willi Apel quickly moves on to the "great days of improvisation," the era of Bach, Handel, Mozart, and Beethoven, who were, he says, known as much for their ability to improvise as for composing.

In *Grove's* third edition, H. C. Colles asserts that "extemporization," is "the primitive act of music-making, existing from the moment that the untutored individual obeys the impulse to relieve his feelings by bursting into song. Accordingly, therefore, amongst all primitive peoples musical composition consists of extemporization subsequently memorized" (Colles 1935). Colles insists, significantly, that all composition without notation begins as improvisation. The *Grove's* series made little progress from the first edition, with its short article "Extempore Playing" (Taylor 1896a), through "Extemporization" in the much larger fifth edition, (Colles 1954), an abridgment of the third edition's entry. The association of improvisation with the mere absence of notation is emphasized in the article "Extemporizing Machine" in the first edition (Taylor 1896b), which describes a kind of melograph connected with keyboard mechanisms that records on paper what has been played. It is interesting that this early stage of transcribing machinery, conceptually so central to ethnomusicology, arose out of the concept of improvisation.

The distinction between improvisation as an aspect of the interpretation of established compositions and as an independent art plays a role in some musicological literature. Robert Haas's (1931) extensive survey of performance practice brings up improvisation at many points, as composition technique in nonliterate societies, in South Asian art musics, and as a requirement in many European art music genres. The parallel work published sixty years later by Danuser, this time titled *Musikalische Interpretation,* makes the distinction more explicit, giving attention to improvisation in the performance of masterworks but excluding genres that are explicitly improvisatory (Danuser 1992, 8). Yet the distinction between the concepts of performance practice, improvisation, and, indeed, composition in (at the very least) oral traditions is as yet an unsolved issue.

Looking, then, at the position of improvisation in musical scholarship and in the Western art music culture in which musicology is grounded, we find it to be regarded as (1) something definitely distinct from performance and precomposition, (2) imitation of precomposition with the helping hand of notation withdrawn, (3) the essence of composition where there is aural transmission, (4) an art at which the great composers particularly excelled, (5) a craft but not an art, (6) something to be evaluated along the same lines as composition, (7) a process that cannot be explained or analyzed, and (8) a kind of music making that sets apart the musical cultures outside the Western art music establishment.

Points of Departure
One occasionally hears statements to the effect that improvisation cannot be explained, analyzed, or described. Indeed, Derek Bailey (1992, ix) discourages

explanation: "any attempt to describe improvisation must be, in some respects, a misrepresentation, for there is something central to the spirit of voluntary improvisation which is opposed to the aims and contradicts the idea of documentation."

The essays here at hand suggest otherwise, but it is easy to sympathize with Bailey's view. For compositions, we believe that all components are equally and definitely intended by the composers to be as presented; never mind that for some compositions, several versions may have been successively created. In improvisation, one must face likelihood that some of the material may be precisely intended while other passages are thrown in without specific thought, possibly to permit the performer to think of "what to do next." To be sure, there may be analogies in composition as, say, in the distinction between thematic and episodic material in eighteenth-century sonata forms. Even so, while one may analyze the transcription of an improvisation virtually as if it were a sonata or a rhapsody by Brahms, in an improvisation the relative significance of the various components would be harder to establish.

One approach that sets off improvisation from composition, and that helps the understanding of the improvisatory processes of individual performances as well as established practices, involves the identification of a point of departure (for which the term "model" has been used: see Zonis 1973, 62; and Lortat-Jacob 1987, 54–57) which the improvisor uses as a basis for his or her art. Used in a number of studies of music in several cultures, this approach comes closest to providing a paradigmatic method for improvisation research. These points of departure or models exhibit enormous variety throughout the world.

In some kinds of Western art music, thematic material and standardized form may be typical points of departure. The improvising organist has a given theme and the characteristics or requirements of fugal structure upon which he builds his creation. For a concerto cadenza, motifs and themes of the movement or work, along with musical gestures (scales, double-stops, arpeggios) that are characteristic for exhibiting virtuosity are, taken together, the model. Jazz musicians, obviously, use sequences of harmonies ("changes") and tunes which may be the basis of variation or which may lead to unrelated solo improvisations.

In Carnatic music, the large form, *ragam-tanam-pallavi*, proceeds from very general gradually to more restricted models. For *alapana* or *ragam*, there is the *raga* itself, in its broadest manifestation—an abstraction embodying scale and typical kinds of tone order, along with the tendency to show musical movement or progress. This is achieved by moving gradually to higher tessitura along with a greater degree of intensity, more ornamentation, and increased virtuosity, and it is followed by a rapid descent and relaxation of tension. *Tanam* contains the same requirements, to which is added a characteristic nonmetric rhythm. *Niraval* is based on the tonal characteristics of the *raga* as well, but the model also includes a theme from a composition (pallavi) which is subjected to a set of variations. In *kalpana swaram* the musician uses the tonal characteristics of the *raga,* some thematic material from a composition, and a characteristic and formally predictable rapid-fire staccato delivery. Moving through the *ragam-tanam-pallavi,* performers gradually have less choice, and the model upon which they improvise increases in specificity.

Persian classical music has developed a unique model, the body of material known as the *radif,* described and analyzed in some detail by a number of authors (e.g., Zonis 1973; Farhat 1990; Nettl 1992; During 1992). It is unique in the sense that it has become a revered canon, a body of specific and memorized music (and associated concepts), which functions as the fundamental repertory and a corpus of pedagogical material, as well as a guide to improvisatory techniques, formal patterns, and overall structure of performances. It is a point of departure for improvisation as a whole, but its individual components provide guidance for various types of improvisation.

Iranian musicians distinguish several ways of using the *radif* as model (Caron and Safvate 1966, 133): (1) One may simply perform the *radif* as memorized but, as it were, in one's own way, slightly or moderately varying the canonic material, a degree of improvisation somewhat like the performance of a baroque work with improvised ornaments. (2) One may perform a kind of fantasia upon one mode, or *dastgah* in the *radif,* alternating virtually direct quotations with creative departures, but adhering in the broad sense to the *radif*'s structure. In Western music, this might correspond to certain kinds of jazz, or perhaps to concerto cadenzas (when actually improvised). (3) A technique called *morrakab-khani*—"in the way of the composer-singer" or "singer-creator"—consists of modulating among *dastgahs,* putting together materials not ordinarily combined, using components of the *radif* but violating their canonic arrangement and order. This kind of performance might be compared to the eighteenth-century quodlibet or to a nineteenth-century practice of German student singing in which lines from unrelated songs would be combined ad lib.

In some respects, the Persian *radif* is comparable to the themes or tunes sometimes used in Western art music improvisation; in other ways, it corresponds to *ragas,* or to the even less specifically prescribed Arabic *maqams.* Then again, in its various components (thematic and stylistic, motivic and rhythmic) it also corresponds to units of musical content such as gestures or motifs that may be called building blocks, and whose manipulation is a major component of improvisation in some cultures, as seen in some West African drum ensembles.

In the musical aspect of South Slavic epic traditions, whose verbal building blocks have been described in Albert Lord's distinguished book (1965, 30, 38–41), short musical phrases that accompany the ten-syllable lines are the relevant units. One epic may use a stock of six or eight musical lines which are repeated, varied, alternated, and manipulated in ways that are in part determined by the movement of plot and action in the verbal text. These six or eight lines are the building blocks of the musical improvisation of which the epics consist.

For the music of the Shona people of Zimbabwe, we find an interesting dilemma. Berliner (1978) suggests a complex of theoretical concepts, themes, and rhythmic interactions which provide a vocabulary. On the other hand, Dumisani Maraire's (1971, 14) notes accompanying his own recording of performance on the *nyunga-nyunga mbira* or *karimba* indicate that the model for his work is a sequence of nine steps or sections of which a piece must consist, and whose order provides increased tension but finally, in a circular structure, goes back to the content and mood of the beginning. This form, plus the identity of a theme, is the material which the performer (who may often be making music for his personal entertainment or solace) uses as the basis of performance. Maraire's theory does not appear to be shared by other Shona musicians, and one must ask to what extent apparently credible and reasonable musicians' interpretations of their own culture must be accepted by their peers in order to have authenticity.

In the Arabic *taqsim,* the principal instrumental nonmetric improvised form, we can identify several levels of building blocks (Touma 1971; Touma 1975, 57–69; Reichow 1971; Elkholy 1978). First there are the tones of the *taqsim*'s principal *maqam,* from which the performer draws more or less at will, observing typical sequences of order, although the melodic movement must be largely scalar. Motifs of three to five tones associated with each *maqam* that must appear at least occasionally are building blocks of a higher order. Beyond this, a *taqsim* is composed of different kinds of sections, most easily characterized by their length, and these sections as well as their lengths may also be regarded as building blocks. Musicians arrange them in appropriate but individual order, permitting each to carry out a particular musical function. Thus, the long sections contain modulations to secondary *maqams,* the shorter ones may serve to establish the main *maqam,* and the shortest ones provide relief from the building intensity. The wider use of the "building block" concept, existing at various levels, is developed by Lortat-Jacob (1987, 56–57) with the use of the terms *systèmes monomodulaires* and *plurimodulaires.*

These building blocks, individually and in their options of interrelationship, are, as it were, the vocabulary on which the improvisor may draw. Observing the manipulation of the components of a musical vocabulary may also be an analytical technique for composed music, but the supply of building blocks in an improvised style is likely to be less extensive than in precomposed music. Conceivably an improvisatory repertory can be developed only if the options are limited, satisfying the needs of both spontaneity and oral transmission.

It may be stated as an article of faith that improvisers always have a point of departure, something which they use to improvise upon. There are many types, extending from themes, tunes, and chord sequences to forms, from a vocabulary of techniques to a vocabulary of motifs and longer materials, from what is easy or "natural" for the hand to what is intellectually complex.

What is it that actually happens in the mind of the improviser in the course of a performance? This may be the most significant question for scholars investigating the process. In one way or another, it has resulted in the largest body of studies. But to generalize from these? Again, Berliner's study of jazz (1994) suggests that musicians may have much to say about this, but it is difficult to establish patterns of thought process and attitude. One cross-culturally valid approach is examining the musician's need to balance "doing your own thing" with sticking to the rules. There is the recognition of a risk factor, the belief that improvisers purposely place themselves in difficult situations in order to prove their ability to escape from them by solving their musical problems of logic and consistency. Ferand proposes a kind of joy, an attitude of enthusiasm, that lies at the bottom of the activities (Bailey 1992, ix), while Jairazbhoy asserts a virtual dialogue between the musician and his music: "when the musician is performing beyond his normal capacity . . . the music becomes alive" (Jairazbhoy 1971, 31).

Recognizing the significance of singling out improvisation for specific studies as if it were one kind of thing, we will nevertheless probably find it necessary to discard this simple line of demarcation between improvisation and precomposition, or to draw lines at different points. We may wish to reexamine the significance of paper and notation as diagnostic features of true music, and to stop thinking that the mark of a true work of art is the time devoted to its explicit preparation. And of course we will increasingly have to look at improvisation as a group of perhaps very different phenomena.

* * *

This collection of essays is not an attempt to provide a survey of improvisation in the world's musics, past and recent. But the selection of studies presented herewith cuts across the world of improvisation in several ways. Emphasizing three areas that have received the greatest amount of attention—jazz, South Asia, and West Asia—it pays attention also to several other parts of the musical world. While it has not been possible (nor has it been the purpose) to provide representation of all musics or areas of musical culture in which improvisation plays a major role, the contributions provided here touch on many points of the globe; and while contemporary practice is at the forefront, the recent and more distant past also appear.

More important than geographic and chronological representation is the series of approaches that are represented. Four essays (including the present introduction) approach the issue of improvisation most broadly, and together function as an introduction to the rest of the work, which consists principally of case studies. Stephen Blum, taking a view that combines philosophy, ethnography, and philology, integrates the concept of improvisation with other processes in human behavior and musicality in a detailed, cross-cultural study of the uses of various terms relating to improvisation—providing in particular an analysis of these relationships in Arabic and Persian culture, literature, and musical thought. Jeff Pressing's approach draws from the related subdiscipline of systematic musicology and from the discipline of psychology to look at improvisation in the light of analysis of various forms of behavior. He suggests the use of expertise theory as an explanatory device for understanding ways in which various psychological and cultural constraints shape improvisational strategizing. R. Anderson Sutton asks fundamental questions about the existence and nature of improvisation, using gamelan music as a template. In his title—"Do Javanese Gamelan Musicians Really Improvise?"—he tackles one of our major questions: the line between composition and improvisation, and how we can deal with it interculturally. Looking at gamelan music from a broad intercultural perspective, he concludes that Javanese musicians improvise, but Javanese music is not really improvisatory.

Although the four introductory papers do study specific cases, the rest of our presentation is more explicitly devoted to case studies. They are divided into two groups, but they will readily be seen to overlap. The second group is concerned particularly with the work of individual artists. Although the initial purpose was not to present essays on prominent improvisers, five of our studies are about the work of artists who are unquestionably among the world's greats.

Two studies concern outstanding figures in the history of jazz. Lawrence Gushee analyzes the stature of Louis Armstrong, wrestling with the musicologist's perennial question about the great ones—What did they do that made them so great?—and grounding much of his essay on the facts of Armstrong's life and relationship to other musicians, as well as the analysis of a multitude of recordings. Christopher Smith turns to Miles Davis from the viewpoint of semiotics and the quest for musical meaning, seeing whether one can move from the improvised performance to a sense of what the musician and what African-American music as a whole try to say. Smith's study of Miles is based on analysis of audio and video recordings and accounts by colleagues.

In a historical study quite different from and yet related to the many studies on individual jazz artists, Valerie Goertzen studies the art of Clara Schumann as performer and composer, teasing out of information on biographical and historical context, and out of notations, a portrait of the improvisatory art of this great musician and the role of improvisation in her life.

Stephen Slawek concentrates on several distinguished Hindustani musicians, most significantly his teachers, Pandit Ravi Shankar and Dr. Lalmani Misra, in order to take apart the concept of improvisation in the context of Hindustani music. Using as a starting point a teacher's emphasis on "keeping it going," he explains the "given" or point of departure and the performer's contribution, and the complexity of concepts and terms with the use of close analysis of several performances, showing the interaction of the learned and the created, of terminology and musical sound.

The study of Jihad Racy's performances of *taqsim nahawand,* a case study attempting to show norms and boundaries, what is typical, required, rare, and forbidden in a restricted corpus, by Ronald Riddle and myself, was first published in 1974. It is presented here in a revised version, and brought up to date by comparison with Racy's performances some twenty years later, a period during which Racy rose to great distinction as one of the best-known performers of Arabic music in North America.

These studies, concentrating on individuals, are preceded by a larger group of essays that deal with the role of improvisation in musical culture more broadly. In some, the focus is genre or repertory, but each of them contributes as well to an understanding of the broader relationships of music and society. Here too, however, the perspective of the individual musician plays a major role. Thus we provide two studies by scholars who write about music in which they themselves participate as improvisers. T. Viswanathan, a leading figure in the world of Carnatic music in Madras and in North America, and his colleague and former student, Jody Cormack, provide an explanation of three types of improvisation in South Indian classical music, balancing the performer's and the analyst's perspectives. A. Jihad Racy, of Lebanese origin and himself the subject of an essay, a performer and distinguished scholar (and thus also able to balance cultural and musical insider's and outsider's perspectives), looks at the importance of the audience in stimulating the improviser, and further analyzes the concept of ecstasy in performance by deconstructing the statements of a distinguished Egyptian singer.

Several studies relate to Racy's in their perspective of the cultural role of improvisation, but with widely divergent scope. Eve Harwood looks at the concept of improvisation as a way of understanding social and artistic relationships in children's games, as several girls in an Illinois school playground and several of their games lead to an account of a number of roles that improvisation can play. In contrast to this study of one localized venue, Peter Manuel's essay views a broad spectrum of Latin American music with European and African heritage and explains the interaction of formal structure and improvisation in a number of genres, identifying common patterns and practices.

Ingrid Monson's study of modal jazz, particularly in the work of George Russell and John Coltrane, analyzes a genre that is self-contained and yet reaches out across stylistic and national boundaries, and provides interpretation from social, cultural, and political perspectives. Sau Y. Chan, turning to Cantonese opera, a genre not ordinarily included as among improvisational styles, examines the several ways in which the concept of improvisation can be used to shed light on the structure of an entire musical work, and the various kinds of improvisation that appear.

Several of the case studies make significant contributions to the methodology of studying improvisation in an ethnomusicological context. This is particularly true of Tullia Magrini's work on Italian folk music. Accounting for

Italian lyrical singing as musical and social behavior, she analyzes several performances from a number of viewpoints and suggests a new model for the analysis of the relationship of point of departure to performance. Importantly, she illustrates the function of group improvisation in enacting social relationships.

Besides pointing out the significance of the principal grouping of the papers in the table of contents, it may be instructive to suggest other features by which they are related. The essays range from studies of specific venues and individual musicians (e.g., those of Harwood, Gushee, Smith, Goertzen) to broad syntheses (e.g., Blum, Viswanathan and Cormack, and Sutton); from studies of the "typical" musician (e.g., the studies of Chan, Sutton, and Magrini) to studies of outstanding and perhaps culturally exceptional artists. In several essays we see how improvisation lives, as it were, in a musical culture (e.g., in the essays of Sutton, Magrini, Viswanathan and Cormack, and Monson), and how individual musicians contribute to its development (e.g., in the essays of Goertzen, Gushee, and Smith). Several essays—notably those of Slawek, Chan, and Smith—provide discussion of the role of mistakes in shaping the improvisational outcome. We see improvisation in music of folk cultures (Magrini), in everyday modern life (Harwood), in popular music (Manuel), along with the better-represented areas of classical or canonic musics and jazz. While the majority of studies are based on field work or the analysis of twentieth-century recordings, the reader will also find the use of old source material that gives a distant sense of musical sound (for example, in the studies of Goertzen and Blum), and of materials generated specifically for the purpose of the research (e.g., Nettl and Riddle, Viswanathan and Cormack).

We (editors and authors) are happy to provide a wide range of studies that view improvisation from many perspectives, though naturally less happy with the inevitable gaps in the representation of places, peoples, genres, periods, and approaches. We are grateful for the opportunity to contribute to the understanding of music created in the course of performance.

References

Alperson, Philip. 1984. "On Musical Improvisation." *Journal of Aesthetics and Art Criticism* 43:17–29.

Apel, Willi. 1969. *Harvard Dictionary of Music.* 2d ed. Cambridge: Harvard University Press.

Bailey, Derek. 1992. *Improvisation: Its Nature and Practice in Music.* New York: Da Capo Press.

Berliner, Paul. 1978. *The Soul of Mbira.* Berkeley: University of California Press.

———. 1994. *Thinking in Jazz: The Infinite Art of Improvisation.* Chicago: University of Chicago Press.

Blacking, John. 1995. *Music, Culture, and Experience: Selected Papers.* Edited by Reginald Byron. Chicago: University of Chicago Press.

Campbell, Patricia. 1991. *Lessons from the World.* New York: Schirmer Books.

Caron, Nelly, and Dariouche Safvate. 1996. *Iran: Les Traditions Musicales.* Paris: Buchet/Chastel.

Cavanagh, Beverley A. 1986. "Inuit." In *The New Grove Dictionary of American Music,* edited by H. Wiley Hitchcock and Stanley Sadie vol. 2, 494–97. London: Macmillan.

Chan, Sau Y. 1991. *Improvisation in a Ritual Context: The Music of Cantonese Opera.* Hong Kong: Chinese University Press.

Clark, Eric F. 1988. "Generative Principles in Music Performance." In *Generative Processes in Music,* edited by John A. Sloboda, 1–26. Oxford: Oxford University Press.

Colles, H. C. 1935. "Extemporization." In *Grove's Dictionary of Music and Musicians,* 3d ed., edited by H. C. Colles, vol. 2, 184–86. London: Macmillan.

———. 1954. "Extemporization." In *Grove's Dictionary of Music and Musicians,* 5th ed., edited by Eric Blom, vol. 2, 991–93. London: Macmillan.

Danuser, Hermann, ed. 1992. *Musikalische Interpretation.* Vol. 11 of *Neues Handbuch der Musikwissenschaft,* edited by Carl Dahlhaus. Laaber: Laaber-Verlag.

Durant, Alan. 1989. "Improvisation in the Political Economy of Music." In *Music and the Politics of Culture,* edited by Christopher Norris, 252–82. New York: St. Martin's Press.

During, Jean. 1984. *La musique iranienne: tradition et évolution.* Paris: Editions Recherches sur les Civilisations.

Einstein, Alfred. 1951. *Schubert: a Musical Portrait.* New York: Oxford University Press.

Elkholy, Samha. 1978. *The Tradition of Improvisation in Arab Music.* Giza, Egypt: Rizk.

Erlmann, Veit. 1985. "Model, Variation and Performance: Ful'be Praise Song in Northern Cameroon." *Yearbook for Traditional Music* 11:88–112.

Farhat, Hormoz. 1990. *The Dastgâh Concept in Persian Music.* Cambridge: Cambridge University Press.

al-Faruqi, Lois Ibsen. 1985. "Music, Musicians, and Muslim Law." *Asian Music* 17: 3–36.

Fédorov, V. 1957. "Improvisation." In *Larousse de la musique,* vol. 1, 463–64. Paris: Larousse.

Ferand, Ernst. 1938. *Die Improvisation in der Musik.* Zurich: Rhein-Verlag.

———. 1957 "Improvisation." In *Die Musik in Geschichte und Gegenwart,* edited by F. Blume. vol. 6, 1093–135. Kassel: Bärenreiter.

Gerson-Kiwi, Edith. 1963. *The Persian Doctrine of Dastga-Composition.* Tel Aviv: Israel Music Institute.

Gramit, David. 1993. "Constructing a Victorian Schubert: Music, Biography, and Cultural Values." *Nineteenth Century Music* 17:65–78.

Gurlitt, Willibald, and Hans Heinrich Eggebrecht, eds. 1967. *Riemann Musiklexikon, Sachteil,* 12th ed. Mainz: Schott.

Gushee, Lawrence. 1981. "Lester Young's 'Shoeshine Boy.'" In International Musicological Society, *Report of the Twelfth Congress, Berkeley, 1977,* edited by Daniel Heartz and Bonnie Wade, 151–69. Kassel: Bärenreiter.

Haas, Robert. 1931. *Aufführungspraxis der Musik.* Vol. of *Handbuch der Musikwissenschaft,* edited by Ernst Bücken. Potsdam: Athenaion.

Hall, Edward T. 1992. "Improvisation as an Acquired, Multi-level Process." *Ethnomusicology* 36:223–36.

Herzog, George. 1936. "A Comparison of Pueblo and Pima Musical Styles." *Journal of American Folklore* 49:283–417.

Hood, Mantle. 1971. *The Ethnomusicologist.* New York: McGraw-Hill.

Horsley, Imogene, Michael Collins, Eva Badura-Skoda, and Dennis Libby. 1980. "Improvisation: Western Art Music." In *The New Grove Dictionary of Music and Musicians,* edited by Stanley Sadie, vol. 9, 31–52. London: Macmillan.

Jairazbhoy, Nazir A. 1971. *The Rāgs of North Indian Music.* London: Faber and Faber.

———. 1980. "Improvisation: Asian Art Music." In *The New Grove Dictionary of Music and Musicians,* edited by Stanley Sadie, vol. 9, 52–56. London: Macmillan.

Jung, Angelika. 1989. *Quellen der traditionellen Kunstmusik der Usbeken und Tadschiken Mittelasiens: Untersuchungen zur Entstehung und Entwicklung des Šašmaqam.* Hamburg: Karl Dieter Wagner.

Kaeppler, Adrienne. 1987. "Spontaneous Choreography: Improvisation in Polynesian Dance." *Yearbook for Traditional Music* 19:13–22.

Kartomi, Margaret J. 1980. "Childlikeness in Play Songs: A Case Study Among the Pitjantjara at Yalata, South Australia." *Miscellanea Musicologica* 11:172–214.

———. 1991. "Musical Improvisations by Children at Play." *World of Music* 33, no. 3:53–65.

Kassebaum, Gayathri Rajapur. 1987. "Improvisation in Alapana Performance: A Comparative View of Raga Shankarabharana." *Yearbook for Traditional Music* 19:45–64.

Katz, Ruth. 1968. "The Singing of Baqqashot by Aleppo Jews." *Acta Musicologica* 40:65–85.

Kernfeld, Barry. 1981. "Adderley, Coltrane and Davis at the Twilight of Bebop: The Search for Melodic Coherence (1958–59)." Ph.D. dissertation, Cornell University.

Khatschi, Khatschi. 1962. *Der Dastgah.* Regensburg: Bosse.

Kippen, James. 1988. *The Tabla of Lucknow: A Cultural Analysis of a Musical Tradition.* Cambridge: Cambridge University Press.

Koskoff, Ellen, ed. 1987. *Women and Music in Cross-Cultural Perspective.* New York: Greenwood Press.

Kramer, Lawrence, ed. 1993. "Schubert: Music, Sexuality, Culture." Special issue of *Nineteenth Century Music* 17, no. 1.

Kunst, Jaap. 1959. *Ethno-Musicology.* 3d ed. The Hague: Nijhoff.

Levy, Kenneth. 1990. "On Gregorian Orality." *JAMS* 42:185–227.

Lord, Albert B. 1965. *The Singer of Tales.* New York: Athenaeum.

Lortat-Jacob, Bernard, ed. 1987. *L'improvisation dans les musiques de tradition orale.* Paris: Selaf.

Malm, William P. 1975. "Shoden, A Study in Tokyo Festival Music: When Is Variation an Improvisation?" *Yearbook of the International Folk Music Council* 7:44–66.

Maraire, Abraham Dumisani. 1971. "Introduction." *Mbira Music of Rhodesia.* Seattle: University of Washington Press. Booklet accompanying recording (UWP 1001).

Marcus, Scott L. 1992. "Modulation in Arab Music: Documenting Oral Concepts, Performance Rules and Strategies." *Ethnomusicology* 36:171–96.

Massoudieh, Mohammad Taghi. 1968. *Awâz-e Sur.* Regensburg: Bosse.

Merriam, Alan P. 1964. *The Anthropology of Music.* Evanston: Northwestern University Press.

Merriam, Alan P., and Raymond W. Mack. 1960. "The Jazz Community." *Social Forces* 38, no. 3 (March):211–22.

Monson, Ingrid. 1991. "Musical Interaction in Modern Jazz: An Ethnomusicological Perspective." Ph.D. dissertation, New York University.

Moser, Hans Joachim. 1955. *Musik Lexikon.* 4th ed. Hamburg: Sikorski.

Nattiez, Jean-Jacques. 1990. *Music and Discourse: Toward a Semiology of Music.* Translated by Carolyn Abbate. Princeton: Princeton University Press.

Nettl, Bruno. 1974. "Thoughts on Improvisation, a Comparative Approach." *Musical Quarterly* 60:1–19.

———. 1986. "Improvisation." In *The New Harvard Dictionary of Music,* edited by Don M. Randel, 392–94. Cambridge: Harvard University Press.

———. 1989. *Blackfoot Musical Thought: Comparative Perspectives.* Kent, Ohio: Kent State University Press.

———. 1992. *The Radif of Persian Music.* Rev. ed. Champaign, Ill.: Elephant and Cat.

———. 1994. "Persian Classical Music and the Twentieth Century: The Changing Value of Improvisation." In *To the Four Corners: A Festschrift in Honor of Rose Brandel,* edited by Ellen Leichtman, 57–66. Warren, Mich.: Harmonie Park Press.

———. 1995. *Heartland Excursions: Ethnomusicological Reflections on Schools of Music.* Urbana: University of Illinois Press.

Nettl, Bruno, with Bela Foltin, Jr. 1972. *Daramad of Chahargah: A Study in the Performance Practice of Persian Music.* Detroit: Detroit Monographs in Musicology.

Neumann, Frederick. 1986. *Ornamentation and Improvisation in Mozart.* Princeton: Princeton University Press.

Owens, Thomas. 1974. "Charlie Parker: Techniques of Improvisation." Ph.D. dissertation, University of California, Los Angeles.

Porter, Lewis. 1985. "John Coltrane's 'A Love Supreme': Jazz Improvisation as Composition." *JAMS* 38:593–621.

Pressing, Jeff. 1984. "Cognitive Processes in Improvisation." In *Cognitive Processes in the Perception of Art,* edited by W. Ray Crozier and Antony J. Chapman, 345–63. Amsterdam: Elsevier.

———. 1988. "Improvisation: Methods and Models." In *Generative Processes in Music,* edited by John A. Sloboda, 130–77. Oxford: Oxford University Press.

Racy, Ali Jihad. 1991. "Creativity and Ambience: An Ecstatic Feedback Model from Arab Music." *World of Music* 33, no. 3:7–28.

Reichow, Jan. 1971. *Die Entfaltung eines Melodiemodells im Genus Sikah.* Regensburg: Bosse.

Rycroft, David. 1962. "The Guitar Improvisations of Mwenda Jean Bosco." *African Music* 3, no. 1:86–102.

Saba, Abolhassan. 1970 (ca.) *Dure-ye avval-e tār va setār.* Reprint, Tehran: n.p.

Sartori, Claudio, ed. 1964. *Enciclopedia della Musica.* Milan: Ricordi.

Sawyer, R. Keith. 1996. "The Semiotics of Improvisation: The Pragmatics of Musical and Verbal Performance." *Semiotics* 108, nos. 3–4:269–306.

Slawek, Stephen. 1987. *Sitar Technique in Nibaddh Forms.* Delhi: Motilal Banarsidass.

Smith, Gregory. 1983. "Homer, Gregory, and Bill Evans? The Theory of Formulaic Composition in the Context of Jazz Piano Improvisation." Ph.D. dissertation, Harvard University.

———. 1991. "In Quest of a New Perspective on Improvised Jazz: A View from the Balkans." *World of Music* 33, no. 3:29–52.

Song, Bang-Song. 1986. *The Sanjo Tradition of Korean Komun'go Music.* Seoul: Jung Eum Sa.

Stewart, Milton L. 1979. "Some Characteristics of Clifford Brown's Improvisational Style." *Jazzforschung/Jazz Research* 11:135–64.

Stolba, K. Marie, 1990. *The Development of Western Music: A History.* Dubuque, Iowa: Wm. C. Brown.

Sudnow, David. 1978. *Ways of the Hand: The Organization of Improvised Conduct.* Cambridge: Harvard University Press.

Susilo, Hardja. 1987. "Improvisation in Wayang Wong Panggung." *Yearbook for Traditional Music* 19:1–12.

Sutton, R. Anderson. 1987. "Variation and Composition in Java." *Yearbook for Traditional Music* 19:65–96.

Tambiah, S. J. 1985. *Culture, Thought and Social Action: An Anthropological Perspective.* Cambridge: Harvard University Press.

Tarasti, E. 1993. "From *Mastersingers* to Bororo Indians: On the Semiosis of Improvisation." In *Proceedings from the Congress of Improvisation,* edited by T. Bram, 62–81. Luzern.

Taylor, Franklin. 1896a. "Extempore Playing." In *A Dictionary of Music and Musicians (A.D. 1450–1889),* edited by Sir George Grove, vol. 1, 498–99.

———. 1896b. "Extemporizing Machine." In *A Dictionary of Music and Musicians (A.D. 1450–1889),* edited by Sir George Grove, vol. 1, 499.

Tirro, Frank. 1974. "Constructive Elements in Jazz Improvisation." *JAMS* 27:285–305.

Touma, Habib Hassan. 1968. *Der Maqam Bayati im arabischen Taqsim.* Berlin: H. Touma.

———. 1971. "Maqam Phenomenon: An Improvisation Technique in the Music of the Middle East." *Ethnomusicology* 15:38–48.

———. 1975. *Die Musik der Araber.* Wilhelmshaven: Heinrichshofen.

Treitler, Leo. 1991. "Medieval Improvisation." *World of Music* 33, no. 3:66–91.

Trimillos, Ricardo D. 1987. "Time-Distance and Melodic Models in Improvisation among the Tausug of the Southern Philippines." *Yearbook for Traditional Music* 19: 23–36.

Viswanathan, Tanjore. 1977. "The Analysis of Raga Alapana in South Indian Music." *Asian Music* 9:13–71.

Wilkens, Eckart. 1967. *Künstler und Amateure im persischen Santurspiel.* Regensburg: Bosse.

Wiora, Walter. 1983. *Das musikalische Kunstwerk.* Tutzing: Hans Schneider.

Zonis, Ella. 1973. *Classical Persian Music: An Introduction.* Cambridge: Harvard University Press.

THE CONCEPT AND ITS RAMIFICATIONS

CHAPTER ONE

Recognizing Improvisation

STEPHEN BLUM

Responding to Unforeseen Challenges

Although the noun "improvisation" and its cognates are relatively new words in European languages, they have quickly become indispensable terms for talking about music and about many other areas of social life. Their importance in ethnomusicology stems from the fact that performers in so many cultures are expected to respond appropriately to "unforeseen" challenges and opportunities—perhaps by composing a performance that fits and enhances the moment and situation in which it takes place, perhaps by serving as the vehicle of a superhuman agent or connecting with a source of inspiration that suddenly becomes available. We are not likely to speak of improvisation unless we believe that participants in an event, however they are motivated, share a sense that something unique is happening in their presence at the moment of performance.

Of course, experiences or impressions of uniqueness are not enough to distinguish improvisation from other activities—such as executing a rigorously prescribed sequence of ritual actions at precisely the right moment, or presenting a composition that has been carefully prepared for an important occasion. Before extending the reference of the term "improvisation" to a particular type or aspect of performance, we need at least a rudimentary understanding of what the performers are expected to accomplish and how they prepare themselves to meet those expectations. Performers are almost never responding to challenges that were *entirely* unforeseen.

In every part of the world we can observe activities that would fail to achieve their ends if performers were unable to improvise effectively in the presence of other participants. More often than not, for example, praise singers or lamenters must show that they are sensitive to the immediate needs and desires of those to whom their performances are addressed: presentation of a "prefabricated" lament or praise song might be taken as a sign of insincerity. When one purpose of repeating a sequence of motions in dance or ritual is to generate feelings of euphoria, one or more participants may need to decide when to replace one pattern with another. When one of the aims of a ceremony is to invite gods or ancestors to take part, the performers must know how to react appropriately at any sign that the invited guests have arrived or are on their way. Rules of improvisation (where they exist) are often rules of courtesy and hospitality, which need not prevent them from also being rules of competition.

Jeff Titon has identified a potential blind spot in the motivations of American ethnomusicologists: "Perhaps at some deep level we prize improvisation not just because of the skills involved but because we think it exemplifies human freedom" (Titon 1992, 11). The obvious implication is that we can easily be mistaken, through ignorance of the pertinent constraints.[1] Many of the activities we are inclined to call improvisation are evidently taken for granted as basic obligations of performers toward themselves, toward fellow members of ensembles, and toward patrons or other listeners. Moreover, such obligations may well go without saying. Ethnomusicologists are often in the position of trying to describe processes of social interaction that participants have little or no interest in describing. It is fortunate for all concerned that performers can never tell us every last detail about their modes of performance; if they could, the performances would be superfluous as well as lifeless.[2] Still, we might expect to find various ways of contrasting improvisation with other modes of action—and we do. While some of the contrasts are binary choices (*either* this type *or* not), others involve discriminations between *more or less* improvised aspects of performance.

Improvisation (like "freedom" or "music") is a topic that forces us to confront formidable problems of translation. Different translations are always possible, and we must ask what alternative terms might have been used by performers or by outside observers to denote each component in a sequence of actions. Terms that overlap in one way or another with our notions of improvisation will point to specific respects in which one type of action differs from other types. The pertinent contrasts are not always those between improvisation and reproduction of an existing composition, or between improvisation and creation of a scheme or work designed for performance at a later time.

Responses Commensurate to the Situation

Discussions of improvisation in Near Eastern writings and oral literatures tend to emphasize the immediacy and the appropriateness of a performer's response to a given situation. It is often assumed that competent performers can repeat whatever they have just heard, with significant additions or alterations. A Kurdish narrative *(beyt)* tells of two singers who sought out a master performer in order to learn a *beyt* known to him alone. After they had listened to his performance over a period of four nights, the master asked them to repeat the entire *beyt,* and in doing so they added 28 new stanzas—all of which were "appropriately placed" *(be rê we cê lêyan)* (Fattāhi Qāzi 1970, 10). The implication of the story is that a fully competent singer knows how to compose new stanzas in performance—a higher level of competence, presumably, than the ability to make adjustments in conventional rhythmic and tonal frameworks while singing familiar stanzas. The two guests showed that they had been worthy of the master's hospitality and that they were capable of receiving his gift of the *beyt*.[3]

Generally speaking, a need to specify whether poetry or oratory has been memorized in advance or composed during performance seems to have arisen more often than any need to apply the same distinction to vocal or instrumental music. George Sawa (1989, 145) notes that the Arabic verb *irtajala*, used for improvising poetry, was extended by Henry George Farmer to musical improvisation but is not used in this sense in al-Isfahāni's massive *Kitāb al-aghāni* (fourth century A.H./tenth century A.D.).[4] The examples of spontaneous creation of music that Sawa does cite from the *Kitāb al-aghāni* are actions carried out with respect to existing poems: "she set it [the poem] to music at once" *(min waqtiha)*; "I set it to music at once" *(min sā'ati)*. The use of adverbial phrases to qualify actions that might have been performed "in advance" rather than "at once" has been one of the most common ways of marking performances as improvised, particularly in Europe. The most common implication of these usages is that patrons and other listeners were ready to admire a demonstration of skill in spontaneous composition.

The rewards bestowed on poet-singers by their princely patrons "have been gained through improvisation *(badihe)* commensurate to the situation *(ḥasb-e ḥāl)*." Such is the advice offered to neophytes by the Persian writer known as Nezāmi 'Arūzi in the second of his *Chahār maqāle* ("Four Discourses," written in the mid-sixth century A.H./twelfth century A.D.). Successful improvisation "fires up" *(bar afrūzad)* the assembled listeners and makes the king favorably disposed to reward the performer (Qazvini 1910, 31–36). Nezāmi 'Arūzi praises the celebrated poet-musician Rudaki (d. A.H. 329/A.D. 940–41) as the master who attained rewards which "no one else has seen." The effect of improvised verses must have depended, in part, on how they were presented musically, but the term *badihe* (borrowed from Arabic) applies here to the creation of new verses, not to the performer's use of conventional musical resources in presenting the verses.

A situation in which two poet-musicians perform newly created verses is described at length toward the end of the poem *Khosrow and Shirin* by Nezāmi of Ganja (d. ca. 605/1209; not to be confused with the essayist Nezāmi 'Arūzi). From within a tent, Shirin calls for a musician who will produce concord *(sāz)* "commensurate to my emotional state" *(be ḥasb-e ḥāl-e man)*; the harpist Nakisā is given a seat near the tent and told to shape his sung poetry and instrumental accompaniment according to Shirin's instructions. The lutenist Bārbad acts as Khosrow's spokesman and responds to each of Nakisā's *ghazals* with one of his own, in a different melodic system *(parde)*. After four such exchanges using eight melodic systems, Shirin herself sings a newly created melody, to which Khosrow responds harmoniously in the same *parde*. In this long scene of 326 verses, Nezāmi repeatedly emphasizes the freshness of the melodies:

from the *parde* called *Ḥesār*, Nakisā "drew out" *(bar āvord)* a tune "like the firstborn in a litter."[5]

Persian writers have also discussed other ways, besides the spontaneous composition of sung poetry, in which performances are made "commensurate to the situation." From the viewpoint of a prince, as presented in the *Qābūs-nāme* of Kai Kā'ūs (late fifth/eleventh century), "the greatest art of a professional musician" *(khonyāgar, moṭreb)* lies in "penetrating the listener's temperament" and in exercising patience toward even the most intoxicated listeners (Yūsufi 1966, 196–97). A musician who happens to be in love should avoid all temptation to make music that is commensurate to his own state *(ḥasb-e ḥāl-e khish);* instead he should choose a melody type *(rāh* or *ṭariq)* and a song *(sorud)* that suit the time, the season, and the temperament of any listener who seems prepared to reward him. His selection of just the right items from his repertoire is taken to be the decisive factor, not his command of variation or recomposition at the moment of performance. Musicians are also expected to sing "something" *(chizi)* in each of the ten melodic systems *(parde),* beginning with *Rāst.* At no point does Kai Kā'ūs urge them to shape each phrase or each verse according to their perceptions of the dynamics of the situation; whatever their choices in this respect, performers can be certain that some listeners will become intoxicated.

The resources of the musician's art *(ṣan'at),* as Kai Kā'ūs describes them, have been codified by earlier practitioners; neophytes who wish to become familiar with these resources must understand the purposes they were invented to serve (one reason for writing about music in the first place). Given the preference of older, more serious listeners for songs in heavy poetic meters, it was necessary to create melody types *(rāh* or *ṭariq)* appropriate to these meters. The rule that a song in a heavy meter should be followed by one in a lighter meter (and hence with a different melody type) takes into account the preferences of younger listeners (Yūsufi 1966, 193–94). Whatever the accuracy of these claims, they are good examples of *constraints* on combinations that are either simultaneous (melody type plus poetic meter) or successive (heavy followed by light). The language in which such understandings are expressed may apply equally well whether composition is carried out mainly in advance or mainly at the moment of performance, even when authors or speakers make no mention of social interactions that might distinguish improvisation from other options.

Experienced performers would necessarily associate the name of each *rāh* or each *parde* with an appropriate set of habits—procedures used in the past and available for use in future performances. Kai Kā'ūs speaks of the invention of melody types *(rāh* or *ṭariq)* for the heavy and light meters but says nothing about meters or topics that are more effectively handled in one *parde* than in another; perhaps a *parde* was somewhat more flexible than a *rāh.* In general, musical entities bearing their own proper names but treated as a collection (or "population") are likely to have identities (or "personalities") with varying degrees of complexity, so that musicians become better acquainted with the most complex through increased experience. Identities are partly a matter of the combinations that are recommended, permitted, or prohibited; hence discussion of what does and does not fit with the constitution of a given *parde* or *maqām* has been a major concern of Persian and Arabic theorists. Learning verses that are appropriately sung in each *parde* (or, more recently, *gushe*) has long been seen as an indispensable part of a Persian musician's education.[6]

We might expect conventional combinations and associations to be highly significant but not altogether binding on the best performers. ʿAbdolqadir ibn Gheybi Marāghi (d. 838/1435), the most prolific writer of Persian treatises on music, makes precisely this point in his commentary on the fourteenth chapter of the famous *Kitāb al-adwār* by Ṣafi al-Din al-Urmawi (d. 693/1294): the performer whose artistry is "complete" and "ineffable" will have sufficient command of both singing *(āvāz)* and enunciation *(makhraj)* to arouse emotions of pity and sadness in listeners, even while using a *parde* associated with strength and courage (Binesh 1991, 278). We can recognize this as something that may happen in improvisation, when singers know how to articulate the same text in ways that create very different meanings. Marāghi might also have been thinking of compositions designed to challenge performers by requiring them to work against the conventional associations of a *parde*.

Some of the rules formulated by Persian and Arabic theorists apply to all acts of composition—those taking place in the presence of listeners no less than those directed toward performance at a later time. In the writings of Marāghi and of Qotb al-Din al-Shirāzi (d. 710/1311), the term *talḥin* sometimes denotes composition in this broad sense, embracing various arts of combination and conjunction—above all, those that coordinate text and tune—but also such common problems as how to move from one component to another within a modal system. According to Qotb al-Din, "one should know that these groups *(jumūʿ)* and branch-modes *(shoʿab)* are related to one another and that, in *talḥin,* passing *(enteqāl)* from any [group or branch-mode] to a related one is a way to increase [the music's] splendor *(rownaq)* and freshness *(tarāvat)*" (Wright 1978, 292).[7]

The difference between producing a new melody on a specific occasion and composing melodies that are remembered by others is possibly indicated by the choice of different verbs, as in the Chaghatay Turkish text of the memoirs of Bābur (1483–1530), the Timurid ruler of Kabul and the first Mughal emperor of India. In his description of musicians at the court of Sultan-Husayn Mirza at Herat, Bābur mentions one performer who "did not compose many melodies" *(xaylî iš bağlamaydur)* and another who, on one occasion, "drew out, quite nicely, a melody from the *ney*" *(bir išni naydin xūb čiqarur)* (Thackston 1993, 381, 379).

Theorists and pedagogues have a reason to mark improvisation as a special

case when they wish to indicate where it diverges from general rules of composition. An interesting early example occurs in the Arabic treatise *Kitāb kamāl
adab al-ghinā'* of al-Ḥasan (fifth/eleventh century): a musician should avoid
passing with a jolt *(hazzāz)* from one octave species *(naw')* to another, "except
when he is improvising *(yaqtariha)*" (al-Hefni and Khashabah, 1975, 127; for
French translation see Shiloah 1972, 177). Al-Ḥasan also points to situations
where rules offer little or no help: some melodies in the standard repertoire are
relatively complete but need to be embellished by performers, drawing on their
natural gifts rather than on their knowledge of rules. Other melodies are much
less complete, as their composers have not exhausted all the possibilities; here
the outermost boundary might be defined as what we would consider a framework for improvisation. Al-Ḥasan urges performers to refrain from enlarging
or contracting a melody if the composer has already exploited its possibilities
to the full (al-Hefni and Khashabah 138; Shiloah 193–94). His discussion
makes it clear that musicians did not always agree on the extent to which recomposition was permissible or desirable, but we can be certain that in some
situations it was unavoidable. The discussion amounts to a classification of
models according to one criterion: the extent to which they offer options as
well as obligations.

The *rate* at which various obligations need to be met, though it may well
provide one means of classifying some melodic repertoires, does not always
furnish a basis for distinguishing improvisation from other modes of performance. In most of the situations discussed above, the pertinent distinctions
have more to do with problems of coordination: adjusting text and tune to one
another, fitting a performance to a patron's mood, and so on. Performers cannot
know in advance how listeners, or even how they themselves, will respond
to the conjunctures and moments of coordination that occur in performance.
Evaluation of what has happened, or of what should happen, may place greater
emphasis on the behavior of all parties than on the performer's manipulation
of "models."

Performers and listeners learn not only when to act and what to do but also
when not to act and what not to do. This brief excursion through a few Persian
and Arabic writings has not yet arrived at one of the central meanings of the
word *ḥāl:* the anomalous state that performers and auditors can only receive
as one of God's "gifts" *(mavāheb)* or "favors" *(afzāl)*. It is this conception, first
articulated in the *Kashf al-mahjūb* of al-Hujviri (mid-fifth/eleventh century)
and developed in the theory and practice of Sufism, which has made improvisation so important in Persian musical culture for several centuries (see also During 1994, 138–83). The fundamental situation is the ceremony called *samā'*
after its main purpose, "audition." Those who take part in the ceremony (and
in situations that are derived from or analogous to it) are "auditors," to whom
al-Hujviri's advice is applicable: "The auditor must have enough perception

[didār] to be capable of receiving the Divine influence [*vāred-e Ḥaqq*] and of doing justice to it. When its might is manifested on his heart he must not endeavour to repel it, and when its force is broken he must not endeavour to attract it" (Zhukovsky 1994, 545; for translation see Nicholson 1976, 419). This doctrine creates many openings for spontaneous behavior, not least from performers whose station in life allows them to become "auditors" (in this special sense), rather than "service professionals," whose responses are shaped according to the needs and desires of their superiors. The dynamics of performance situations in Sufi ceremonies and their numerous analogues is a rich topic, which ought to be approached from many perspectives (see also Rouget 1980, 350–428; Qureshi 1986).

Development and Progress

If improvisation has often been described with respect to the expectations and responses of listeners in a familiar milieu, it can also be treated as an art that enables performers to control their dependence on habitual responses. This is al-Fārābi's approach in the *Kitāb al-mūsiqi al-kabir* (fourth/tenth century), where he describes three levels of practical musical art *(sinā'a)* and a few intermediate levels—each defined in terms of relationships between sense perception, imagination, and reasoning.

At the first level, musicians are dependent on the habits they have formed with respect both to an instrument and to a specific ambience or set of circumstances; outside this milieu, or away from the instrument, they cannot imagine or perform anything. Their development has been arrested in the first stage of musical education, in which neophytes try to imitate the motions of accomplished artists in order to reproduce what they have seen and heard—"inscribing" it in the imagination as they gain experience (Ghattās and al-Hefni 1967, 53–54, 81; for French translation see d'Erlanger 1930, 8–9, 23).

Other musicians also remain dependent on sense perceptions but acquire the capacity *(hai'a)* of forming *(siyāgha)* melodies that "were not inscribed *(murtasim)* in the mind at an earlier time" but are "worked out *(tartasim)* only at the moment *(fi-l'hin)* of perception" (Ghattās and al-Hefni 1967, 56, d'Erlanger 1930, 10). The newly shaped melody is an immediate response to what has just been done by someone else, or by the same performer, perhaps introducing very subtle changes. A strong example of the first possibility is the Persian practice known as *javāb-e āvāz,* in which an instrumentalist improvises a response *(javāb)* to each of the singer's phrases; certain instrumentalists are recognized for their excellence in *javāb-e āvāz* (which should not be described as "reproduction" of the *āvāz).*

The faculty of imagination *(takhayyul),* as al-Fārābi describes it, allows musicians to become less dependent on the senses as it becomes strengthened through social interaction. Only those who have attained the third and highest level of practical musical art are capable of talking coherently about whatever their imagination has conceived. As an example, al-Fārābi mentions Isḥāq al-Mawsili (d. 235/850), the most famous of all 'Abbasid musicians. Art does not become knowledge until one can describe not just what happens, but *why* it happens.

Performers who merely reproduce melodies that are already "inscribed" in their minds have not advanced beyond the initial stage of musical education and are not yet ready to participate in the competition among musicians that leads to improvements in practical musical art. These improvements include recomposition of existing melodies, shortening the parts that were too long and lengthening the parts that were too short (d'Erlanger 1930, 20). Whether the recomposition is carried out "in advance" or "at once" does not seem to matter, so long as musicians are capable of stating their reasons for each decision.

The uses that al-Fārābi found for his hierarchical ordering of three "levels of practical musical art" differ significantly from Boethius's discussion of "what a musician is," which concludes the first book of his *De institutione musica* (early sixth century A.D.). For Boethius, reason *(ratio)* is more honorable than skill *(artificium),* just as the mind is superior to the body; hence, "a musician is one who has gained knowledge of making music by weighing with the reason, not through the servitude of work, but through the sovereignty of speculation." If manual labor and intellectual labor are the two extremes, "those who are engaged in the musical art" can be classified according to their distance from these extremes; musicians of the lowest class are "dependent *(positum)* upon instruments" and "totally lacking in thought" *(totius speculationis expertes).* Those of the highest class, being "totally grounded *(positum)* in reason and thought," are able to carefully weigh *(perpendere)* rhythms and melodies and the composition as a whole. In between the two extremes come "those who compose songs"—the poets who are "led to song not so much by thought and reason as by a certain natural instinct" (Bower 1989, 50–51; Friedlein 1867, 224–25).

Al-Fārābi's discussion can be read as an account of a complete musical education, in which development of the imagination is crucial. Boethius was more concerned with social divisions—with authority, honor, and "classes" of musicians (only one of which deserves the name in its true sense). He did not invoke a faculty of imagination to mediate between mind and body, skill and reason. Starting from these or from other schemes based on Aristotle's hierarchy of faculties, one might choose to emphasize either what improvisors *can do* or what some of them *don't know*. Both options have been selected many times over.

Compelling reasons for talking about improvisation have included not only an interest in how musicians gain competence, but also a desire to imagine the historical development of performing arts. Aristotle's remarks on the origins of Greek drama (*Poetics* 1448b7 and 1449a14) are the most famous example:

> Given, then, that mimetic activity comes naturally to us—together with melody and rhythm (for it is evident that metres are species of rhythms)—it was originally those with a special natural capacity who, through a slow and gradual process, brought poetry into being by their improvisations [*autoschediasmāton*]. . . .

> At any rate, having come into being from an improvisational origin [*arches autoschediastike*] (which is true of both tragedy and comedy, the first starting from the leaders [*archōnton*] of the dithyramb, the second from the leaders of the phallic songs which are still customary in many cities), tragedy was gradually enhanced as poets made progress with the potential which they could see in the genre. And when it had gone through many changes, tragedy ceased to evolve, since it had attained its natural fulfilment. (Halliwell 1987, 34–35)[8]

Different strands of Aristotle's account have been singled out for emphasis in the translations and commentaries of Near Eastern and European writers. Aristotle's view of the initial, improvised activities as directed toward the perfected form of tragedy invites commentators to elaborate on what is missing from the improvised activities, or what is "natural" according to their own conceptions. Ibn Rushd (late sixth/twelfth century), echoing the earlier commentary of Ibn Sinā, finds evidence of natural inclinations in what his own contemporaries do in response to one type of challenge: "He said: a sign that these kinds are the first to occur to souls, is that in disputes people improvise these kinds of hemistichs for their arguments when hard pressed" (Butterworth 1986, 71).[9]

The Latin and Italian terms chosen by sixteenth-century translators and commentators form a cluster of closely associated notions (table 1.1), all of which turn up (perhaps with different associations) in accounts of European performance genres from the Renaissance to the present. We could learn much about the history of European musical thought by tracing the usage of each word or phrase in this cluster—that is, how groups of terms have been formed, then reconfigured, in order to describe contemporary models of performance and contemporary views of the ever-changing past.[10]

Studies of musical terminology require close analysis of the narratives in which the terms are used (and of the social actions in which the narratives are used). Europeans have been aggressive in presenting their histories of "culture" to themselves and others. It would be worthwhile to investigate the various ways in which European and "non-European" myths and stories of origin make comparisons between spontaneous creation, playful experiment, careful structuring over a period of time, and other alternatives.

Table 1.1 Terms used in seven translations/commentaries on Aristotle's *Poetics*, 1448b and 1449a

---

à principio rudes essent, planéque informes (Pazzi 1536, 8ᵛ)
un principio quasi casuale & isproveduto (Piccolomini, 1575, 80)

Cum ab initio extemporanea esset (Robortelli 1548, 39)
Nata igitur initio extemporanea (Vettori 1560, 40)
ex ipsis extemporariis, id est, ex carminibus ruditer factis genitam esse Poesim (Maggi and Lombardi 1550, 76)

sine meditatione ulla aliquid scribere (Robortelli 1548, 39)
subitò alicui, nulla meditatione adhibita, in mentem venerant (Vettori 1560, 34)

subito in mentem vel buccam potius ipsis venisset (Vettori 1560, 40)
quasi all'improvista di bocca à i lor genitri uscisse (Piccolomini 1575, 80)
procreaverunt poësim ex subitis studijs, & ijs quae ex tempore dicerentur (Vettori 1560, 33)

la poesia con inventioni fatte dapprima all'improviso (Segni 1549, 284)
la poesia versificando sprovedutamente (Castelvetro 1570, 35)
la poesia, quasi all'improvista facendo versi in essa, formassero, & generassero (Piccolomini 1575, 71)

From Adverb to Verbal Noun

The development of European terms for improvisatory practices began with adverbs and adverbial phrases (table 1.2), then continued with verbs and nouns for specific practices or genres (e.g., *sortisare* and *sortisatio, ricercare* and *ricercar*), and nouns for agents (e.g., Italian *improvvisatore*). Only in the nineteenth and twentieth centuries have the newer verb *improvise,* the noun *improvisation,* and their cognates in other languages been treated as general terms, applicable to a number of practices (though sometimes used as substitutes for older terms with a more restricted reference).

One of the reasons why a general term proved useful is evident in a question posed by Sir John Hawkins, after listing the names of some ancient Greek poet-singers: "Did the music of these, and many other men whom we read of, consist of mere Energy, in the extemporary prolation, of solitary or accordant sounds; or had they, in those very early ages, any method of notation, whereby their ideas of sound, like those of other sensible objects, were rendered capable of communication?" (Hawkins 1963, 1)[11] More often than not, "improvise" or "improvisation" becomes a "marked" rather than an "unmarked" term, designating an activity that somehow diverges from (or precedes, as in the case of Hawkins's "extemporary prolation") the routines one can name with unmarked terms.

Through the sixteenth, seventeenth, and eighteenth centuries, the European terms for improvised music making form two rather distinct groups, referring to vocal and instrumental practices and centered around the adverbial phrases used to qualify "singing," "playing," or "composing." Some verbs refer to spe-

Table 1.2. Selective list of adverbs and adverbial phrases in European writings, to 1810

Latin	Italian	French	German	English
ex improviso	de improviso	à l'impourvue	unvorsehender Weise	unexpected
ac improvisa	all' improviso	à l'improviste	unversehens	
	all' improvistà			
	alla sproveduta			
	sprovedutamente			
ex tempore	estemporaneamente	impromptu		
	all' impronto	sur-le-champ	auf der Stelle	on the spur of the moment
ex sorte	a caso		aus dem Stegereif	by chance
fortuita			auf zufällige Art	on the sudden
				accidently
repente	alla mente	de tête	aus dem Kopfe	
ad placitum	a piacere	à plaisir		
ad libitum	ad arbitrio			
	di fantasia	à phantasie		
sine arte	senza arte			
sine meditatione		sans règle ni dessein	unbedachtsam	

cific types of improvised singing (e.g., Latin *sortisare*) or playing (e.g., German *fantasiren* and *capriciren,* Italian *ricercare,* French *rechercher* and *préluder*). Nouns related to the verbs designate the activity (*sortisatio*), the results of the activity (an instrumental *fantasia, capriccio, ricercar, recherche, prélude*), or the imaginative capacity that enables the musician to act (his or her *fantasia* or "caprice"). Nouns that name the actors involved (e.g., *descanter,* "one that can extempore sing a part upon a playnesong" in Morley 1597, 70) are much less common, the most notable being the Italian *improvvisatore.*

One consequence of the existence of different clusters of terms is that writers and speakers could choose whether or not they wished to transfer connotations of one type of activity to discourse concerned with another way of acting. Difficult though it may have been to discuss improvisation by a solo instrumentalist without drawing on the terminology of rhetoric and imagining the player as a "speaker" (see Kirkendale 1979), writers did not need to compare instrumental solos with verses composed by the *improvvisatori* in the presence of spectators. Madame de Staël chose to make precisely this comparison: "On occasion [in Germany] I entered impoverished households blackened by tobacco smoke and at once heard not just the mistress but the master of the house improvising at the keyboard, as the Italians improvise verses" (Staël 1958, i, 45–46).[12] She seems to have been surprised to find men improvising at the keyboard in their own homes. The composer Grétry described domestic improvisation as an appropriate and satisfying activity for a young unmarried woman with a vivid imagination (adding in a footnote that the Italian *improvvisatori* were likewise drawn to music by their "vivid imaginations"): "To improvise on a full instrument, such as the piano, the harp, etc., is a source of happiness for lively imaginations"; a young woman's modesty "is never compromised by unfurling her entire soul in the language of melody" (Grétry 1797, iii, 109–10).[13] In Grétry's usage the verb *improviser* is merely a synonym for the more familiar *jouer de tête* and *préluder* (as in his manual of 1803). The Germans who received Madame de Staël would have described their keyboard performances as *fantasieren* or *präludieren.* The (relatively new) verbal noun *Improvisieren* has only one meaning in Koch's *Musikalisches Lexikon* (1802): a composer's skill in setting to music a poem he has never seen while at the same time performing the new setting.[14] Rousseau, who incorrectly claimed to have added the verb *improviser* to the French language by adopting it from Italian (1768, 252), had defined it as a singer's simultaneous composition of words and melody alike, to the accompaniment of a guitar or other string instrument.[15]

The extension of the verb to cover both vocal and instrumental practices, already evident in Grétry's *Mémoires* and Staël's book on Germany, was confirmed in the *Dictionnaire de musique moderne* of Castil-Blaze (1821).[16] The availability of a general verb in French and other languages made it possible, perhaps even necessary, to argue about what types of interaction were best described as improvising. One of the key variables was the responsiveness of performers to their listeners and to themselves.

The demands of others who happen to be present can be interpreted as inhibiting rather than motivating acts of improvisation. For Chopin, the true sense of the verb *improwizować* included the freedom to play as he wished, which was apt to be more readily available in an intimate situation than in a theater (Sydow 1955, 115–16).[17] Even in a small group, it was not so easy to improvise in response to someone's request if the instrumentalist felt more like sleeping; a good musical idea (*myśl*) was more likely to arrive early in the morning, when only one friend was present (87).[18]

An individual's receptiveness to such ideas and impulses as may make themselves felt was one of the conventional topics of writings concerned with instrumental fantasias and preludes. The language of recommendations that one should catch ideas without really paying attention may approach the paradoxical, as in Beethoven's remark about the activity of *fantasiren* in a sketch of 1807 or 1808:

> Man fantasirt eigentlich nur wenn man gar nicht acht giebt, was man spielt, so—würde man auch am besten, wahrsten fantasiren öffentlich—sich ungezwungen überlassen, eben was einem gefällt. (Kinsky 1916, no. 215)

Ernst Ferand misquoted this passage in a general survey of "Improvisation," replacing Beethoven's verb *fantasiren* with *improvisieren,* a word he may never have heard or used (Ferand 1957, 1123).[19] In English, however, "improvise" is as good a choice as any, so long as we remember that the result is a "fantasia":

> One is actually improvising [a fantasia] only when one is heedless of what one plays, so that—were one to improvise in public in the best and truest manner—one [would] yield quite freely to whatever comes to mind.

A keyboardist who thought of *fantasiren* in these terms would presumably pay no attention to the responses of listeners.

At the opposite extreme are arguments that improvisation depends on exchanges between participants who are present in a particular type of venue. Stendhal, pretending to dispel the illusions of young ladies studying piano, vigorously denied that any interaction between instrumentalists and listeners could equal the warmth of the bonds between opera singers and listener-spectators in a theater: "Young ladies [studying piano] who know a bit about music will easily understand that the *nuances* which are to some extent improvised according to the immediate demands of spectators can only exist in song. They will understand that the miracles of music result from these nuances—miracles which can be transferred to instruments after the fact, in ordinary discourse, but which instruments are not capable of engendering" (Stendhal 1960, 380).[20] These remarks seem to imply that, detached from the circumstances in which they were generated, the "miracles" retain at least the possibility of evoking their original associations, but in fantasy rather than in face-to-face contact. (Chopin, of course, was by no means least among those who succeeded in transferring vocal "miracles" to instrumental discourse.)

Needless to say, arguments about how human musicality is activated (or inhibited) have not been confined to discussions of improvisation. Whether or not it is "proper" to compose a notated work at the keyboard is a familiar example of an issue that can only be debated by appealing to one or another conception of the musician's field of action. Historians and theorists seldom recognize how many fields of action were recognized and explored by the musicians of a given time and place. We often find it difficult to interpret the figurative language in which conceptions of the self in relation to others are articulated.

Without denying that studies of improvisatory practices must consider a number of factors, this essay has concentrated on certain ways of naming and talking about the types of human interaction that are presupposed, initiated, or enriched by improvisation. The fact that so many people have found such matters worthy of discussion helps to refute Maurice Bloch's well known thesis that "In a song . . . no argument or reasoning can be communicated, no adaptation to the reality of the situation is possible" (Bloch 1974, 71). Most improvisors know how to argue with plenty of songs and how to adapt to the reality of variable situations.

Notes

1. It is not uncommon for ethnomusicologists to observe that "recordings of apparently 'spontaneous' improvised African music reveal a consistency of performance which suggests that the musicians hold in their heads both the grammar of a musical system and the equivalent of a musical score" (Blacking 1995, 224; cf. Arom 1984, 51).

2. Compare Pierre Bourdieu's remark that "doubtless there are . . . grammarians of decorum able to state (and elegantly, too) what it is right to do and say, but never presuming to encompass in a catalogue of recurrent situations and appropriate conduct, still less in a fatalistic model, the 'art' of the *necessary improvisation* which defines excellence" (Bourdieu 1977, 8).

3. I am grateful to Amir Hassanpour for providing me with a copy of this text along with his English translation and notes. The story lays great emphasis on the zeal with which the younger singers do everything that the master (*westa*) might expect of a guest (*meyvan*), beginning with elaborate compliments and an offer to serve him "as long as we are alive."

4. In his translations of the musical portions of the *'Iqd al-farid* of Ibn 'Abd Rabbih, Farmer rendered the word *murtajal* as "improvising" (1941, 129) and as "extemporaneously" (1943, 278), both times in a context where the word refers to unaccompanied singing that is not necessarily improvised. His error found its way into al-Faruqi's glossary of Arabic musical terminology (1981, 110).

5. In Vahid Dastgerdi's edition of Nezāmi's *Khosrow and Shirin* (1954), this sequence is printed on pp. 355–78.

6. In the important treatise *Bohūr al-alhān* ("Meters of Melodies"), Nasir Forsat al-

Dowle Shirāzi (d. 1920) gives the texts of several *ghazals* of Ḥāfez and other poets (including himself), naming at least one *dastgāh* or *gūshe* to which each *ghazal* might be sung (Forsat al-Dowle Shirāzi, 1966). For those of Ḥāfez, at least three of his recommendations are consistent with choices made by the great singer Mahmūd Karimi, whose *radif* has been carefully transcribed and analyzed by Massoudieh (1978, 148–60, 130). Karimi's recorded performance in *dastgāh-e Navā* (OCORA 558 563) includes the *ghazal* "Dar hame deyr-e moghan nist chu man sheidā'i," for which Forsat recommends either *Navā* or *Chahārgāh* (Forsat 1966, 174). In the published *radif*, the *darāmad* of *Rāst Panjgāh* is presented with a *ghazal* ("Dar azal par to ve hosnat ze tajalli dam zad") that is appropriately sung in *Chahārgāh* or *Rāst Panjgāh* according to Forsat (155); likewise the *gūshe Neyshāburak* in the *dastgāh* of *Māhūr* is presented with one verse from a *ghazal* ("Vaqt rā ghanimat dān ūn qadr ke bet'vānî") that Forsat (180) describes as particularly effective in the *gūshe Azerbāyjāni*, which occurs in close proximity to *Neyshāburak*.

7. Owen Wright (1978, 180) unduly restricts the meaning of *talḥin* in this passage merely by adding an indefinite article: "to pass from each one to another related to it in the course of *a* composition is a source of greater splendour and freshness."

8. For the connotations of *autoschediasmāton* and *autoschediastike* in these sentences, consider the references in the *Iliad* (12.192, 15.510, 17.294) and the *Odyssey* (11.536) to fighting "at close quarters" *(autoschedios)*—i.e., with minimal opportunity to plan one's moves before making them. In Plato's dialogues, Socrates (*Euthyphro* 16a) speaks of "no longer through ignorance acting carelessly" *(autoschediazo),* and he maintains (*Menexenus* 235c) that "it is in no wise difficult to improvise" *(autoschediazein)* a speech. To a small group of listeners, Socrates (*Euthydemus* 278e) declares that "in my eagerness to listen to your wisdom I shall venture to improvise in your presence." Responding to Socrates on another occasion, Hermogenes (*Cratylus* 413d) charges that "you must have heard this from some one and are not inventing it yourself." (These translations are from the Loeb Classical Library editions.)

9. Ibn Sinā's commentary on this portion of the *Poetics* is translated by Dahiyat (1974, 79, 82): "[Poetry's] birth is, in the main, attributable to those natively endowed poets who extemporized poetry. . . . [Aristotle] added that the evidence that this is natural is that men, during debates and disputations, may extemporize, and by natural disposition, as much as half a line, i.e., six syllables."

10. For a penetrating study of the language used in translations and commentaries on Aristotle's *Rhetoric,* see Kirkendale 1979, 2–12, 42–44.

11. Charles Burney offered a more realistic answer to the question of how people managed before the invention of musical notation: "before that period, music must have been played extempore, or by memory" (1789, 152n).

12. "Il m'est arrivé d'entrer dans de pauvres maisons noircies par la fumée de tabac, et d'entendre tout à coup non-seulement la maîtresse, mais le maître du logis, improviser sur le clavecin, comme les Italiens improvisent en vers."

13. "Improviser sur un instrument complet, tel que le piano, la harpe, &c., est une source de bonheur pour les imaginations vives: il y a, je le sais, du plaisir à exécuter la musique des bons auteurs; mais il est impossible de se complaire à répéter souvent la meilleure sonate; car, de même que l'on rougit en société de raconter deux fois la même chose devant les mêmes personnes, on a une sorte de honte à reproduire les mêmes morceaux de musique. Combien au contraire il y a de resources à improviser! La mod-

estie d'une jeune femme, d'une demoiselle, n'est jamais compromise en nous dével-
oppant son âme toute entière dans le langage de la mélodie. Quel heureux expédient de
la pudeur, d'oser dire avec des sons ce qu'à peine le coeur ose avouer!"

14. "*Improvisieren*—die Geschicklichkeit eines Tonsetzers, über ein ihm noch unbe-
kanntes Gedicht sogleich aus dem Stegreife eine Komposition zu verfertigen und solche
zugleich singend unter der Begleitung eines Instrumentes vorzutragen. Dieses Improvisieren, wenn es nemlich nicht ohne alle vorhergegangene Überlegung des Textes ge-
schieht, kann sehr oft für den Tonsetzer ein Mittel werden, die Thätigkeit seines Genies
zu reitzen, oder sich in denjenigen Zustand zu versetzen, den man die Begeisterung
nennet" (Koch 1802, 778)

15. Rousseau's definition goes beyond that given in Oudin's *Dictionnaire* of 1660
("chanter sans préparation"): "*improviser*—C'est faire & chanter impromptu des Chan-
sons, Airs & paroles, qu'on accompagne communément d'une Guitarre ou autre pareil
instrument. Il n'y a rien de plus commun en Italie, que de voir deux Masques se rencon-
trer, se défier, s'attaquer, se riposter ainsi par des couplets sur le même air, avec une
vivacité de Dialogue, de Chant, d'Accompagnement dont il faut avoir été temoin pour
la comprendre. Le mot *improvisar* est purement Italien: mais comme il se rapporte à la
musique, j'ai été constraint de la franciser pour faire entendre ce qu'il signifie." Rousseau may not have been aware of the extent to which the *improvvisatori* made use of
conventional melody types.

16. "*improviser*—C'est faire et exécuter impromptu un morceau de musique vocale
ou instrumentale. Il y a d'excellens improvisateurs parmi les pianistes. En Italie,
on rencontre des chanteurs qui *improvisent* en même temps les paroles et la musique"
(Castil-Blaze 1821).

17. See Chopin's letter of 27 March 1830 to his friend Titus Woyciechowski, describing his improvisation in the National Theater of Warsaw five days earlier: "Nareszcie
improwizowałem, co się pierwszopiętrowym łożom bardzo podobało.—Jeżeli Ci mam
szczerze powiedzieć, to improwizowałem nie tak, jak miałem ochotę, bo to nie dla tego
świata było" (Sydow 1955, i, 115–16). French translation in Sydow 1953, 147: "Enfin,
j'improvisai, ce qui plut beaucoup aux loges du premier balcon. A te parler sincèrement
je n'improvisai pas de la manière dont j'avais envie de le faire, car cette manière n'aurait
point plu à ce monde-là."

18. See Chopin's letter of 23 December 1828 to Woyciechowski: "Wiesz, jak to wy-
godnie, kiedy się spać chce, a tu proszą o improwizacją. Dogódźże wszystkim! Rzadko
zdarzy się myśl podobna tej, co nieraz rano na Twoim pantalionie tak snadnie weszła
mi pod palce!" (Sydow 1955, i, 87). French translation in Sydow 1953, i, 93: "Tu sais
combien il est commode alors qu'on a envie de dormir d'improviser parce que quel-
qu'un vient de vous le demander. Il arrive bien rarement que l'on ait alors une idée
comparable à celles qui me venaient sous les doigts chez toi le matin lorsque je m'assey-
ais à ton pantaléon!" (Although the *pantaleon* was originally a large dulcimer invented
by Pantaleon Hebenstreit in the late seventeenth century, the term was later used for
small square pianos.)

19. The verb *phantasiren* is also used in Beethoven's conversation books for 1823
with respect to Liszt's concert of 13 April in Vienna (Köhler, Beck, and Brosche 1983:
186–87, 189).

20. "Les jeunes personnes qui savent un peu de musique comprendront facilement
que les *nuances* en parties improvisées d'après les exigences actuelles des spectateurs

ne peuvent exister que dans le chant, et que ce sont ces nuances qui produisent les miracles de la musique, miracles que l'on prête ensuite aux instruments dans le *discours ordinaire,* mais qu'ils sont incapables de faire naître."

References

Arom, Simha. 1984. "The Constituting Features of Central African Rhythmic Systems: A Tentative Typology." *The World of Music* 26(1):51–64.

Binesh, Taqi, ed. 1991. *Shahr-e Adwār-e 'Abdolqāder b. Gheybi al-Marāghi.* Tehran: Iran University Press.

Blacking, John. 1995. *Music, Culture, and Experience: Selected Papers of John Blacking.* Edited by Reginald Byron. Chicago Studies in Ethnomusicology. Chicago: University of Chicago Press.

Bloch, Maurice. 1974. "Symbols, Song, Dance and Features of Articulation: Is Religion an Extreme Form of Authority?" *Archives Européennes de Sociologie* 14:55–81.

Bourdieu, Pierre. 1977. *Outline of a Theory of Practice.* Translated by Richard Nice. Cambridge Studies in Social Anthropology, 16. Cambridge: Cambridge University Press.

Bower, Calvin, trans. 1989. *Fundamentals of Music* [by] *Anicius Manlius Severinus Boethius.* New Haven: Yale University Press.

Burney, Charles. 1789. *A General History of Music from the Earliest Ages to the Present Time.* Vol. 1. 2d ed. London: Charles Burney.

Butterworth, Charles E., trans. 1986. *Averroes' Middle Commentary on Aristotle's Poetics.* Princeton: Princeton University Press.

Castelvetro, Lodovico, trans. 1575. *Poetica d'Aristotele vulgarizzata et sposta.* Vienna: Stainhofer.

Castil-Blaze. 1821. *Dictionnaire de musique moderne.* Paris: Magasin de Musique de la Lyre Moderne.

Dahiyat, Ismail M., trans. 1974. *Avicenna's Commentary on the Poetics of Aristotle.* Leiden: E. J. Brill.

d'Erlanger, Rodolphe. 1930. *La musique arabe.* Vol. 1. Paris: Paul Geuthner.

During, Jean. 1994. *Quelque chose se passe: le sens de la tradition dans l'Orient musical.* Lagrasse: Éditions Verdier.

Farmer, Henry George. 1941. "Music: the Priceless Jewel." *Journal of the Royal Asiatic Society,* 22–30, 127–44.

———. 1943–44. "The Minstrels of the Golden Age of Islam." *Islamic Culture* 17: 273–81, 18:53–61.

al-Faruqi, Lois Ibsen. 1981. *An Annotated Glossary of Arabic Musical Terms.* Westport, Conn.: Greenwood Press.

Fattāhi Qāzi, Qader. 1970. *Manzūme-he kordi: Shor Mehmud-û Merzêngan.* Tabriz: Dāneshkade-he Adabiyāt-e Tabriz.

Ferand, Ernst T. 1957. "Improvisation." In *Die Musik in Geschichte und Gegenwart,* edited by Friedrich Blume, vol. 6, 1093–135. Kassel: Bärenreiter.

Forsat al-Dowle Shirāzi, Nasir. 1966 *Bohūr al-alhān.* 1913. Facsimile reprint, Tehran: Ketābforūshi-ye Forūghi.

Friedlein, Gottfried, ed. 1966. *Anicii Manlii Torquati Severini Boetii: De institutione arithmetica libri duo; De institutione musica libri quinque.* 1867. Reprint, Leipzig: B. G. Teubner.

Ghattās, 'Abd al-Malik Khashabah, and Mahmud Ahmad al-Hefni, eds. 1967. *Kitāb al-mūsiqá al-kabir, ta'lif abū Nasr Muhammad b. Muhammad b. Tarkhān al-Fārābi.* Cairo: Dar al-Katib al-'Arabi lil-Tibaah wa-al-Nashr.

Grétry, André Ernest Modeste. 1797. *Mémoires.* Paris: Imprimerie de la République.

————. 1803. *Méthode simple pour apprendre à préluder en peu de temps avec toutes les ressources de l'harmonie.* Paris: Imprimerie de la République.

Halliwell, Stephen. 1987. *The Poetics of Aristotle: Translation and Commentary.* Chapel Hill: University of North Carolina Press.

Hawkins, John 1963 *A General History of the Science and Practice of Music.* 1776. Reprint, New York: Dover.

al-Hefni, Mahmud Ahmad, and 'Abd al-Malik Khashabah Ghattās, eds. 1975. *Al-Kātib: Kitāb kamāl adab al-ghinā'.* Cairo: al-Hayat al-Misriyat al-Ammah lil-Kitab.

Kinsky, Georg. 1916. *Musikhistorisches Museum von Wilhelm Heyer in Cöln: Katalog.* Vol. 4. Cologne: J.P. Bachem; Leipzig: Breitkopf und Härtel.

Kirkendale, Warren. 1979. "Ciceronians versus Aristotelians on the Ricercar as Exordium." *Journal of the American Musicological Society* 32:1–44.

Koch, Heinrich Christoph. 1802. *Musikalisches Lexikon.* Frankfurt: Hermann.

Köhler, Karl-Heinz, Dagmar Beck, and Günter Brosche, eds. 1983. *Ludwig van Beethovens Konversationshefte.* Vol. 3. Leipzig: VEB Deutscher Verlag für Musik.

Maggi, Vincenzo, and Bartolomeo Lombardi. 1550. *In Aristotelis Librum de poetica communes explanationes.* Venice: Vincenzo Valgrisio.

Martini, Giovanni Battista. 1781. *Storia della musica.* Vol. 3. Bologna: Lelio della Volpe.

Massoudieh, Mohammad Taghi. 1978. *Radīf vocal de la musique traditionelle de l'Iran par Mahmūd-e Karīmī: transcription at analyse.* Tehran: Vezārat-e Farhang va Honar.

Morley, Thomas. 1597. *A Plaine and Easie Introduction to Practicall Musicke.* London: Peter Short.

Nezāmi Ganjavi. 1954. *Khosrow u Shirin.* Edited by Vahid Dastgerdi. Tehran: Ebn Sinā.

Nicholson, Reynard A. 1976 *The Kashf al-Mahjūb of al-Hujwiri: The Oldest Persian Treatise on Sufism.* 1911. Reprint, E. J. W. Gibb Memorial Series, 17. London: Luzac.

Pazzi, Alessandro. 1536. *Aristotelis Poetica . . . in latinum conversa.* Venice.

Piccolomini, Alessandro. 1575. *Annotationi . . . nel libro della Poetica d'Aristotele.* Venice: Guarisco.

Qazvini, Mirza Mohammad, ed. 1910. *Nezāmi 'Arūzi: Chahār Maqāla.* E. J. W. Gibb Memorial Series, 11/1. Cairo and Leiden: E. J. Brill.

Qureshi, Regula Burckhardt. 1986. *Sufi Music of India and Pakistan: Sound, Context and Meaning in Qawwali.* Cambridge Studies in Ethnomusicology. Cambridge: Cambridge University Press.

Robortelli, Francesco. 1548. *In librum Aristotelis De arte poetica explicationes.* Florence: Torrentino.

Rouget, Gilbert. 1980. *La musique et la transe: esquisse d'une théorie générale des relations de la musique et de la possession.* Paris: Gallimard. Published in English as *Music and Trance: A Theory of the Relations Between Music and Possession.* Chicago: University of Chicago Press, 1985.

Rousseau, Jean Jacques. 1768. *Dictionnaire de musique.* Paris: Duchesne.

Sawa, George. 1989. *Music Performance Practice in the Early Abbasid Era, 132–320* A.H./*750–932* A.D. Toronto: Pontifical Institute of Medieval Studies.

Segni, Bernardo, trans. 1549. *Rettorica et Poetica d'Aristotile tradotta di greco.* Florence: Torrentino.

Shiloah, Amnon, ed. and trans. 1972. *Al-Hasan b. Ahmad b. 'Ali al-Kātib: La perfection des connaissances musicales/Kitāb kamāl adab al-Ġinā'; Traduction et commentaire d'un traité arabe du XIᵉ siècle.* Paris: Paul Geuthner.

Staël, Germaine de. 1958. *De l'Allemagne.* 1813. Edited by la Comtesse Jean de Pange. Paris: Hachette.

Stendhal. 1960. *Vie de Rossini.* 1823. Edited by V. del Litto and Ernest Abravanel. Lausanne: Éditions Rencontre.

Sydow, Bronislaw Edouard, ed. and trans. 1953. *Correspondence de Frédéric Chopin: Vol. 1 L'aube, 1816–1831.* Paris: La Revue Musicale.

———, ed. 1955. *Korespondencja Fryderyka Chopina.* Warsaw: Państwowy Instytut Wydawniczy.

Thackston, W. M., Jr., ed. and trans. 1993. *Zahirüddin Muhammed Bâbur Mirza: Bâburnâma, Part Two.* Sources of Oriental Languages and Literatures, 18. Cambridge: Harvard University, Department of Near Eastern Languages and Civilizations.

Titon, Jeff Todd, ed. 1992. *Worlds of Music: An Introduction to the Music of the World's Peoples.* 2d ed. New York: McGraw-Hill.

Vettori, Pietro. 1560. *Commentarii in primum librum Aristotelis de Arte poetarum.* Florence: Successors of Bernardo Giunti.

Wright, Owen. 1978. *The Modal System of Arab and Persian Music,* A.D. *1250–1300.* London: Oxford University Press.

Yūsufi, Gholām Hossein, ed. 1994. *Oābus nāme-he 'Unsur al-Ma'āli Kai Kā'ūs b. Iskandar b. Qābus b. Wushmgir b. Ziyār.* Tehran: Enteshārāt-e 'Ilmi va Farhangi.

Zhukovsky, V.A., ed. 1994. *Kashf al-Mahjūb, tasnif-e Abu l-Hasan 'Ali b. 'Osmān al-Jullābi al-Hujviri al-Ghaznavi.* 1926. Reprint, Tehran: Ketābkhāneh-e Tahvori.

Chapter Two

Psychological Constraints on Improvisational Expertise and Communication

Jeff Pressing

This chapter builds on foundations set out in several previous publications, which surveyed fundamental issues in the psychology of improvised behavior and interdisciplinary resources for its modeling, culminating in a potentially computational theory of musical improvisation (Pressing 1984, 1988). The theory was applied to the micro- and macroanalysis of improvised keyboard music in a separate report (Pressing 1987). In this chapter I extend certain aspects of that previous work and evaluate its potential for further development. In particular, I pursue the idea of improvisation as a system of expertise, examining how improvisers adapt to or circumvent the psychological and cultural constraints under which they inevitably operate in the quest for increased fluency and efficacy of musical expression. I shall aim to draw cross-cultural conclusions, and not to confine the discussion to any particular repertoire, but the reader is urged to be alert to the possible effects of disproportionate extrapolation from my own areas of musical specialization.

General Principles of Expertise

Before focusing on improvisational expertise, it will be useful to review some general findings in the psychology of expertise. "Folk" Western psychology and lay opinion have, for many centuries, but particularly since the Renaissance, regarded expertise as the predominant result of natural gifts. This is the "innate talent" view of high accomplishment. In line with this traditional view, Galton (1979 [1869]) spelled out three central factors in developing expertise: innate ability, motivation, and effort. If the main effects of training are to asymptotically develop skill towards a plateau characteristic of the individual's potential, then it follows that innate ability will be the dominant distinguishing factor in expertise (Ericsson and Charness 1994).

In music, the idea of specially gifted individuals is virtually axiomatic in Western cultures, reflecting their emphasis on the individual. Naturally enough, it is built into the structure of musical instruction, particularly at intermediate to higher levels. University instructors speak of students with "cloth ears" who founder due to their lack of basic aptitudes required for competence.

But, as is now well known—at least among anthropologists and ethnomusicologists—the innate talent view of excellence is hardly a cultural universal.

As has often been noted, in a number of traditional cultures virtually everyone has a palpable degree of professional musical status (e.g., Blacking 1973; Feld 1984). Training is inclusive and competence seemingly pervasive, reflecting the effects of cultural and environmental factors. In fact, it appears that attribution of causes to outcomes in some traditional societies may more heavily and correctly weight contextual and interpersonal factors than in Western societies, which favor explanations based on individual traits, a bias called *fundamental attribution error* (Gleitman 1995). However, the idea of specialized and differential musical aptitude exists within the vast majority of all cultures.

The innate talent view has also been undermined by a range of more recent studies by psychologists, which are congruent with the ethnomusicological perspective. Substantial evidence now exists that it is primarily intensive practice of the right kind ("deliberate practice") that is linked with expert status, and that the sources of expertise might well be sought in the factors that predispose individuals towards such intensive practice (Ericsson, Krampe, and Tesch-Römer 1993). This kind of practice is individually tailored and targets particular subgoals that stand in definable relation to the central task. Typically, a deliberate practice regime is designed and executed under the guidance of an experienced teacher, operating within clear traditions. With respect to improvisation, the guidance component of deliberate practice may be achieved by working with a teacher in a directed situation, but also by aural absorption of examples of expert performance, study of theory and analysis, and interactive work in peer group ensembles during rehearsal and performance, which typically moves from an apprenticeship phase to full status membership, as documented by Berliner (1994) for the American jazz community.

Note that this emphasis on practice does not boil down to a simple nature/ nurture dichotomy. Instead we may note that deliberate practice taken to the degree required for high levels of skill is not typically pleasurable and ask: Why do people do it? Practice-predisposing factors will be partly, perhaps largely, environmental, based on the degree of support of parents, teachers, friends, peer groups, and general cultural forces. But they will also be affected by such personal factors as temperament, intrinsic motivation, ambition for rewards (high status, personal distinction, material gain, etc.), pleasureableness of the activity, and preferred activity level, which evidently may have genetic components.

These more personal factors have been the subject of considerable research, though primarily outside the field of music. And while personality is not the main focus here, a few comments are in order. For example, Cattell (1963) found that eminent researchers in the fields of physics, biology, and psychology could be distinguished from teachers and administrators in the same fields and from members of the general population on the basis of personality characteristics. Distinguished researchers were more self-sufficient, emotionally unstable, dominant, introverted, and reflective than the other groups. While there do not appear to be any structured examinations of personality profiles of improvisers along these lines, biographies of the personal lives of significant jazz musicians and eighteenth- and nineteenth-century Western improvisers seem at least roughly concordant with such conclusions. We do, however, have increasingly differentiated accounts of performing musicians' and composers' personality traits (e.g., Kemp 1996). It is found that personality traits of instrumentalists may vary with instrument, within the general ambit of musical personality, whereas composers show dispositions similar to those found in other creative fields, typically exhibiting introversion, independence, sensitivity, imagination, radicalism, and an attraction for complex and ambiguous symbolic enterprises (Kemp 1996). Although the cross-cultural limitations of these conclusions have been little examined, a reasonable starting suggestion for improvisers would appear to be that they would exhibit temperament and personality traits reflecting their dual status as real-time composers and musical performers.

One traditional aspect of the innate talent view has been the notion that expertise is founded on exceptional basic abilities: markedly superior levels of such things as vigilance or attentional focus, muscular strength, memory, hand-eye coordination, reaction speed, logical fluency, spatial perception, or speed and depth of associative thinking (Ericsson and Charness 1994). Yet when such ideas have been put to the test, they have not stood up well (Ericsson and Smith 1991): correlations of these factors with expertise are weak, and much stronger correlations are obtained with deliberate practice. For example, champion athletes perform remarkably in the context of their sport, but do not exhibit reaction times or perceptual acuity to simple stimuli that distinguish them from ordinary athletes or the public at large (Ericsson, Krampe, and Tesch-Römer 1993). Rather, experts develop domain-specific subskills. Although expertise should be facilitated by a good fit between an individual's palette of dispositions and the domain skill components, such dispositions may have a large environmental component.

In line with this, it turns out to be quite difficult in general to predict which children will become eventual experts. In music, despite the well-known anecdotal accounts of distinguished composers, many early blossoming prodigies do not later develop their projected potential and are often eventually surpassed by later starters (Ericsson and Charness 1994; Sloboda, Davidson, and Howe 1994). The effects of early intervention can be seen from two examples of the development of musical skills in children: (1) the success of the Suzuki method of piano and violin instruction, which has produced many instances of prodigy-like skill levels in those without apparent pre-existing dispositions to music; and (2) strong evidence that the learning of absolute pitch is highly linked to a critical assimilation period of approximately three to seven years of age, and that if suitable pitch labelling training is given in this period, a substantial fraction (perhaps 50 percent of all children, rather than the current 0.01 percent) can develop absolute pitch (Takeuchi and Hulse 1993).

To receive optimal benefits from training and practice, individuals need to monitor their results with full and sustained attention. This level of concentration is effortful and fatiguing, and can only be maintained to a limited extent each day. In many cases this period is about four hours, and several studies point to the morning as the best time for it within the day (Ericsson and Charness 1994).

Overall, what are the results of all this deliberate practice? Across domains the story is the same: the development and refinement of domain-specific skills and knowledge structures, and progressive physiological and cognitive adaptations. Highly expert performance typically reflects extreme adaptations, achieved through decades of effort, to a quite specific constellation of task requirements. The scope and importance of various constituent subskills will typically develop and change over the course of learning and training. Transfer of expertise between different skills is weak; experts do not show natural advantages outside their specialist domains, unless the new and old skills are extremely congruent. From this vantage point, it is not surprising that the musical skills of sight-reading, memorized performance, composition, and improvisation are seemingly quite independent, even though they share an extensive knowledge base. This independence further refines the idea of a separate musical intelligence (Gardner 1983), and indeed there are a number of reported cases of selective loss of musical subskills due to neurological damage (e.g., Sergent 1993, describing Ravel) and instances of "idiot savants" with considerable skill in musical improvisation (Hermelin, O'Connor, Lee, and Treffert 1989).

Overall, fluency in real-time adaptive skills that mirror improvisation is less well researched, but in many real situations, adaptation to changing conditions is one hallmark of expertise. This has been examined in the classroom teaching of mathematics, for example, which can be considered a case of improvised speech. Livingston and Borko (1990) found that experts showed greater fluency than novices in improvising activities and explanations in response to student questions and comments. They attributed this to the fact that the novices' cognitive schemata for content and pedagogy are "less elaborated, interconnected, and accessible than those of the experts" (Livingston and Borko 1990).

Psychological Foundations of Improvisational Expertise

In many ways, improvisational skill fits in quite well with the general principles of expertise enunciated above. However, there are some further considerations.

Sloboda (1991) has drawn attention to the distinction between receptive and productive musical expertise, which parallels the competence/performance split in natural language theory (Chomsky 1957), pointing out that members of the society at large achieve a sound level of culturally based receptive "expertise" without any formal instruction. Such knowledge is implicit, and it may be represented, for example in the specific case of traditional tonal relations, as a set of (hard and soft) rules (e.g., Lehrdahl and Jackendoff 1983), a framework of probabilities of note incidence or pairs (Krumhansl 1990), distances between notes in a tonal space (Shepard 1982), or weights in a neural network (Bharucha 1987), to mention only some of the better known approaches. The idea that such perceptual "expertise" is common to experts and nonexperts is supported by studies showing similar segmentation of atonal melodies by the two groups (Deliege and El Ahmahdi 1990), similar structural classification of tonal melodies by the two groups (Bigand 1990), and similar patterns of preferential structural level recall by musicians and nonmusicians (Sloboda and Parker 1985). In the last case, higher order structural features were found to be preserved at the expense of detail for both groups.

In one sense, this is not surprising. Most musicians primarily play and compose for nonmusicians, so it is to be expected that similar cognitive structures will emerge in music perception. Such shared knowledge must form the foundation for appreciation by nonexperts of improvisational skill. Yet there is a well-known gap between the preferences of progressive professional musicians, notably including contemporary Western improvisers, and those of nonmusicians, which is particularly evident outside of mainstream classical and popular repertoires. This may be due to very different perceptual emphases. For example, Wolpert (1990) found that musicians and nonmusicians focused on quite different aspects of the music in performing a recognition task: nonmusicians responded overwhelmingly to instrumentation, whereas musicians based their responses overwhelmingly on melodic structure and harmonic accompaniment. Such differences are probably widespread: specialist appreciation of specialist music occurs in many cultures (e.g., within classical traditions of India and Indonesia).

One central thread will be developed in the sections below: how improvisation is critically shaped by often rather severe constraints on human information-processing and action. For the improviser must effect real-time sensory and perceptual coding, optimal attention allocation,[1] event interpretation, decision-making, prediction (of the actions of others), memory storage and recall, error correction, and movement control, and further, must integrate these processes into an optimally seamless set of musical statements that reflect both a personal perspective on musical organization and a capacity to affect listeners. Both speed and capacity constraints apply. To circumvent these limitations, certain tools are used, representing the results of deliberate practice. Only if the coherence problem is addressed with a sufficiently powerful set of skills and tools can the performer operate substantially on a high level of musical thinking and interaction, exhibiting sensitivity to nuance, context, development, and reference structures.

THE REFERENT

To achieve maximal fluency and coherence, improvisers, when they are not performing free (or "absolute") improvisation, use a *referent,* a set of cognitive, perceptual, or emotional structures (constraints) that guide and aid in the production of musical materials (Pressing 1984). In jazz, for example, the referent is the song form, including melody and chords; a survey of examples is given in Pressing 1984.

The use of a referent helps to enhance performance outcome in a number of ways: (*a*) Since the referent provides material for variation, the performer needs to allocate less processing capacity (attention) to selection and creation of materials. (*b*) Since the referent is normally available well before performance, pre-analysis allows construction of one or more optimal structural segmentations of the referent and also a palette of appropriate and well-rehearsed resources for variation and manipulation, reducing the extent of decision-making required in performance. (*c*) Specific variations can be precomposed and rehearsed, reducing the novelty of motoric control and musical logic of successful solutions of the improvisational constraints, and providing fallback material in the case of a temporary lack of invention, possibly helping to reduce performance anxiety. (*d*) Since referent information is shared, the need for detailed attention to the perception of the parts of other performers is reduced—for example, a more limited set of cues may suffice to track the behaviour of other performers. In addition, (*e*) when the referent is *in-time* (that is, it specifies time relations, either ordinally, absolutely, or relatively), as is common, it reduces the attention required on the task of producing effective medium to long-range order, since the referent, in part, provides this. By common channeling of thought and action across the ensemble, it also increases the likelihood of synergetic serendipity, which can have a boosting effect on the course of an improvisation.

The degree of processing reduction enabled by referent use will depend on the information content of the referent and on the performers' depth of familiarity with it—and on its developmental potentials. The effect of this reduction is to free up more processing resources for perception, control, and interplayer interaction, increasing the chances of reaching a higher artistic level.

The referent's role is not only that of increasing processing efficiency. It also provides material with emotional and structural foundations honed to engage the listener and performer and reinforce piece identity within and across different performances. Such foundations will guide the production of expectancies in musical improvisation (Schmuckler 1990). Since one prominent cognitive theory of the origin of musical emotion is via the creation and selective frustration, delay, or confirmation of expectancies (Meyer 1956, 1973; Dowling and Harwood 1986; Narmour 1977; Jackendoff 1991), this suggests that referent interaction may have a powerful role in the capacity of improvisation to communicate emotion, which presumably is heightened by the immediacy of relevance and topicality of control that improvisation can reflect.

THE KNOWLEDGE BASE

Another tool for improvisational fluency arises from the creation, maintenance, and enrichment of an associated knowledge base, built into long-term memory. One difference between experts and nonexperts is in the richness and refinement of organization of their knowledge structures. Chase and Simon (1973) established immediate access to relevant knowledge as a major dimension distinguishing masters, experts, and novices. This results in better solutions, determined faster, and is clearly applicable to musical improvisation.

The novice has a set of techniques that are incomplete in detail and poorly linked. In other words, the invocation of a technique or class of techniques is strongly context-specific. (For example, the novice jazz improviser may only be able to execute a riff in certain keys.) Links between techniques and materials are sparse, limiting the capacity for generalization. The distinguished expert has materials that are known in intimate detail, and from differing perspectives, and the various materials or modules are cross-linked by connections at various levels of the hierarchical knowledge structure. Part of the effect of improvisational practice is to make motorically transparent by overlearning what has been conceptually mastered. (For example, in achieving top-level jazz improvisational expertise, chord voicings are typically practiced in all inversions and spacings; motifs are mastered in all keys and with varying rhythmic designs and tempi.) Declarative knowledge (facts) about procedures are folded in with direct procedural knowledge, as part of the process of constructing useful generalized motor programs. (A generalized motor program, as described in Keele, Cohen, and Ivry 1986, is a parametrically tunable control structure used by the motor system to effect a result.)

The improviser shares the culturally predicated "passive expertise" referred to above, and also more specialized and explicit knowledge from his or her role in nonimprovisational production activities like composition, sight-reading, and recreative performance. There is also a large knowledge set accrued via improvisational practice, rehearsal, analysis, selective listening, and performance, and it contains elements that may be declarative or procedural (Pressing 1988), object- or process-oriented (Pressing 1984), and either explicit or implicit.

Overall, the knowledge base will include musical materials and excerpts, repertoire, subskills, perceptual strategies, problem-solving routines, hierarchical memory structures and schemas, generalized motor programs, and more. It is a cauldron of devices collected and fine-tuned on the basis of optimizing improvisatory performance. One task of pedagogy is to systematize these elements, but this systematization can never be complete; individual differences in subskills and orientations to artistic output require that programs of optimal operation be individually tailored.

As with the referent, the musical knowledge base is not purely "engineered" by considerations of performance efficiency; it encodes the history of compositional choices and predilections defining an individual's personal style. Two drives, one towards efficacy of action, and one towards artful expression, primarily shape the selection of information and performance resources in real time, and guide their integration.

SPECIALIST MEMORY
Experts have excellent domain-specific memory coding aptitudes, which they achieve by chunking simple memory elements into larger groups, based on developed special structures in long-term memory (Ericsson and Charness 1994). For example, chess masters remember chess positions with an accuracy and rapidity far exceeding that of novices, but only when the positions correspond to plausible game positions. Their memory for random arrangements of pieces is not superior (Chase and Simon 1973).

Specific training has been shown to produce some remarkable effects, circumventing well-established "universal" memory limitations, notably the short-term memory capacity of 7 ± 2 "chunks" (Miller 1956). For example, Chase and Ericsson's (1981) subject "SF," starting with normal short-term memory capacity of about seven numbers, learned over the course of about 250 hours of practice to memorize random eighty-digit strings of numbers (presented one per second) after only one hearing. This memory skill was confined to numbers; his ability to retain syllables or other small items remained at a normal level.

Chase and Ericsson showed that SF's remarkable development was based on the construction of an elaborate system of mnemonics. Primarily, SF segmented numbers into groups of three or four, interpreting these groups for the purpose of storage and recall predominantly as times to run a race. Significantly, SF was himself a talented long-distance runner. When the race time mnemonic could not apply, he used other techniques, such as interpretation of three digits as ages (with one decimal point). This circumvention of normal basic human capacities via specialized training has also been found for some other variables, notably reaction time (Ericsson and Charness 1994).

Nearly all cases of exceptional memory are domain-specific, and retention of sequences or arrays of digits is the most common locus. However, dedicated "memory experts" can achieve wider powers of generalization, apparently due to the expenditure of time to create special memory structures in a range of domains.

These and other studies have shown that memory experts go to a great deal of trouble to have handy coding and "chunking" facilities available. The order in the information needed to allow chunking is either discovered by analysis, or, if it is not present, imposed by a personally meaningful correspondence scheme (a repertoire of pattern reference and analysis routines). These studies raise the possibility that special training may be able to improve musical memory dramatically, with potentially powerful effects on improvisation.

The ability to remember music in nearly complete detail after only one or two hearings and reproduce it on an instrument is a rare and valuable skill. We have anecdotal evidence of such aptitudes in some musical prodigies, such as the young Mozart, and also more systematic studies, such as Revesz's (1925) examination of the Hungarian prodigy Erwin Nyherigazy. Some studies of autistic savants have reported this ability (Sloboda, Hermelin, and O'Connor 1985), suggesting that it can be fairly independent of other musical subskills.

We also have anecdotal evidence about such effects in Renaissance and baroque requirements for candidates for employment as organists. It was commonly stated that candidates should be able to improvise to a set melody and then subsequently notate the improvisation (Ferand 1961). By the standards of today's workers in improvisation, or indeed any form of music, this qualifies as exceptional memory. Although this evidence is anecdotal in the sense that it does not occur under well-defined task conditions, the fact that it was written into position descriptions and formed the basis of commercial evaluations means that its reality was accepted by the experts of the day. On balance, it seems possible that one or more sets of successful training techniques for exceptional musical memory have been lost. Interestingly, although researchers have shown that many exceptional memory powers can actually be taught to the general population, efforts to teach this immediate musical memory skill to novices have not been successful (Ericsson and Charness 1994).

Nevertheless, impressive memory feats not linked to improvisation are routinely required of highly trained Western musicians. Some orchestral conductors conduct without the score. Classical concerto or solo performers perform vast stretches of fixed music from memory, aided presumably by tonal "chunking" procedures. Studies have shown that memorization of atonal works is much more difficult (Sloboda, Hermelin, and O'Connor 1985). Yet a small fraction of performers can readily memorize complex twentieth-century works that do not follow traditional tonal schemas, and the techniques they use to do so are so far not well understood. For example, Michael Kieran Harvey is a distinguished Australian pianist who selectively performs such contemporary music, sometimes memorizing highly complex pieces such as Carl Vine's recently composed twenty-minute *Piano Sonata* in a few weeks' time for a premiere. Harvey recounts that he sometimes practices improvising in the style of the piece as a safety net against memory lapses, and he also consciously codes the musical materials in a number of parallel independent formats to facilitate remembering (M. Harvey, personal communication).

The optimal memorization skills required of performers are inevitably linked to the nature of the music, and particularly its position on the improvisation/composition continuum. For example, in traditional drum ensemble music of the Ewe people of Ghana, the master drummer functions as a master of ceremonies, and his selective recall of patterns from a vast repertoire of possibilities triggers corresponding precomposed steps from the dancers. He (or rarely, she) may also embellish the patterns to prolong and heighten their effect (Locke 1979). In some cases, the cuing may operate in reverse—the lead dancer may begin a dance pattern which the master drummer and the support drums must respond to appropriately (Kobla Ladzkepo, personal communication). In this case the memory is not based on the idea of a through-composed piece, but on a palette of materials which may be drawn on to bring forth a certain range of musical and choreographic effects, a system closely allied to the formulaic composition model of improvisation (Smith 1991).

GENERATIVE AND EVALUATIVE PROCESSES
Pressing (1988) developed a theory of the improvisational generation of musical behavior, based upon the continuity of parallel representations of musical structure in motor, musical, acoustic, and other aspects. Each aspect was decomposed into three kinds of arrays: features (e.g., loudness), objects (e.g., a motif), and processes (e.g., sequencing of a motif). An interruptable associative process based on ongoing evaluation of previous musical events was considered to guide the generation of new material, subject to constraints such as training, the referent, memory, and an apposite knowledge base. Motifs and other related events were considered to form event clusters, groupings of events representing structural boundaries in the produced material. The theory was applied to the analysis of two piano improvisations (Pressing 1987) and has been reviewed and addressed by a number of writers. It is necessary to mention that it has been on occasion drastically misrepresented (Sawyer 1992). For further details see Pressing (1988).

The theory is quite general, which is both its strength and its weakness. It can show how musical materials of any particular class can be generated, based on the inputting of a highly detailed compositional/improvisational knowledge base. It operates at a general level, and does not spell out exactly how real-time constraints of memory and attention are to be accommodated. It cannot claim to represent uniquely, or even minimally (in the sense of Occam's razor), cognitive and other processes underlying improvisation. It seems likely that no theory will be able to do this because there is no unique way to generate or analyze a certain set of musical patterns, and we lack a convincing evaluative protocol for creative musical output which might unambiguously distinguish between alternative cognitive models (Pressing 1988), although brain imaging techniques may yet provide some valuable insights. The same problem occurs in the analysis of "fixed" music. Even well-known and very short examples (e.g., the single *Tristan* chord) can generate marked analytical disputation and diversity. Small wonder, then, that a theory of generative processes underlying adaptive musical creation should be nonunique.

CULTURAL CONSTRAINTS
The constraints of the culture on improvisational expertise are in many ways shared by the traditions of composed music, and include such things as musical styles, repertoire, effects of media, employment opportunities, instrument types and availability, social status of musicians, degree of incorporation of music in rituals and social events, and so on. Specific improvisational constraints also occur, such as the degree of developmental priming of improvisational competence, the status given to creative or novel musical behavior, and the size and number of societal subgroups that provide a subculture of appreciation for real-time musical composition.

IMPROVISATION AND EMOTION
One function of music is to suggest or mediate a range of emotional responses (Sloboda 1991). One prominent theory of musical emotion, as mentioned above, is based on the creation of expectation. Such expectations can only be created in listeners if they are engaged by the music and if they understand enough of the musical language (implicitly) to perceive expectancy manipulations, such as key modulations, delayed nonharmonic tone resolutions, added rhythmic and dynamic nuance, or, in the case of improvisation, unexpected notes, timbres, or rhythmic devices.

Adult listeners from a common cultural base tend to agree about the emotional associations of different passages of (composed) music, as measured by the adjectives used to describe the passages (Hevner 1936). This consensus of judgment of emotion has also been found for improvised music. Behrens and Green (1993) showed that the improvisations of vocalists and string, brass, and percussion players could successfully express particular emotions (sadness, anger, fright), as judged by listeners of varied levels of musicianship. Success in transmission, however, did vary with instrument and emotion expressed.

Such commonality of judgment of affect acts as a foundation for the societal functions of music. Emotional interchange between performers and listeners is a vital part of a great many formats for music presentation, and it assumes a particular power in the ecstatic improvisatory components of certain types of music, such as the call-and-response church and cult traditions of Africa and the Americas, and much secular Arabic musical performance, as in the modern *tarab* style. This culminates in a view that creativity is not individual-centered and creator-focused, but collectively based and socially inspired (Racy 1991).

Musical improvisation continues to be used in therapeutic situations to facilitate arousal and engagement and enhance social interaction, and can succeed in drawing out patients, for example some autistic children, who are otherwise nearly unreachable (Preistley 1987; Edgerton 1994; Gunsberg 1991).

External Aids for Improvisational Coherence

The coherence problem in improvisation can also be addressed with external aids. Here I will discuss the two main forms these take in contemporary Western music: notation and real-time computer assistance.

THE NOTATIONAL CODING OF REFERENTS

Memory is one repository for the referent; real-time display, that is, notation, is another. Many improvisation traditions use no notation; of those that do, there is a range of relations between notation and production. Different traditions of improvisation make different uses of notation, and such notation is linked to the compositional partner system, when it exists. Fundamentally, notation for improvisation must use symbols that are meaningful (hence typically related to an allied compositional system), yet substantively indeterminate. There must be some fuzziness or ambiguity or conflict or incompleteness in the symbol set, and this should be an order of magnitude greater than the fuzziness of any associated notated compositional tradition.

The form of this indeterminacy is perhaps best seen by a look at nomenclature in the best known contemporary Western improvisation tradition, jazz. Jazz notation adopts a modified version of classical notation with respect to the placement of notes in time, the difference being largely due to "swing." Chord symbols have also been borrowed from classical notation, but the differences go deeper. Specifically, the jazz chord symbol places the twelve pitch classes into one of two functional sets. For example, the symbol C9(♯11) partitions the twelve pitch classes into the two sets:

> chord tones — {C, E, G, B♭, D, F♯} = *C*, and
> nonchord tones — {D♭, E♭, F, A♭, A, B} = *NC.*

Essentially, a note's membership in one of the two sets triggers a set of constraints on how it may function (its placement in time and register, and in relation to other notes). The precise acts that may be considered consistent with a given chord symbol cannot be exhaustively spelled out, due to the infinite nature of variation, although one could imagine computing a function that would assess the degree of consistency of a given voicing or musical statement with a given chord symbol. (In general, of course, there could be effects due to previous events by the performer and, for group improvisation, previous or concurrent events of other ensemble members.) Such a function would operate by examining the constraints that are implicit in the chord symbol. The constraints are surprisingly extensive, and so I shall not be exhaustive, but simply illustrative.

First, only tones from the *C* set should be presented as stable notes. Second, although the chord symbol does not specify the octave placement of the pitch classes making up the chord, there are certain relational expectations (see below). Third, for a chording support instrument such as the piano or guitar, the chord symbol must be normally realized with a majority of the *C* tones, and although any note may be omitted, the most essential notes are usually considered to be the third (E) and the seventh (B♭). These notes are singled out because they characterize the basic chord color most succinctly (since root and fifth are more readily guided by contextual functional expectations, and upper extensions are less prescriptive). They are also the most important notes from the standpoint of resolution: normally a dominant function chord of this type will proceed to a tonic function or substitution chord of F (e.g., I, vi) of some type, and the resolutions E to F and B♭ to A or A♭ (depending on F chord color) are critical elements in the voice leading. Individual style is partly expressed through patterns of preference in accepting or acting against such constraints.

Chord voicings that fail to meet these criteria will be unsuitable. Example 2.1 shows several voicings built solely from the notes of the *C* set. The chords labeled (a) and (b) are suitable voicing realizations, showing that doubling of tones, the placement of the fifth of the chord in the bass, and omission of the tonic are appropriate variations, as commonly established in jazz. Example 2.1 (c) is an unsuitable realization because, although it does not contradict the tones in the chord set, it does not contain enough essential notes to spell it out, and misleadingly suggests G as a tonic. The chord labeled (d) fails to be suitable for two reasons: weakly, because the F♯–G dissonance is placed at the nonpreferred interval of the minor ninth (Pressing 1978); and more significantly, because the placement of the ninth of the set (D) in the bass creates a configuration there, D-C-F♯, which strongly suggests a D chord, since the bass register arrangement of tones is more powerful than the treble register in suggesting the roots of jazz (and other tonal) chords.

Melodies improvised over chord symbols must also articulate or at least be compatible with the chord symbol, and so the chord symbol can be considered to also present linear (melodic) constraints. Chord tones normally act as (relatively) stable melodic entities; nonchord pitch classes are associated with dependence on other notes, and have roles of dissonance, their genesis and use deriving predominantly from linear factors. Generally, each *NC* tone resolves to a *C* tone.

At a more detailed level, operating upon each set are distinct traditions of note use and connection based on sound ideals and incorporation in the motifs that constitute the foundations of improvisational and compositional repertoire. The chord symbol does not specify the order in which tones must be played, but it does provide a constraint on that order. For example, the dissonant note F in the *NC* set normally resolves to E in the *C* set, although the rarer resolutions to F♯ or G in the *C* set are also possible. Melodies that do not resolve

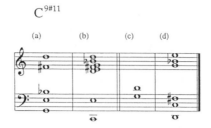

Example 2.1

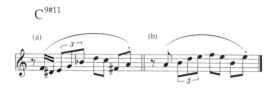

Example 2.2

"correctly" will create effects that may be judged as incompatible with the tradition, uninteresting, or unmusical (e.g., they have not been correctly pre-heard), though of course context can modify such judgments. Melodies that exhibit stability for certain *NC* set elements may be judged wrong. This is shown in Example 2.2. The melodic figure (a) is compatible with the chord symbol because the only *NC* tones, F and D♯, are treated as local neighbor tones and hence are dependent on the following E, a *C* element. The triplet figure also arpeggiates the chordal structure and increases compatibility. Example 2.2 (b) fails to fit, in the absence of other contextual factors, because it emphasizes the note B, an *NC* set member, without providing a linear resolving tone. The motif would be more compatible with a B half-diminished chord, which is structurally incompatible which the given chord symbol.

The interpretation of notes here is also governed by historical accretions, producing, among other effects, ambiguity and multiple reference. For example, the *C* note F♯ may act as a stable tone (e.g., ending a phrase), or it may function dependently and move to G, referencing the traditional tonal resolution of this chromatic alteration of the scale. Because jazz tonality is based on the foundation of classical tonality, such ambiguity is not moot, but a central aspect of the richness of meaning that can be effected by its musical manipulations.

Thus, a flow of chord symbols provides a reference base with which to evaluate ambiguities, deviations, and expectations. This is the nature of creative traditions in music. Only when some norm or context is established can expectations and deviations from the norm make significant psychological contributions to musical perception, cognition, and affect.

What happens when we go beyond, to those symbols whose meanings are somewhat less specific, and whose traditions of interpretation are less well developed? Here it is difficult to make comprehensive statements, and we verge into an area that has substantial overlap with graphic notation.

Without a pretense of comprehensiveness, it may be useful to look at a recent compilation of notated compositions for improvisers as a source of information. This book, Compositions for Improvisers (Pressing 1994), provides a compilation of significant written compositions for improvising musicians dating from the early days of the "white invasion" of Australia. The pieces were collected on the basis of invitation and a national appeal to composing improvisers, and can be classified as shown in table 2.1.

Because of uncertainty about the best classification of some of the pieces, several were entered in more than one category; however, these figures may give a representative impression of types of work in this subfield of improvisation, at least in Australia. All the pieces have referents (obviously), and the majority have a temporal backbone. There is a clear attempt in nearly all pieces to guide the interpretations of the performers in a coherent fashion, as shown by the adoption of traditional devices like melodies, rhythmic vamps, preset material, legends, and chord symbols. However, a minority of pieces are intentionally quite nonspecific in many musical dimensions, as befits a creative art.

Three examples of the less traditional forms follow. Example 2.3 is a tiny excerpt from Keith Humble's massive process *Nunique* (1968–95), entitled *The Anonymous Butchery,* which challenges ideas of special competence and the use of sound in musical performance. Example 2.4 shows *Duo 1,* from *Duos 1.2.3.* by Robert Rooney (1965), which can be played as a duo or, preferably, as a trio, with the third player improvising freely in parallel. This piece has a legend (which space does not permit to be included), which specifies gestural and timbral (but not pitch) meanings for the symbols. Example 2.5 shows two

Table 2.1. Structural classification of notations for improvisers in a recent compilation (Pressing 1994)

Piece Format	Incidence (%)
1. Melody and chord symbols	35
2. Set of accessible resources, largely traditionally notated	20
3. Special graphic notations + legend	15
4. Full score with separate improvisational sections	7.5
5. Verbal instructions alone	7.5
6. Special instrumental preparations* + legend	5
7. Composed parts with parallel improvised parts	5
8. Text without legend	5

*E.g., prepared piano.

THE ANONYMOUS BUTCHERY

For a large number of people.

Material: Each person has a large piece of white paper.
Duration: 15".

Everybody slowly hides their faces behind the paper. They delicately shake the paper - no sounds!
They drop the paper all together.

Example 2.3. From *Nunique* (1968–95) by Keith Humble (Pressing 1994).

Duo 1

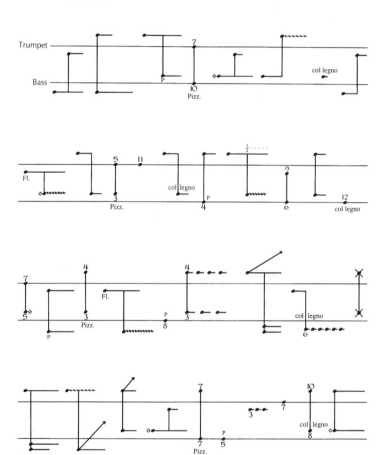

Example 2.4. From *Duos 1.2.3.* (1965) by Robert Rooney (Pressing 1994).

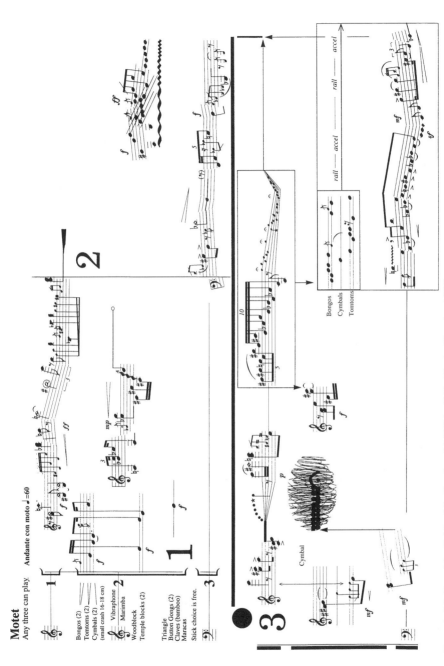

Example 2.5. From *The Guide of the Perplexed* (1993) by Felix Werder (Pressing 1994).

"modules" from Felix Werder's *The Guide of the Perplexed* (1993). The composer has given a legend here but encourages the performers to make their own adaptations and to freely pick and choose among possible interpretations. None of these pieces refers to a standard tradition of improvisational interpretation, although Rooney's work evolved as repertoire for a particular ensemble, which came to its own interpretive traditions over years of work.

INTERACTIVE COMPUTER SYSTEMS

Interactive computer systems have developed extensively since the early 1980s and yielded numerous aesthetic and cultural implications, particularly for music. "Intelligent instruments" have been extensively built with the capacity to do such things as compose along with a performer in real time, act as an improvising accompanist or aural environment, provide a freshly created referent for interaction, or infer tempo and act to drive production of prerecorded material. New terms have come into existence for different kinds of human-computer interaction, among them *composed improvisation, extended instruments, hyperinstruments,* and *real-time performance synthesis,* about which I have written extensively elsewhere (for reviews, see Pressing 1992; Rowe 1992). Virtual musical instruments (instruments existing in virtual computer environments, accessed for example by glove controllers) and musicogenic displays (musical or visual or haptic displays generated by the conversion of information, which may be performance information) have been developed in the 1990s, setting new benchmarks in, if not fundamentally redefining, the improvisation/composition continuum (for a review, see Pressing 1997).

Such systems have considerable potential for providing assisted musical competence, including improvisational competence, to those with mental or physical disabilities. The landscape of musical expertise will never be quite the same, and it remains to be seen to what extent such systems, even if only in an assisting role, can approach the capacity of the autonomous skilled human expert in terms of contextual fluency, interpersonal interaction, and emotional expression.

Conclusion

The discussion here suggests that the approach to improvisation via standard expertise theory is in many ways fruitful. In particular, the existence of psychological constraints to the real-time problem solving which underlies improvisation shapes the construction of special memory, knowledge, decision-making, and generative structures adapted to minimize the impact of those constraints. External tools such as notation and real-time interactive computer systems also serve similar functions, though not exclusively. Such minimization of impact allows the improviser to operate at a higher and more long-range level of musical discourse, leaving attentional resources free for deeper musical control, heightened emotional effects and greater interaction with the audience and co-improvisers.

Notes

1. Standard theories of attention with respect to improvisation are reviewed in Pressing 1984, although attention can be justifiably criticized as a concept whose vagueness limits its explanatory power. However, recent Positron Emission Tomography research makes plausible a neurophysiological description of selective attention as selective activation and deactivation of particular brain structures or regions, a fact which sits well with resource models of attention, particularly multiple resource models. The multiple resource perspective on attention suggests that there are multiple and at least partially distinct pools of attention. This view is favored in so-called "human factors" research (Proctor and Van Zandt 1994). For example, Wickens (1984) proposed a three-dimensional framework of resources based on stage of processing (input, central processing, response), type of information coding, and input/output modality. Evidently, in such a situation, attentional constraints can be reduced by learning to optimally spread processing demands across different resource dimensions; skill in such optimal dynamic allocation may be a significant component of improvisational efficiency.

References

Behrens, G. A., and S. B. Green, 1993. "The Ability to Identify Emotional Content of Solo Improvisations Performed Vocally and on Three Different Instruments." *Psychology of Music,* 21(1):20–33.

Berliner, P. 1994. *Thinking in Jazz: The Infinite Art of Improvisation.* Chicago: University of Chicago Press.

Bharucha, J. J. 1987. "Music Cognition and Perceptual Facilitation: A Connectionist Framework." *Music Perception* 5:1–30.

Bigand, E. 1990. "Abstraction of Two Forms of Underlying Structure in a Tonal Melody." *Psychology of Music* 19:45–59.

Blacking, John. 1973. *How Musical Is Man?* London: Faber and Faber.

Cattell, R. B. 1963. "The Personality and Motivation of the Researcher from Measurements of Contemporaries and from Bibliography." In *Scientific Creativity: Its Recognition and Development,* edited by C. R. Taylor and F. Barron, 119–31. New York: Wiley.

Chase, W. G., and K. A. Ericsson. 1981. "Skilled Memory." In *Cognitive Skills and Their Acquisition,* edited by J. R. Anderson, 141–89. Hillsdale, N. J.: Lawrence Erlbaum.

———. 1982. "Skill and Working Memory." In *The Psychology of Learning and Motivation,* edited by G. H. Bower, vol. 16, 1–58. New York: Academic Press.

Chase, W. G., and H. A. Simon. 1973. "The Mind's Eye in Chess." In *Visual Information Processing,* edited by W. G. Chase, 215–81. New York: Academic Press.

Chomsky, Noam. 1957. *Syntactic Structures.* The Hague: Mouton.

Deliege, I., and A. El Ahmahdi. 1990. "Mechanisms of Cue Extraction In Musical Groupings: A Study of Perception, on *Sequenza VI* for Viola Solo by Luciano Berio." *Psychology of Music* 19:18–44.

Dowling, W. J., and D. L. Harwood. 1986. *Music Cognition.* New York: Academic Press.

Edgerton, Cindy Lu. 1994. "The Effect of Improvisational Music Therapy on the Communicative Behaviors of Autistic Children." *Journal of Music Therapy* 31(1):31–62.

Ericsson, K. A., and N. Charnoss. 1994. "Expert Performance: Its Structure and Acquisition." *American Psychologist* 49:725–47.

Ericsson, K. A., R. T. Krampe, and C. Tesch-Römer. 1993. "The Role of Deliberate Practice in the Acquisition of Expert Performance." *Psychological Review* 100: 363–406.

Ericsson, K. A., and J. Smith. 1991. "Prospects and Limits of the Empirical Study of Expertise: an Introduction." In *Toward a General Theory of Expertise,* edited by K. A. Ericsson and J. Smith, 1–38. Cambridge: Cambridge, University Press.

Feld, Steven. 1984. "Sound Structure as Social Structure." *Ethnomusicology* 28: 383–409.

Ferand, Ernst. 1961. *Improvisation in Nine Centuries of Western Music* (in German). Cologne: Arno Volk Verlag.

Galton, F. 1979. *Hereditary Genius: An Inquiry into its Laws and Consequences.* 1869. Reprint, London: Julian Friedman.

Gardner, Howard. 1983. *Frames of Mind.* London: Fontana Press.

Gleitman, H. 1995. *Psychology.* New York: W. W. Norton.

Gunsberg, A. 1991. "Improvised Musical Play: With Delayed and Nondelayed Children." *Childhood Education* 67(4):223–26.

Hermelin, B., N. O'Connor, S. Lee, and D. Treffert. 1989. "Intelligence and Musical Improvisation." *Psychological Medicine* 19(2):447–57.

Hevner, Kate. 1936. "Experimental Studies of the Elements of Expression in Music." *American Journal of Psychology* 48:246–68.

Jackendoff, Ray. 1991. "Musical Parsing and Musical Affect." *Music Perception* 9(2): 199–230.

Keele, S. W., A. Cohen, and R. Ivry. 1986. "Motor Programs: Concepts and Issues." In *Attention and Performance, XIII: Motor Representation and Control,* edited by M. Jeannerod, 77–110. Hillsdale, N.J.: Lawrence Erlbaum.

Kemp, Anthony. 1996. *The Musical Temperament.* Oxford: Oxford University Press.

Krumhansl, C. 1990. *Tonal Structures and Music Cognition.* New York: Oxford University Press.

Lehrdahl, F., and R. Jackendoff. 1983. *A Generative Theory of Tonal Music.* Cambridge: MIT Press.

Livingston, C., and H. Borko. 1990. "High School Mathematics Review Lessons: Expert-Novice Distinctions." *Journal for Research in Mathematics Education* 21(5): 372–87.

Locke, David L. 1979. *The Music of Atsiabeko.* Ph.D. dissertation, Wesleyan University.

Meyer, Leonard. 1956. *Emotion and Meaning in Music.* Chicago: University of Chicago Press.

———. 1973. *Explaining Music.* Berkeley: University of California Press.

Miller, G. A. 1956. "The Magical Number Seven, Plus or Minus Two." *Psychological Review* 63:81–97.

Narmour, E. 1977. *Beyond Schenkerianism.* Chicago: University of Chicago Press.

Pressing, Jeff. 1978. "Towards an Understanding of Scales in Jazz." *Jazzforschung/Jazz Research* 9:25–35.

———. 1984. "Cognitive Processes in Improvisation." In *Cognitive Processes in the Perception of Art,* edited by Ray Crozier and Anthony Chapman, 345–63. Amsterdam: North Holland.

———. 1987. "The Micro- and Macrostructural Design of Improvised Music." *Music Perception* 5:133–72.

―――. 1988. "Improvisation: Methods and Models." In *Generative Processes in Music,* edited by John Sloboda, 129–78. Oxford: Clarendon Press.

―――. 1992. *Synthesizer Performance and Real-Time Techniques.* Madison, Wisc.: A-R Editions; London: Oxford University Press.

―――. 1997. "Some Perspectives on Performed Sound and Music in Virtual Environments." *Presence* 6:1–22.

―――, ed. 1994. *Compositions for Improvisers: An Australian Perspective.* Melbourne: La Trobe University Press.

Priestley, Mary. 1987. "Music and the Shadow." *Music Therapy* 6(2):20–27.

Proctor, R. W., and T. Van Zandt. 1994. *Human Factors in Simple and Complex Systems.* Boston: Allyn and Bacon.

Racy, A. Jihad. 1991. "Creativity and Ambience: An Ecstatic Feedback Model from Arab Music." *The World of Music* 33(3):7–28.

Revesz, G. 1925. *The Psychology of a Musical Prodigy.* London: Kegan Paul, Trench and Trubner.

Roe, A. 1953. "A Psychological Study of Eminent Psychologists and Anthropologists, and a Comparison with Biological and Physical Scientists." *Psychological Monographs* 67:1–55.

Sawyer, Keith. 1992. "Improvisational Creativity: An Analysis of Jazz Performance." *Creativity Research Journal* 5(3):253–63.

Schmuckler, M. A. 1990. "The Performance of Global Expectations." *Psychomusicology* 9(2):122–47.

Sergent, J. 1993. "Music, the Brain, and Ravel." *Trends in Neuroscience* 16, no. 5:168–72.

Shepard, R. N. 1982. "Structural Representations of Musical Pitch," In *The Psychology of Music,* edited by Diana Deutsch, 344–90. New York: Academic Press.

Sloboda, John A. 1991. "Musical Expertise." In *Toward a General Theory of Expertise,* edited by K. A. Ericsson, and J. Smith, 153–71. Cambridge: Cambridge University Press.

Sloboda, J. A., J. W. Davidson, and M. Howe. 1994. "Is Everyone Musical?" *The Psychologist* 7(8):349–54.

Sloboda, J. A., B. Hermelin, and N. O'Connor. 1985. "An Exceptional Musical Memory." *Music Perception* 3:155–70.

Sloboda, J. A., and D. H. H. Parker. 1985. "Immediate Recall of Melodies." In *Musical Structure and Cognition,* edited by P. Howell, I. Cross, and R. West, 143–67. London: Academic Press.

Smith, Gregory E. 1991. "In Quest of a New Perspective on Improvised Jazz: A View from the Balkans." *The World of Music* 33:29–52.

Takeuchi, A. H., and S. H. Hulse. 1993. "Absolute Pitch." *Psychological Bulletin* 113(2):345–61.

Wickens, C. D. 1984. "Processing Resources in Attention." In *Varieties of Attention,* edited by R. Parasuraman and R. Davies, 63–102. New York: Academic Press.

Wolpert, R. S. 1990. "Recognition of Melody, Harmonic Accompaniment, and Instrumentation: Musicians vs. Nonmusicians." *Music Perception* 8(1):95–106.

CHAPTER THREE

Do Javanese Gamelan Musicians Really Improvise?

R. ANDERSON SUTTON

Much is variable in the realization of a Javanese musical piece. From the songs *(sulukan)* of puppeteers to the cyclical pieces *(gendhing)* for full gamelan ensemble, performances on different occasions, and even immediate repetitions by the same musicians during a single evening, will reveal some significant differences. But are the musicians improvising? The answer, of course, depends on what one means by the term "improvisation." If improvisation is understood simply to require some spontaneous decision making by musicians as they perform, then some Javanese musicians do indeed improvise in some instances, but to what extent? Given what has been written on this subject in Java, one might expect to find much more pervasive use of improvisation in Javanese gamelan performance than seems actually to be the case.

Improvisation is one aspect of the larger issue of performance practice, a topic that has been the primary focus of many recent studies by scholars of Javanese music, replacing an earlier concern with tunings and modal classifications. Some scholars state categorically that Javanese gamelan performance is largely improvisational (Sindoesawarno 1987, 378, Hood and Susilo 1967, 16–24; Hood 1975, 29–30; Susilo 1980, 195; 1987, 1; Jairazbhoy 1980, 53). Some write of "paraphrase" (Groneman 1890, 37; Hood 1954, 11; Kunst 1973, 175), "embellishment" (Sorrell 1990, 97–98), "elaboration" (Hood 1954, 11; Sumarsam 1995, 231), "variation" (Sutton 1978, 1979, 1988, and 1993), and "flexibility" (Vetter 1981). Margaret Kartomi even describes some gamelan music as "semi-improvisational" (1980, 120).

Much of the controversy would seem to hinge not so much on what Javanese musicians do, as on what to call the processes whereby they do it. Based on the list of instruments characterized as "improvising" in Hood and Susilo (1967, 16–24), one is led to conclude that they apply the term improvisation to any instance in which a player (or singer) has even a minimal degree of choice in creating and varying her or his own part. Those parts that are not completely fixed prior to performance, and that are therefore variable (even if in some performances they do not actually vary), are said to be improvised, simply because the musician has the potential to decide some aspect of her or his part and is not constrained by musical convention to reproduce exactly a precomposed part, whether written or memorized. But variability and variation do not necessarily constitute improvisation in the sense in which I and other scholars and musicians use the word. Variation can be worked out prior to the moment of performance.

I am more comfortable with the cautious position offered by Sorrell: "Because the word 'improvisation' has no absolute meaning it must always be used with care and myriad qualifications. To state that gamelan music is improvised is likely to convey the impression of a freedom, even a looseness, which it does not have; but to try and close the matter there would do the greater disservice of denying it that element of choice and interpretive spontaneity that is crucial to any great musical tradition" (Sorrell 1990, 76). Susilo, writing some twenty years after the 1967 booklet coauthored with Hood, points out in the Indonesian summary of his English-language article on improvisation in the Javanese music-dance-drama form *wayang wong panggung* that the term is indeed Western and, though used by some in its Indonesianized form *(improvisasi),* is imprecise in its application to what Javanese do (Susilo 1987, 11). An ample number of Javanese terms exists, he points out, although some of those he discusses are more appropriately applied to the words and gestures of dancer-actors than to the music performed by gamelan players and singers. Yet it is worth noting that Javanese employ the loan words *improvisasi* and *spontan* (meaning "spontaneous"), for lack of exact Javanese equivalents, in discussions of music making (their own and others') in the late twentieth century.

Problematics of Musical Improvisation
One might argue that we should be more concerned with learning what Javanese musicians do than with anguishing over whether to label it as improvisation or as something else. Indeed, a good portion of this chapter will be concerned with what they do and say. But even as we seek to understand things from a Javanese point of view, those of us who are not Javanese engage in an inherently comparative enterprise. The question of improvisation, then, is instructive and legitimate.

IMPROVISATION AND SPONTANEITY
We need to begin with a brief exploration of the meanings and implications of the term improvisation as it is understood and applied cross-culturally, as well as in Javanese performance. Following this, we will investigate some aspects of flexibility in Javanese gamelan performance and attempt to identify what can be called improvisation. And we will also consider the relative importance of any such improvisation in aesthetic evaluation of musical performance in Java. Is it (potentially) good, bad, to be maximized, to be minimized, evident but unimportant? Due to limitations of space, I consider here only the court-derived gamelan tradition of central Java. The findings might well be different if other genres of Javanese music were included.

We can begin with Bruno Nettl's oft-cited conclusions concerning improvisation in his insightful article in which he poses improvisation and composition not as opposite processes, but as two points on a continuum,[1] separated by degree of spontaneity, or, if you will, the time lag between creation and presentation (Nettl 1974). Indeed, writers on the subject concur that improvisation involves at least some degree of spontaneity in musical decision making during the act of performance (e.g., see Ferand 1961, 5, and Horsley et al. 1980, 31). In his exhaustive study of improvisation in jazz, Berliner writes:

> When artists use *improvisation [improvise]* as a verb, however, they focus not only on the degree to which old models are transformed and new ideas created, but on the dynamic conditions and precise processes underlying their transformation and creation. Typically, they reserve the term for real-time composing—instantaneous decision making in applying and altering musical materials and conceiving new ideas. Players distinguish such operations during solos from the recall and performance of precomposed ideas, those formulated outside the current event in the practice room or in a previous performance. (Berliner 1994, 221–22)

This implies some element of surprise on the part of a listening audience and, in ensemble performance, on the part of other performers (who may themselves be contributing to the level of surprise through their own spontaneous choices). Moreover, it would seem that, in some circumstances, the performer her/himself might experience some surprise, as motor impulses occasionally take the fore in creating melodies and rhythms not yet fully worked out in the mind of the performer.[2]

IMPROVISATION AND "THE MODEL"

Most instances of musical improvisation involve the realization of one or more musical parts constrained by a "model"—a melody, rhythmic pattern, or chord progression which, whether actually sounded or not, is known by the improvising musician (Nettl 1974, 11). The improvising musician is expected to play or sing a part that articulates the model—through unison, consonance, or some other type of audible sameness—not constantly, but at certain "points of reference" (12). The successful improviser demonstrates knowledge of the model, correspondence with the model at points of reference with a frequency (Nettl calls this "density") expected within the tradition, and with an appropriate degree of inventiveness. This inventiveness may be evident in the choice of "building blocks" or musical "formulas," and in the manipulation and alteration of these units from one instance to the next. Musical improvisation, then, is not free expression constrained only by the inspiration of the moment, but a complex and multilevel process, one that must be learned and practised.

IMPROVISATION, ORAL TRADITION, ORAL PERFORMANCE

While most ethnomusicologists, along with many other listeners around the world, tend to admire the skill of improvisation, this process has been denigrated by some. Even whole music traditions have been judged unworthy for the very fact that so much of the music is improvised, and therefore presumably *not* worked over, refined and improved as one would expect of a writing composer, working through various drafts. Consider this passage from a book ominously entitled *Verdict on India:* "Indian music is almost entirely a matter of improvisation. Art is not, never has been, and never can be, a matter of improvisation. . . . Indian music has yet to suffer the pangs of birth, the pangs which are the inevitable accompaniment of all artistic creation. It must boldly proclaim itself on paper, in black and white" (Nichols 1944, 134–36). Mantle Hood confronts this kind of attitude with the following:

> If the basic ground rules for the two [composing and improvising] are the same within a tradition, can we say that the essential difference is that the composition can be subjected to greater cultivation through a process of writing and revision? But then, what about those cultures that know only an oral tradition and yet have developed fixed melodies, that is, compositions? And is it not possible that from improvisation to improvisation the same process of revision, polish, and cultivation takes place simply without writing?

He goes on to express essentially the same opinion as Nettl: "the fine line between improvisation and composition may be difficult to establish and . . . possibly, in some instances, such a line may not even exist" (Hood 1975, 26)

Hood here conflates the idea of oral tradition with improvisation, and written tradition with nonimprovised composition. Judith Becker takes issue with this stance, however, by emphasizing the importance of formulas. In her dissertation, she states:

> Until recently, it was believed that oral performances were either memorized or improvised. In fact, they are neither. The basic building block of an oral tradition is the melodic formula, not a fixed formula, but one which can be expanded, condensed or rearranged according to the needs of the musical situation in combination with the fancy of the performer. (Becker 1972, 47)

In the published revision of her dissertation, however, she modifies this to read as follows:

> Too often, oral tradition is equated with oral performance, that is, playing without written music, or with aural learning of a composition, that is memorization through repeated hearings. Or, the term oral tradition may be equated with improvization on a theme or motif as practiced by some jazz musicians. None of these interpretations describes the practice of the musicians in an oral tradition. The musician in an oral tradition, rather, has mastered a *technique* of composition, based upon the manipulation of formulas, which allow him to perform and compose at the same moment. (1980, 20)

Note that in her revision she does not go so far as to claim that oral performance is not improvised. Rather, she tells us, it is not improvisation of the kind prevalent in jazz. But as the questions of improvisation and variation are not central to her study, she does not pursue in any detail what elements *are* improvised. Nevertheless, she alludes to the importance of what she calls melodic formulas, flexible ones, in the creative process of Javanese performance.

Again, the prevailing scholarly discourse on music, largely Western-dominated, has tended to equate use of formulas with a lack of creativity, as if the formulas were the lazy way to make up a piece or make one's way through a piece. This presumes a positive evaluation of originality over such other qualities as accessibility, familiarity, and so forth. In earlier writings, I have argued that central Javanese gamelan musicians, while not averse to some kinds of originality and creativity, still place high value on what is familiar and comfortable, both to hear and to play (Sutton 1987, 1988, 1993). As such, it would seem there is not a strong impetus for individual musicians to develop skills that we might call improvisational.[3]

For many musicians and scholars, the notion of improvisation suggests a significant level of originality. Consider, for example, jazz musician Lee Konitz's ideas on improvisation, as presented by Berliner. Konitz reserves the term improvisation for "the most radical transfigurations of the melody," as distinct from "subtler alterations falling within the realm of variation, embellishment, and interpretation" (Berliner 1994, 221). Might Javanese music, then, be improvisational? It is certainly "less improvisational" than most jazz, if such cross-cultural comparisons can be meaningfully made.

If we take an absolute stance, then, perhaps every performing musician improvises to some degree, as Nettl has noted (1974; 1986; 1991, 4). An accomplished pianist may modify the dynamics in a certain passage, play a trill differently, take a somewhat faster tempo than s/he did in a previous performance. Indeed, at some level, each performance of any piece of music will be unique, differing in some ways from all other performances of it. But this can be so even if the musician has arrived at an interpretation that s/he strives to duplicate in each performance. It makes more sense to reserve the word improvisation for more substantial choices being made at the moment of performance—choices of pitch and rhythmic structure whose difference from previous instances of the "same" piece or passage are intended by the performer to be apprehended by listeners.

IMPROVISATION AND ANALYSIS

How are we to know improvisation when we encounter it? Reference merely to sound structures is inadequate—whether heard live, heard from the playback of recordings, or read from transcriptions. For if we perceive significant differences between two or more performances of a piece, or variation between repetitions within a single performance, how can we know that these differences are the result of spontaneous decision making by the performers? We need to pay heed both to the sound structures and to what musicians who have produced these structures have to say about the process whereby they produced them. One without the other is insufficient in a quest to identify and understand improvisation.[4]

I propose below to consider what several musicians have said about their playing, and to compare and discuss excerpts from transcriptions of recorded performances by the musician I have known best, my teacher Suhardi, in order to illustrate the extent to which one might call his playing improvisational or nonimprovisational. He and I have discussed many elements of Javanese performance practice over a period of more than twenty years, and I have been able to record his playing over this long period and ask him about the processes whereby he creates his parts. In January 1996, Suhardi retired from many years as director of the gamelan musicians at the national radio station (Radio Republik Indonesia) in the city of Yogyakarta, one of two main centers of court-derived gamelan music in contemporary Java. He is one of the most highly regarded musicians in Yogyakarta, respected for his command of the gamelan music styles and repertories associated with the two major court centers, Yogyakarta and Surakarta.[5]

Variation and Improvisation in Javanese Gamelan Performance

Given the long tradition of central Javanese gamelan studies in ethnomusicology, I will dispense with a general introduction to the music and its instruments.[6] Essential to the topic at hand is an awareness of a melody now generally referred to as *balungan,* often multi-octave in conception but sounded by anywhere from one to seven single-octave metallophones *(saron* and *slenthem). Balungan* translates as "skeleton" or "outline," and in Javanese performance practice it serves as the "model" with its "points of reference" that constrain, in various idiomatic ways, the playing of other instrumental parts and, when present, the singing. Yet many central Javanese musicians distinguish the parts which are closely bound to this skeletal melody (and thus could hardly be said to be improvised) and those which routinely diverge from it—often in adherence to a multi-octave melodic model, identified by Sumarsam as "inner melody" and, in somewhat different form, simply as *lagu* (literally, "melody") by my teacher Suhardi.[7] It is the latter, diverging parts which tend to be called *garap* or *garapan* parts. I have translated *garapan* as "treatment," as has Hatch in his translation of the theoretical writings of R. L. Martopangrawit (1984). Perlman also glosses it as "interpretation," although he points out that Indonesian also has the word *tafsiran* (1993, 576). In nonmusical contexts, the word *garap* can mean "to work on," "to cultivate." It implies a kind of busy activity, a working through, in an attempt to produce something suggested but not fully formed, hence also a searching—for something inherent, but perhaps not yet uncovered.

One cannot talk about the possibility of improvisation in Javanese gamelan music without attempting to understand *garapan.* And crucial to the process of *garap*-ing a Javanese piece—that is, rendering it in performance—are terms that might be glossed as "formula," but that denote different levels of fixity and individuality. Javanese musicians often describe the process of *garapan* as the fitting of appropriate *céngkok* to the skeletal melody—or to the implicit melodic model—of a piece. Musicians understand the term *céngkok* in several senses. Some musicians use the term to refer to melodic patterns as performed. The highly influential musician-theorist, the late R. Ng. Martopangrawit (formerly R. L. Martopangrawit), reserved the word *céngkok* for melodic pattern in the abstract, as do his many former students and colleagues. He used the term *wiletan* to refer to the particular realizations of *céngkok* (see Perlman 1993, 569; Martopangrawit 1973). Others use the root form, *wilet,* to refer to these realizations. Both terms suggest winding and twisting, intricate decoration, efflorescence. According to Perlman, Martopangrawit used the term *wilet* for the "intensely individual *je-ne-sais-quoi*" (Perlman 1993, 564)—unnotatable minutiae that differentiate even very nearly identical *wiletan*.[8] Suhardi often used the verb form of *céngkok (nyéngkok)* to refer to melodically active parts that were rather divergent from the skeletal melody and from other parts heard simultaneously. Basically, *céngkok* can be defined as a flexible melodic pattern, normally filling four beats of skeletal melody (or in some cases twice or half that number). Depending on how precisely one conceives of the identity of a *céngkok,* some passages can be acceptably rendered ("*garap*ed") with any of several *céngkok* (rarely more than three), but other passages are, at least nowadays, widely judged to require one *céngkok*. Use of an alternate *céngkok* would simply be "wrong."

In the case where a musician has a choice, though, is that decision made at the moment of performance? Analysis of transcriptions alone cannot answer the question, for variation may not entail improvisation. It is only the musicians who can answer, and the ones I have talked to say that they often make this kind of choice well before a performance, preferring one solution over the other. Addressing the issue of treatment *(garapan)* and improvisation, Perlman asked, "To what extent do musicians regard spontaneity and novelty as important features of *garap?*" Martopangrawit told him, "Spontaneous [playing] only uses what already exists, it doesn't make anything new," though he noted, as Perlman paraphrases it, "You can, of course, devise or develop something new, but this doesn't happen spontaneously." And Suhardi told him, "We should plan our *garap*. While we sometimes happen on to something, while there are discoveries we make while playing, these aren't frequent" (Perlman 1993, 182).

Musicians hold open the possibility of judicious use of alternatives for the sake of variation, and confide that their choices between *céngkok* or aspects of their realization may sometimes be spontaneous, particularly in response to what others are playing at the moment. But one will not find a very high degree of spontaneity in the choice of *céngkok,* due to the finite supply of acceptable *céngkok* in a particular context. Musicians do not, as far as I know, engage in experimental searches for new *céngkok* during performance; and most do not do so in private rehearsal either. I have never heard a musician praised for devising or composing new *céngkok,* although it is evident that the *céngkok* in use have been created, and perhaps gradually developed, in the past. Walton (1995) reports the creation of new *céngkok* by one of the female singers *(pesindhèn)* with whom she conducted research, but she notes that this is unusual.

The level at which one finds a far greater degree of individual input, often spontaneous, though by no means always, is in the detailed realization of a particular *céngkok,* often called (as noted above) *wiletan* or *wilet.* It is clear from the extensive listening I have done—and this is corroborated by what Javanese musicians say themselves—that seasoned musicians develop their own *wiletan* for a particular instrument, drawing on those of their teachers and other musicians. But the process is generally seen as natural, rather than as a self-conscious effort to distinguish oneself with a unique style. Indeed, the various *wiletan,* as instances or versions of a particular *céngkok,* must be similar enough to one another to be recognizable as realizations of that *céngkok.* While the final tone, general contour, and some rhythmic elements must be maintained, some of the tonal material can be altered. In the playing of one individual, even the very most skillful and highly regarded, one hears *wiletan* recur frequently. One may play through a passage many times in an evening without repeating the same *wiletan* in all its details, but constant variation is generally avoided.

How limitless is one person's ability to create or spontaneously vary *wiletan?* Does s/he consciously try to create new *wiletan* in the course of performance, or does s/he draw from a finite *wiletan* vocabulary, a bag of tricks? What my teachers have explained to me is that they may well employ *wiletan* that they have played many times before, but that the choice at this level is *not* worked out prior to performance, generally not remembered from one performance to the next, and not consistently remembered from one statement to its repetitions within a single performance. Musicians make much of the need for a good player to reflect the mood of the piece and of the individual playing. But again, this need can be effectively met largely through skillful choice among extant patterns.

Suhardi, the teacher with whom I studied most intensively, who has devoted much thought to analysis of gamelan music and performance, told me in a conversation in 1994 (eight years after his very similar statement to Perlman) that only very occasionally did he come up with anything new while performing—that is, a new *wiletan* (or *variasi*—the term he generally used, rather than *wiletan* or *wilet,* to refer to realization of melodic patterns). He did not strive to create new *variasi,* did not feel that good performance required it, but nevertheless would sometimes, almost accidentally or inadvertantly, play a new version of a passage (a new *variasi*) and exclaim to himself: Gee, that was nice! He would then attempt to remember it and incorporate it into his vocabulary of patterns for use on another occasion. These are not new *céngkok;* instead, they are new variants of extant *céngkok.*[9]

Other musicians, however, appear to engage in more active exploration during performance. Perlman cites the remarks of Sukamso, a young musician, who "described himself as 'still searching *[masih mencari],* still lacking a large enough vocabulary *[kurang perbendaharaan].* His search involved both imitating other players (he expressed interest, for example, in learning more about Sabdhosuwarno's *gendèr* patterns), and experimenting: at rehearsals he sometimes would end up playing in ways never done before *[menabuh yang belum dilakukan orang]* because he was at the searching stage *[tahap mencari].*" (Perlman 1993:363)

One would probably note greater variety and spontaneous creativity in the playing of this young musician than in the playing of the most venerated performers. Hence, we might say that the evidence of improvisation might bring negative aesthetic appraisal of one's playing as inexperienced, not yet settled and mature.

VARIATION AND IMPROVISATION IN SUHARDI'S PLAYING

Over the past 21 years I have periodically recorded Suhardi playing instrumental parts for several pieces, including three I wish to draw upon here: *Ketawang "Mijil Wedharing Tyas," pélog pathet nem; Ketawang "Puspawarna," sléndro pathet manyura;* and *Gendhing "Gambir Sawit," sléndro pathet sanga.*[10] Though spread out over more than two decades, the circumstances of these recordings were very similar: Suhardi playing the instrument at his house in the course of a music lesson, with another musician playing the skeletal melody for reference. That these recordings did not involve a full ensemble might seem problemmatic. Yet I have observed Suhardi playing with full ensemble in many contexts and can assure the reader that the parts I recorded during the lessons were, in both his estimation and mine, characteristic of his playing style, neither more nor less varied than those played with full ensemble.[11] Below I offer comparative data from performances on *gambang,* a multi-octave xylophone that is played with what musicians characterize as rather greater freedom for variation than is normal for most other parts. I used *gambang* recordings made in 1974 and 1980 as part of my earlier study of individual variation in gamelan playing (Sutton 1988). Here I compare Suhardi's realizations of repeated passages on this same instrument as recorded in 1974, 1983, and 1995, evaluating degree of variation both within a single performance and on separate occasions separated by many years. To present complete transcriptions of these performances with this chapter would far exceed the space limitations of this volume; they are available from the author on request. Rather, I wish to show with excerpts from the transcriptions the surprisingly high degree of stability in many passages, and to discuss some aspects of the variation that is evident in others. Examination of other instrumental parts, other pieces, and the playing of other musicians would be appropriate in a lengthier study, but would not, I am confident, alter the findings significantly.

In accord with current Javanese theoretical conventions, it is appropriate to consider these parts in rhythmic and tonal relation to the skeletal melody part. While *céngkok* and their realizations here may be said to consist of phrases that fill four skeletal melody beats, they can be analyzed more closely as being constituted from shorter units of one or two skeletal melody beats in duration. The norm, readily explained by practically every musician I have spoken with, and demonstrated in performance, is for convergence with the skeletal melody at the end of almost all four-beat "measures" (called *gatra*), and often on the second beat as well. By Javanese convention, it is the final beat that has the greatest weight, with secondary stress on the second beat. The "odd" beats (first and third) are weaker and are usually the points of least constraint for convergence between skeletal melody and other parts, although the other parts may often coincide with the skeletal melody tone on the first beat of the measure. In measures that sustain the same tone throughout (called *gantungan*, literally "hanging"), it is the beginning of the measure that is tonally weighted.

It will be instructive first to consider his several renditions of a two-measure phrase in *Ketawang "Mijil Wedharing Tyas"*—2126 2165, a passage that was repeated several times in each of three recorded performances. The passage is not an unusual one. Each of the two measures are found in countless other pieces in the central Javanese repertory, and have been rendered by *gambang* players in a variety of ways.[12] Reference to the part transcribed in example 3.1 will serve both to illustrate the concepts of *céngkok* and *wiletan/variasi* and to raise questions concerning choices at several levels.[13]

If we look at a full measure (one *gatra*) we can ask whether the same passage was rendered with exactly the same (or very nearly the same) *céngkok* each time. If not the same or nearly so, we can see whether the *gambang* part arrived at the same tones at the point of rhythmic simultaneity with the skeletal melody, thereby tracing the same basic contour but with different paths between these points of reference. If passages contrast, we have variation—possibly planned, possibly spontaneously produced. If they do not, we have fairly strong evidence that it has been planned, of course; but we could also suggest it was spontaneous in that the musician had a choice but in fact chose to play it the same way he did before, or usually has, or always has. The leap from the transcription data to conclusions about improvisation, then, requires my drawing on remarks made by Suhardi and other musicians and on my own listening experience.

Comparing the three statements for skeletal melody 2126 from 1974, we find a high degree of similarity, along with some contrast at several levels of detail. Basically, the first halves of each statement (the sixteen *gambang* beats ending on skeletal melody tone 1) were very similar, as Suhardi not only played unison with both skeletal melody tones, but employed nearly identical contours to reach these tones.[14] With only the subtlest differences in frequency of the slight offset of rhythm between left and right hands, the 1974b and c statements were identical for this portion. Moreover, in these statements (1974b and c) he went on to play melodies that traced nearly identical contours, going back to 2 and then cadencing to low 6. In the 1974a version, Suhardi chose to end this measure with a very common sixteen-beat phrase, leading from 1 to low 6. It is somewhat ambiguous whether this contrast is sufficient to constitute a difference in *céngkok,* or merely in *wiletan/variasi.* Suhardi called it a different *variasi,* despite the marked similarity between the first half of each of these. Others have said these are all instances of the same *céngkok* because they proceed from the previous low 5 to a low 6 via 2 (on the first beat) and 1 (on the second). The more subtle variance between the first halves would, in Martopangrawit's terminology, be referred to as differences in *wilet,* the contrast between the 1974a statement and the other two as differences in *wiletan.*

Turning to the three statements played with skeletal melody 2165, we again find almost exact similarity between two (1974a and b), which actually traced identical contours, differing only in scarcely perceivable changes in left- and right-hand rhythm until the last three *gambang* beats (three conjunct tones ascending from low 2 to low 5 in the first statement and descending from 1 to low 5 in the second). The third statement, however, was very clearly a different *céngkok,* tracing a path up through middle 5 on the first beat to high 1 on the second, and then cadencing on middle 5 at the end of the measure. This was not simply an alternative *céngkok* that Suhardi chose for the sake of variation. Instead, it was dictated by the musical context: specifically, the need to end the measure on middle 5, thereby serving as transition from the mostly low- and middle-register first section *(umpak)* to the mostly high- and middle-register second section, known as *lik* (literally, "little," i.e., high in pitch). What he played was one realization of a *céngkok* leading from the lower to the middle and higher registers, cadencing on middle 5, rather than low 5. In this context it would be unusual for the *gambang* not to reach the upper register somewhere near the middle of the measure, and a substantial error to go to any tone other than middle 5 at the end. The change in *gambang* pattern was motivated by a markedly different interpretation of the passage.

Though the sounding of the skeletal melody on the single octave metallophones does not change from previous statements, the conception (interpreted as "inner melody" or *lagu*) of it does—from something like 2, 1, low 6, low 5, to 2, high 1, middle 6, middle 5. While individual musicians will differ in the way they might describe the different nature of this instance compared to previous instances of 2165 in this piece, all would concur that it "goes high" and "ends on middle 5, not low 5." By convention, this reshaping of the measure is signalled by the melodic leader of the ensemble, the *rebab* (spike fiddle) player, who should move to the middle register just prior to the beginning of

skeletal melody: 2   1   2   6
(from 5)
r.h. 5 6 5 1̇ 1 6 1̇ 2̇ 2̇ 3̇ 3̇ 3̇ 3̇ 1̇ 6 1̇ 1̇ 2̇ 1̇ 2̇ – 6 5 3 2 2 2 5 5 3 5 6
1974a   /   /   /   /   /
l.h. – 6̣ 5̣ 1 5̣ 6̣ 1 2 5 3 2 3 2 1 6̣ 1 3 2 1 2 1 6̣ 5̣ 3̣ – 2̣ 2̣ 5̣ 2̣ 3̣ 5̣ 6̣

r.h. 5 5 5 1̇ 1̇ 6 1̇ 2̇ 1̇ 3̇ 2̇ 3̇ 3̇ 1̇ 6 1̇ 5 5 5 1̇ 1̇ 6 1̇ 2̇ 2̇ 6 5 3 2 3 5 6
1974b   /   /   /   /   /   /   /   /
l.h. – – 5̣ 1 5̣ 6̣ 1 2 5 3 2 3 2 1 6̣ 1 5̣ – 5̣ 1 5̣ 6̣ 1 2 1 6̣ 5̣ 3̣ 2̣ 3̣ 5̣ 6̣

r.h. 5 5 5 1̇ 1̇ 6 1̇ 2̇ 1̇ 3̇ 2̇ 3̇ 3̇ 1̇ 6 1̇ 5 1̇ 1̇ 6 1̇ 2̇ 1̇ 2̇ 2̇ 6 5 3 2 3 5 6
1974c   /   /   /   /
l.h. – – 5̣ 1 5̣ 6̣ 1 2 5 3 2 3 2 1 6̣ 1 5̣ 1 5̣ 6̣ 1 2 3 2 1 6̣ 5̣ 3̣ 2̣ 3̣ 5̣ 6̣

skeletal melody: 2   1   2   6
r.h. 5 6 5 1̇ 1̇ 6 1̇ 2̇ 2̇ 3̇ 2̇ 3̇ 3̇ 1̇ 6 1̇ 1̇ 6 1̇ 2̇ 3̇ 5̇ 2̇ 6̇ 6̇ 6̇ 5̇ 3̇ 5̇ 2̇ 1̇ 6
1983a /   /   /   /   /
l.h. 1 6̣ 5̣ 1 5̣ 6̣ 1 2 5 3 2 3 2 1 6̣ 1 5̣ 6̣ 1 2 3 5 2 6 6 6 5 3 5 2 1 6̣

r.h. 5 6 5 1̇ 1̇ 6 1̇ 2̇ 2̇ 3̇ 2̇ 3̇ 3̇ 1̇ 6 1̇ 1̇ 6 1̇ 2̇ 3̇ 5̇ 2̇ 6̇ 6̇ 6̇ 5̇ 3̇ 5̇ 2̇ 1̇ 6
1983b /   /   /   /   /
l.h. 1 6̣ 5̣ 1 5̣ 6̣ 1 2 5 3 2 3 2 1 6̣ 1 5̣ 6̣ 1 2 3 5 2 6 6 6 5 3 5 2 1 6̣

r.h. 5 6 5 5 5 6 1̇ 2̇ 5 6 5 6 1̇ 5 6 1̇ 1̇ 6 1̇ 2̇ 3̇ 5̇ 2̇ 6̇ 6̇ 6̇ 5̇ 3̇ 5̇ 2̇ 1̇ 6
1983c /   /
l.h. 1 6̣ 5̣ – 5̣ 6̣ 1 2 5̣ 6̣ 5̣ 6̣ 1 5̣ 6̣ 1 5̣ 6̣ 1 2 3 5 2 6 6 6 5 3 5 2 1 6̣

skeletal melody: 2   1   2   6
r.h. 5 6 5 6 1̇ 6 1̇ 2̇ 5 6 5 6 1̇ 5 6 1̇ 1̇ 6 1̇ 2̇ 1̇ 2̇ 1̇ 2̇ 2̇ 6 5 3 5 3 5 6
1995a   /   /   /   /
l.h. 5̣ 6̣ 5̣ 6̣ 1 6̣ 1 2 5̣ 6̣ 5̣ 6̣ 1 5̣ 6̣ 1 5̣ 6̣ 1 2 3 2 1 2 1 6̣ 5̣ 3̣ 2̣ 3̣ 5̣ 6̣

r.h. 5 3 5 6 1̇ 6 1̇ 2̇ 1̇ 6 1̇ 5 6 1̇ 6 1̇ 1̇ 6 1̇ 2̇ 1̇ 2̇ 1̇ 2̇ 2̇ 6 5 3 5 3 5 6
1995b /   /   /   /   /   /
l.h. 2̣ 3̣ 5̣ 6̣ 1 6̣ 1 2 5̣ 6̣ 1 5̣ 6̣ 1 2 1 5̣ 6̣ 1 2 3 2 1 2 1 6̣ 5̣ 3̣ 2̣ 3̣ 5̣ 6̣

r.h. 5 3 5 6 1̇ 6 1̇ 2̇ 1̇ 6 1̇ 5 6 1̇ 6 1̇ 1̇ 6 1̇ 2̇ 1̇ 2̇ 1̇ 2̇ 2̇ 6 5 3 5 3 5 6
1995c /   /   /   /   /   /
l.h. 2̣ 3̣ 5̣ 6̣ 1 6̣ 1 2 5̣ 6̣ 1 5̣ 6̣ 1 2 1 5̣ 6̣ 1 2 3 2 1 2 1 6̣ 5̣ 3̣ 2̣ 3̣ 5̣ 6̣

Example 3.1. *Gambang* playing for repeated passage from *Ketawang "Mijil Wedharing Tyas," pélog pathet nem* in three performances by Suhardi.

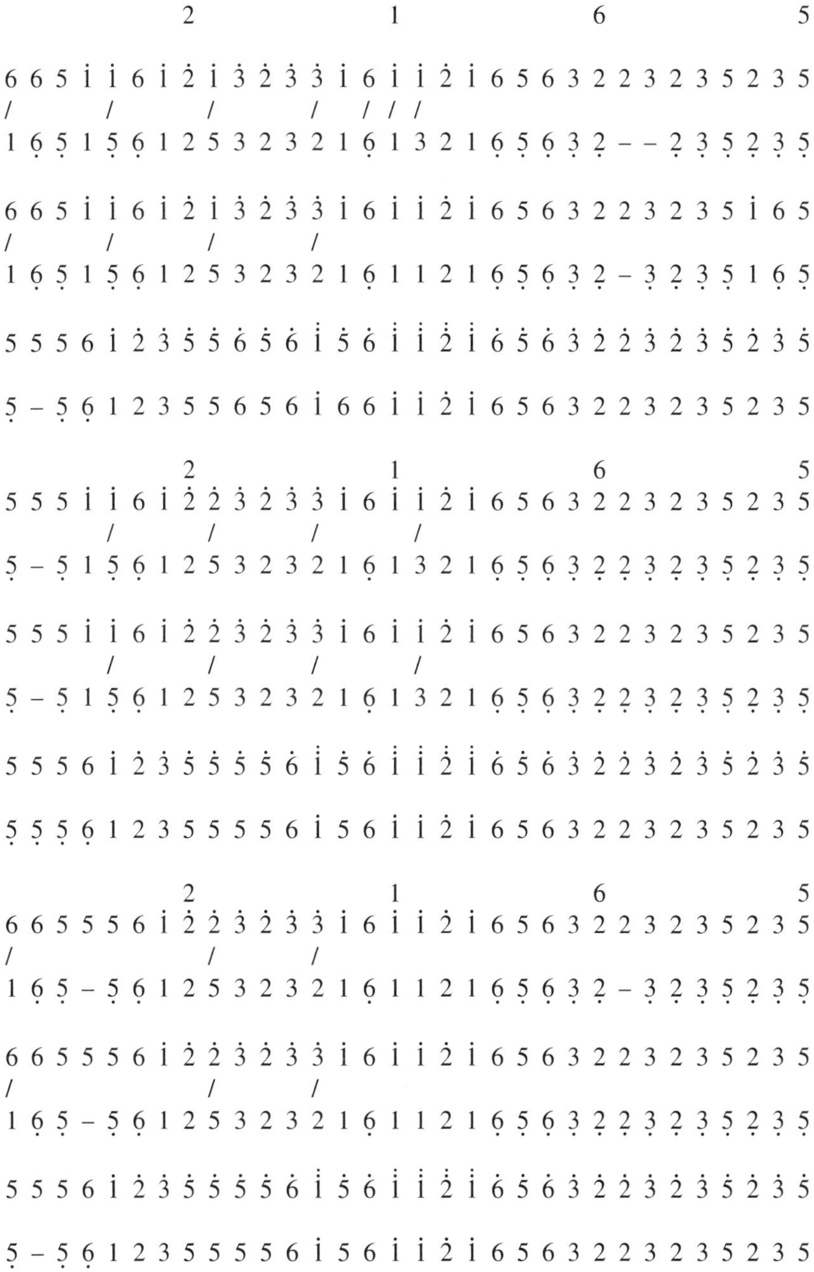

this measure so that the other musicians have at least a moment's warning to alter their choice of *céngkok.*

The three statements of this same passage recorded in 1983 reveal remarkable internal consistency. Indeed, the second statement of the entire two-measure phrase was identical, at least with respect to details of pitch and rhythm (as shown in the transcription), to the first statement: employing identical eight-*gambang*-beat contours to proceed from low 5 to 2, 1, 6, low 6, 2, 1, low 2, and low 5 (corresponding with most of the skeletal melody points of reference). In the third statement, first measure, he proceeded through the same tones, but chose a slightly different eight-*gambang*-beat pattern to go from low 5 up to 2 (at the beginning of the passage), and a more audibly different pattern to move to 1: (left hand) 5̣ 6̣ 5̣ 6̣ 1 5̣ 6̣ 1, instead of 5 3 2 3 2 1 6̣ 1. The last half of the measure was the same in each of the three 1983 statements.

Concerning this first measure, Suhardi told me that he had not planned ahead of time to play identical versions twice, with contrast the third time. It just came out that way, he said, allowing that he probably was trying to make his third statement a little different. He said it was not completely a conscious mental process, however, and that his hands seem to make the choice by themselves. This would appear to be an instance of documented spontaneity, albeit extremely limited. And it should be pointed out that what he played each time consisted of eight- and sixteen-*gambang*-beat patterns he has played countless times before in this and the many other pieces with these same measures.

For the second measure, again, the third statement was an entirely different *céngkok* used as transition between sections. As we compare this to the same thirty-two–*gambang*–beat passage in the 1974 recording, we find that the two differ only by slight contrasts on the second and tenth *gambang* beats (the absence in the 1983 version of a left-hand rest on the second, and the choice of 5 rather than 6 on the tenth). The realizations of this measure in the first two 1983 statements (when the *garapan* is to end on low 5, rather than middle 5) resemble very closely those recorded in 1974, differing only in the choice of a few tones at the beginning of the first eight-*gambang*-beat pattern, the choice of 1 or 3 on the first *gambang* beat of the second half of the measure, and the presence or absence of left-hand rests near the end of the passage.

Comparing the playing of the first measure in 1983 with that from 1974, we find close resemblance between the patterns played during the first half of the measure, but in the second half a marked contrast between the pattern Suhardi played each of three times in 1983 and either of the patterns he played in the 1974 performance. He explained that the 1983 pattern was *"lebih nyéngkok"* (more divergent from the skeletal melody and *lagu*) than those used in 1974. He had not made a conscious decision to play in a divergent style in 1983, but he happened to play this pattern during the first statement in the 1983 performance and liked its sound enough that day to reiterate it in both of the subsequent statements of the same passage. Far from constituting a new *céngkok* or even new *wiletan/variasi,* his choice in 1983 was simply to employ one of a number of preexisting sixteen-*gambang*-beat patterns that navigate from 1 to low 6 in conformity with constraints of the *pathet* (modal classification—here *pathet nem* of the *"sanga"* variety; discussed further in Sutton 1975, 41–42, and Martopangrawit 1984, 137).

In the 1995 performance, the first two statements (1995a and b) of the entire two-measure passage are nearly identical, tracing the same path at each skeletal melody beat (from low 5 to 2, 1, 2, low 6, 2, 1, low 2, and low 5) with the same or nearly the same patterns between these tones. In the third statement (1995c), the first measure is identical to that of the second statement (1995b); and the second measure, serving as transition to the high and middle registers, moves via 5, high 1, and 2, to 5. Suhardi played not only the same *céngkok* that he did in 1974 and 1983, but used the same *wiletan/variasi* (note for note!) that he did in 1983. Further comparing the 1995 performance with those of 1983 and 1974, we find a consistent preference in 1995 for (1) a slightly different opening eight-*gambang*-beat pattern in both measures (entirely conjunct in each of the 1995 versions and in none of the previous ones); (2) a leap from 2 down to low 5 to begin the second eight-*gambang*-beat pattern in the first measure (in each of the 1995 versions and in 1983c, but not used otherwise); and (3) convergence with skeletal melody tone 2 on the third beat of the first measure (in each of the 1995 versions and in 1974b and c, but not otherwise).

With these few exceptions, then, the 1995 performance resembles closely both prior performances, strongly supporting Suhardi's verbal claim that once he arrives at a treatment *(garapan)* for a passage, he is not likely to alter it. It also supports the conclusion that he did not plan out his playing note for note, and thus that each performance is unique even though it consists, perhaps entirely, of preexisting patterns that the player has used many times before—not only in this piece, but in others that share similar phrases. One may call the part "improvised" only if one stresses that originality and invention are evident at only a very subtle level and that too much of either will result in unidiomatic playing, with the musician judged either to be ill-prepared or to be seeking a level of individual attention inappropriate within the largely communal ethos of gamelan playing. This speaks not only to the resistance on the part of the player to maximizing variation within a single performance, but also to the high degree of observable fixity over time in parts that are described as relatively "free" or "variable."

Further evidence for the recurrent choice of the same *céngkok* with very similar or even identical realizations can be drawn from many sources. In performances I recorded and transcribed of Suhardi playing Ketawang *"Puspawarna," sléndro pathet manyura,* again spanning a period of twenty-one years (1974–95), his choice of *céngkok* and the details of their realization were very nearly the same, even in passages where the skeletal melody tones are articulated only on the second and fourth beats, thus at least potentially allowing the player greater freedom (fewer points of reference) than in measures with four tones (such as those in ex. 3.1, above).

The similarity in Suhardi's choices, not only in successive repetitions of a passage within one performance but also between performances over many years, is particularly remarkable given the Javanese characterization of the *gambang* as one of the least constrained *garapan* instruments. Suhardi and others informed me that, compared to *gendèr* and *rebab*, for instance, the *gambang* part is freer *(lebih bebas)*, not only as regards the path between tones corresponding with skeletal melody beats, but also in sounding unison with the skeletal melody tones. In exercising this freedom, for example, Suhardi's *gambang* playing never arrived at tone 2 in the middle of the skeletal melody measure–2–1 in *Ketawang "Puspawarna"* (i.e., where the skeletal melody sounds the tone 2), but it *always* (ten out of ten occurrences) arrived at tone 3 at that point.[15]

Lest one get the impression that Suhardi lacks a sufficiently large vocabulary of *gambang* patterns with which to realize this or other pieces, consider that from my transcription and analysis of six pieces performed by Suhardi in 1974, some of them rather lengthy, I identified over two hundred *gambang* "motifs" (eight *gambang* beats in length), which could be transposed and combined in numerous ways to create a far greater number of one-measure-length *céngkok* (see Sutton 1975). When I asked him about the remarkable similarity between his renditions over the years, he simply replied that his treatment was sufficiently pleasant *(kepénak)* and his hands were used to *(kulina)* doing it that way. Attempting to vary it more might have resulted in his inadvertently starting to play a pattern that would lead naturally to a different tone, causing an awkward and uncomfortable moment as he put himself back on course.

One might argue that my findings are somewhat prejudiced by my choice of very well known pieces (or passages)—that any musician is more likely to have a set way of performing *Ketawang "Puspawarna"* or the passage from *Ketawang "Mijil Wedharing Tyas"* than other more rarely played pieces or passages, for which even someone as senior as Suhardi might still have the urge (or the need) to keep searching for slightly different and slightly more pleasant *garapan*.[16] Yet in the less popular pieces which I have observed him play over this same span of twenty-one years, Suhardi has demonstrated a similarly constrained impetus to vary. Different occurrences of some passages are identical, or nearly so; others may vary somewhat, but not radically.

To provide another perspective on improvisation in *gambang* playing, let us consider seven renditions of a short passage (one measure) from *Gendhing "Gambir Sawit,"* a popular but more complex piece. The measure is sounded on the skeletal melody instruments as – – 5 6, with tone 5 from the end of the previous measure sustained for the first two beats. This is a measure whose "inner melody" or *lagu* can be interpreted either as closely tied to the skeletal melody, or as a more active contour going to high 2 (written by Suhardi as

skeletal melody:	–		–		5		6

(from 5)

r.h. 5 3 5 5 5 6 5 5 5 6 5 1 1 6 1 2 2 3 2 1 6 1 5 3 2 2 2 5 5 3 5 6
1974a / / /
l.h. 2 3 5 5 1 6 5 – 1 6 5 1 5 6 1 2 2 3 2 1 6 1 5 3 2 2 2 5 2 3 5 6

r.h. 5 3 5 5 5 6 5 5 5 6 5 1 1 6 1 2 2 3 2 1 6 1 5 3 2 2 2 5 5 3 5 6
1974b / /
l.h. 2 3 5 5 1 6 5 – 5 – 5 1 1 6 1 2 2 3 2 1 6 1 5 3 2 2 2 5 2 3 5 6

skeletal melody:	–		–		5		6

r.h. 5 6 5 2 3 5 3 5 5 6 5 5 5 6 5 5 5 6 1 2 1 2 1 2 2 6 5 3 5 5 3 5 6
1983a / / / /
l.h. 1 6 5 2 3 5 6 5 1 6 5 – 1 6 5 – 5 6 1 2 3 2 1 2 1 6 5 3 2 3 5 6

r.h. 5 6 5 5 5 5 5 1 1 6 1 2 1 2 1 2 2 6 5 5 5 6 5 3 2 2 2 5 5 3 5 6
1983b / / / / /
l.h. 1 6 5 – 5 – 5 1 5 6 1 2 3 2 1 2 1 6 5 – 1 6 5 3 2 – 2 5 2 3 5 6

skeletal melody:	–		–		5		6

r.h. 5 5 5 3 5 2 3 5 6 1 6 5 6 1 6 5 5 6 5 5 5 6 5 3 2 2 2 5 5 3 5 6
1995a / / /
l.h. 5 – 5 3 5 2 3 5 6 1 6 5 6 1 6 5 1 6 5 – 1 6 5 3 2 – 2 5 2 3 5 6

r.h. 5 5 5 3 5 2 3 5 6 1 6 5 6 1 6 5 5 6 5 5 5 6 5 3 5 3 5 3 5 3 5 6
1995b / / /
l.h. 5 – 5 3 5 2 3 5 6 1 6 5 6 1 6 5 1 6 5 – 1 6 5 3 2 3 5 3 2 3 5 6

r.h. 5 3 5 2 3 5 3 5 6 1 6 5 6 1 6 5 5 6 5 5 5 6 1 2 2 6 5 3 5 3 5 6
1995c / / /
l.h. 5 3 5 2 3 5 6 5 6 1 6 5 6 1 6 5 1 6 5 – 5 6 1 2 1 6 5 3 2 3 5 6

Example 3.2. *Gambang* playing for repeated passage from *Gendhing "Gambir Sawit," sléndro pathet sanga* in three performances by Suhardi.

1 2 1 6). The *gambang* player may choose to stick close to the skeletal melody, to trace the contour of the implicit 1 2 1 6, or to diverge somewhat from either of these approaches.

As we can see in the transcription given in example 3.2, Suhardi chose to move to high 2 by the middle of the measure in both statements from 1974 and in statement b from 1983, and to move to high 2 by the third skeletal melody beat of the measure in statement a from 1983 and in statement 1995c. In the instances in which he did not reach high 2 by the middle of the measure, he performed what is considered a sustain of pitch 5 by playing eight-*gambang*-beat patterns that ended on 5 with the skeletal melody beats (here the two "rests," through which the skeletal melody instruments sustain the previous tone 5). In this case, he told me he wished *not* to be committed to one or another interpretation, as other players tend to maintain several interpretations of this measure. Yet he said he would not simply follow the *rebab* or *gendèr*—that is, going to high 2 if one or both of those instruments did so, or sustaining 5 if one or both of those instruments sustained 5. Rather, in conformity with the aesthetic he has articulated as *nunggal-misah* (literally, "converge-diverge"), he would resist slavish convergence with these other *garapan* parts just as he would resist convergence with every tone of the skeletal melody.

IMPROVISATION AS RECOVERY AND "FAKING"

Before concluding, I need to mention two areas of musical performance in which improvisation clearly does take place. In a tradition such as Javanese gamelan music, in which musicians play for many hours at a stretch (often all night long), loss of concentration, slips, and errors of various kinds are not uncommon. Even the best musician will have a lapse, and one of the measures of a good musician is her/his ability to execute a quick recovery, one that will almost inevitably involve a moment of improvisation to get back on track. Another instance of clear improvisation of far greater duration is the case of a musician who is insufficiently familiar with the piece being played and attempts to follow certain lead instruments, but makes false starts towards certain erroneous goal tones or points of reference only to have to turn away, all the while striving to reveal as little of his confusion as possible. This kind of playing can be quite remarkable to outside observers (such as myself), who may well marvel at the superior aural skills that enable a musician to fake it through extended passages without falling apart. But knowledgeable Javanese listeners and performers are quick to recognize this kind of playing *(ngawur)* and, while acknowledging that some are better at it than others, tend to evaluate it as undesirable.

Conclusion

In conclusion, we can say that, even outside the cases of recovery from a slip or faking through a passage, Javanese musicians make choices among extant patterns, sometimes during rather than prior to performance; and they may spontaneously alter some elements of these extant patterns; and, therefore, indeed they improvise. But does good performance require improvisation? For the most part, based on the testimony of a number of revered musicians, and the musical transcriptions presented and discussed above, I would say it does not. In fact, the inexperienced performer is likely to do more improvising than the experienced one. Pressing my teacher Suhardi on the relative value of spontaneity, I asked him about several hypothetical approaches to playing the special nine-keyed *saron wayang* (which, unlike the more numerous six- and seven-keyed *saron,* plays not the skeletal melody melody but embellishments or elaborations thereof). Player A plays with an exuberance of variation, but in that exuberance, occasionally misses the periodic congruence with the points of reference required by current performance conventions (generally every four beats of the skeletal melody). Player B has memorized one part, which he plays without variation in each repetition of the piece. Furthermore, B's part is, in itself, rather unimaginative, consisting mostly of conjunct motion away from and back to the points of convergence. Suhardi laughed that he wouldn't relish listening to either of these players! But he said he supposed the latter would be preferable. Only when I reduced the number of errors by player A to just one did he indicate he might prefer A; but he felt uncomfortable with this imaginary dilemma—two poor choices![17]

Not all Javanese musicians hold identical opinions on aesthetic matters, of course. But among the other musicians with whom I studied, I feel confident in stressing that, while very little is *entirely* fixed beforehand in a Javanese performance, a great deal is *almost* fixed (or is expected to be). I believe most Javanese musicians and listeners enjoy the element of flexibility, but there is a strong aversion on the part of many musicians to major musical risk taking and to bold originality. There are surprises, and these keep each performance fresh and unique, but the surprises are almost always little ones. Listeners and performers, then, can be comfortable and not startled. The extent to which this aesthetic sensibility may be related to the long legacy of colonialism in Java is difficult to determine, but we should note that such sensibility also characterizes other forms of social interchange in Java. Indeed, maintaining a smooth and unprovocative demeanor was a quality encouraged by Dutch colonial rulers in their Javanese subjects (see Pemberton 1994), and has come to be a defining component in conceptions of "Javanese-ness" held by Javanese and non-Javanese alike.

As promised, we must concede that Javanese musicians improvise, but would we wish to characterize Javanese music as improvisatory? I would say not, for the aesthetic emphasis is not on originality, spontaneity, or even planned variability, though for many of the *garapan* parts some degree of variation is both normal and expected. I would conclude simply by positing that we view gamelan music performance as the combination of individually composed parts, with relatively little determined spontaneously during performance and hardly anything presented without prior planning. It would not be a contradiction, then, to say that Javanese musicians improvise, but that Javanese music is not improvisatory.

Notes

1. Kartomi echoes this view, stating that "since improvising and composing both involve workings and reworkings of creative ideas, they are essentially part of the same process" (1991, 55).

2. Sanctioned spontaneity, of course, involves responsibility—the responsibility of the performer to create (that is, "compose") and execute passages that are aesthetically acceptable to most listeners. And with this responsibility comes potential risk—that what is spontaneously composed and performed will not be favorably received. But are writing composers free of such risks? One may work over a piece prior to its initial presentation to a listening audience, but one still shoulders the responsibility of arriving at something to be judged. What written composition does, of course, is to remove much of the creative responsibility from the performer, leaving the performer to be judged largely on matters of technique and nuance. The writing composer may still risk embarrassment in the press, but not in a face-to-face encounter with the audience during or immediately after the performance of the music.

3. Cf. Becker's remarks: "At a Javanese *wayang kulit* [shadow puppet performance], a musician in the gamelan may be creating particularly fine *gender* [multi-octave metallophone] patterns during the playing of the *talu* or introduction. Some in the audience will notice and appreciate, some will not. Either way, it does not matter much to the *gender* player. He is part of a whole, and the integration of his part into the whole is more important than the creation of exquisite *cengkok* or melodic patterns" (1979, 6–7).

4. I have often had students describe the musical features of a recording as "improvised," but when I press them for the criteria behind this description they realize that improvisation is a process, not a product with definable, audible traits.

5. On regional differences in traditions of Javanese gamelan musical, see Sutton 1991.

6. For an introduction to central Javanese gamelan music, see Sorrell 1990, Lindsay 1992, and Sutton 1993.

7. Sumarsam's notion of "inner melody" is outlined in Sumarsam 1975a and explored at length in Sumarsam 1984. Suhardi's conception of *lagu* is outlined in Sutton 1979. Marc Perlman's recent dissertation (1993) skillfully explores the nature of these unplayed melodic models and questions the extent to which they are shared by central Javanese musicians, particularly outside of academic circles.

8. See further Perlman's intelligent and wide ranging discussion of these and related terms (1993, 55–77).

9. These would be called *variasi* in Suhardi's terminology, and *wiletan* (or *wilet*) in the terminology prevalent among musicians and students affiliated with Sekolah Tinggi Seni Indonesia (STSI), the academic institution where Martopangrawit taught in Surakarta.

10. For *balungan* notation, brief discussion of overall form, and transcription and analysis of *gambang* (multi-octave xylophone) parts for these pieces, see Sutton 1975 (116–59 and 238–93). For comparative transcriptions and discussion of *gambang* variation in different passage from Ketawang "Puspawarna," see Sutton 1988 (172–87) and 1993 (168–84).

11. I made the first set of recordings with the purpose of learning about Suhardi's playing style on two *garapan* instruments (*gendèr*, multi-octave metallophone, and *gambang*, multi-octave xylophone). With subsequent recordings (in 1979–80, 1983 and

1995) I wished to discover possible changes in his playing style and found, as can be seen in the data presented in this article, a high degree of stability over many years, leading me to conclude that his style had not really changed at all.

12. The two *gatra* constitute one *kenongan,* a phrase marked by the sounding of a large kettle gong (called *kenong*) on the final (eighth) beat of the phrase. In this piece, the first and second *kenongan* have the same *balungan.* At the end of the second *kenongan* in this and all pieces in *ketawang* form, a large gong (called *gong*) is sounded simultaneously with the *kenong* and the final beat.

13. The musical examples here employ the Javanese cipher notation system *(titlaras kepatihan),* which enjoys widespread popularity throughout Java. Each numeral represents one pitch degree within one of two scale systems: *sléndro* (1 2 3 5 6, with nearly equidistant intervals) or *pélog* (1 2 3 4 5 6 7, with small and large intervals). When outside the middle register for a particular instrument or part, register is indicated by subscript dots (lower octave) and superscript dots (higher octave). Ranges on the *balungan* instruments (*saron* and *slenthem*) and on the *gambang* are as follows: *saron* and *slenthem* (in *sléndro*): $\underset{\cdot}{6}$–$\dot{1}$; (in *pélog*): 1–7; *gambang* (in both scale systems): $\underset{\cdot}{1}$–$\overset{\cdot\cdot}{3}$. Whether *sléndro* or *pélog,* the *gambang* has only five tones per octave (in order to facilitate transfer of patterns from one scale system to the other). Thus in *pélog,* the tones available in each octave are either 1 2 3 5 6 or 2 3 5 6 7. The last beat of a grouping is the most heavily weighted, comparable to the first beat of a measure in Western staff notation. For example, the skeletal melody phrase 2 1 2 6 has the greatest stress on the 6, with secondary stress on the 1. Skeletal melody and *gambang* parts are both characterized by great rhythmic regularity, the skeletal melody proceeding with four even beats per measure, and the *gambang* part subdividing each skeletal melody beat here by eight even *gambang* beats (in other contexts, where *balungan* may be slower or faster, the *gambang* subdivision is always an even multiple of two, up to thirty-two *gambang* beats per skeletal melody beat). Sustaining of a previous tone, involving a physical "pause" by the player (although not the same as a rest in Western notation) is indicated by a dash, and is referred to in the body of the text as a rest. Instances in which right and left hand tones are slightly offset rhythmically are shown with a slash: $\overset{5}{\underset{1}{/}}$ indicates the right-hand 5 is played just perceptibly prior to the left-hand 1.

14. Because *gambang* playing consists almost entirely of doubling at the octave, Javanese talk of the *gambang* part as a single melodic line. For the purposes of analysis here, in discussing convergence with skeletal melody and *lagu,* I refer to the octave combination $\underset{\cdot}{\overset{5}{5}}$ as *gambang* tone 5 (low 5), octave combination $\overset{\cdot}{1}$ as 1, etc.

15. This was not a deliberate dissonance against skeletal melody tone 2, Suhardi told me, but rather a "comfortable" *(kepénak)* midpoint on the way from high 3 down to 1—"comfortable" in the sense that he uses well-established patterns. A dissonance with the skeletal melody at midpoint of the measure, while not consistently sought, is often acceptable and may represent a consonance with other parts (e.g., *gendèr*); and a dissonance creates some tension to be resolved at the end of the measure (where, in this case, Suhardi *always* reaches tone 1).

16. For more extensive discussion of the notion of "searching" in relation to Javanese performance practice, particularly for *garapan,* see Perlman 1993 (364–70).

17. Cf. Nettl's remarks: "The musician who is highly creative and tries to avoid using the points of reference and the building blocks of the model is chastised for his ignorance of the model; an identical performance each time is almost equally unacceptable,

but perhaps not quite as culpable, and this point is of great import because it strengthens our view that the improviser is really simply the performer of a traditional piece, establishing his own way of rendering it" (1974, 18–19).

References

Becker, Judith. 1972. "Traditional Music in Modern Java." Ph.D. thesis, University of Michigan.

———. 1979. "People Who Sing; People Who Dance." In *What Is Modern Indonesian Culture?* edited by Gloria Davis, 3–10. Southeast Asia Series, no. 52. Athens, Ohio: Ohio University Center for International Studies.

———. 1980. *Traditional Music in Modern Java: Gamelan in a Changing Society.* Honolulu: University of Hawaii Press.

Berliner, Paul F. 1994. *Thinking in Jazz: The Infinite Art of Improvisation.* Chicago: University of Chicago Press.

Ferand, Ernest T. 1961. *Improvisation in Nine Centuries of Western Music: An Anthology with a Historical Introduction.* Cologne: Arno Volk Verlag.

Groneman, J. 1890. *De Gamelan te Jogjakarta.* Foreword by J. P. Land. Amsterdam: Johannes Müller.

Hood, Mantle. 1954. *The Nuclear Theme as a Determinant of Patet in Javanese Music.* Groningen and Jakarta: J. B. Wolters. Reprint, New York: Da Capo Press, 1977.

———. 1975. "Improvisation in the Stratified Ensembles of Southeast Asia." *Selected Reports in Ethnomusicology* 2, no. 2:25–33.

Hood, Mantle, and Hardja Susilo. 1967. *Music of the Venerable Dark Cloud: Introduction, Commentary, and Analysis.* Los Angeles: University of California Press.

Horsley, Imogene, Michael Collins, Eva Badura-Skoda, and Dennis Libby. 1980. "Improvisation." In *The New Grove Dictionary of Music and Musicians,* edited by Stanley Sadie, vol. 9, 31–52. London: Macmillan.

Jairazbhoy, Nazir A. 1980. "Improvisation: Asian Art Music, East and South-East Asia." In *The New Grove Dictionary of Music and Musicians,* edited by Stanley Sadie, vol. 9, 52–53. London: Macmillan.

Kartomi, Margaret. 1980. "Musical Strata in Sumatra, Java, and Bali." In *Musics of Many Cultures: An Introduction,* edited by Elizabeth May. Berkeley: University of California Press.

———. 1991. "Musical Improvisations by Children at Play." *The World of Music* 33, no. 3:53–65.

Kunst, Jaap. 1973. *Music in Java: Its History, Its Theory, and Its Technique.* 2 vols. Translated by Emile van Loo. 3d ed., revised and enlarged by E. Heins. The Hague: Martinus Nijhoff.

Lindsay, Jennifer. 1992. *Javanese Gamelan: Traditional Orchestra of Indonesia.* 2d ed. Singapore: Oxford University Press.

Martopangrawit, R. L. 1973. *Titilaras Cengkok-cengkok Genderan dengan Wiletannya* [Notation of Gendèr Melodic Patterns with their Realizations]. Surakarta: Akademi Seni Karawitan Indonesia.

———. 1984. "Notes on Knowledge of Gamelan Music." Translated by Martin Hatch. In *Karawitan: Source Readings in Javanese Gamelan and Vocal Music,* edited by Judith Becker and Alan Feinstein, vol. 1, 1–244. Ann Arbor: University of Michigan,

Center for South and Southeast Asian Studies. First published as *Catatan-Catatan Pengetahuan Karawitan,* 2 vols., Surakarta: Akademi Seni Karawitan Indonesia, 1969–72.

Nettl, Bruno. 1974. "Thoughts on Improvisation: A Comparative Approach." *The Musical Quarterly* 60:1–19.

———. 1986. "Improvisation." In *The New Harvard Dictionary of Music,* edited by Don Randel, 392–94. Cambridge: Harvard University Press.

———. 1991. Preface to "New Perspectives on Improvisation." *The World of Music* 33, no. 3:3–5.

Nichols, Beverley. 1944. *Verdict on India.* London: Jonathan Cape.

Pemberton, John. 1994. *On the Subject of "Java."* Ithaca: Cornell University Press.

Perlman, Marc. 1993. "Unplayed Melodies: Music Theory in Post-Colonial Java." Ph.D. thesis, Wesleyan University.

Sindoesawarno. 1987. "Knowledge about Gamelan Music." Translated by Martin Hatch. In *Karawitan: Source Readings in Javanese Gamelan and Vocal Music,* edited by Judith Becker and Alan H. Feinstein, vol. 2, 311–87. Ann Arbor: University of Michigan, Center for South and Southeast Asian Studies. First published as *Ilmu Karawitan,* Surakarta: Konservatori Karawitan Indonesia, 1955.

Sorrell, Neil. 1990. *A Guide to the Gamelan.* London: Faber and Faber.

Sumarsam. 1975a. "Inner Melody in Javanese Gamelan Music." *Asian Music* 7, no. 1:3–13.

———. 1975b. "Gendèr Barung, Its Technique and Function in the Context of Javanese Gamelan." *Indonesia* 20:161–72.

———. 1984. "Inner Melody in Javanese Gamelan." In *Karawitan: Source Readings in Javanese Gamelan and Vocal Music,* edited by Judith Becker and Alan H. Feinstein, vol. 1, 245–304. Ann Arbor: University of Michigan, Center for South and Southeast Asian Studies.

———. 1995. *Gamelan: Cultural Interaction and Musical Development in Central Java.* Chicago: University of Chicago Press.

Susilo, Hardja. 1980. "Indonesia: Central Java, Classical Music." *The New Grove Dictionary of Music and Musicians,* edited by Stanley Sadie, vol. 9, 189–96. London: Macmillan.

———. 1987. "Improvisation in Wayang Wong Panggung: Creativity within Cultural Constraints." *Yearbook for Traditional Music* 19:1–11.

Sutton, R. Anderson. 1975. "The Javanese Gambang and Its Music." M. A. thesis, University of Hawaii.

———. 1978. "Notes Toward a Grammar of Variation in Javanese *Gendèr* Playing." *Ethnomusicology* 22:275–96.

———. 1979. "Concept and Treatment in Javanese Gamelan Music, with Reference to the Gambang." *Asian Music* 9, no. 2:59–79.

———. 1987. "Variation and Composition in Java." *Yearbook for Traditional Music* 19:65–95.

———. 1988. "Individual Variation in Javanese Gamelan Performance." *Journal of Musicology* 6:169–97.

———. 1991. *Traditions of Gamelan Music in Java: Musical Pluralism and Regional Identity.* Cambridge: Cambridge University Press.

————. 1993. *Variation in Central Javanese Gamelan Music: Dynamics of a Steady State.* DeKalb: Northern Illinois University, Center for Southeast Asian Studies.

Vetter, Roger. 1981. "Flexibility in the Performance Practice of Central Javanese Music." *Ethnomusicology* 25:199–214.

Walton, Susan Pratt. 1995. "One Singer's Transformation of a Traditional Javanese Gamelan Composition: Agency and Spiritual Power in a Composition by Ibu Supadmi." Paper presented at Midwest Chapter Meeting of the Society for Ethnomusicology, University of Illinois at Urbana-Champaign, 22 April 1995.

Improvisation as Music and in Culture

CHAPTER FOUR

Improvisation, Ecstasy, and Performance Dynamics in Arabic Music

ALI JIHAD RACY

What do musicians' articulations about their creative musical endeavors tell us about music making as a process? Can such articulations help us reconstruct cultural models of musical creativity and eventually enable us to better understand related phenomena such as improvisation, inspiration, musical excellence, and performance ambience? This chapter investigates one Arab musician's views on creativity, a concept that Western thinkers have generally associated with newness and value and addressed in three related areas: the agent or the creating person, the creative process, and the created object (Rothenberg and Hausman 1976, 6). Defining creativity in broad and flexible terms as a complex phenomenon with cultural and personal dimensions, I refer to contrastive examples from outside the Arab world. Particularly emphasized is the tradition of modal improvisation in the Near Eastern Arab world and the role played by various contextual dynamics in the improvising process.

Today, the male singer Ṣabāḥ Fakhrī (born in Aleppo, Syria, in 1933) is widely recognized as an icon of traditional Arab music. A major proponent of Aleppo's established musical legacy, Fakhrī is heard in live performances and on cassettes and videotapes in various Arab communities throughout the East Mediterranean world, North Africa, Europe, and North America. In a conversation I had with the celebrated artist, the notion of creativity was explained as follows:

> As a matter of fact, I feel delighted when I see the people understanding me and judiciously following what I am performing *(bīḥāsbūnī)*. Indeed, I prefer an audience that is fully able to fathom my music, one that is artistically enlightened. First and foremost, a listener has to love music because the more he loves it, if he is also able to understand the words and the tunes, the more his presence delights me. Such a listener knows the value of the music, as the jeweler tells diamond from glass. Of course I sense people's reactions from their movements and by observing their inner emotional tribulations *(infiʿāl)* and their responses *(tajāwub)* to what I am singing.
>
> In order for me to perform best, first I have to be sure that I am physically in good condition and that I am accompanied by good musicians as well as equipped with an appropriate sound system, one that I have tried out and adjusted in advance. Beyond that it is the audience that plays the most significant role in bringing the performance to a higher plateau of creativity

(ibdāʿ). . . . I like the lights in the performance hall to remain on so that I can see the listeners and interact with them. If they respond I become inspired to give more. As such we become reflections of one another. I consider the audience to be me and myself to be the audience.

Of course, the performer has also to be in a state of ecstasy *(maṭrūb)* in order to perform in the most inspired fashion. Obviously, in order to deliver something you must have it yourself first and then reflect it, as the moon shines by reflecting the light it receives from the sun. In a large measure, this state emanates from the audience, particularly the *sammīʿah* (talented and sensitive listeners), although the singer must also be endowed with *rūḥ* (soul) and *iḥsās* (feeling), in addition to being in a state of elation and ecstasy (*basṭ* and *tajallī*) at the time of performing. Indeed, elation causes the talented artist to shine.[1]

Throughout history, societies have held different views on the role of the artist in the creative process and the sources of his or her inspiration. In ancient Greece, inspiration was considered a form of guidance stemming from external powers, for example, a person's own "genius" or attendant spirit, and similarly in Arabia poets and musicians were inspired by the *jinn* (Farmer 1973, 7). Plato, who associated inspiration with the literary arts, maintained that it was received through emotional frenzy, supernatural possession, and "divine madness" (Rothenberg and Hausman 1976, 31; Rouget 1985, 199). In Europe's nineteenth-century culture, articulations of creativity and inspiration turned away from external attributions and instead treated the artist himself as the center of attention and a source of clues to the creative process (Osborne 1977, 242–44). Such focus on the individual artist is implicit in the following excerpts from the letters and memoirs of Hector Berlioz (1803–1869). Here the romantic composer reflects upon his own creativity while composing:

> I got up with the intention of working exclusively at my score today; my fire was lighted and my door shut; there was no chance of importunate callers or fools of any kind, when your letter arrived . . . .
> You ask me what I am doing. I am finishing the *Troyens*. . . .
> You can have no idea, my dear Bulow, of the ebb and flow of opposite feelings which have agitated my heart since I have been working at this composition. . . . One more huge effort, and we shall both reach the top of the mountain, one carrying the other.
> The thing which would be absolutely fatal to Sisyphus now, would be any fresh discouragement from without; but nobody can discourage me, nobody knows anything about my score, no callousness can reach me through the impressions of anybody else. Even if you, you yourself, were here, I would not show you anything. I am too much afraid of being frightened. (Dunstan 1882, 274, 277, 278–9)

In his memoirs he gives a more general statement of his musical philosophy:

The predominant features of my music are passionate expression, inward intensity, rhythmic impetus, and a quality of unexpectedness. When I say passionate expression, I mean an expression bent on reproducing the inner meaning of its subject, even when that subject is the opposite of passion, and gentle, tender feelings are being expressed, or a profound calm. (Cairns 1969, 478)[2]

Berlioz's remarks can be linked to the intellectual, philosophical, and artistic climate of mid-nineteenth-century Europe. The statement by Ṣabāḥ Fakhrī, on the other hand, represents a traditional facet of secular Arab music, specifically the modern *ṭarab* style of the East Mediterranean world and Egypt, a style that emphasizes live musical performance, gives prominence to instantaneous modal creations, and treats music as an ecstatic experience.

A comparative interpretation of the above two statements can shed further light upon the musical worlds of the two artists. More specifically, it can inform on the physical, emotional, and social components of the creative process, as well as the nature of the created musical product in each of these musical worlds. Incidentally, the two seemingly contrastive worldviews are discussed in order to demonstrate the variety and complementarity of creative patterns rather than to represent culturally demarcated or mutually exclusive approaches. In this chapter, a basic premise is that these and other creative modes tend to coexist, interact, and overlap with one another.

For convenience, the social-aesthetic complex represented by Fakhrī's statement is referred to here as "the first model" to differentiate it from the cultural-artistic complex expressed by Berlioz's statement (the "second model"). Accordingly, the first model, representing the *ṭarab* musical culture, appears to emphasize the operative component of the musical process. Without necessarily negating the intrinsic value of musical works as such, this approach derives its significance and effectiveness from the immediate physical and temporal context. An integral part of the performance event, the creative process is considered place and time specific. To compare, the second model implies that the creative process generates aesthetic works that are valuable in themselves, or according to Kant's philosophical view of art, imbued with an objective, universal, and transcendental aesthetic value (Schott 1989, 81). Furthermore, the first model, which treats society (specifically the initiated listeners) as an indispensable source of inspiration, is in essence collectively based, socially experienced, and outwardly directed. In contrast, the second model portrays creativity as being highly introspective, individual-centered, and creator-focused. Accordingly society, or the public, is a potential source of distraction and a threat to the artist's solitude, composure, and concentration.

The first model demonstrates a distinct awareness of the role of the audience and places the creative process largely within the domain of social accessibility. By comparison, the second model depicts the creative endeavor with an air of elitism, awe, and exclusivity, thus bringing to mind an attitude expressed by a major twentieth-century European composer:

> I believe that a real composer writes music for no other reason than that it pleases him. Those who compose because they want to please others, and have the audience in mind, are not real artists. They are not the kind of men who are pressed to say something whether or not there exists one person who likes it, even if they themselves dislike it. They are not creators who must open the valves in order to relieve the interior pressure of a creation ready to be born. They are merely more or less skillfull entertainers who would renounce composing if they could not find listeners. (Schoenberg 1947, 69–70)

Furthermore, the first model implies recognition of the mysterious and complex nature of creativity but also reveals a natural or practical outlook toward it, reminding us of Mozart's description of his own spontaneous, down-to-earth delivery of musical ideas (Ghiselin 1952, 44–45). In the second model a composer might seek his creative material inwardly in an act of retrieval and pursue inspiration within his own mental and emotional realms, which may be imaginatively portrayed or metaphorically expressed. Similarly, the created work, as Berlioz's remarks seem to indicate, may become a product of emotional belaboring, soul searching, and even physical tribulations, a process perhaps analogous to giving birth. Whereas Fakhrī's remarks are voiced in response to specific questions[3] rather than written in a published memoir or autobiography, Berlioz's statements obviously reflect an interest in self-analysis and fascination for the intriguing nature of the composer's inner psyche.

Moreover, the first model links inspiration to a specific condition of ecstasy which in turn depends on the artist's own physical and emotional state, input from the accompanying musicians, possible inexplicable outside controls, and above all, a musically educated and responsive audience. Berlioz's interest in the realm of ecstasy, through the potential effects of mind-altering substances, may have stemmed from a desire to experience the extraordinary, the shocking, and the fantastic, or perhaps from an interest in distancing oneself from ordinary reality. In Fakhrī's model, however, ecstasy tends to sharpen the performer's relationship with his immediate world, represented by the direct listening context.

Furthermore, in the first model, creativity involves both the artist and his listeners (or to put it differently, both the listeners and their artists) and relies on direct and instantaneous input from the audience. However, in the second model creativity seems vicarious and mediated by the musical score and the interpreter, thus leading to an indirect or delayed input from the audience. The first model exhibits tendencies to impress, affect, re-create, perfect, and reinterpret. The second model does not necessarily preclude such ideals, but it demonstrates an effort to express, create, produce, or as the above quote from Schoenberg seems to indicate, release inner energy in the form of catharsis.

Finally, in the first model, music derives its momentum and emotional efficacy from human interplay, through a feedback process involving active and direct communication between the artist and the initiated listener. Whereas the modern concept of "listening" tends to imply a cerebral aesthetic process distinct from the mere physical sense of "hearing," the *ṭarab*-related concept of *samaʿ* means both "listening" and "hearing." Like the related Sufi concept of *samāʿ*, or "auditioning," the concept of *samaʿ* tends to present music as a visceral experience. In view of its transformative emotional and physical powers, Arab music has been historically linked to both mystical transcendence and mundane sensuality. As *ṭarab* artists say, *al-fann iḥsās*, "art is feeling," or "music is to be felt."

Creative Ecstasy

Fakhrī's statement gains its legitimacy from established practice. It attests to the emotional, physical, and musical conditions that enhance the creative musical experience and prepare the performer to become an effective generator of *ṭarab*. Traditional performers whom I have interviewed maintain that the *ṭarab* process first requires that the singer or the instrumentalist be rooted in the *ṭarab* tradition. Like his audience members, he must be well versed in the *ṭarab* idiom so that he can "feel" the music, or as Fakhrī explains, he must understand it and sense it properly. He is expected, for example, to play the neutral (microtonal) Arab intervals correctly and "feel" their musical effect. Similarly he must understand and respond to the *qaflāt* (singular *qaflah*), the emotionally charged cadential formulas at the end of each melodic phrase, particularly in modal improvisations.

In addition, such a performer must be endowed with *ruh*, "soul" or "feeling," namely the emotional power and talent to musically affect or engage the listener ecstatically. Without this innate quality, a performer may still be accepted for his technical performance skills or his ability to display musical innovations, but he is also criticized and even dismissed as someone who plays but does not communicate emotions, or as Ṣabāḥ Fakhrī puts it, "He can play his instrument, but cannot make it speak." Musically, *iḥsās* implies correct intonation, rhythmic accuracy, and good judgment regarding modal progressions and tonal emphases. "Feeling" also refers to an intuitive ability to affect—for example, carefully avoiding renditions that are too static and too repetitive to be emotionally engaging, or those that are too excessive and digressive to generate and maintain a true sense of musical ecstasy. A talented *muṭrib,* or *ṭarab* singer, is someone who knows how to manipulate the music in order to engage the initiated listeners, a skill that requires that the performer be able to "feel" the music himself as well.

The *ṭarab* process also calls for conditions that have to be present at the time of performing. Creativity on the part of a *ṭarab* artist presupposes suitable physical, emotional, musical, and according to some performers, cosmological states. As Ṣabāḥ Fakhrī's statement suggests, a singer should be physically comfortable, having had enough sleep, and should have refrained from foods and drinks that are detrimental to singing, instead selecting those that suit the voice. He should also be in an agreeable mood, having avoided upsetting concerns or experiences such as personal conflicts immediately prior to performing.

Another basic temporary condition is the development of ecstasy. A performer must experience an ecstatic state that musicians describe in general terms as *tajallī, basṭ,* and *kayf* but often refer to specifically as *salṭanah.* The general concept of *ṭarab* refers to both the traditional secular music as a genre and to the overall ecstatic sensation connected with that music and experienced by various participants in the musical process. By comparison, the musical term *salṭanah* (apparently from the verb *tasalṭana,* "to dominate," "to reign over," or "to experience a sense of authority") may be translated as "modal ecstasy." It applies mainly to performers and refers specifically to a state developed prior to, as well as during, the generation of *ṭarab* proper. Of special concern to traditional *ṭarab* performers, modal ecstasy is recognized as the road to excellence and emotional effectiveness in performance (Racy 1987, 20 3; 1988, 146).

Today musicians attribute *salṭanah* to a number of factors. Some established musicians from Cairo, Damascus, and Aleppo, including Ṣabāḥ Fakhrī, are aware of medieval Arabic treatises that discuss musical cosmology and celestial influence upon humans on various days or times of the day. Rooted in Pythagorean doctrines linking musical ethos to the shifting configurations of planets and zodiacs (Shiloah 1981, 38), the notion implies direct causalities between the momentary appeal of specific modes and the momentary configurations of heavenly entities. Performers cite a practice that in some Arab countries was common until the early decades of this century. Accordingly, the call to prayer was rendered in a cosmologically "correct" melodic mode each time it was performed. The cosmological explanation as to why at certain times we feel inclined to perform in specific *maqāmāt* (plural of *maqām,* or "melodic mode") is not explicitly subscribed to by practicing musicians in general. However, some musicians still allude to a possible external source for *salṭanah,* primarily because at times modes "impose" themselves in ways that seem mystifying and compelling.

On another level, *salṭanah* can be voluntarily produced and maintained. Although some musicians imply that the deliberate inducement becomes fruitful only when it happens to agree with the externally determined modal "energy," *salṭanah* has been traditionally acquired through actual modal suggestions prior to performing. Solo improvisations or short ensemble pieces such as the *dūlāb* heard prior to a performance are known to establish within the artist *salṭanah* in the mode of such preludes and enable him or her to excel in performing in that mode. In the traditional *waṣlah,* the multisectional compound form found in Cairo before World War I, the linear order and the stylistic content of the inner components was dictated in part by ecstatic considerations.

The *waṣlah* structure was well suited to the generation and maintenance of *salṭanah* within the musicians, especially the leading vocalist, and subsequently for instilling *ṭarab* emotions into the listeners (Racy 1983).

In modern practice, the state of *salṭanah* is acquired through a preparatory phase of modal "conditioning," which includes hearing music in the mode of an ensuing performance, sometimes even listening to a short *taqāsīm* passage either live or recorded. A musician may also develop modal ecstasy if he or she actually performs in a certain mode for a period of time, long enough to feel the captivating effect of the *maqām* and to sense an effortless and ineffably effective power to create music in that mode. As metaphorically expressed by Muḥammad al-ʿAqqād, a prominent *qānūn* player from Egypt, "When you have *salṭanah* you become like a king; you are invincible; nobody can conquer you,"[4] a view reminiscent of the magical connotations of the *duende* state experienced by Spanish flamenco musicians and dancers (Papenbrok 1985, 54). Despite such confidence, musicians acknowledge that the carefully developed and nurtured modal ecstasy is fragile as well as transient. A performer's intense modal ecstasy may be diminished or disrupted if he hears bad intonation or experiences an abrupt shift to an unrelated *maqām*, or if he has to make a sudden transposition to another tonal level. Indeed, relative tonal stability and intervallic consistency are both conducive to modal ecstasy, as for that matter, drones are recognized for their potent ecstatic suggestibility. Modal ecstasy is essentially tonal as well as intervallic.

Beyond these voluntary and involuntary conditions, the *ṭarab* culture attributes creativity to the interactive cycle of communication involving the performer and the audience. The dynamic exchange between a talented performer who is ecstatically transformed *(maṭrūb)* and a compatibly talented and emotionally transformed audience is viewed as a primary condition for the rise of *salṭanah* and the attainment and maintenance of excellence during a performance. Such an interactive atmosphere with its ideal human and physical surroundings is summed up by the musical concept of *jaww,* best translated as "ambience" or "atmosphere."

Creative Listening

In the *ṭarab* culture, the listener is considered a primary player in the creative *ṭarab* process. The key role of the *sammīʿ* is underscored by the Arab tradition of articulating *ādāb* ("manners" or "codes of behavior") pertaining to music. This tradition is rooted in the same cultural matrix that led to the listening and conduct manuals prepared by Sufi authorities such as al-Ghazālī (n.d., 236–69) and al-Suhrawardī in Medieval Islam (Milson 1975, 62), and to the idealized performance mannerisms associated with Medieval ʿAbbasid courts (Sawa 1989, 118–27). The desire to promote a cadre of good listeners, which in Sufi traditions led to specific rules regarding *samāʿ* and *wajd* (spiritual ecstasy), had counterparts in the modern secular world. In an early twentieth-century treatise on Arab music, Kāmil al-Khulaʾī of Egypt articulated musical *ādāb* for both performers and listeners, approaching the topic of listening in ways similar to those he applied to performing (al-Khulaʿī [1904?]). Distressed by the moral, educational, and behavioral standards of the Cairean musical public of his time, he discussed the importance of knowledge about music and about how musicians function, what their needs are, how they feel, and the circumstances under which they perform and excel. Also stressed were other desirable factors pertaining to the listeners' behavior during a performance and their basic attitudes toward music and musicians.

Accordingly, the *muṭrib* would lose his ecstatic modal power if his performance was disrupted by listeners' persisting requests or if he were forced to switch abruptly to another *maqām*. Indeed, such a switch would have been technically difficult since at al-Khulaʿī's time the *qānūn* lacked tuning levers and was tuned in advance to the *maqām* of each *waṣlah*. Al-Khulaʿī warned that because of ignorance in the rudiments of the art *(uṣul al-fann)*, the listener may not realize how disturbing or inappropriate his request is, particularly since the tune he is requesting may be in a *maqām* different from the one being performed, or from the mode that "has become sweet and has dominated the ears of the singer" (al-Khulaʿī [1904?], 83). Here, al-Khulaʿī was referring to the predominance of the *salṭanah* state. The singer does not have time to fulfill the requests of everyone attending the performance, and furthermore, "if the singer were not possessed by *ṭarab* himself he would not be able to instill *ṭarab* in anybody," a statement echoed by Fakhrī almost ninety years later. Furthermore, the listener has an obligation to take into consideration the feelings of the performer and to put him in the right mood through sweet and tender speech: "That is what gives the singer the sense of comfort and the right disposition to create *ṭarab* in you in as much as God [at that moment] has bestowed upon him," a statement that clearly refers to the audience's role in preparing an ambience conducive to *salṭanah* within the *muṭrib*.

Today, musicians critique their audiences along the same criteria outlined by al-Khulaʿī. Often stressed are the listeners' sensitivity regarding the time needed for tuning, their concern for the right musical ambience, their ability to listen, and their sincere display of *ṭarab* feelings, including voicing exclamations of approval that indicate genuine ecstasy. Musicians complain about the lack of truly active performer-listener communication and the domination of one of two extremes, either apathy or excessively impassioned behavior, often marked by drunkenness, dancing, clapping, and singing loudly with the *muṭrib*, extremes that can stifle the finesse of the music and put an end to the performer's sense of ecstasy. Musicians often summarize the lack of creativity in their performances by referring to the overall atmosphere of the performance. A phrase typically expressed is *mā fīsh jaww* ("there is no ambience").

The interaction between the performer and the audience develops gradually and requires certain preparatory procedures. In a *haflah*, or large public performance, the *muṭrib* first needs to locate and establish communication with the *sammī'ah* in the audience. He also has to establish basic rapport with the audience members, to ascertain their musical interests and inclinations, and to select the song repertoire accordingly. This process demands charisma, intuition, and talent on the part of the *muṭrib;* as Ṣabāḥ Fakhrī puts it, a good *muṭrib* must be a psychologist (*'ālim nafs*). The *muṭrib* may begin to create a *jaww* by talking to the audience. In some large *ḥaflāt* (the plural of *ḥaflah*), he may test basic audience reactions through a few musical trials. Ṣabāḥ Fakhrī explains that in his case the *ḥaflah* proper begins after about one hour of singing, because until that time he is trying pieces in different styles, *muwashshaḥāt, qudūd,* a *dawr,* and others.

Such musical scanning is accompanied by visual surveillance on the part of the *muṭrib,* whose ability to see and hear his audience is of crucial importance. Adequate lighting in the performance hall enables the singer to monitor audience reactions and to maintain visual contact with the listeners throughout the performance.[5] Once a healthy rapport is established, the artist attempts to keep the audience emotionally engaged. According to Fakhrī, the repertoire is conceived and manipulated in such a way as to prevent the *ṭarab* momentum from slackening or dissipating. For example, if the singer felt his *mawwāl* was becoming too long and tedious he would follow it immediately with a metrically animated precomposed song.

In a *jalsah,* or small gathering, and to some extent in a nightclub, the process of interaction tends to be more intimate and more direct than in the large public performance. In an informal gathering, the performer, often an unpaid artist, may know the *sammī'ah* in the audience personally and may have already established a social rapport with them. Often, *jalsah* audiences consist almost entirely of *sammī'ah* who listen in subtle and circumspect ways, but who communicate their intense reactions directly and unequivocally. In such a context, the performer is less dependent upon personal charisma than upon effective musical communication. Indeed, *ṭarab* musicians I have interviewed, including those who perform mostly in large public performances, cherish the inspiring ambience created by small, musically select groups.

The Role of Improvisation

Improvisation, viewed broadly as "the creation of a musical work, or the final form of a musical work, as it is being performed" (Horsley et al. 1980, 31), is a natural adjunct to the ecstatic feedback process. Composing while performing is intimately linked to the interactive nature of the *ṭarab* event. In effect, the full shape of a *ṭarab* performance depends on three interrelated factors: first, an emotionally meaningful stock of compositional devices shared by participants in the *ṭarab* process; second, the skill of the *ṭarab* artist who possesses "soul" and may be able to render his performance in an appropriate ecstatic state; and third, the listener's musical disposition and sensitivity communicated through direct emotional-musical input.

don't have a categorical distinction [?]

The *ṭarab* culture recognizes improvisation primarily in tacit and indirect ways. In fact, the modern *ṭarab* jargon does not include a standard term that means "improvisation."[6] Similarly, the modal theory expounding the various *maqāmāt* makes no distinction between improvisation and precomposition and provides only an implicit correlation between the unfolding of a mode and the application of a genre that is metrically free and suitably flexible. Furthermore, concepts such as *taqāsīm, layālī,* and *mawwāl,* despite their improvisatory nature, refer literally to such components as structure, text, and literary content. This lack of specificity about improvisation, a categorical distinction that may stem mostly from Western analytical perspectives, appears compatible with the *ṭarab* culture's fundamental acceptance of flexibility and spontaneity as norms of musical creativity. Such acceptance is implicit in Ṣabāḥ Fakhrī's statement and in the performance criteria and mannerisms of traditional *ṭarab* artists.

In *ṭarab* performances, the levels of compositional flexibility, spontaneity, and instantaneity exist in a wide continuum ranging from the most to the least structured. The music "may involve the work's immediate composition by its performers, or the elaboration or adjustment of an existing framework, or anything in between" (Horsley et al. 1980, 31). Within this continuum, however, we may speak in terms of two creative formats or levels; one we may arbitrarily call "modal," and the other "interpretive."

The modal improvisatory format is represented by the instantaneous realization of the *maqāmāt* and is illustrated by such genres as the *taqāsīm,* the *layālī,* and the improvised *qaṣīdah,* which are typically non-metric, through-composed, and soloistic. Despite the existence of binding, often unarticulated, modal rules, the contents of such improvisatory creations exhibit a relatively wide latitude of flexibility in such areas as length of performance, arrangement of sections, and modulations to secondary *maqāmāt* (Nettl and Riddle 1973, 18). In the *ṭarab* culture, improvisatory creations are valued because they are "the perfect synthesis . . . of originality and tradition, freedom and convention" (Elkholy 1978, 17), and because in addition to exemplifying established modal rules, they provide the performer with both compositional challenges and avenues for instantaneous creativity. Emotionally potent genres such as the *taqāsīm* and *layālī* are also considered highly reflective of the performer's ecstatic condition and of the performance ambience in general.

Such reflectiveness can be studied musically by comparing performances from different contexts, although such a treatment is likely to be troubled by the numerous variables affecting each performance. Among such variables are the circumstances of performing, the musician's emotional condition during the performance, the musician's own musical style, and the premium on modernity and innovation in today's musical practices (Racy 1982). However, we can still learn about the contextual as well as individual dimensions of improvisation by analyzing three sets of improvisatory performances. The *'ud taqāsīm* of the late Farīd al-Aṭrash, performed for relatively heterogeneous and outwardly enthusiastic audiences, display fast tempo, dense picking, frequent use of trem- olos, and highly energetic *qaflāt,* typically followed by the listeners' loud cheers and exclamations. Usually restricting modulations to the more "popu- lar" *maqāmāt,* they also make frequent allusion to Spanish guitar music. Mean- while, a number of *'ūd taqāsīm* by the late modernist composer Muḥammad al-Qaṣabjī, played before a smaller group of listeners at Cairo's Music Acad- emy some forty years ago, present relative modal instability, a kaleidoscopic display of modal shifts, most often with nebulous and unconventional transi- tions, and an excessive use of accidentals. In these performances the artist seems much less interested in creating *ṭarab* than in displaying his innovative modal technique. A third set of *taqāsīm* performances by the celebrated com- poser Riyāḍ al-Sinbāṭī are relatively subdued but imbued with tremendous ec- static efficacy. These *taqāsīm* display a stately and consistent pace; economy in the use of the plectrum; effective use of silence; impeccable intonation; ample emphasis on the mode of the performance before modulations are exe- cuted; frequent reference to the tonic; varied, carefully timed, and often subtle *qaflāt;* and an effective ambient quality in the form of an echo effect, perhaps added in the recording process. The performances of al-Sinbāṭī appear to have stemmed from a conducive emotional state marked by a contagious sense of *salṭanah,* a state that the artist may have experienced in the presence of a few highly sensitive *sammī'ah* as he performed.[7]

It is also possible to observe how the same musician may perform in varied styles and demonstrate different levels of creativity, depending largely upon his emotional state during the performance and upon the nature of his audi- ence. Ṣabāḥ Fakhrī's fans cherish some of his recordings in part because the listeners on those recordings consisted mostly of *sammī'ah.* From the perform- er's perspective, I can cite inconsistencies in my own playing. During an in- vited lecture to a University of California at Los Angeles seminar on musical aesthetics, I played three recordings of my *taqāsīm* on the *nāy,* all in *māqām Ṣabá.* The students were mostly Westerners and included only a few who had taken a course or two on Arab music. Asked to guess how I ranked the perfor- mances from the most to the least creative, the majority favored the one I con- sidered the worst, giving it such descriptions as "smooth," "soothing," and "pretty," but referred to the one I thought best as being "choppy," "erratic," "delivered in piecemeal," and periodically interrupted by a "noisy" audience. Somewhat amused by their classmates' choices, the few who were familiar with Arab music had no problem recognizing that the one I favored was the product of intense interaction with a group of enthusiastic Arab listeners.

In fact, the performance I ranked the least inspired was presented to a polite, appreciative, and mostly non-tradition-based, American West Coast audience. I remember performing before a group of listeners who appreciated the music and in their own ways probably enjoyed it, but were not genuine *sammī'ah,* for they did not "feel" the music in the traditional ecstatic sense of the word. I played without *saltanah* and felt that the physical presence of a large group of individuals unable to respond idiomatically to my improvisation was a musical liability. The *taqāsīm* piece displayed correct intonation, accurate intervals, and a pitch progression that was modally correct. However, the phrases appeared aimlessly stretched out and seamlessly joined together, leaving little room for pauses. The tonal centers and the modal levels received insufficient emphases, the overall progression seemed to use long-winded and somewhat lyrical melodic configurations, and perhaps most importantly, the *qaflāt* were either perfunctory and ineffective or nonexistent.

The performance I had considered to be emotionally most efficacious and also musically most sophisticated was given in Beirut as part of a musical *jalsah* with an audience consisting of young *tarab* fans and highly skilled musicians, including some music teachers and instrumentalists employed by the Lebanese radio station. My *nāy* solo came after about two hours of performing in addition to socializing with the rest of the group. Reflecting the *muhāsabah* (judicious listening) of the seasoned musicians, as well as the passionate responses of the younger aficionados, the performance was organized largely in terms of discrete and clearly demarcated phrases or vignettes. In each of these phrases a specific modal or thematic idea appeared to develop and to reach a distinct resolution. Some of these microevents included tonal, modal, and thematic deviations that seemed particularly to impress the analytically minded. However, such digressive elements were used sparingly, thus ensuring the tonal and scalar consistencies needed to preserve the sense of *saltanah* in the *Sabá* mode. The tempo was stately, the low tonal area of the mode was amply explored in the first few phrases, and although sometimes subtle and uncommon, the *qaflāt* were unequivocal. The overall structure paralleled the auditory-emotional behavior of the listeners, whose communicative silence alternated with ecstatic and correctly timed exclamations voiced increasingly as the *qaflah* began to approach its conclusion. In a sense, the content was the sonic manifestation of a social interactive process. From an insider's vantage point, such an ecstatically conceived and interactively produced rendition was creatively distinct and qualitatively different.

Meanwhile, the interpretive improvisatory format is marked by the musician's ability to reinterpret, modify, alter, and elaborate on already existing works. Some literary-minded Arab musicians refer to this format as *tasarruf,* which literally means "taking liberties," for example in translating or paraphrasing a literary text. Interpretations of musical works require introducing one's own choice of ornaments, melismatic elaborations, and melodic and rhythmic nuances to the tune. Such interpretations characterize the performances of both the leading vocalist and the instrumentalists, who all perform heterophonically with one another. In view of such compositional liberties, "the process of music making is the mutual contribution of the combined efforts of composer and performer" (Elkholy 1978, 8). Furthermore, members of the *ṭarab* culture generally maintain that the traditional art of interpretation not only demonstrates musical experience, talent, and innate sensitivity, but also, like other improvisatory forms, reflects the artist's own condition of *salṭa-nah* and rapport with the audience.

The role of instantaneous interpretation can be best illustrated by the model set by the celebrated Egyptian female singer, Umm Kulthūm (1903–1975), who played a highly creative role in shaping the content of the long precomposed songs she performed in public, particularly during the 1940s and 1950s. According to Niʿmāt Fuʾād, one of Umm Kulthūm's main biographers, the final rendition of the work was indeed the fruit of collaborative efforts and the product of both precomposition and spontaneous and context-inspired creations (Fuʾād 1976). At the initial phase, the composer created the song as he internalized and envisioned Umm Kulthūm's vocal ability and style, in terms of range, ornaments, melismatic elaborations, and so on. At the same time he anticipated that the final touches to the composed tune would be worked out during rehearsals. In turn, Umm Kulthūm left it to her *qānūn* player, whose musical judgment she trusted, to hold the first conference with the composer in order to examine the tune. In light of his experience with Umm Kulthūm's abilities and his knowledge of what would suit her and win her approval, the *qānūn* player would suggest appropriate changes and modifications. After the changes were incorporated, Umm Kulthūm would learn the tune in its basic format through a process of *tahfīẓ,* during which the composer, using his own voice and often his *ʿūd,* assisted her in learning the tune by rote.

After the singer had memorized the new song, orchestral rehearsals began. At this point, the *qānūn* player served the important intermediary function of coaching other instrumentalists and helping them learn the new tune. During these work sessions, usually occurring every other day for a month, Umm Kulthūm listened to the tune repeatedly as it was being taught "in order to become more intimate with it and to live it very closely" (Fuʾād 1976, 410). However, in the process she often asked the composer to replace and modify certain parts "on the basis of the musical executions she had heard, and her inner reactions *(tafāʿulāt)* to the tune and the musical ensemble altogether." Finally, when she performed the new song before the public she added her own touches again "in such ways that were not anticipated by the composer, and that even she herself did not anticipate before she had begun to sing." Reportedly, the singer's musical liberties with the composers' works brought her great admiration from the composers themselves.

The example of Umm Kulthūm here represents a confluence of two cultural forces: the increasing importance, authority, and specialization of the twentieth-century Arab composer; and the *ṭarab* artist's traditionally recognized prerogative to reinterpret precomposed musical works. More significantly, perhaps, the example clearly demonstrates the different levels and modalities of creativity utilized among the various players in the creative process, including Umm Kulthūm herself, during the different stages of the compositional endeavor.

Conclusion

The feedback approach to creativity, or the first model discussed in this chapter, places prime emphasis on the process of music making. Music is seen as a participatory phenomenon that involves direct emotional exchange between performers and listeners. *Tarab* artistry is intimately intertwined with the ecstasy-based and interactive dynamics of the performance event.

Given the organic links among the artist, the creative process, and the created work, ethnomusicologists and Western scholars in general appear to take an extremely compartmentalized approach to studying the creative phenomenon. Ethnomusicological research tends to exhibit distinct selectivity and to gravitate toward particular themes and concerns. The literature most relevant to the *tarab* model of creativity emphasizes the domain of mode and improvisation. Addressing topics such as the musical structure of modal improvisations (Gerson-Kiwi 1970, 66) and the tonal elements characterizing a typical improvisation in a specific *māqām* (Touma 1980, 30), current writings give in-depth analyses of established musical modalities. Meanwhile, recent seminal studies exploring fundamental issues such as the essential similarity between composition and improvisation as processes (Nettl 1974, 6) and the scope of variance and consistency in the modal creations of one specific performer (Nettl and Riddle 1973) broaden the inquiry to include the musical creators and their mental operations. Many works, however, continue to deal with the subject primarily in terms of the created musical materials and from this particular angle seem more compatible with the second rather than the first model discussed above. Although the ecstatic requirements for an effective modal improvisation and the improvisatory devices that creative artists employ to influence their listeners are occasionally alluded to in the works of Near Eastern scholars (see, e.g., Elkholy 1978, 18; Qujamān 1978, 84–97), current research seems to exhibit little interest in musical ambience and its role in the creative process.

Meanwhile, in the modern *tarab* culture the ecstatic feedback process can operate in conjunction with other, even contrastive, creative processes. Some Arab informants state, for example, that Riyāḍ al-Ṣinbāṭī is known to have composed his tunes in the quiet seclusion of his bedroom, alone with his *'ūd* and tape recorder. Others describe situations in which emotionally powerful tunes come to them at unpredictable moments of inspiration, tunes that are later developed and modified through conscious calculations and trials before they reach their final compositional form. Adherence to the second model of composing, without a participating audience, is best exemplified by the artistic approach of the Western-minded modernist Muḥammad 'Abd al-Wahhāb. Although acknowledging the traditional significance of the live performance, this major Egyptian composer and singer eschews what he calls the practice of "singing at the people" *(yughannī ʿalá al-nās)* and likens himself to a writer who produces his literary work away from the public rather than a journalist whose commentaries are directly suggested by immediate events.[8] As such, ʿAbd al-Wahhāb's sentiments are in league with those of Berlioz, and perhaps with those of Schoenberg. At the same time, there is no reason to assume that both models are not consciously or unconsciously integrated or used alternately throughout the creative pursuits of individual *ṭarab* artists.

Moreover, the two models seem to share certain characteristics. Despite the opposition exhibited by the two implied musical worldviews, there may be an element of Ṣabāḥ Fakhrī in Berlioz and vice versa. In the case of Western music, some analysts have spoken of a nonconceptual mutual "tuning-in" relationship that connects composers, performers, and listeners as members of the same musical culture and extends experientially beyond the limits of the musical score (Schultz 1977, 106–19). On a broader and more abstract level, creativity in general has been explained in terms of the perceptual congruities among participants in the artistic process, whether such congruities are the "collective unconscious" in Jung's analysis of poetic art (Rothenberg and Hausman 1976, 120–26), or the inner psychic experiences and tensions we all share (Nieman 1978, 53).

In both models studied in this article, we sense a love-hate relationship with the audience, which in either case is directly or indirectly a key player. In both articulations there is an underlying sense of particularity and caution. Whereas Berlioz is disdainful of the antimusical and destructive attitudes in the audience at large, Fakhrī stresses the importance of the listening initiates, a stance that reminds us of Sufi leaders' watchfulness toward the outside world and their criticism of disingenuous and sensually minded individuals who misconstrue the inner meanings of *samāʿ*. Fakhrī's analogy regarding those who cannot tell diamond from glass echoes al-Ghazālī's statement that songs with symbolic amorous texts must be barred for those who are superficial and passionately inclined, as donkeys are barred from eating flowers and aromatic herbs (al-Ghazālī n.d., 248). In both models the artists devise their own defensive strategies vis-à-vis their public. The notion of sheltering oneself from the bad effects of society, as expressed by Berlioz, is paralleled by *ṭarab* artists' concern about having enough *sammīʿah* to counterbalance those who are excessively disruptive or apathetic. In the absence of good listeners, members of a performing ensemble usually play the double role of musicians and *sammīʿah,* supporting and ecstatically reinforcing the performances of one another.

The ecstatic feedback model becomes even more comparable to other models of music making if we define ambience and audience participation in flexible, nonliteral terms. The *ṭarab* artist, like a symphonic composer, can create his work alone without the direct input of a physically present audience. *Ṭarab* musicians stress that playing for oneself can be a profoundly ecstatic and creative experience, and can lead to a state of *sal̲ṭanah* conducive to improvising or composing emotionally affective tunes. Thus, when the *ṭarab* artist creates alone, his ecstatic state can be self-induced and the feedback process can be internalized as he becomes both a *ṭarab* initiator and a *sammīʿ*. In this sense, the *ṭarab* maker constitutes a microcosm of the entire *ṭarab* process.

Similarly, *ṭarab* music itself can be emotionally experienced outside the immediate ecstatic and interactive ambiance that originally led to its creation. Whether in the form of recordings of live performances by Ṣabāḥ Fakhrī or radio broadcasts of *taqāsīm* by Riyāḍ al-Sinbāṭī, *ṭarab* works can serve as ecstatic codes capable of establishing a *ṭarab* ambience for the culturally trained and musically initiated listener. Musical works too can be looked at as microcosms of creative processes.

In short, musicians' articulations about their own pursuits bring to focus the aesthetic, stylistic, and social systems these musicians belong to and identify with. In the case of Arab music, they enable us to better understand how improvisation works as a compositional process, as well as provide us with frameworks for studying the creative patterns and strategies of individual artists. From a broader perspective, musicians' personal statements provide insights into the complex and multifaceted nature of the creative musical process.

Notes

This chapter is a revised version of an earlier work that appeared as "Creativity and Ambiance: An Ecstatic Feedback Model from Arab Music" in *The World of Music* 33, no. 3 (1991):7–28. I wish to thank the editor of the above journal, Max Peter Baumann, for granting me permission to publish this adaptation of the original work.

1. I conducted this interview in Arabic with Ṣabāḥ Fakhrī in Santa Monica, California, on 24 January 1990. I am deeply grateful to the artist for his graciousness and the valuable information he generously provided. All quotes of Fakhrī in this chapter are from this interview. I have provided my own English translations of this and other Arabic quotes throughout the chapter.

2. I am indebted to Professor Robert Winter, musicologist and colleague of mine at the University of California at Los Angeles for calling my attention to the quote from Cairns's *Memoirs of Hector Berlioz*.

3. Within Fakhrī's quote, the opening statement regarding the audience was specifically in response to an inquiry that my wife, Barbara Racy, had voiced regarding the phenomenon of performance anxiety, currently a topic of concern in Western psychological research.

4. From an interview of al-ʿAqqād which I conducted in Los Angeles in the summer of 1984.

5. In his statement Fakhrī was referring to a specific performance he gave in Los Angeles in 1990. In fact, before performing he requested that the lights be turned on after the attending technicians had routinely dimmed the lights in the hall.

6. In formal Arabic usage the word *irtijāl*, often used by modern musical scholars to mean "improvisation," refers to creating things impromptu, but it also has strong liter-

ary connotations and subtle indications that the delivery is premature or inadequately prepared.

7. Recordings by the three artists discussed above can be obtained from a variety of sources. Those of Farīd al-Aṭrash can be heard on a number of commercially available LP recordings of live performances. Those of al-Qaṣabjī are found mostly on non-commercial tapes, although some of his more traditional renditions are available on a commercial CD release featuring both al-Qaṣabjī and Iraqi 'ūd player Munīr Bashīr (Club Du Disque Arabe, AAA 003, CDA 401, Paris 1988). I acquired my examples through the courtesy of Simon Shaheen, a concert violinist and 'ūd player now living in New York. The taqāsīm of al-Sinbāṭī have appeared sporadically on commercial cassettes and lately have been featured as a collection on one CD release titled Riyāḍ al-Sinbāṭī; Taqāsīm 'ūd, produced by Ṣawt al-Qāhirah, manufactured and distributed by SIDI, P.O. Box 13241, Jeddah 21483, Saudi Arabia.

8. This information comes from a recorded interview that Simon Shaheen conducted with 'Abd al-Wahhāb in Cairo. I am grateful to Mr. Shaheen for providing me with a copy of the interview.

References

Cairns, David, trans. and ed. 1969. The Memoirs of Hector Berlioz. New York: Alfred A. Knopf.

Dunstan, H. Mainwaring, trans. 1882. Life and Letters of Berlioz. Vol. 1. London: Remington and Co.

Elkholy, Samha. 1978. The Tradition of Improvisation in Arab Music. Giza, Egypt: Imprimerie Rizk.

Farmer, Henry George. 1973. A History of Arabian Music. 1929. Reprint, London: Luzac and Co.

Fu'ād, Ni'māt. 1976. Umm Kulthūm wa 'Aṣrun min al-Fann ('Umm Kulthūm and an Age of Artistry). Cairo: al-Hay'ah al-Miṣriyyah lil-Kitāb.

Gerson-Kiwi, Edith. 1970. "On the Technique of Arab Taqsim Composition." In Festschrift Walter Graf, Wiener musikwissenschaftliche Beiträge 9, 66–73. Vienna: Hermann Bohlaus Nachf.

al-Ghazālī, Abū Ḥāmid. n.d. Iḥyā' 'Ulūm al-Dīn (The Revival of Religious Sciences). Vol. 2. Damascus: Maktabat'Abd al-Wakīl al-Durūbī.

Ghiselin, Brewster, ed. 1952. The Creative Process. London: The New English Library.

Horsley, Imogene, Michael Collins, Eva Badura-Skoda, Dennis Libby and Nazir A. Jairazbhoy. 1980. "Improvisation." In The New Grove Dictionary of Music and Musicians, edited by Stanley Sadie, vol. 9, 31–56. London: Macmillan.

al-Khula'ī, Kāmil. [1904?]. Kitāb al-Mūsīqá al-Sharqī (The Book of Eastern Music). A.H. 1322. Cairo: Maṭba 'at al-Taqaddum.

Milson, Menahem, ed. and trans. 1975. A Sufi Rule for Novices; Kitāb Ādāb al-Murīdīn of Abū al-Najīb al-Suhrawardī. Cambridge: Harvard University Press.

Nettl, Bruno. 1974. "Thoughts on Improvisation: A Comparative Approach." The Musical Quarterly 60:1–19.

Nettl, Bruno, and Ronald Riddle. 1973. "Taqsim Nahawand: A Study of Sixteen Performances by Jihad Racy." Yearbook of the International Folk Music Council 5:11–49.

Nieman, Alfred. 1978. "The Composer and Creative Tension." In Tension in the Performance of Music, edited by Carola Grindea, 41–55. London: Kahn and Averill.

Osborne, Harold. 1977. "Inspiration." *The British Journal of Aesthetics* 17, no. 3: 242–53.

Papenbrok, Marion. 1985. "The Spiritual World of Flamenco." In *Flamenco,* edited by Claus Schreiner, 49–56. Portland, Ore.: Amadeus Press.

Qujamān (Kojaman), Y. 1978. *Al-Mūsīqà al-Fanniyah al-Muʾāsirah fī al-ʿIrāq* (Contemporary Art Music in Iraq). London: ACT Arabic Translations.

Racy, Ali Jihad. 1982. "Musical Aesthetics in Present-Day Cairo." *Ethnomusicology* 26:391–406.

———. 1983. "The *Waṣlah:* A Compound Form Principle in Egyptian Music." *Arab Studies Quarterly* 5, no. 4:396–403.

———. 1987. "Music, Trance, and Music-Trance Relations: A Symposium." *Pacific Review of Ethnomusicology* 4:20–23, 35.

———. 1988. "Sound and Society: The Takht Music of Early-Twentieth Century Cairo." *Selected Reports in Ethnomusicology* 7:139–70.

Rothenberg, Albert, and Carl R. Hausman, eds. 1976. *The Creative Question.* Durham: Duke University Press.

Rouget, Gilbert. 1985. *Music and Trance.* Chicago: University of Chicago Press.

Sawa, George. 1989. *Music Performance Practice in the Early ʿAbbasid Era 132–320* A.H./750–932 A.D. Toronto: Pontifical Institute of Medieval Studies.

Schoenberg, Arnold. 1947. "The Musician: Heart and Brain in Music." In *The Works of the Mind,* edited by Robert Heywood, 68–89. Chicago: University of Chicago Press.

Schott, Robin. 1989. "Kant and the Objectification of Aesthetic Pleasure." *Kant-Studien* 80, no. 1:81–92.

Schultz, Alfred. 1977. "Making Music Together: A Study in Social Relationship." In *Symbolic Anthropology,* edited by Janet L. Dolgin, David S. Kemnitzer, and David M. Schneider, 106–19. New York: Columbia University Press.

Shiloah, Amnon. 1981. "The Arabic Concept of Mode." *Journal of the American Musicological Society* 34:19–42.

Touma, Habib Hassan. 1980. *Maqam Bayati in the Arabian Taqsim.* Berlin: Das Arabische Buch.

CHAPTER FIVE

Go On Girl! Improvisation in African-American Girls' Singing Games

EVE HARWOOD

In North American playgrounds, back yards, and front stoops, children acquire through oral tradition a body of children's lore including folk stories, jokes, superstitions, charms, games, and other pastimes. Some of these are musical entertainments such as camp songs, parody songs, counting-out chants, ring games, and jump rope rhymes. While individual children often accompany their private play with spontaneous humming, singing, and rhythmic chanting, the repertoire they share as a group—their traditional music lore—contains relatively little scope for individual innovation. The musical genres in which improvisation[1] regularly occurs include handclap games performed in dyads, small groups, and large circles; ring games; line formation singing games; call-response step-and-clap songs; and group line dancing.

In contemporary North America, such games are generally viewed as the province of girls.[2] The descriptions of improvisational activity that follow draw primarily on fieldwork among African-American girls, whose repertoire of traditional singing games, line dancing, and handclapping is particularly rich (Abrahams 1966; Brady 1975; Eckhardt 1975; Harwood 1987; Jones and Hawes 1972; Merrill-Mirsky 1988; Riddell 1990).[3] I have relied on my own fieldwork at an after-school club attended primarily by African-American girls ranging in age from seven to fourteen as the principal source of anecdotal description and informant testimony (Harwood 1992, 1993). To appreciate why improvisation appears in the forms it does in these girls' play, it is helpful to articulate assumptions about constancy and change that are an integral part of children's oral tradition, for it is within this framework that individual melodic, rhythmic, gestural, and textual improvisation occurs.

You Doin' It Wrong: Deviation as Error
Playground values generally discourage individual improvisation.[4] Among African-American girls, for instance, the reprimand "You doin' it wrong" is likely to greet any variant performance of standard items such as handclaps or jump rope chants. William Newell, an early collector of American children's lore, described the strong conservative tendency of children: "The formulas of play are as Scripture, of which no jot or tittle is to be repealed. Even the inconsequent rhymes of the nursery must be recited in the form in which they first

became familiar; as many a mother has learned, who has found the versions familiar to her own infancy condemned as inaccurate, and who is herself sufficiently affected by superstition to feel a little shock, as if a sacred canon had been irreligiously violated" (Newell 1963, 28). This conservative instinct is also apparent when discussions about the proper performance of specific repertoire occur. At the girls club one day I witnessed a conversation among several players who were communally trying to re-create a handclap that ends, "that's the way my story goes." It was not one regularly played at the club, but a couple of girls had heard it. They sent for authorities (girls at the club who had learned the game elsewhere), tried several times to reconstruct the complete text and actions, and listened to shouted suggestions from informed onlookers until they arrived at what they agreed was the complete, authentic version. They did not consider that one might legitimately omit the missing parts, or simply make up the tune or the hand pattern.

While players occasionally argued about the right way to perform a given song, no one questioned the notion that there was a "right" way. This mindset is fairly common in reports of fieldwork among English-speaking children in various parts of the world. When newcomers to a given setting enter a handclap circle, for instance, they are expected to conform to the conventions for play in the established group. In Great Britain, Iona and Peter Opie report that newcomers to a scene are eagerly listened to for new items to add to the local repertoire, but "the local children, while willing to enlarge their store of jokes and rhymes, will not consciously brook any alteration to what they already know" (Opie and Opie 1959, 35). Merrill-Mirsky similarly reports that among her Los Angeles informants, newcomers might become sources for new repertoire, but they had to adapt to the local customs of play in established games in order to be socially accepted. One informant reported: "In Detroit we didn't say words. We just did it. And here I had to learn the words, the new clap, and all that. In Detroit we just, it was just, like this, like that's the way we did it" (Merrill-Mirsky 1988, 195). From conversations at the girls' club it was clear the girls knew that in other places people played the games differently, but deviations from their normal play were invariably viewed as errors, not as legitimate alternatives.

Without a written retrieval system, everyone in an oral tradition becomes responsible in some sense for maintaining the authenticity of the repertoire. One outcome of this circumstance is the blending of roles between performer, critic, and audience. Everyone feels entitled to comment on the style and the accuracy of the game as it is played, and there was often encouragement and vocal criticism from onlookers when games were performed. Even girls who could not themselves perform a particular item recognized a good performance and often identified the item as a song they knew. "I know that one but I can't do it" was one revealing response to the question, "Do you know that song?"

Against this backdrop, where everyone is a critic, where performing the correct way is the only socially acceptable way, and where correctness means faithful adherence to the existing tradition, it is little wonder that improvisation, in the sense of individual melodic, rhythmic, or textual embellishments of the "right" tune, does not flourish. But balancing children's fiercely conservative impulse is the attraction they have for innovation and novelty. The many fads in speech and dress that inexplicably emerge and vanish, songs that come and go in fashion, and the variants of old favorites that crop up over time are testament to the winds of change that regularly sweep through children's folk culture. African-American girls are no different from other children in this regard.

The tension between conservatism and innovation has been observed by many children's folklorists and has elicited commentaries on the paradoxical phenomenon of two conflicting loyalties coexisting in the play life of children.[5] A detailed examination of African-American girls' musical play reveals that improvisation provides one avenue for resolving the paradox. Their approach to improvising allows them to negotiate the territory between the polar opposites of conservatism and invention.[6] I suggest the following as four different examples of such resolution.

1. Teneka, She Know All the Games: Special Dispensation

Where standard repertoire is concerned, a few select individuals are allowed to suggest alterations or innovations that are then accepted into practice. That they are acknowledged master players appears to bring a legitimacy to their musical or gestural additions without challenging the generally held rule that deviations are errors. Masters are allowed to break the rules in a way that novices and regular folks are not.

Selected girls were identified as ones who could make up new handclaps or routines and who taught new repertoire to others at the club. These informally designated game leaders were also acknowledged handclap masters. When I asked one of the girls what makes for a really good handclap player, her response was to name Teneka, with the explanation, "She know all the games." When players had difficulty recalling a game, arbitrating the rules, or simply needed someone to organize a group, Teneka was sent for. She had mastered a wide personal repertoire and was very adept at performing the games, and she could maintain the tune, text, and clap pattern herself while looking around a clap circle to identify and remove a player who had "messed up."[7] Her sister Maya added the information that Teneka could also make up handclaps. She gave as an example the clap pattern they had invented to go with "Uno Dos y Esso" after they heard it performed on television on "The Cosby Show." Teneka suggested they repeat their hand motion on the words "quick quick quick." "We can just hear one and fit it" was Maya's explanation. The repetition of the same motion when a word in the text repeats is, in fact, a fairly common occurrence in other games. This particular deviation is therefore well within stylistic conventions and to an adult may not seem particularly exciting or novel. What is significant is the conscious, deliberate deviation from the normal clap pattern, and Maya's conviction that this ability to fit a new hand pattern to a given aural source is unique to her sister Teneka and herself.

2. Dancing on the Bases: Improvisation as Transition

African-American girls use spontaneous bursts of rhythmic vocalizations, accompanying step/clap patterns, and dance movements as transitions from one activity to the next. Referred to as "dancin'," such activity can last anywhere from a few seconds to a few minutes. When invitations to join the next game are called or some other formal activity begins, the improvisation breaks off. There is no conflict in values, because the improvised dancing begins in a sound vacuum and is used to fill time not organized in other ways.

Sometimes the dancing is individual, a way of passing time while waiting. During a kickball game, for instance, I observed girls who were waiting on base dancing and humming to themselves. The parent of an informant made a similar observation regarding her daughter and her friends, that at picnics when playing baseball they were "dancing on the bases," and they always liked to have a walkman or boom box with them to provide music so they could dance (Harwood 1987). On numerous occasions girls at the club would half-strut, half-dance while walking from room to room or while players were deciding what game to do next.

Sometimes the dancing is communal, with several participants using body percussion and unpitched rhythmic vocalizations to provide a textured rhythmic background for movement. Two informants described it this way:

> *Tosheba:* [trying to recall a cheer] I can't stomp on this floor, I can't get my beat.
> *Rachel:* Well stand up.
> [They both begin clapping, dancing, vocalizing]
> *EH:* What was that you were doing? Were you making that up?
> *Tosheba:* We just do that to dance on.
> *Rachel:* That's what we dance off.
> *EH:* And you make it up as you go along?
> *Rachel:* Yeah, it don't have no words to it, you just go— [demonstrates].

As I studied videotapes of the girls playing at the club, I gradually began to see what I had first overlooked in my eagerness to learn traditional game repertoire. There in the background of a formal game, or between formal games, were many examples of this spontaneous eruption of physical gesture and vocal backup extending into short dance, one or two players moving, clapping, and vocalizing. It now seems to me that these girls carry a sense of rhythmic flow and energy close to the surface of their everyday conduct and it bursts through as dance when not channeled in other ways.

3. Don't Show No One: Routines

More advanced players and older girls of various ability generally abandon performance of traditional genres such as handclaps and ring games in favor of genres known variously as cheers, drill teams, and routines. Here individuals improvise and then practice to refine an extended set of movements to the accompaniment of a traditional cheer text or a contemporary rap or pop song. Routines are sequences of choreographed dance steps, drawn from a recognizable vocabulary of line dancing and MTV dance video moves. They are first improvised, then practiced and taught to selected individuals, and are jealously guarded by their originators. At the club the music was sung by the girls themselves, using text and melody from popular Top 40 songs. Although the kinds of movement are clearly an outgrowth of those used in standard playground singing games and line dances, there is no conflict between the communal need to conserve what is inherited from tradition and the individual desire to invent new material. The inventors of routines are seen to own their repertoire and are solely responsible for passing it on if they so choose.

A number of features mark routines as the property of individuals rather than the group. For instance, I was not allowed to see Teneka's routines while she was teaching them to a group of girls she had selected. She would only allow what she considered a finished performance to be viewed. On another occasion a girl who was visiting the club shared a routine she had made up with a small group, but then expected to learn one in return. This initiated a discussion regarding who could learn routines and where you could perform them. One girl wanted to practice a club routine at home but the older girls said no emphatically, because once you do it at home it goes to school, "then everybody know it." As one girl said, "When somebody teach me something I keep it," meaning she did not share it without express permission from the owner. Receiving a routine is a trust.

Only a few girls at the club made up routines, and they were generally older, in junior high school. Teneka describes a routine she is working on with some friends at the moment:

> *Teneka:* It's "Shake It Baby Twist and Shout." See with the "Ding Dong" stuff we just . . . we be . . . I sing the verse, they dance, like in the back and do creative stuff in there. Then they walk around. We do anything that comes to our mind.
>
> *Friend:* And then after the girls come we all go to Teneka's house and make up some . . . like we're getting the "Ice Ice" thing ready for the July 11th [a community event for which girls club members will be performing].

4. Go On Girl: Mandatory Improvisations

Many standard game forms incorporate within them a space, albeit a fairly circumscribed one, for individual invention. The simplest kind of improvising occurs in games that require players to create motions or fill in missing lines of text. A variety of such games are known by most girls, and by convention each participant takes a turn. Through such games the players gradually acquire a vocabulary of stylistically acceptable stock responses which will do if no inspiration comes to mind.[8] Some excel and produce novel movements or rhymes, while others stick to formulaic improvisations, relying on imitation rather than invention. In any case, there is no conflict of values, since the conventional method of play itself demands improvised elements.

IMPROVISED MOVEMENT

Elementary steps in learning to improvise are taken in games where a few seconds of free movement occur. It may be as simple as suddenly striking a pose, as in the game "Bump Up Tomato," which ends with the command, "Freeze!" The more outrageous or dramatic the pose, the more giggling and appreciation comes from fellow players. In other cases, one player at a time is required to improvise a short movement while standing in place, and this movement is then copied by the group. An example is "Jigalo" (ex. 5.1).

More complicated games are performed in circles or lines, and require one player at a time to improvise movements in the center, or to strut past a line of other players. One version of the ring game "Sally Walker" exhorts Sally (the girl in the center) to "go on girl, shake that thing, shake that thing. " Part of the goal is to outdo other performers in boldness and sophistication of moves. Other players call out encouragement and laugh appreciatively at the more dar-

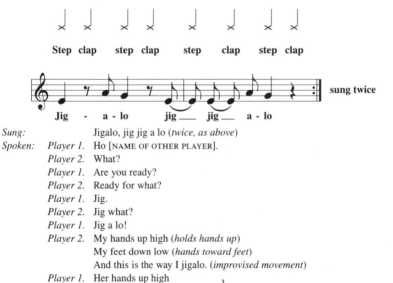

Sung:		Jigalo, jig jig a lo (*twice, as above*)
Spoken:	Player 1.	Ho [NAME OF OTHER PLAYER].
	Player 2.	What?
	Player 1.	Are you ready?
	Player 2.	Ready for what?
	Player 1.	Jig.
	Player 2.	Jig what?
	Player 1.	Jig a lo!
	Player 2.	My hands up high (*holds hands up*)
		My feet down low (*hands toward feet*)
		And this is the way I jigalo. (*improvised movement*)
	Player 1.	Her hands up high
		Her feet down low } (*imitates movements of player 2*)
		And this is the way she jigalo.

Example 5.1. "Jigalo."

Example 5.2. "Jump in the Car."

ing shakers. The texts of some games include words of encouragement for the featured individual. "Jump in the Car" (ex. 5.2), is one such game. Players stand in a line and all move to demonstrate the actions suggested in the first four measures. On measures 5 through 8, the named girl passes down the line, strutting and shaking, while others shake, step, and sway in place.

IMPROVISED TEXT

Some standard songs include space for individuals to improvise short phrases or whole lines of text. An imperative is that the words must fit the time and accent pattern established in the meter of the song. The audience is appreciative of clever or unusual verbal solutions that meet this goal. In a circle game called "Concentration" (also known as "Categories"), players establish the pulse through a repeated pattern of handclaps begun with the initial verbal chant. At specified places each player in turn has to name something fitting the given category (such as colors or automobile names). Players who hesitate or repeat another player's answer or whose answers deviate from the category are out of the circle. Players who fail to maintain the pulse are also out. From such games, girls learn to fit their individual contributions within the context of an ongoing musical performance, to enter and exit at the moment defined by the gestural and metrical structure, and to develop the presence of mind requisite for many kinds of improvisation. Although it seems simple enough, in the context of play it requires considerable concentration.

A more complex example of verbal improvisation occurs in songs such as "Ding Dong" (ex. 5.3). Here one player sings the solo calls supported by a vocal backup group which sings the responses and maintains a step/clap rhythmic accompaniment throughout. The invented text not only must fit the metrical structure but also must rhyme. Cleverness and audacity of lyrics are appreciated by onlookers and accompanying performers. Unlike games such as "Concentration" and ring or line games, where everyone is expected to take a turn, the requirement to improvise is voluntary in this kind of song. That is, only two or three girls out of a much larger group typically step forward to take the soloist's role. One girl might lead the group for several verses, then another strong singer might take over. "I got one" is the indication for a new leader to begin. The leaders for "Ding Dong" were for the most part the same girls that were most proficient at handclapping and other singing games.

IMPROVISED MELODY

The most complex musical improvisation at the girls club was evident in a number of different songs they called "the blues." These were not performed nearly as often as were traditional singing games, line dances, and handclaps. The same few soloists who led "Ding Dong" led this kind of song, again supported by a backup vocal group who maintained a step/clap pattern and sang short interludes between solo lines. The girls performed a number of different melodies under the title "the blues," and there appeared to be no fixed words. Krondalette gave the following explanation of requirements for making up a blues: "You can just make up anything you want to. . . . We made one up for my brother cause he locked his shoes in the room at the baby-sitter. It gotta rhyme." At my prompting she demonstrated a version of the blues, transcribed here as example 5.4.

The text of a blues generally contains four lines, with the second and fourth rhyming. Each line is introduced by a chant, performed with a nasal tone, perhaps in imitation of an electric guitar or some other instrument. These introductions or punctuations are generally performed by a group of singers who also maintain a step/clap pattern on the main pulses. There seemed to be no prescribed version of the tune for the soloist. Krondalette's version was intoned (rather than formally sung) on two pitches roughly a minor third apart. Other girls sang more melodically adventurous versions on occasion.

Conclusion

To some extent, what has been suggested as an African-American solution to the paradox of improvisation in a musically conservative tradition is evident in the play of Anglo-American girls as well. "Sally Walker" and other games

Example 5.3. "Ding Dong." An arrow (↗) indicates that the tone begins below the pitch noted and slides up.

Example 5.4. "The Blues" (improvised version).

calling for individual improvised movement are played by girls of both her-itages. And certainly there are genres sung by both boys and girls where play-ers invent rhyming lines of text, such as the familiar camp song "Down by the Bay."

However, several aspects of the improvisation described in this chapter ap-pear to be particularly characteristic of African-American girls' play. One is the supportive and encouraging response of the community to individual solo effort. Improvisation is nurtured by the receptive attitude of the girls to individ-ual displays of competence as part of musical play. It is evident in their sponta-neous dancing, in call-and-response songs, and in line games where everyone shows off for an equal turn. Bess Lomax Hawes's description of Bessie Jones and some Georgia Sea Islanders playing ring games is equally apt for the games at the girls club:

> The emotional climate of ring play is humorous, if not uproarious. . . . they
> provided an opportunity for the hottest dancing, the most ridiculous miming,
> the most exaggerated horseplay. . . . For one thing, the usual family taboos
> and prohibitions are suspended. Black children are not encouraged in "real
> life" to "put on airs" or to flaunt themselves publicly. In the ring play, they
> may strut and tease, flirt and wiggle while everybody claps for them. (Jones
> and Hawes 1972, 89)

Hawes goes on to reflect on her own discomfort when asked to join in ring plays. But her informants knew, as did mine, that "the surrounding group would support the shy or the awkward just as strongly as it would the bold or the graceful, and that no dancer would get more or less time than any other."

Another noteworthy feature of African-American girls' musical play is the apparent link between the kinds of stylized movements incorporated within formal game or line dance structures and the world of spontaneous, improvised dancing that appears to lie just under the surface of everyday life. Bess Lomax

Hawes makes a similar observation regarding her principal informant, Bessie Jones:

> The more I watched Mrs. Jones and the Islanders, the more convinced I became that all their music-making activities involved basic body movement, or what the white community would call "dance." The point is, as Mrs. Jones puts it, "you've got to get it all over." All singing was accompanied by swaying, weight shifts, and hand, head, and body movements of greater or less degree, all suggesting a dance that was not yet quite visible. Their "real" dances seemed, then, simply broader, more explicit statements of the dances they were already doing while they stood still to sing. (Jones and Hawes, 1972, 43)

The short individual moves learned and practiced in ring and line games played by younger girls (age 7 to 10 or so) form the basis of a movement vocabulary from which longer routines are invented by some individuals in the next age group (10 to 13). A logical extension of this kind of choreographed group movement is the "stepping" tradition associated with African-American sororities and fraternities on college campuses.

A final observation about the role of improvisation among African-American girls is that the repertoire accommodates differing levels of musical competence. The ability to improvise develops over time, and one may see in their game repertoire a hierarchy of improvisational opportunities, from the simplest performed routinely by everyone, to more demanding musical tasks reserved for a few. They progress from simple repeated single movements, to chanting textual improvisations, to complete melodic and textual improvisations such as solo lines in the blues. There is also variety in the duration of individual and group improvisatory activity. The space for vocal, textual, or movement improvisation within a formal game is defined by the song or chanted text. Group dancing to their own spontaneously generated percussive vocalizations may last from a few seconds to a few minutes.

While it is individuals who perform improvised movements, make up lines of text, or sing solo calls, the community of fellow players is essential for musical and social support. For some genres, such as group dancing, a number of singers is mandatory, some to provide responses or vocal and step/clap accompaniment and some to sing solo lines and improvise solo dance steps. The improvisations may be on a miniature scale but they are significant within this community, where informants are sensitive to and highly critical of even slight deviations from the prescribed texts, tunes, and methods of play for their standard repertoire. In an environment where there is considerable emphasis on performing in accordance with the stylistic conventions of the existing tradition, improvisation is a form of musical risk taking, requiring audacity as well as practice. The exhortation "Go on girl" characterizes African-American girls' communal acceptance of the challenge.

Notes

1. There is a large body of literature on children's improvisation using different meanings of the term. Music education research in this area includes studies of solitary musical play, group improvisations using classroom instruments as part of school music programs, and independent instrumental or vocal compositions by children created as a result of extended and repeated improvisation, among others. The meaning of the term for this chapter is much narrower, limited to describing improvisation as it occurs within the context of a traditional, standard body of repertoire in oral circulation among children.

2. The informants referred to in this discussion are mostly girls, not because they are more important than boys, but because they have proved to be a more fruitful source of musical material. While some musical genres such as parody songs and chanted taunts are performed by girls and boys alike, over the course of the twentieth century singing games have become virtually the exclusive province of girls (Sutton Smith and Rosenberg 1961; Opie and Opie 1985).

3. Many handclaps and singing games in their repertoire are shared by English-speaking girls in New Zealand, Canada, Australia, and Great Britain. Even common items, however, are performed with African-American flavor and style that often calls for more hip swaying and accompanying body percussion than is evident in performances by their Anglo-American counterparts. Their line dances, call-response stepping games, and use of spontaneous vocalizing to accompany dancing appear to be uniquely African-American in origin.

4. Improvisation, for the purposes of this discussion, has the following features. First, an individual improvises within the context of a group performance of a standard item in the repertoire. Second, improvisation includes musical, gestural, or textual elements spontaneously generated without apparent premeditation or formal composition. Last, the improvised elements conform to stylistic conventions accepted by the community. They are not random, arbitrary or unduly idiosyncratic in nature, nor are they simply the result of mistakes in performance.

5. Newell was the first to describe both characteristics of children, in two introductory pieces to his major collection of singing games. One is titled "The Inventiveness of Children," and the other, "The Conservatism of Children." For three alternative solutions to Newell's paradox, see Fine 1980.

6. I am indebted to Jay Mechling for the characterization of these and other polar opposites as themes in children's folklore. See Mechling 1986.

7. Merrill-Mirsky (1988, 226–27) ascribed various qualities to the playground game leaders in her study, including being likely to introduce new games into existing repertoire. Teneka's function at the girls club matches Merrill-Mirsky's list very well.

8. This marks the traditional repertoire as different from the more idiosyncratic and faddish nature of songs children learn from radio and television, for instance, where individual or group improvisation takes on a different meaning. Merrill-Mirsky notes that rapping play depends on the players' having memorized texts individually, away from peers, whereas girls' handclaps are learned in the course of performing them with a group. Also, girls' handclap repertoire is constant, maintained across generations, whereas raps are transient repertoire. Their air time on radio and MTV determines their popularity on the playground.

References

Abrahams, Roger. 1966. "There's a Black Girl in the Ring." In *Two Penny Ballads and Four Dollar Whisky,* edited by K. Goldstein and R. Byington, 121–36. Hatboro, Pennsylvania: Folklore Associates.

Brady, M. 1975. "This Little Lady's Gonna Boogaloo: Elements of Socialization in the Play of Black Girls." In *Black Girls at Play: Perspectives on Child Development,* edited by Richard Bauman, 1–55. Austin: Southwest Educational Development Laboratory.

Eckhardt, R. 1975. "From Handclap to Line Play." In *Black Girls at Play: Perspectives on Child Development,* edited by Richard Bauman, 57–99. Austin: Southwest Educational Development Laboratory.

Fine, Gary. 1980. "Children and Their Culture: Exploring Newell's Paradox." *Western Folklore* 39:170–83.

Harwood, Eve. 1987. "The Memorized Song Repertoire of Fourth and Fifth Grade Children in Champaign, Illinois." Ed.D. dissertation, University of Illinois.

———. 1992. "Girls' Handclapping Games: A Study in Oral Transmission." *Bulletin of the International Kodaly Society* 17(1):19–25.

———. 1993. "A Study of Apprenticeship Learning in Music." *General Music Today* 6(3):4–8.

Jones, B., and B. L. Hawes. 1972. *Step It Down: Games, Plays, Songs and Stories from the Afro-American Heritage.* New York: Harper and Row.

Mechling, J. 1986. "Children's Folklore." In *Folk Groups and Folklore Genres: An Introduction,* edited by E. Oring. Logan, Utah: Utah State University Press.

Merrill-Mirsky, C. 1988. "Eeny Meeny Pepsadeeny: Ethnicity and Gender in Children's Musical Play." Ph.D. thesis, University of California.

Newell, W. 1963. *Games and Songs of American Children.* 1883 and 1903. Reprint, New York: Dover.

Opie, I., and P. Opie. 1959. *The Lore and Language of School Children.* London: Oxford University Press.

———. 1985. *The Singing Game.* London: Oxford University Press.

Riddell, C. 1990. "Traditional Singing Games of Elementary School Children in Los Angeles." Ph.D. thesis, University of California.

Sutton-Smith, B., and B. G. Rosenberg. 1961. "Sixty Years of Historical Change in the Game Preference of American Children." *Journal of American Folklore* 79:17–46.

CHAPTER SIX

Improvisation in Latin Dance Music: History and Style

PETER MANUEL

Latin dance music constitutes one of the most dynamic and sophisticated urban popular music traditions in the Americas. Improvisation plays an important role in this set of genres, and its styles are sufficiently distinctive, complex, and internally significant as to merit book-length treatment along the lines of Paul Berliner's volume *Thinking in Jazz* (1994). To date, however, the subject of Latin improvisation has received only marginal and cursory analytical treatment, primarily in recent pedagogical guidebooks and videos.[1] While a single chapter such as this can hardly do justice to the subject, an attempt will be made here to sketch some aspects of the historical development of Latin improvisational styles, to outline the sorts of improvisation occurring in mainstream contemporary Latin music, and to take a more focused look at improvisational styles of one representative instrument, the piano. An ultimate and only partially realized goal in this study is to hypothesize a unified, coherent aesthetic of Latin improvisation in general.

In this chapter, the term "Latin music" is used not to denote the realm of Latin American music in its entirety, but instead to refer to popular musics based on Afro-Cuban rhythms, as developed and performed throughout the Hispanic Caribbean basin and its diaspora, including New York City. Our focus thus comprises the interrelated genres *rumba, danzón, son, guaracha, mambo,* and *chachachá,* both in their traditional forms and as incorporated under the stylistically ambiguous rubric "salsa." Due to space limitations and the natural affinities of this particular set of genres, this article will not deal with Dominican *merengue,* Colombian *cumbia* and *vallenato,* or Puerto Rican *bomba, plena,* and *música jíbara,* however rich the improvisatory styles therein may be. Likewise, only passing reference will be made to Latin jazz; although improvisation plays a more prominent role in Latin jazz than in Latin dance music itself, the distinctive features of Latin improvisation styles are more visible in the latter than in the former, much of which overlaps with mainstream jazz itself. In contrast with jazz and Latin jazz, Latin dance music, as the term indicates, is quintessentially designed for accompanying social dancing. However, if its improvisatory styles are ideally intended to support this function rather than to command attention in themselves, their sheer sophistication and uniqueness amply justify critical regard.

Sources: The African and European Heritages

While Latin improvisational styles are original products of Hispanic Caribbean musicians in the twentieth century, they did not emerge out of a vacuum, but can be seen to have evolved from a specific set of sources. One influence of increasing importance from the 1920s on was jazz, whose impact will require further mention below. On the whole, however, Latin improvisation has evolved as a form parallel to jazz rather than derivative from it; indeed, since the beginnings of jazz history, the influences between the two genres have been mutual rather than unidirectional (see, e.g., Fiehrer 1991). The more immediate, original, and profound sources for modern Latin improvisational traditions were the diverse varieties of musics flourishing in Cuba at the turn of the century, which can be seen as occupying places on a continuum according to their predominance of European-derived or African-derived features.

The music genres on the European-derived side of this spectrum comprise a heritage of remarkable richness. At the same time, their contributions to the emergence of a distinctive improvisation style are in some respects indirect or unverifiable. The most substantial body of Spanish-derived folk music in Cuba is the set of regional varieties of the *punto,* whose aesthetic emphasis is on the text (generally in ten-line *décima* form) rather than the music per se. Although the modern *punto* does feature lively improvisations on the mandolin-like *laúd* between verses, there is no evidence that this tradition exerted any significant role on improvisation styles in urban popular music.[2] Similarly, improvisation does not appear to have played a significant role in the local creole *contradanza (habanera)*, as it flourished in bourgeois circles in the nineteenth century. It is true that such pieces were performed not only from written scores as parlor piano works, but also as popular vernacular dances by ad hoc ensembles for working-class audiences. Performance styles in such contexts may well have accommodated some flexibility, but there is no documentation of such a tradition. There is somewhat more evidence for the role of improvised trumpet flourishes in the *pasadobles* and other genres played by regimental bands (Edgardo Díaz Díaz, personal communication), and bombardino improvisations were important features of the late nineteenth-century Puerto Rican *danza* (Veray 1977, 32). However, the extent to which such traditions constituted direct precedents and sources for subsequent mainstream brass improvisation styles is unclear. Rather, the contribution of these traditions to Latin improvisation appears to lie more in the eventual application of instrumental technique and knowledge of formal theory to improvising—a process that evidently commenced in the *danzón* in the latter 1920s.

If the European-derived contribution to Latin dance music is as great as the African-derived one, it is the latter which appears to account for most of what is distinctive in this music, thereby justifying the music's designation as "Afro-Cuban." On the most basic level, the Afro-Cuban contribution to mainstream dance music comprises the use of a set of interrelated rhythmic cells. As shown

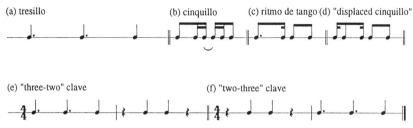

Example 6.1. Afro-Cuban rhythmic cells.

in example 6.1, these include the *tresillo,* the *cinquillo,* the *ritmo de tango,* the figure (ex. 6.1d) which could be regarded as a "displaced *cinquillo,*" and, most importantly, the *clave,* in its "3–2" and "2–3" variants. The notion of *clave* comprises not only these two specific patterns and the hardwood sticks on which they are played, but also the conception of these patterns as generative structures underlying the entire composite rhythm of two-bar ostinatos.[3]

Most of these rhythms came to pervade creole musics as well as Afro-Cuban genres; the *ritmo de tango* and *cinquillo,* for example, were fundamental ostinatos in the *contradanza* and *danzón,* respectively. Nevertheless, the ultimate origins of all these patterns in prior Afro-Caribbean or African musics appear well established, especially if *clave* is understood in the more general sense of connoting what could be analyzed as a two-measure open/closed or syncopated/unsyncopated ostinato format. In mainstream Latin dance music, these rhythms constitute basic building blocks for composition as well as improvisation, thereby illustrating Nettl's observation (see the introduction to this volume) that the same principles tend to underlie the two processes in most cultures.

The Afro-Cuban musical heritage includes styles associated with neo-African syncretic religions (primarily *santería, palo, iyesá,* and *arará*), with the *abakuá* societies, and with the *conga* genre featured in Carnival processions. Improvisation figures prominently in only a few of these styles; in the realm of *santería* music, for example, while *bembé* drumming foregrounds elaborate solos by a lead drummer, the more widespread and better-known *batá* music consists primarily of standardized patterns, however loosely and flexibly rendered. Nevertheless, knowledgeable percussionists do assert that such styles are the sources for many of the rhythms used in percussion improvisation in secular dance music (Orlando Fiol, personal communication).

By far the more direct source, however, is the traditional rumba, which flourished in the early twentieth century as a lower-class, predominantly Afro-Cuban dance and music genre, performed by voices and percussion. The rumba's formal structure, as determined by the lead vocalist, consists of a few short vocal warm-up phrases (the *diana*), followed by an extended text *(canto, largo)*, leading to a longer *montuno* section sung in call-and-response with a chorus. This structure is evidently the source and model for that of *son* and salsa, including the semi-improvised calls *(soneo, inspiración)* of the lead vocalist in the responsorial *montuno*. The rumba's instrumental accompaniment consists of a composite ostinato most typically rendered on two conga drums, *clave,* and *palitos* (two sticks beaten on a hard surface).[4] Throughout the song, a lead drummer improvises rhythms on a third, higher-pitched conga (the *quinto*), ideally interacting with the dancers (solo male in *rumba columbia,* and a single couple in *yambú* and the more popular *guaguancó*). As we have suggested, *quinto* patterns may incorporate certain features evidently derived from Afro-Cuban religious musics, but they appear to derive more directly from equally old secular dance traditions (e.g., the Congolese-derived *yuka*), and in terms of basic rhythmic principles and structures they have close affinities to traditional African drum musics. Especially important for purposes of this chapter is the way the *quinto* rhythms exhibit structural devices which, I submit, are basic to Latin improvisation as a whole. Specifically, these devices include the use of binary phrasing of triplet passages and ternary phrasing of passages in binary subdivisions, of which more will be said below. In more general terms, these affinities involve a percussive aesthetic which pervades all solo styles.[5]

The *Son* and *Danzón* until 1940

While negrophobic repression to some extent confined the rumba—and especially the obstreperous conga drum—to lower-class Afro-Cuban tenements, its influence eventually came to permeate Cuban musical culture. By the 1920s and '30s, *danzón* composers were omnivorously borrowing popular Afro-Cuban tunes (Díaz Ayala 1994, 104), and *teatro bufo* troupes and stage bands like the Lecuona Cuban Boys were presenting their own vaudeville-style versions of rumbas. A more significant vehicle for the mainstreaming of Afro-Cuban structural features was the *son,* which emerged in the first decades of the century and by the '30s had become Cuba's most popular dance music genre, as played primarily by septets (vocals, guitar, *tres,* trumpet, maracas, *güiro* scraper, cowbell, and string bass).

The *son* resists compartmentalization as exclusively Afro-Cuban or Euro-Cuban, instead constituting a felicitously balanced and definitive fusion of the two streams. The European heritage of the early *son* is obvious in its predominantly nonpercussive texture (unlike that of the rumba, for example), the presence of trumpet, guitar, and the guitar-like *tres,* and the use of functional harmonies and chordal harmonic progressions in the initial, "song"-like first section (now often called *guía*), which came to frequently rely on the 32-bar AABA form typical of American popular music. At the same time, the *son,* which was performed mostly by Afro-Cuban musicians, adopted from the rumba the *clave,* the *canto/guía-montuno* formal structure, the presence of a continually improvising drum (the bongo, rather than the *quinto*), many particular compositions, and the tradition of texts foregrounding Afro-Cuban culture and often extolling the rumba itself. For its part, the role of the *tres* in the *son* is as much rhythmic as melodic or chordal, consisting primarily of syncopated, standardized accompanimental ostinatos called *guajeos*. The use of the *marimbula* bass—an enlarged version of the African *mbira*-type lamellophone—further illustrates the fundamentally syncretic nature of the early *son*.

The improvisational styles of the early *son*, which are fairly well documented in recordings of the 1920s and '30s, are the direct ancestors of their counterparts in modern Latin music. The bongo, as suggested, perpetuates the role—and many specific techniques and rhythms—of the rumba's *quinto*, although without the function of interacting with a specific dancer (the *son* being danced by loosely embracing couples). The *montuno* usually commences with the trumpet player improvising two-bar phrases in alternation with the choral refrains (*coros*); typically, after four of these exchanges, the lead singer improvises his own *soneos* in alternation with the *coro*, which may continue indefinitely, perhaps interrupted by a solo on the bongo or, less often, the *tres*. The syllabic, relatively unadorned *soneo* style is essentially identical to that of the rumba, except for the occasional use of a more European, vibrato-laden vocal production. For its part, the trumpet style, rather than being flashy or markedly idiomatic, closely resembles the vocal *soneo* style, from which it presumably derives. (Similarly, contemporary jazz trumpet style was also essentially vocal in character, as can be heard, for example, in the marked affinities between Louis Armstrong's singing and cornet playing.) The occasional *tres* solos, unlike the flashy styles of the *laúd* and Puerto Rican *cuatro*, stress syncopated percussive chords and *guajeo*-type passages rather than fast single-note runs.

Until the late 1930s, piano and wind instruments aside from the trumpet were not used in the *son* septets. Instead, flute and piano styles evolved in the context of the *danzón*, as played since the first decade of the century by *charanga* ensembles consisting of flute, two violins, piano, bass, and percussion. In 1910 José Urfé's "El bombín de Barreto" had initiated the practice of adding a harmonically static, vamp-like final section to the *danzón*. Pianist and bandleader Antonio María Romeu was evidently the first to introduce improvised solos in this section. Díaz Ayala (1994, 135) refers to a "timid hint" of a solo in two Romeu recordings of 1925. John Santos (1982) cites as famous and seminal the extended solo in Romeu's 1926 recording of "Tres Lindas Cubanas," which is re-created by Romeu on a subsequent release (FE 4066). This solo, somewhat like those recorded in the 1930s by Armando Orefiche of the Lecuona Cuban Boys, consists of an amalgam of classical-style snippets, evoking Czerny rather than Earl Hines. By modern standards, many aspects of the solo appear manneristic and archaic, including its tinkling Alberti bass patterns, quaint Schubertian arpeggios, and block chords reminiscent of Rachmaninoff or, closer to home, Lecuona. At the same time, the solo contains features that would become trademarks of Latin piano; these include vigorous

Lisztian double- and triple-octave runs (occasionally with parallel thirds added), an emphasis on syncopation and rhythm in general, and, most presciently, the juxtaposition of discrete passages in contrasting rhythms and textures rather than extended thematic continuity or development.

According to Max Salazar (1992, 13), Romeu was one of the very few pianists to improvise solos before the late 1930s. The idiosyncratic nature of his playing, the scarcity of recorded flute solos, statements by elderly informants,[6] and the relative simplicity of trumpet playing in the *son* septets all suggest that until this time Latin improvisation styles had not really developed a distinctive character. The notable exceptions, of course, were the dynamic styles associated with the lowly bongo and *quinto,* whose richness and vitality would animate all the instrumental styles maturing in the next decade.

It was in the 1940s that a definitive mainstream Latin dance music style coalesced, comprising norms of composition, arranging, and improvisation that remain structurally fundamental even in the salsa of today. The most salient developments included the following: the popularization of the *conjunto* format, in which conga, piano, and second or third trumpets were added to the *son* septet; the incorporation of the *timbales* into the standard dance band ensemble; the standardization of accompaniment parts; the use of more sophisticated and elaborate horn arrangements (in the case of the mambo big bands, adopting sectional arrangement principles from swing jazz); the adaptation of these techniques (whether in *conjuntos, charangas,* or larger groups) to playing pieces in up-tempo Afro-Cuban rhythms (especially as derived from the rumba via the *son*); and, finally, the unprecedented emphasis on instrumental solos and the concomitant emergence of mature, distinctive instrumental improvisatory styles. The mambo big band of Machito and Mario Bauzá is sometimes credited with being the first to feature sophisticated instrumental solos, although the practice had clearly commenced earlier.

Salazar (1992, 13) indicates that the inclusion of improvised piano solos in arrangements became popular from about 1938, perhaps first inspired by a *tres* solo recorded by Arsenio Rodríguez. The transitional period to more modern styles can be traced in the early recordings of Arsenio, Conjunto Casino, Orquesta Casino de la Playa, and the Sonora Matancera. The piano playing featured on most of these records (especially by Anselmo Sacasas, Pérez Prado, Agustín Mercier, and Roberto Alvarez) indicates the rapid emergence of the modern accompaniment and solo styles. The solo playing includes archaisms and eccentricities like oompah left-hand patterns and Alberti bass passages, along with what would become standard features: runs in doubled and tripled octaves, occasional *guajeo*-type accompaniment patterns, and a delight in quasi-atonal nonsense riffs (typically involving chromatic descending sequences) introduced for their rhythmic and textural irregularity. As archaisms disappeared in the latter '40s, the playing of Lílí Martínez, Pedro "Peruchín" Jústiz, Noro Morales, and Jesús López essentially codified the modern piano style.

By 1950 a mainstream Latin dance music style in general had congealed which continues to form the basis of modern salsa. Indeed, the relabeling of Cuban dance music as "salsa" in the latter 1960s involved a socio-musical resignification rather than a fundamental stylistic change (Manuel 1994, 264–80), such that Díaz Ayala may have been only slightly exaggerating to state, "In the legacy of Arsenio, salsa was already complete" (1981, 174). Within this general body of music, however, one can distinguish substyles which are self-consciously *típico* (loosely, "traditional"), as opposed to more modern approaches. The former would include most *charanga* groups (see Murphy 1991) as well as salsa *conjuntos* led by Johnny Pacheco and Pete "El Conde" Rodríguez, modeled on 1950s Cuban performers like Felix Chappotín and the Sonora Matancera. Aside from Latin jazz, the stylistic vanguard of Latin dance music has been represented by ensembles of Eddie Palmieri, Ray Barretto, Jerry and Andy Gonzalez, and others. Both these sets of substyles, as well as the familiar mainstream, rely on a core of improvisation norms inherited from the latter 1940s. It is to this mainstream core that we may now turn.

Modern Latin Music: Accompanimental Improvisation

Popular and academic discourse on improvisation naturally tends to focus on featured instrumental solos by virtuoso performers. In many types of music, however, improvisation also plays a crucial role in accompaniment styles; such is certainly the case in Latin dance pieces, wherein improvised solos are often short or entirely absent. Improvisation in Latin music accompaniment ranges from microrhythmic nuances by individual players to overtly audible passages involving spontaneous collective collaboration.

Much of the expressive essence of Latin music lies in the intricate composite rhythm created by the percussion, bass, and piano, which together constitute the rhythm section. This composite rhythm is the product of a set of standardized accompanimental ostinatos, such as are illustrated in the *montuno* excerpt in example 6.2. These patterns, or alternative versions thereof, are maintained with a limited amount of variation throughout a given song. In the words of pianist Oscar Hernandez, "You have to perform as a unit—a team player" (in Gerard and Sheller 1989, 35). At the same time, the composite rhythm is enlivened by judicious amounts of improvised variation, along the lines of what Berliner calls "controlled flexibility" (1994), Keil terms "participatory discrepancies" (1995), and Leonard Meyer would subsume under the term "simultaneous deviation" (1956, 234–46). As pianist Sonny Bravo notes, within certain limitations, "anyone in the [rhythm] section can alter what he's doing a little bit to build the groove" (in Doerschuk 1992, 317).

Because some of these improvised variation techniques have been outlined elsewhere (esp. Mauleón 1993, Gerard and Sheller 1989, and Doerschuk 1992), our observations here will be brief. The ostinato generally played on the side (*cascara, paila*) of the *timbales* or on its attached cowbell is perhaps the least subject to variation (Gerard and Sheller 1989, 50); it functions as a funda-

Example 6.2. *Montuno* excerpt.

mental time-keeper roughly analogous to the "time line" of West African percussion. Somewhat greater flexibility is allowed to the conga drum, which was
incorporated into dance band ensembles in the 1940s. However, the conga's
role in this context is not comparable to that of the *quinto* in the rumba. That
is, it is not featured as a foreground, constantly improvising instrument, but
rather as a secondary cog in the composite rhythm, reiterating, with some creative latitude, a standardized ostinato (the *tumbao*). As mentioned above, the
quinto's role in the *son* septets had been usurped by the bongo, which improvised freely throughout a given song. With the coalescence of the standardized
composite rhythm in the mainstream style, the bongo's improvisatory flexibility was also reduced to performing variations *(repiques)* on a stock ostinato
(the *martillo* or "hammer") during the *guía* (the bongo player generally switch-
ing to cowbell during the *montuno*). These variations, while more free than
those played on the conga, generally maintain a steady eighth-note pulse.

As in jazz, the bass plays an important role in maintaining the composite
rhythm. As bassist Andy Gonzalez states, "In Latin music you have to approach
the bass as a drummer would approach the drums—with the same sense of
percussiveness and attacks" (in Gerard and Sheller 1989, 42). The most typical
accompanying pattern is the "anticipated bass" ostinato such as is shown in
example 6.2, or variants thereof. The bass player enjoys some latitude to alter
his part, with the "sense of percussiveness" noted by Gonzalez. These variations might consist of alternate ostinatos, or, as in jazz drumming, they might
comprise subtle, microrhythmic nuances referred to, for example, as "pushing
the beat" or "playing on top of the beat"; musicians state that such nuances,

however incremental, can greatly intensify the music when deployed effectively (Chris Washburne, personal communication).

If jazz piano accompaniment consists of "comping" chords in a loose, desultory, irregular manner, the Latin pianist must maintain a regular ostinato pattern, at least throughout the *montuno*. These standardized patterns themselves are called *guajeo* or *montuno* and derive ultimately from counterparts played on the *tres* in traditional *son*. Generally a pianist will maintain a given *guajeo* (such as that in ex. 6.2) throughout an entire section of the *montuno,* altering it primarily during the ensemble horn breaks (mambo, *moña*). Excessive or even slight but inappropriate alterations can be seen by aficionados as distracting and reflective of immaturity, and extensive reiteration of the same ostinato, rather than being monotonous, can help create a hypnotic intensity. However, skilled pianists can also introduce discreet variations which can heighten rather than muddy the effect, even, for example, behind horn solos. In general, as Mauleón notes (1993, 118), "a solid *montuno* is one that creates a balance between repetition and variation."

One of the most distinctive forms of improvisation in Latin music is the spontaneous creation of *moñas* by the horn section. A *moña* is an instrumental interlude which is typically introduced between *soneos* or *montuno* sections, or during the latter part of an instrumental solo. It generally features two or three layered, interlocking or overlapping horn lines, played, for example, by the trombones and trumpets.[7] While a typical salsa chart may contain one or more precomposed *moñas,* horn players in the better salsa bands often improvise *moñas* in longer songs. A good *moña* can greatly intensify the "groove" in an extended solo, while providing a creative outlet for horn players otherwise relegated to reading parts from scores.

Improvising a *moña* requires a remarkable collective interaction. Typically, the trombone player might initiate a line, which a trumpeter would answer with a complementary riff; the other horn players would then join in. Ideally, the *moña* should sound as if it were precomposed. Once, for example, after watching the Ray Sepulveda band play what seemed to me an entirely precomposed song (except for the solos), I was quite surprised to hear from the group's trombonist, ethnomusicologist Chris Washburne, that the final *moña* had been spontaneous. Washburne explained to me after the set:

> What happened there was that Ray started to cue us during the piano solo to go into the final mambo and end the song, but I thought the music was just getting hot, and that we should build on it, so I signalled to him that we would do a *moña.* Then I sang the trombone part I had in mind to the other trombonist, so we came in together, and the trumpet players, who were ready, answered it right away with their own line. And it worked.

Collectively improvising *moñas* involves a dimension of risk, as well as expressivity, different from that in soloing. The initiator of a *moña* may feel exasperated if his colleagues respond with an incompatible line (see, e.g., Sonny

Bravo quoted in Doerschuk 1992, 318) or if they fail to answer at all, whether due to fatigue, laziness, or incompetence. As Washburne relates,

> It's like having a gun to your head, but if you want to hang with the big boys and not just be a B-grade hack playing on autopilot, you have to rise to the occasion. So sometimes we try something, and it's a disaster. Or perhaps I'm tired myself, or not in the most creative mood, so I just recycle a riff that I know, perhaps varying it to fit the situation. But then it can turn into something completely different. And if a night goes by where I don't try something new, I'm not growing as a musician. (Personal communication)

As Washburne observes, the tradition of improvising *moñas* persists in the live performances of bandleaders like Sepulveda who are appreciative of their accompanists' virtuosity, and even in studio recordings, where scores may be quite incomplete. Nevertheless, the practice has declined significantly since the "classic" salsa era of roughly 1965–78. The change may be due in part to the tendency of modern pop *salsa romántica* to stress the singer's star image over musicianship, such that contemporary bands tend to mechanically follow scores rather than improvise on stage.[8] The increasingly rigid adherence to recorded versions of songs perpetuates this decline, especially since modern recordings are generally done by overdubbing individual parts, rendering impossible any form of spontaneous group interaction (see Manuel 1995:88).

Modern Latin Music: Solo Improvisation
Although in Latin music the role of improvisation in accompaniment styles is important, solo improvisations are naturally more conspicuous. While clearly incorporating features from jazz and from African and European sources, Latin solo styles have evolved as highly original and distinctive idioms. Solos generally take place not in the short, largely precomposed *guía*, but in the longer *montuno* section, which can be extended indefinitely by solos, perhaps punctuated by mambos and *moñas*.

Although instrumental solo styles are the most elaborate, improvisations by the lead singer are in their own way at least as prominent. Indeed, Latin music vocalists have often been bandleaders and star attractions, whether because of their musical skills or, as is often the case today, the pop-star image projected around them by the commercial music industry. Talented vocalists can function as musical leaders in spite of being musically illiterate and ignorant of theory. The classic example is Cuban singer and bandleader Beny Moré (d. 1963), who, although lacking formal musical knowledge, was, in Acosta's words, "three-quarters of the band" (1993, 16).

Aside from interpretative nuances in rendering the melody of the *guía*, vocal improvisation occurs primarily in the context of the lead singer's *soneos* or *inspiraciones* performed responsorially with the *coro*. This style, consisting generally of two- or four-bar phrases in overlapping call-and-response style, derives directly from the traditional rumba, which itself evolved primarily from African predecessors. According to some singers, the lyrics of the *soneos* should relate to the story or subject of the song lyrics proper, whether consisting of quotes from the *guía* lyrics or original (if precomposed) snippets of verse (see, e.g., Miguelito Valdés's comments in Salazar 1992, 11). Often, however, vocalists simply sing stock and thematically unrelated phrases, typically in colloquial slang (Gerard and Sheller 1989, 30–32). Since the phrases are so short, involve both text and tune, and are often sung by vocalists lacking technical musical knowledge, it is natural that they often consist more of flexible reiterations of vocalists' favorite phrases than truly spontaneous creations. Such is particularly the case with many of the modern pop *salsa romántica* singers, who tend to adhere timidly to the recorded versions of their songs, and who, at any rate, may be promoted less for their talent than for their star image.[9] These tendencies serve to throw into greater relief the few contemporary singers such as Gilberto Santa Rosa who are fluid improvisers.

As we have suggested above, the Latin improvisational piano and wind instrument styles that coalesced in the 1940s continue to form the bases for their modern counterparts. Such changes as have occurred in the interim consist mostly of jazz influences, whose incorporation has led to the use of the term *típico* to distinguish older styles. *Típico,* as in reference to music or food, implies "traditional" or "old-fashioned," or redolent of island life. As John Murphy (1991) documents, the *charanga* ensemble, with its somewhat quaint flute-and-violins format, is itself regarded as *típico,* suggestive as it is of bygone days in Cuban bourgeois salons and cotillions. Although *charangas* have largely forsaken the archaic *danzón* for the up-tempo Afro-Cuban *son* and *guaracha,* the flute improvisation style associated with *charanga* remains distinctively *típico.* Murphy observes that this *típico* aesthetic can be understood partly as the avoidance of jazz-type chromaticisms, and also as the self-conscious use of a vocabulary of familiar phrases and riffs (1991, 121–22). Example 6.3a, cited by Murphy, is a typical and ubiquitous stock phrase,[10] as is the figure shown in example 6.3b.

Equally popular are arpeggios and other patterns reflective of the classical (rather than jazz) background of most *charanga* flautists. Although heavily reliant on such a finite repertoire of stock riffs, *charanga* flautists often improvise not only in solos but throughout entire songs. *Charanga* violinists also solo, and they have their own somewhat idiosyncratic *típico* style.

Latin trumpet playing evolved in different contexts, namely, the *son*-based septets and, later, *conjuntos.* In the traditional *son,* the trumpet would improvise in the opening of the *guía* and in call-and-response style with the first four *coros* of the *montuno* (the latter practice remaining standard in modern salsa). As mentioned above, trumpet playing in the septets was fairly simple; indeed, it closely resembled the vocal *soneo* style, and might incorporate snippets of contemporary songs (Orlando Fiol, personal communication). In the 1940s,

(a)   (b)

Example 6.3. *Típico* flute phrases.

however, improved technical standards led trumpet playing to depart from vocal models and develop in its own direction, as happened contemporaneously
with jazz; the better soloists also cultivated an interest in jazz and freely incorporated elements from it. Despite such influences, Latin trumpet playing acquired and retained its own character, especially in the *típico* style represented
by players like Alfredo "Chocolate" Armenteros. As with *charanga* flute, the
típico style comprises both a reiteration of favorite, typical phrases as well as
an avoidance, whether deliberate or ingenuous, of jazz mannerisms. As dance
bands incorporated saxophones and trombones, characteristic Latin styles of
soloing on these instruments also evolved.

We have outlined the sorts of improvisatory latitude accorded to the bongo,
timbales, and conga in their accompanimental roles. *Montunos* may also feature improvised solos on these instruments, and percussionists like Patato Val-
déz and Tito Puente may acquire considerable renown as soloists. To some
extent, solo styles on these instruments have their own distinct histories and
idiosyncracies. Modern bongo playing has natural affinities with the bongo
style of the *son* septets, as does conga soloing with the *quinto* style of the
traditional rumba; however, the presence of conga solos in dance band music
dates only from the mid-century decades, when it was popularized by Mongo
Santamaría. The use of the timbales as a solo instrument for up-tempo Afro-
Cuban dance music commenced around the same time, when Tito Puente popularized its usage, along with a colorful and flamboyant improvisatory style.

In other respects the solo styles associated with the three instruments are
quite similar, drawing from a common vocabulary of motives and devices. Accordingly, most modern percussionists learn to perform on two or three of the
instruments, using many of the same rhythmic principles and techniques. Some
of these are evident in the bongo solo schematically transcribed as example
6.4. Brief as this solo is, it exhibits some quintessential features of the *típico*
idiom, including the emphasis on artful syncopation rather than gratuitous
speed and virtuosity[11]; the tendency—as pervasive in West African drumming
as in the solos of *charanga* flautist Dave Valentín—to establish a given phrase
that can be repeated (with or without slight variation) a few times, and then
move to another discrete phrase; and lastly, the sequential use of contrasting
syncopations, particularly different articulations of either ternary phrasings of
binary subdivisions, or, conversely, binary phrasing of triplets. In this case, the
solo quickly progresses through the following phrases: ternary-phrased single
strokes (mm. 1–3); reiterations of a four- or five-stroke sextuplet figure (mm.
4–6); an extended series of regular triplet strokes (mm. 11–13); and lastly, a

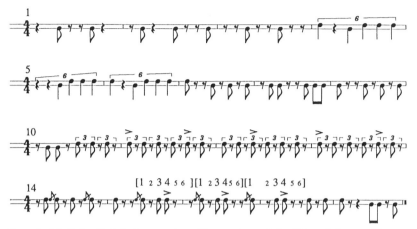

Example 6.4. Carlos Embale, bongo solo on "Los rumberos de La Habana," *Soneros Mayores,* EGREM PRO-067.

stock phrase consisting of threefold repetition of a pattern with ternary phrasing of binary subdivision (such as could be schematized: **1** 2 3 **4** 5 6 **1** 2 3 **4** 5 6 etc.), all in eighth-notes (mm. 15–17).

Omitted from this and other transcriptions in this article are the numerous and subtle microrhythmic nuances (playing "behind the beat," straddling triplet and quadratic subdivisions, and the like) which can be judiciously introduced (and perhaps subsequently avoided) in all instrumental styles in order to heighten rhythmic drive and tension (see Washburne 1998).

Latin Piano Improvisation

Latin piano style constitutes one of the most original and distinctive features of Latin music. Because of its uniqueness and the way it embodies what can be seen as certain quintessential features of Latin improvisation, it merits more expansive discussion in this article. Essentially, the solo style comprises a set of standardized patterns or techniques having contrasting textures, which, in a given solo, are introduced in the form of relatively short, discrete phrases. In several of these typical patterns, rhythm and texture are of greater importance than melody and harmony. The most common patterns include the following: (1) repeated ternary-phrased, three-pitch, eighth-note arpeggios, usually with doubled or tripled octaves, alternating between tonic and dominant chords (as in ex. 6.5, or mm. 3–5 of ex. 6.7, or, in triplets, mm. 19–24 of ex. 6.7); (2) melodies played in double, triple, or quadruple octaves (e.g., mm. 16–19 in ex. 6.7, or throughout ex. 6.8); (3) phrases using parallel thirds (or tenths), also generally played in doubled octaves (mm. 9–14, 30–32 in ex. 6.7); (4) syncopated patterns repeating short, double-octave right-hand phrases (usually one or two pitches) with left-hand chords (mm. 9–18 of ex. 6.8); (5) *guajeo/mon-*

Example 6.5. Typical piano pattern.

Example 6.6. Anselmo Sacasas, piano solo on "Esto es los último" (excerpt), Orquesta Casino de la Playa, *Memories of Cuba*, Tumbao TCD 003.

tuno-like passages; (6) block chords; (7) quasi-atonal, and often a-rhythmic nonsense riffs (often descending sequences like the passage in ex. 6.6); (8) single-note right-hand runs, with occasional left-hand "comping" chords, as in mainstream jazz piano.

The affinities with jazz are apparent mostly in the realm of chord voicings, which often use ninths, thirteenths, and, in less *típico* contexts, piled fourths such as were popularized by McCoy Tyner.[12] However, the differences from jazz are perhaps more striking. Since the emergence of bebop in the early 1940s, mainstream jazz piano style has consisted overwhelmingly of single-note right-hand runs, punctuated by occasional left-hand chords (comping). That is, it is essentially a one-handed style (such as prompted Art Tatum to state of bebop pianist Bud Powell, "He ain't got no left"). This texture does occur in Latin piano (pattern 8 above), but as merely one of several more common textures. In general, Latin piano stresses volume, power, textural contrast, and rhythm more than intricacy of melodic line. As Sonny Bravo states, half in jest, "We're not dealing with subtle music here; we're dealing with savages from the jungle" (in Doerschuk 1992, 323). It may also be noted that such textural variation works much more naturally with harmonically static or repetitive *montunos* than it would with extended harmonic progressions used in jazz standards; pattern 1 (ex. 6.5), for example, is designed to fit over a repeated tonic-dominant ostinato, and would be difficult to introduce in a jazz song with extended chord progressions. Conversely, it would be difficult to sustain interest in a solo over an extended *montuno* ostinato by using only jazz-style single-note right-hand runs. Accordingly, when Latin jazz pianists play songs with sequential harmonic progressions, they tend to lapse into the single-note format, reserving the more varied textures for chordal ostinato sections.

Example 6.7, a typical piano solo by Larry Harlow, illustrates how some of these textures are performed. A brief introductory two-octave phrase leads to a

Example 6.7. Larry Harlow, piano solo on "Anacaona," from *Salsa del Barrio: 14 exitos originales,*
Profono TPL 1403.

two-bar ternary arpeggio figure (mm. 3–4), using the familiar device of ternary phrasing of duple (eighth-note) subdivisions. Following this is a passage in doubled parallel thirds, structured, as are many phrases in Latin improvisation, in the form of what could be seen as an antecedent-consequent or call-and-response pattern (mm. 9–14). In the next passage (from m. 15), an ascending line in quadruple octaves climaxes in a double-octave call, which, after a pause, segues to a triplet arpeggio ostinato figure in doubled octaves, alternating tonic and dominant chords (mm. 20–25). A transitional phrase leads to a descending, ternary/*montuno*-type figure (mm. 28–29), and the solo concludes with another passage in doubled parallel thirds. (This solo, it may be noted, also reflects one of the basic principles of *clave*, that is, the tendency to stress downbeats only on the "2" side—here, odd-numbered bars—eliding the others.)

There is an obvious parallel between the aesthetic evident here and that in percussion solos, such as example 6.4. In both cases, the emphasis is not on extended thematic development, nor even on overt textural or rhythmic continuity per se, but rather on the sequential presentation of discrete contrasting phrases. Like percussion improvisations, these often take the form either of antecedent-consequent phrasing, or of a pattern repeated, perhaps with variation, twice or thrice, generally lasting less than five seconds. At the same time, the effect is not one of a disjointed pastiche, but of a continuous flow.

Latin Improvisation and Jazz

By this point it should be quite clear that Latin improvisation, although influenced by jazz, is best regarded as a parallel tradition, which, indeed, has exerted its own influence on jazz. Since the 1940s, many Latin musicians have informally studied jazz and freely incorporated elements from it into their playing. More than one instrumentalist has told me that since he grew up immersed in Latin music and eventually performing it, he presently cultivates a more active interest in jazz than Latin music. Further, jazz pedagogy has generally had much more to offer students in terms of publications, classes, "music minus one" records and the like. Jazz horn players have also regularly been featured as guest soloists in Latin jazz groups, especially in the 1940s and '50s, when the distinctive Latin solo styles were just taking shape. The overlap between the two styles is formalized in the genre of Latin jazz, which uses the rhythms and often the *montuno* ostinatos of Latin music, while sharing with jazz the emphasis on solo improvisation, the predominantly instrumental (rather than vocal) format, and a function as music for listening rather than dancing.

In other respects, the realms of Latin music and jazz remain distinct. There are many Latin horn players who are fluent at improvising over *montunos*, but who would be hard-pressed to play a solo over a jazz standard like "Stella by Starlight." Conversely, jazz players who delve into Latin music must be able to perform interesting solos over chordal ostinatos, and they must develop some feeling for the aesthetic, and, ideally, for rhythmic subtleties like *clave*.[13] Of course, a fundamental distinction between the two genres is that Latin music, unlike jazz since the swing era, is dance music. Solos must ideally intensify the groove for dancers, and soloists learn to gauge the success of their improvisations by the degree to which dancers are "getting down."

Toward an Aesthetic of Latin Music Improvisation

Latin music, like any mature musical genre, comprises not a random grab bag of diverse techniques and mannerisms, but a cohesive set of idiomatic substyles which have been organically cultivated by generations of musicians. As such, Latin improvisation may be presumed to be animated by a consistent underlying aesthetic, which may, however, be difficult to describe analytically. In attempting to abstract an aesthetic of Latin music improvisation per se, prior research on West African music may provide some useful models, especially because of the close affinities and historical bonds between the two culture areas. Robert Farris Thompson (1973) and, in a somewhat different manner, John Chernoff (1979) have posited a certain "aesthetic of the cool" pervading much of West African music and dance, and one might be tempted to seek parallels in Afro-Latin music. Latin percussionists do indeed articulate the importance of control and economy of style, rather than ostentatious and gratuitous display;[14] similar notions, of course, can be found in many improvisational styles, from jazz to Hindustani music. However, extending the analogy is problematic; Latinos certainly do not praise music as *fría* or "cool," but instead speak of salsa and rumba as *caliente* (hot) or *brava* (wild, fierce). At the risk of generalizing, I would opine that Latin music strives for intense drive and exuberance (implicit in the oft-used term *sabor*) rather than coolness and restraint.

David Locke presents a somewhat less abstract, more practical set of aesthetic guidelines in his pedagogical study of Ghanaian drum Gahu (1987, 127–28). Among the goals Locke recommends to students are intensity, momentum, power, humor, orientation toward dance, interaction with other musicians, and thinking in terms of phrases rather than individual strokes. Such guidelines would apply well to Latin music, as indeed they might to other musics such as jazz.

A more analytical and perhaps less ambitious approach to hypothesizing a consistent aesthetic of Latin music would be to locate specific technical features that appear to recur as common denominators in all or most instrumental improvisational idioms. I have mentioned above, for example, the tendency toward short, discrete, contrasting phrases evident in both melodic instrument and percussion solos. Such phrasings may suggest question-answer-type patterns, or, alternately, formats in which a phrase is introduced, repeated or varied twice or thrice, and then dropped. Such tendencies reflect a continuity with traditional rumba drumming and dancing and, on a slightly more general level, with the essentially percussive orientation of modern piano and even wind instrument styles. In this sense, Latin improvisation (and composition) could be said to be unified by a common and quite distinctive approach to rhythm, just as "swing" is sometimes posited as the essence of jazz. Several of the distinguishing features of Latin rhythm can be abstracted and enumerated. These would include the following: (1) the importance of *clave* as an underlying regulating rhythmic ostinato; (2) the use, as basic building blocks, of a set of stock rhythmic patterns, including the cells presented in example 6.1 (and others presented in Mauleón 1993); (3) a fondness for stressing offbeats, and especially anacruses (as in mm. 1–3 of ex. 6.4 above); (4) a particular approach to syncopation, involving the aforementioned use of binary subdivision with ternary phrasing, and conversely, triplet subdivision with binary phrasing.

The latter principle merits further discussion here. These two techniques pervade improvisations on percussion, piano, and, to a somewhat lesser extent, wind instruments, and innumerable examples of each technique could be presented. Ternary phrasing of binary-subdivided notes is the essence of what is one of the most familiar stock Latin piano riffs, described as pattern 1 in the list of common piano patterns above, as illustrated in example 6.5. Another cliché using the same principle is the aforementioned "1 2 3 4 5 6" pattern (or variants thereof), such as is found in the conclusion of example 6.4 and in measures 9–13 of example 6.8, a piano solo by Papo Lucca.[15]

The converse device, binary phrasing of triplet-subdivided notes or beats, is similarly common. Measures 10–13 of the bongo solo in example 6.4 show one typical application of this technique, in the form of an extended roll accented as 1 2 3 4 1 2 3 4 (etc.), using triplet subdivisions. Papo Lucca's piano solo (ex. 6.8) illustrates two other forms of this syncopation: first, triplet (or sextuplet) quarter notes are melodically phrased as descending four-note sequences (indicated by dotted brackets, mm. 1–5), and subsequently as bases for a quadratic ostinato in the rhythm 1 2 3 4 1 2 3 4 (etc). Indeed, the entire second half of this excerpt (mm. 9–18) constitutes a series of percussive variations on a simple melodic phrase, employing the two basic syncopation principles outlined here.

Much of the expressivity of these latter techniques lies in the way that they establish a temporary but quite overt sense of polyrhythm. Their usage can be seen as preserving in Afro-Latin music some of the polyrhythmic complexity that was otherwise sacrificed when quadratic-metered popular music forms replaced the structural ("12/8") polymeters pervading so much of African and neo-African music.[16] Also lost in the Middle Passage were most of the traditional African social structures and ways of life that, as Thompson and Chernoff persuasively show, ultimately informed the "cool" aesthetic itself. A more expansive and holistic study of the aesthetics of Latin music improvisation would ultimately seek not only to identify more of the fundamental technical tropes unifying the style, but to situate them ethnographically in the contexts of their associated cultures and social histories.

Example 6.8. Papo Lucca, piano solo on "Ritmo, Tambor y Flores," on Celia Cruz, *Celia, Johnny, Justo y Papo: Recordando el Ayer,* Vaya 52.

Notes

1. Cf. e.g., Mauleón 1993, and the videos *Conga Virtuoso: Giovanni Hidalgo* (DCI Music Video, 1995), *Jerry Gonzalez and Afro-Caribbean Rhythms, Jerry Gonzalez: Congo Mania,* and *Manny Oquendo on Timbales* (Alchemy Pictures).

2. Nor, for that matter, have *laúd* players been featured in Cuban dance bands, as has Puerto Rican *cuatro* virtuoso Yomo Toro in salsa formats.

3. Shown here is the *son clave;* in the *rumba clave*—i.e., that used in traditional rumba—the third note of the "3" side falls an eighth-note later. For further discussion of *clave,* see Mauleón 1993, ch. 3; Gerard and Sheller 1989, ch. 2; and Manuel 1995, 38–41; regarding the other rhythmic cells, see Behague 1980 and Mikowsky 1988.

4. For transcriptions of these patterns, see Gerard and Sheller 1989, ch. 6; Manuel 1995, 25.

5. Singer (1983) notes that the highest compliment that can be paid to a melodic instrumental player is to be likened to a drummer.

6. Such as pianist Agustín Mercier of Conjunto Casino, as interviewed by Delfín Pérez (personal communication).

7. Although terminology is occasionally inconsistent, *moñas* are generally distinguished as retaining the chordal ostinato of the *montuno,* whereas the otherwise similar mambos depart from it. Because they involve coordination of the piano and bass as well as horns, mambos are precomposed. See Mauleón 1993, 156, for a transcribed example of a *moña.*

8. Informants like trumpeter Hector Colon claim that this trend is particularly marked in bands from Puerto Rico (personal communication).

9. Producer Sergio George, for example, comments, "You've got singers who are selling a lot of records who don't have a clue how to *sonear*" (Boggs 1993, 18).

10. Orlando Fiol states that this figure comes from Cuban *comparsa* ditties (personal communication).

11. Modern percussionists like Archie Flores and Giovanni Hidalgo have popularized more flashy, virtuoso styles of playing.

12. See, e.g., the left-hand voicings of the F-minor chord in m. 10 of example 6.8. I call the use of these features in Latin music "affinities" rather than "influences," since they may to some extent derive from common roots in popular and late Romantic harmony rather than solely from imitation of jazz.

13. I have, however, heard conflicting reports on this issue. While some Latin soloists stress the importance of *clave,* jazz sax player Chico Freeman, who toured extensively with the Machito band, told me, "*Clave* isn't really important for us soloists; it's mostly for the arrangers" (personal communication).

14. E.g., Orlando Fiol (personal communication), and Ray Barretto, who states of the younger percussionists, "Their action is based on speed and rapid-fire, and sometimes open space is as important as what you play" (Tamargo 1994, 14).

15. This riff can also be heard in the timbales solo in "Reina Rumba" on the same LP.

16. This fundamental shift, from polymetric African structures and Spanish triple meter to the quadratic rhythms of modern Latin music, remains to be analytically explored, although a somewhat problematic attempt is found in Pérez Fernández 1987.

References

Acosta, Leonardo. 1993. *Elige tú que canto yo.* Havana: Editorial Letras Cubanas.

Behague, Gerard. 1980. "Improvisation in Latin American Musics." *Music Educators Journal* 66:118–25.

Berliner, Paul. 1994. *Thinking in Jazz: The Infinite Art of Improvisation.* Chicago: University of Chicago Press.

Boggs, Vernon. 1993. "Don Salsa: Sergio George." *Latin Beat* 3, no. 1:16–19.

Chernoff, John. 1979. *African Rhythm and African Sensibility: Aesthetics and Social Action in African Musical Idioms.* Chicago: University of Chicago Press.

Díaz Ayala, Cristobal. 1981. *Música Cubana del Areyto a la Nueva Trova.* San Juan: Editorial Cubanacan.

———. 1994. *Discografía de la Música Cubana: Vol. 1/1898–1925.* San Juan: Fundación Musicalia.

Doerschuk, Robert. 1992. "Secrets of Salsa Rhythm: Piano with Hot Sauce." In *Salsiology: Afro-Cuban Music and the Evolution of Salsa in New York City,* edited by Vernon Boggs, 312–24. New York: Greenwood Press.

Fiehrer, Thomas. 1991. "From Quadrille to Stomp: The Creole Origins of Jazz." *Popular Music* 10, no. 1:21–38.

Gerard, Charley, and Marty Sheller. 1989. *Salsa: The Rhythm of Latin Music.* Crown Point, Ind.: White Cliffs Media.

Keil, Charles. 1995. "The Theory of Participatory Discrepancies: A Progress Report." *Ethnomusicology* 39, no. 1:1–20.

Locke, David. 1987. *Drum Gahu.* Crown Point, Ind.: White Cliffs Media.

Manuel, Peter. 1994. "Puerto Rican Music and Cultural Identity: Creative Appropriation of Cuban Sources from Danza to Salsa." *Ethnomusicology* 38, no. 2:249–80.

————— (with Kenneth Bilby and Michael Largey). 1995. *Caribbean Currents: Caribbean Music from Rumba to Reggae.* Philadelphia: Temple University Press.

Mauleón, Rebecca. 1993. *Salsa Guidebook for Piano and Ensemble.* Petaluma, Calif.: Sher Music Co.

Meyer, Leonard. 1956. *Emotion and Meaning in Music.* Chicago: University of Chicago Press.

Mikowsky, Solomon. 1988. *The Nineteenth-Century Cuban Danza and its Composers, with Particular Attention to Ignacio Cervantes (1847–1905).* Havana: Editorial Letras Cubanas.

Murphy, John. 1991. "The Charanga in New York and the Persistence of the Típico Style." In *Essays on Cuban Music: Cuban and North American Perspectives,* edited by Peter Manuel, 115–35. Lanham, Md.: University Press of America.

Pérez Fernández, Rolando. 1987. *La binarización de los ritmos ternarios africanos en América Latina.* Havana: Casa de las Américas.

Salazar, Max. 1992. "The Miguelito Valdés Story, Part 1." *Latin Beat* 2, no. 1:10–13.

Santos, John. 1982. Liner notes to *The Cuban Danzón: Its Ancestors and Descendants.* Folkways FE 4066.

Singer, Roberta. 1983. "Tradition and Innovation in Contemporary Latin Popular Music in New York City." *Latin American Music Review* 4, no. 2:183–202.

Tamargo, Luis 1994. "Ray Barretto Speaks." *Latin Beat* 4, no. 5:11–14.

Thompson, Robert Farris. 1973. "An Aesthetic of the Cool." *African Arts* 7, no. 1:40–43, 64–67, 89.

Veray, Amaury. 1977. "Vida y desarrollo de la danza puertorriqueña." In Rosado, ed., *Ensayos sobre la danza puertorriqueña,* edited by Marisa Rosado, 23–37. 1956. Reprint, San Juan: Instituto de Cultura Puertorriqueña.

Washburne, Chris. 1998. "'Play It con Filin!' The Swing and Expression of Salsa." *Latin American Music Review* 19, no. 2.

CHAPTER SEVEN

Oh Freedom: George Russell, John Coltrane, and Modal Jazz

INGRID MONSON

Improvisation has often been taken as a metaphor for freedom both musical and social, especially in jazz. The image of improvisation as freedom became especially pronounced in the jazz world of the early 1960s when the free jazz of Ornette Coleman, Cecil Taylor, Albert Ayler, and others catalyzed aesthetic and political debates within the jazz community and music industry. The political contexts of the civil rights movement in the U.S. and the independence movements on the African continent surely informed the accelerated conflation of musical and political freedom, but standard historical accounts of jazz in the decade prior to the emergence of free jazz tend to emphasize a linear succession of musical styles that move from cool jazz to hard bop on an inevitable trajectory toward the modernism and musical avant-gardism of the sixties (Baraka 1963; Schuller 1986). This history is far too self-contained to meet the demands of an ethnomusicology concerned with multiple factors of determination.

In this essay George Russell, John Coltrane, and the history of modal jazz provide a way to rethink jazz history in the fifties and early sixties within a web of interlocking contexts that include aesthetic modernism, spiritual transcendence, transnationalism, the civil rights movement, and African independence. Considering modal jazz within these contexts poses, in addition, several interpretive challenges for an ethnomusicology of improvisation. How can we establish a set of interrelationships between constantly changing musical processes and equally fluid social and cultural ones? What should we make of the ideological and cultural meanings attached to improvisation by performers and audiences at particular moments in time? And what if these meanings conflict with currently fashionable modes of cultural and social interpretation?

Russell's *Lydian Chromatic Concept of Tonal Organization,* first published in 1953, is a theory of music that systematizes the relationship of chords to scales (and, by extension, close to distant harmonic relationships) through the identification of a family of modalities (or scales)[1] related to a particular chord (Russell 1953). In the 1950s and early 1960s Russell's theoretical explorations and expertise on mode were well known among leading jazz musicians including Art Farmer, Bill Evans, Miles Davis, Herbie Hancock, Carla Bley, and Eric Dolphy. Russell's conceptions of modality predated the idea of "modal jazz" that emerged in the wake of Miles Davis's *Milestones* (1958) and *Kind of Blue* (1959) recordings, and indeed, Russell discussed the Lydian Chromatic Concept in detail with Davis at least a year prior to the recording of *Milestones* (Nisenson 1993, 55–56).[2]

Historical accounts of modal jazz nevertheless take Miles Davis's album *Kind of Blue* (Davis 1959) as a point of departure—with particular attention to the composition "So What."[3] The structure of "So What," indeed, has become the canonical example of a modal composition. The A sections of this 32-bar AABA form present a theme in D dorian and the B section transposes the same idea up a half-step to E-flat dorian. Lead sheets represent the harmonic structure of the composition as two chords—Dm7 for the A sections and Ebm7 for the B section. In the 1959 recording, pianist Bill Evans realized the sonority in quartal harmony (Tirro 1993, 363). Improvising soloists, however, were not restricted to the notes of the dorian mode. While the improvisations of Davis and Evans remain close to the mode, John Coltrane and Cannonball Adderly play more freely over the tonally stable background (Porter and Ullman 1993, 294).[4] The term "modal jazz" has come to be associated with these two musical characteristics: fewer chords (than jazz standards or bebop compositions) and (consequently) greater freedom of note (and scale) selection over a relatively more stable tonal background.

The rhythmic implications of tonally open frameworks have less often been emphasized. Freed from the necessity of delineating frequently changing harmonies, bassists expanded their use of pedal points, pianists accompanied long sections with intricate vamps and riffs, and drummers played with greater rhythmic density and cross-rhythms than had been customary in earlier styles. Some of the most spectacular realizations of the rhythmic as well as tonal implications of modal structures can be found in the recordings of the John Coltrane Quartet between 1960 and 1964 and the Miles Davis Quintet between 1963 and 1968. These ensembles featured two of the most revered rhythm sections in jazz: McCoy Tyner, Jimmy Garrison, and Elvin Jones; and Herbie Hancock, Ron Carter, and Tony Williams.[5]

The implications of modal jazz were not, however, restricted to formal musical considerations. More significant from the point of view of ethnomusicology is how more open tonal frameworks served as musical crossroads facilitating the incorporation of transnational (especially non-Western) approaches to improvisation, timbre, and spirituality. The work of John Coltrane, for example, drew from India, Africa, and the Middle East, and George Russell has always viewed his engagement with music theory as a spiritual as well as intellectual quest. Modal jazz implies an interrelated set of musical and cultural issues, in which music functions, in David Stowe's felicitous phrase, as a "sign of a larger field of social forces" (1994, 9). What follows touches on four themes that are central to this larger field of social and historical forces: (1) the content of George Russell's *Lydian Chromatic Concept of Tonal Organiza-*

tion; (2) George Russell's and John Coltrane's interest in spirituality, especially non-Western spirituality; (3) John Coltrane's interest in the musics of Africa and India, and how modal jazz became a musical framework and sign of this internationalist perspective; and (4) how these transnational spiritual and musical interests relate to the American civil rights movement and to current debates about essentialism/anti-essentialism in cultural interpretation.

The Concept

Russell began his professional musical life in the early 1940s as a drummer working with Benny Carter, but soon turned his full attention to writing and arranging.[6] Russell humbly explained his change of direction: "Once I heard Max [Roach], I really knew that I couldn't ever reach that level of drumming" (Russell 1995). Benny Carter replaced Russell with Max Roach at the drum set, but he also bought Russell's first big band arrangement, "New World." Russell used the arrangement as something of a calling card: "I think I sold that to about ten bands and one of them was Dizzy [Gillespie]. It was always my entrée to a band" (1995). Just after he sold the arrangement to Gillespie and had begun to establish a reputation in New York as an arranger, Russell suffered a severe relapse of tuberculosis that left him hospitalized for fifteen months at St. Joseph's Hospital in the Bronx in 1946–47.[7] *The Lydian Concept of Tonal Organization* (1953) was the fruit of a quest that Russell began during this hospitalization. When asked the source of the impulse to systematize his ideas about harmony, Russell remarked: "Well, first of all, it gave me a lot to do in the hospital. . . . Because even when I couldn't get out of bed for six months, bed wasn't a boring place" (1995).

Russell, who was interested in the relationship between chords and scales, pondered two issues. The first was a statement by Miles Davis that his highest musical goal was to "learn all the changes"; and the second was Russell's observation that many bebop musicians ended their tunes on a raised fourth. As Russell told it:

> Miles sort of took a liking to me, when he was playing with Bird [in clubs] along the Street [52nd Street]. And he used to invite me up to his house. We'd sit down and play chords. He liked my sense of harmony. And I loved his sense so we'd try to kill each other with chords. He'd say check this out. And I'd say wow. And I'd say listen to this. . . . I asked him one day on one of these sessions, what's your highest aim?—musical aim—and he said, to learn all the changes. That's all he said [laughs]. At the time I thought he *was* playing the changes, you know. That he was relating to each chord and arpeggiating, or using certain notes and extending the chord and all that. The more I thought about that, the more I felt there was a system begging to be brought into the world. And that system was based on chord-scale unity which traditional music had absolutely ignored. The whole aspect of a chord having a scale—that was really its birthplace. (1995)[8]

In the *Lydian Chromatic Concept of Tonal Organization* (1964), Russell argues that the C lydian mode—C D E F♯ G A B—comes closest to expressing the harmonic (vertical) sonority of a C-major triad, and consequently is the parent scale for this chord. The argument Russell presents employs two ideas from Western musical theory: (1) the importance of the circle of fifths (and its implications for the fifth as a tonic-defining interval), and (2) the ability of linear tetrachords to imply a tonic. From this perspective the lydian mode expresses a C-major tonality more perfectly than the major scale for two reasons. First, the lydian mode is generated by a symmetrical series of perfect (tempered) fifths—the first seven fifths in the series when linearized produce the lydian scale (fig. 7.1a). Secondly, the location of half-steps when the lydian scale is partitioned into two disjunct tetrachords implies that the first tetrachord resolves to G and the second tetrachord resolves to C (fig. 7.1b). The tonal centers generated by these linear segments form the interval of a perfect fifth. The major scale by the same procedure produces tonal centers on F and C. Citing Paul Hindemith, Russell points out that the tonic of a perfect fifth is the bottom note, while the tonic of a perfect fourth is the upper note (Russell 1964, iii). Since the C lydian scale produces tonal centers a perfect fifth and perfect fourth apart (on C, G, and C), Russell argued that both segments of the lydian scale reinforce C as the tonic and consequently the lydian mode is more vertically aligned with a C-major triad than the major scale. The major scale, by contrast, produces tonal centers on F and C. Since they are a perfect fourth and perfect fifth apart (C–F and F–C), the first tetrachord of C major reinforces F as a tonic, while the second tetrachord reinforces C. The tension between F

a. Lydian scale as linearization of circle of fifths

Circle of fifths

$$C \rightarrow G \rightarrow D \rightarrow A \rightarrow E \rightarrow B \rightarrow F\sharp \rightarrow$$
$$D\flat \rightarrow A\flat \rightarrow E\flat \rightarrow B\flat \rightarrow F \rightarrow C$$

C Lydian scale
(first seven fifths)

C   D   E   F♯   G   A   B   C

b. Lydian and major scales in tetrachords
(tones of resolution are underlined)

C lydian

first tetrachord	C D E F♯
second tetrachord	G̲ A B C̲

C major

first tetrachord	C D E F̲
second tetrachord	G A B C̲

Figure 7.1. Lydian Chromatic Concept of Tonal Organization.

Example 7.1. The six lydian scales (from Russell 1964, 4–5).

and C in the major mode is resolved to the tonic of C by the fundamental
I–IV–V–I progression of Western music. Russell summarizes his case for the
importance of the lydian mode: "The major scale *resolves* to its tonic major
chord. The lydian scale *is* the sound of its tonic major scale" (Russell 1964,
iv). The distinction is crucial, for Russell does not claim that the major mode
is unimportant, only that it has a different function.[9]

Having established his case for the lydian mode as the parent scale of the C-
major triad, Russell worked out the appropriate parent scales for every other
chord quality. In so doing he constructed a family of six lydian scales (ex. 7.1)
that combine to produce the twelve tones of what he termed the lydian Chromatic Scale (Russell 1964, 9).[10] Russell systematized the harmonic implications of the lydian scales in a "Tonal Gravity" chart listing chord qualities and
the lydian scales that produced them. His interest lay not only in locating a
parent scale for every chord type, but in helping the improviser identify a series
of possible scales arranged according to their increasing harmonic distance
from the parent scale. When Russell speaks of "vertical polymodality," he is

referring not only to a parent scale, but to a group of scales—a set of possibilities for the musician to explore.

The formidable vocabulary of "the Concept" (as Russell and his students refer to his system) has perhaps contributed to its image as forbiddingly complicated or theoretical. But Russell's apparatus for logically determining parent scales and sets of modes related to particular chords is only one aspect of his thinking. One of the most intuitively appealing aspects of the Concept to improvising musicians has been his notion of three types of "Tonal Gravity": vertical, horizontal, and supravertical. The improviser, in Russell's view, can choose to relate to tonal gravity (the chords of a composition) in three general ways. The musician may (1) allow each chord as it passes to determine his or her choice of scales ("Vertical Tonal Gravity"; see Russell 1964, 22); (2) impose a single scale on a sequence of chords that resolve to a tonic ("Horizontal Tonal Gravity");[11] or (3) improvise his or her chromatic melody in relationship to the overall tonic of the entire piece ("Supravertical Tonal Gravity"). Examples of music embodying these principles include John Coltrane's "Giant Steps" (1959) for vertical improvisation, Lester Young's solo on "Dickie's Dream" (Basie 1939) for a horizontal approach, and Ornette Coleman's "Lonely Woman" (1959) for supravertical improvisation.

Freedom is ultimately what Russell is after, but a freedom with full awareness of all tonal possibilities. With the Concept, Russell argues, *"you are free to do anything your taste may dictate,* for you can resolve the most 'far out' melody since you always know where home is (the parent member scale within the parent Lydian Chromatic Scale)" (1964, 27; emphasis in original). It should be emphasized that Russell's theory is ultimately more comprehensive than the connotations which the term modal jazz later took on (fewer chords and greater freedom of choice over a relatively stable tonal background), for modes underlie his approach to all harmonic situations.[12]

Spirituality and Essence

The *Lydian Chromatic Concept of Tonal Organization* may seem entirely music theoretical at first glance, but for Russell it is a "philosophy of tonality" rather than simply a theory (1964, 1). Indeed Russell's relationship to music theory, systematicity, and unity is better placed in the context of a pan-denominational spirituality merging elements of religion, science, self-knowledge, and mysticism. Russell stressed the intuitive quest for knowledge that the Concept represents: "This is intuitive intelligence. It's intelligence that comes from putting the question to your intuitive center and having faith, you know, that your intuitive center will answer. And it does. I had gone through a number of religious experiences as a child. I was sort of forced into it. My mother was very religious. Searching for something desperately" (1995).

Russell grew up with what he calls "deep black church music," and credits this music with allowing him to experience not only notes and beauty, but the "life" in music. "It opened a door to a life that wasn't stagnant and that was exploratory and that was an open door to the universe." Indeed, Russell recoils from the idea that his theory is academic. "See, a lot of people feel that it's academic. [Especially] if they have an academic feeling. I'm not really an academic. It just made perfect sense for me to educate myself, but once I educated myself I didn't mean to stumble on something that I had to make a complete commitment to—absolute commitment" (1995).

The quest for deeper knowledge and inner exploration, for Russell, is linked to his interest in a variety of religious and spiritual beliefs, including those of G. I. Gurdjieff. Russell acknowledges that there is "a lot of correlation" between the Lydian Chromatic Concept and the thinking of Gurdjieff (Russell 1995). A number of the terms that Russell employs can be found in Gurdjieff's series of books entitled *All and Everything* (1973, 1974, 1991).[13] Russell refers to the Concept as the "all and everything of tonality" and the "all and everything of music" (Russell 1995). Indeed, Gurdjieff's talks about gravity, harmoniousness, space travel, the planet Saturn,[14] unity, and the idea of spiritual essence seem to have provided a fertile means for Russell to combine his interests in tonality, philosophy, the non-Western world, and self-awareness. Gurdjieff, an Armenian, traveled to Egypt, Saudia Arabia, Turkey, Tibet, and India in the early years of the twentieth century in his search for knowledge of ancient metaphysical traditions.[15] He synthesized elements of Hindu, Buddhist, Sufi, and Christian religious ideas into a body of teachings including music and dance which gained adherents in France, Germany, and the United States. Russell's identification with international spiritual ideas underlies his assertion that the Concept is "the first theory to unite the music of the East and the West and be applicable to both of them" (1995).

I suspect that Russell also identified with Gurdjieff's autodidacticism, for in his opening chapter Gurdjieff announces that he has never written anything before, doesn't possess "bon ton literary language," and doesn't intend to be hindered in the least by the conventions of professional writing (1973, 6). Russell rejected the rigidities of formal education sometime during his high school years: "I always dreaded the small life, the small mind, which I sensed controlled the educational system. . . . The streets would be my school and food for my art" (1995). Gurdjieff's admonition, "in life never do as others do" (1993, 27), likewise must have resonated with Russell's point of view, as well as with the rebellious aesthetic of bebop in the late forties and fifties.

Here we have a crucial paradox: the use of modernism—in the form of music theory—to legitimate jazz artistic production in conjunction with an ethereal, almost exotic interest in non-Western spirituality as a whole. What curious bedfellows they seem, at least at first glance. Yet the two interests aren't quite as far fetched as they might at first appear. Music theory functioned both as a tool to legitimate the music as an art music, and as a discourse with which African American musicians could prove their modernist musical intelligence to the classical musical world and white modernist competitors such as Stan Kenton and Dave Brubeck. Interest in spirituality and the non-Western world, on the other hand, balanced with "roots" issues: the importance of feeling and soul, and the potential political and symbolic links between jazz and the successful anticolonial struggles of India and the African continent.

George Russell's music theory and his ideas of spiritual essence mobilized contemporary discourses in the service of needs that were shared by a broader spectrum of the African American jazz intelligentsia: (1) the need to prove the intellectual worth of jazz by demonstrating mastery of the rationalist tools of music theory (thereby undermining the racist idea that the jazz improvisation sprang from the instinctual outpourings of the untutored), while at the same time (2) retaining the romantic trope of music as a means of soulful, emotional, and spiritual transcendence.

One reason for my interest in Russell is that in the current intellectual climate, the Lydian Chromatic Concept might be taken simply as an example of formalism. The vocabulary of the poststructural critique of modernism and essentialism, I am arguing, will only go so far toward addressing the complex circulation of ideological ideas, music theories, and cultural practices (such as improvisation) in the world of jazz in the 1950s and '60s. However central poststructural ideas of relationality and the contingency of categories have been in shaping ethnomusicology's current interest in multiplicity and multidimensionality (Foucault 1972; Derrida 1982), they do not lend themselves easily to situating George Russell's or John Coltrane's use of the term "essence," or their particular beliefs about unity and universality within the historical and social contexts of the 1950s and '60s.

The critique of essentialism has been directed primarily toward the relationship between biological substances (such as blood and genes) and the legitimation of socially constructed ideas of race, ethnicity, gender, purity, and authenticity.[16] The emphasis in postcolonial literature has been to expose any remnants of ideas of fixed essence that survive in strategies for cross-cultural research and interpretation in the social sciences and humanities.

When George Russell speaks of essence or "people of essence" (1995), and when John Coltrane speaks of searching for the ultimate musical essence (Nisenson, 191), they are talking about spiritual depth rather than biological essence. The person of essence, from this point of view, constantly questions, revises, and remakes him or herself in a life-long spiritual journey that is not fixed. While there are timeless and absolute ideas underlying this idea of spiritual self-discovery, they are not particularly biological. Indeed the political positions taken by both men would likely be considered anti-essentialist in today's vocabulary: both musicians emphasized the power of music to break down categories of race, color, and nation—even while they both retain the romantic idea of music as a pathway to a transcendent spiritual truth.

Russell's idea of essence interfaces well with his and Coltrane's upbringing in the African American church (and with its idea of soul); but it also works well with the African American ideological emphasis in the fifties on breaking down the color line through integration. The stress that Russell places on unity, science, and self-development, I would argue, must be seen in the context of both his metaphysical beliefs and his awareness of the worldly politics and social struggles of his own time.

> I think the driving force for bebop, coming out of swing, was the dissatisfaction of black intellectuals, and especially after the return from World War II. They felt they were coming back to the same old thing and they were. And this whole feeling of blacks as an inferior intellect, you know. . . . I think it was a very muscular drive that bebop represented. To convince—to try again to convince small-minded people that if you have any kind of sensitivity at all, you can see that this music does not come from someone who lacks complexity. (1995)

I would like to suggest that ideas of spiritual essence and universality that circulated within the jazz community in the 1950s and '60s had little in common with meanings currently attached to these concepts in contemporary critiques of essentialism and that they require recontextualization within appropriate historical and cultural frameworks.[17] My interest here is in how spiritual ideas of essence, unity, and transcendence served as one of several factors shaping the deepening interest of jazz musicians in non-Western religious and musical expressions, and how that interest was embodied musically in the more open forms generated by modal improvisational thinking. The twin impulses of defending the integrity of the race through modernist achievement and simultaneously emphasizing the transcendent, internationalist possibilities of improvisational musical experience is quite common in the late 1950s and '60s.

John Coltrane and Transnationalism

Russell was not alone in thinking about the spiritual ideas of the East and West or theories of harmony. Among others, John Coltrane stands out as a major artist who explored these ideas. In 1958 Coltrane recorded Rodgers and Hart's "Manhattan" with George Russell (Russell 1958). Russell had reharmonized the tune from the vantage point of the Concept, and he tells of how Coltrane spent an hour in the studio reharmonizing the reharmonization to incorporate his own perspective on harmony (Nisenson 1993, 64–65). Russell mentions the story not to claim an influence on Coltrane, but to emphasize that at the time, Coltrane "had a highly developed theoretical system [of his own], and he was just trying to work it into this arrangement for the purposes of his solo" (65). Coltrane also developed a transnational religious and spiritual stance that included a search for the essential in music (52, 191) and a personal synthesis of Christian, Hindu, Muslim, and Judaic ideas of God (153, 193). Coltrane read widely on the subjects of religion and mysticism, including Yogananda's *Autobiography of a Yogi,* the Bhagavad Gita, Quran, Torah, Kabbalah, and

Bible (153, 185, 134). Coltrane's interest in spiritual ideas from around the world was accompanied by listening to musics from India, the Middle East, and Africa. Coltrane even studied North Indian music for a brief time with sitarist Ravi Shankar, and members of his group, according to bandmember McCoy Tyner, were also quite interested in Indian music (Nisenson 1993, 185; Westendorf 1994, 84).

Indeed a considerable segment of the jazz community seems to have been exploring the sounds of non-Western improvisational musics in the late fifties and early sixties. Bassist Ahmed Abdul-Malik produced concerts that included sounds of the Middle East and India (Abdul-Malik 1959). He entitled one concert "East Meets West," and it included darabeka, drum set, bongo, conga, cello, and trumpet (1962); he called yet another "Oriental and Jazz: Sounds of the Middle and Near East" (1960a). He also recorded an album entitled *East Meets West* (1960b).

Music that included allusion to Africa and the Afro-Caribbean began to increase at this time as well. Russell's own *Cubana Be/Cubana Bop* (1947), in which he first explored ideas of modality, was written for Dizzy Gillespie in collaboration with Cuban percussionist Chano Pozo.[18] Art Blakey's *Orgy in Rhythm* albums (1957) include an Afro-Cuban percussion section, and *African Beat* (1962) includes several musicians from African countries, including Michael Babatunde Olatunji. Randy Weston's *Bantu Suite* (1958) and *Uhuru Africa* (1960), Max Roach's *Freedom Now Suite* (1960), and John Coltrane's *Africa Brass* (1961a) all invoke Africa through composition titles. What is significant here is that the sound of modal jazz—with its open harmonic structures and greater rhythmic possibilities—came to symbolize and musically frame both Africa and other non-Western culture areas, including India and the Middle East.

The idea of the "East" in the jazz community at this time included the African continent as well as India and the Middle East (Russell 1995; Nisenson 1993, 114).[19] There are musical as well as historical reasons that perhaps explain why these three non-Western areas came to be grouped together in the musical, spiritual, and political thinking of American jazz musicians. It is surely no surprise that jazz musicians would recognize kindred musical spirits in the improvisational, melodically rich classical musics of India and the Middle East. An interest in fewer chords, more open improvisational forms, and modality had already been kindled, in part by Russell's theories and music, and in part by Miles Davis's popular realization of "modal jazz" in *Kind of Blue* (1959). Jazz musicians who listened to Indian classical music could recognize in the drone a device to unify long stretches of melodically elaborate improvisation, and in *tala* a cyclicity in time structure to support it. John Coltrane's lengthy solos over drones, often in intensive duet with drummer Elvin Jones, had obvious parallels with the interplay between soloist and tabla in North Indian classical music, as Nisenson has observed (1993, 111).

George Russell would describe the tonal gravity of North Indian classical improvisation as supravertical—improvisation with respect to the overall tonality of a piece. In the early 1960s, the performance of "modal jazz" pieces, whether Coltrane's extended versions of "My Favorite Things" (1960) and "Africa" (1961a) or the Miles Davis quintet's lengthy explorations of tunes such as "Milestones" and "So What" (1964), became increasingly supravertical and drone-like in orientation. To use Russell's terms, there was a move from horizontal to supravertical tonal organization as performers expanded the boundaries of modal tunes. To frame the change in terms of the ethnomusicological literature, as musicians began improvising over fewer chord changes, improvisation moved toward the open-ended "linguisticity" of Indian and Middle Eastern musics described by Harold Powers (1980).[20] Indeed, John Coltrane's solos, which after 1961 frequently lasted an hour or longer (Nisenson 1993, 116), were comparable in length to North Indian performances, much to the distress of some critics.

Coltrane's compositions "Africa" (1961a) and "India" (1961c)—two of his many modal pieces—illustrate this expanded idea of the East through their musical similarities. Both performances proceed over a drone and include two bassists.[21] In "Africa" one bass player sustains the drone, while the other interacts melodically and rhythmically with the rest of the ensemble (more like the traditional role of the bass in jazz); in "India" the bass pattern is less rhythmically driving. But both performances set up a continuous vamp that is constantly varied in its details, particularly through the variety of drummer Elvin Jones's ride cymbal, cross-rhythms, and contrapuntal dialogue with John Coltrane. Coltrane's solos are polymodal in Russell's sense of the term: he employs the melodic and harmonic implications from a wide variety of scales—some closely, some distantly related to the prevailing drone or pedal.

The two basses in the introduction to "Africa" are in call and response. One articulates a rhythmicized low E drone, while the other plays a responding figure an octave higher (ex. 7.2). The time feel combines aspects of swing and Afro-Cuban mambo. The first measure of ride cymbal pattern resembles that used in the mambo (in 2–3 clave), while the second measure is basically the swing ride cymbal rhythm. Since Jones plays his hi-hat on beats 2 and 4, a richly varied swing feel predominates.[22] The original liner notes to the album tell of Coltrane listening to many African records (genres and locations unspecified) and noticing one in particular that "had a bass line like a chant" (Coltrane 1961a). Coltrane's melody outlines a descent from A to D—a descending fifth that produces a suspended feeling in relationship to the drone on E. The large brass section (arranged by Eric Dolphy)—including trumpet, trombone, euphonium, four french horns, and tuba—provides thickly voiced riff accompaniment figures as well as shrieks, cries, and wails at various points in Coltrane's extended solo.

"India," recorded several months later, builds on similar principles. Two ver-

Example 7.2. "Africa" (from Coltrane 1961a).

sions of the piece were released; the first was included on Coltrane's widely known album *Impressions* (1961b). The second version, recorded two days later but released only after Coltrane's death, included two added instruments—Garvin Bushell on oboe and Ahmed Abdul-Malik on tamboura (Coltrane 1961c).[23] To the two double basses, then, are added the "Eastern flavor" of the tamboura's drone, and the oboe (perhaps intended to evoke the sonority of a shenai). The drone is a perfect fifth between G and D. The melody played by Coltrane (on soprano sax) and Dolphy (on bass clarinet) likewise begins with this interval (ex. 7.3). The sustained D of the melody, if the analogy to India can be extended, resembles a *vadi:* indeed Coltrane begins the melodic explorations of his solo interlude with a phrase that ascends to a high D and melodically descends to G.[24]

Transnationalism, India, and the Civil Rights Movement

The literal resemblances among musical devices in Indian, African, and jazz improvisation, however, may not be what is most significant about Coltrane's nod towards India and Africa. Of greater interest may be how a broad range of social, spiritual, transnational, and political meanings became attached to the improvisational tendencies implied by the term modal jazz. John Coltrane's

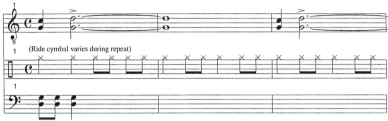

(Ride cymbal varies during repeat)

This bass strumming pattern begins at various
points in the bar throughout the performance

Example 7.3. "India" (from Coltrane 1961b).

use of drones, more open-ended approaches to melodic and harmonic improvisation, and greater variety in the rhythmic polyphony of jazz drumming in "India" and "Africa" served his personal musical aesthetic and spiritual quest, but at the same time resonated intensely with a broader interest in India and Africa on the part of the developing civil rights movement.

Elsewhere I have described the importance of the civil rights movement and African independence in the wrenching debates over race within the jazz community in the early 1960s, and the simultaneous coverage of both movements in the African American press of the 1950s (Monson 1997). Here I would like to describe the importance of India and Mohandas Gandhi as symbols of anticolonialism and nonviolent resistance in twentieth-century African American thought, especially for civil rights organizations in the 1940s. Early in the century, both W. E. B. Du Bois and Marcus Garvey expressed solidarity with the independence struggles of India and Egypt (Kapur 1992, 11, 17), and African American newspapers regularly covered Gandhi's mass protests as early as 1919. After the Salt March of 1930, Kelly Miller, writing for the *New York Amsterdam News,* argued that the "American Negro can learn valuable lessons from Mahatma Gandhi" (Kapur 1992, 43). Several civil rights leaders in the 1940s, including A. J. Muste (Fellowship of Reconciliation), James Farmer (Congress of Racial Equality), and Bayard Rustin (FOR and CORE), did just that: in adapting the Gandhian principles of activism, nonviolence, and mass protest in the early 1940s, they developed what would become the mainstream civil rights strategy of the 1950s and early 1960s. W. E. B. Du Bois, in celebration of India's independence on 15 August 1947, wrote in *The Crisis* that the event should be remembered as "the greatest historical date of the nineteenth and twentieth centuries: for on that date four hundred million colored folk of Asia were loosed from the domination of the white people of Europe. . . . Moreover, it was accomplished, not by blood and war, but by peace and grim determination" (Du Bois 1947, 301).

African American newspaper coverage frequently stressed the resemblance of Gandhi's nonviolent resistance with Christian passive resistance and civil disobedience. Indeed Gandhi was frequently compared to Christ. In this way Gandhi's image was shaped to African American spiritual and political concerns, in a manner that Richard Fox (in press) has termed "over-likeness." By "over-likeness" Fox means that in a world characterized by global circulation, it is easy to see complete similarity when it is only partially there. If many Americans saw in Gandhi a true spiritual ascetic and inspirational champion of passive nonresistance, Fox reminds us that Gandhi "did not believe in 'turning the other cheek' in every situation," and that his opposition to untouchability earned him much criticism from orthodox Hindus on spiritual grounds. Similarly, the mapping of freedom, spiritual development, and identification with an undifferentiated non-Western world onto modal jazz improvisation and musical devices such as drones, modes, and rhythm suggests an "over-likeness" perceived by members of the jazz community in relation to India, Africa, and the Middle East. The characteristics of the "East" that were emphasized within and without the jazz community—including spirituality, civil disobedience, color, and freedom—were firmly rooted in contemporary African American social concerns. The collapsing of the non-Western world into a single, undifferentiated entity resonated especially with the mainstream goals of the civil rights movement which stressed similarity: integration, unity, common moral purpose, and equality before the law.

By the mid-1960s, however, the rhetoric of unity had fragmented in the wake of the violent resistance on the part of whites that met even the most moderate demands of the civil rights movement: integration of the schools, equal access to public accommodations, and the right to vote. To the rhetoric of universality and color-blindness was counterposed the rhetoric of self-determination, nationalism, and autonomy (with an emphasis on difference rather than likeness). The newly independent African nations,[25] as well as the leadership of Malcolm

X, increasingly offered a model and inspiration to African Americans who found Martin Luther King Jr. and the strategy of nonviolence to be too moderate. The tension between philosophies of universality and black nationalism played themselves out within the jazz community just as they did within the American culture at large. In the process cultural, political, and spiritual meanings became attached to musical forms such as modal jazz and free jazz that deserve reexamination within the larger historical framework outlined here: spirituality, anticolonialism, the civil rights movement, as well as Western aesthetic modernism and science.

Conclusions

That it might be possible to experience or even create freedom through improvisation—a process simultaneously musical, personal, and cultural—was a belief held by many in the jazz world of the 1950s and 1960s. This utopian vision remains prominent in contemporary jazz aesthetics, however tempered by a simultaneously unfolding debate about ethnic particularity. It has become customary to analyze the political and cultural positions taken in debates about ethnicity through the interpretive lens of essentialism/anti-essentialism and poststructuralism; yet I believe the examples of George Russell, John Coltrane, and modal jazz illustrate the tension between historically particular understandings of culture, politics, and meaning in the jazz world and today's debates over cultural theory and identity.

George Russell took a central principle of Western music theory—the circle of fifths—and developed a theory of tonal organization adapted to the particular needs of jazz improvisers striving to attain a "modern" sound in the wake of the harmonic inventiveness of bebop. In so doing he developed a theoretical underpinning for what later was termed "modal jazz," earning the respect of several of the principal figures of jazz of the time, including Miles Davis, Bill Evans, Art Farmer, and John Coltrane. In combining his interest in the modernism of Western European music with spiritual ideas from Gurdjieff and the "East," Russell's personal quest—like John Coltrane's intense interest in the non-Western world—resonated with a complex of discourses current within the interracial jazz community, American and African American society, and the global circulation of spiritual, political, and musical ideas.

Music truly served as a crossroads through which this wide range of social discussions were brought into dialogue. The musical structures that came to be associated with modal jazz—fewer chords, greater freedom in melodic and harmonic choices during improvisation, and more open forms over which to improvise—opened the door to a more international dialogue in the musical community, but did not by themselves determine its direction. Coltrane, at least at this point in his career, stressed engagement with non-Western traditions, but these same musical structures, when employed by artists like Ornette Coleman and Cecil Taylor, also generated an intense engagement with Western ideas of the avant-garde. What seems most important to bear in mind is that the meaning of improvisation is multiply determined: musical structures and processes as well as a broad range of social discourses and practices all leave their imprint on our historical and cultural hearings. The challenge of a reinvigorated international discussion of improvisation is to keep the full range of multiplicity: neither losing ourselves in musical description for its own sake, nor in ideologies and politics to the point of excluding what musicians actually do.

Notes

1. In the *Lydian Chromatic Concept of Tonal Organization* (1964), Russell uses "mode" as synonymous with "scale." He does not use "mode" in Harold Powers's sense of "melodic type" (1980).

2. In an interview with Nat Hentoff (1958, 11) Davis mentions Russell, Gil Evans, and Bill Evans as understanding of the possibilities of scales and chords. Bill Evans was the pianist on Russell's highly praised *Jazz Workshop* recordings (1956).

3. The first modal composition is generally taken to be "Milestones" (or "Miles" as it was titled on the album), which was recorded in April 1958. The entire album *Kind of Blue* is pervaded by modal ideas. For discussions of *Kind of Blue* in three recent jazz history texts see Tirro 1993 (361–364), Gridley 1994 (226–230), and Porter and Ullman 1993 (291–294).

4. See Porter and Ullman 1993 (293) for a transcription of the theme and Davis's solo.

5. Recordings with these rhythm sections include Davis 1964 and 1965 and Coltrane 1960, 1961a and b.

6. My account of George Russell's early professional years is drawn from Harrison 1983, the liner notes of Russell 1958, and my interview with Mr. Russell (1995).

7. Some accounts say sixteen months (Harrison 1983). Russell mentioned fifteen months as the length of time he was hospitalized. Tuberculosis claimed the lives of several prominent musicians in the 1940s, including guitarist Charlie Christian and trumpeter Fats Navarro.

8. In an interview done in 1958, Davis credited Russell along with Bill Evans and Gil Evans for opening him up to modal approaches to improvisation (Hentoff 1958), but he later emphasized the effect of having seen the Ballets Africains on his modal thinking (Davis 1989, 225). Keita Fodeba's Ballets Africains presented a mixture of traditional musical genres from Guinea and Senegal (Ballets Africains n.d.). The program notes mention praise songs from Senegal, Ashanti song, Manding music, and a "song of the Soudan" as included in the performance.

9. In Russell's system the lydian mode functions vertically; the major scale functions horizontally.

10. Russell followed the familiar procedure in Western music of stacking thirds above the notes of the lydian scales. The 1959 version of the *Lydian Chromatic Concept of Tonal Organization,* with a technical appendix added in 1964, is the edition most widely available. Russell told me that "the 1953 book clearly made chord-scale associations and told why the scale is a unity with virtually all the definable chords in music" (1995).

11. Russell calls the resolving points "tonic stations," defined as "tonics to which two or more chords tend to resolve" (1964, xix).

12. It should be noted that a chord-scale approach in improvisational pedagogy has become dominant through the books of Jamey Aebersold (1976) and many others. Although these methods do not take the lydian mode as a point of departure, Russell's book set the conceptual stage for their emergence. See also Berliner (1994, 161–62).

13. Gurdjieff describes *All and Everything* as "ten books in three series" (1973, front matter). The first three books are included in *Beelzebub's Tales to His Grandson* (1973), the second three in *Meetings With Remarkable Men* (1974), and the last four in *Life is Real Only Then, When I Am* (1991). Russell left unspecified the other religious and spiritual ideas he explored, but told me that his religious interests were not restricted to Gurdjieff.

14. Sun Ra, who viewed himself as coming from Saturn, was apparently acquainted with Gurdjieff's thinking as well (Szwed 1997, 108, 135, 138).

15. James Moore's (1991) biography of Gurdjieff describes Gurdjieff's travels in detail. Moore addresses the issue of how Gurdjieff financed his trips (accompanied by a group of followers known as the "Seekers of the Truth"), and suggests that at points he may have worked as a political agent for the Tsarist government (27).

16. The critique of essentialism has also been directed at the belief that things and ideas have absolute characteristics that need only to be discovered, but the most vituperative debates have centered on issues of biological essentialism. See Appiah 1992; Butler 1990; Gilroy 1992, 1993, 1994; and Spivak 1988a and b, 1990, and 1992.

17. Caroline Bynum has made a similar case about contemporary critiques of essentialism in her recent discussion of medieval conceptions of the body. Bynum argues that medieval conceptions of the body were not dualistic, but included a tripartite conception of the body *(corpus),* spirit *(animus* or *spiritus),* and soul *(anima)* (1995, 13).

18. The idea for the project came from Gillespie. Although Russell later said that he never thought much would come of mixing Latin music in jazz (Cerulli 1958), his album *New York, N. Y.* (1958) includes a piece entitled "Manhatta-Rico" that makes use of Latin percussion, with Russell himself playing chromatic drums.

19. This condensation of the non-Western world into one no doubt included some of the "Orientalist" presumptions that Edward Said (1978) has justly critiqued. My aim is to show the particularity of the African-American identification with the idea of the "East."

20. Briefly, Powers argues that musics that are subject to fewer ensemble constraints lend themselves more readily to the more expansive type of improvisation found in North Indian classical music (something more akin to a melody type than a scale). Powers contrasts Javanese gamelan and Renaissance music based on a cantus firmus with North Indian *alap* in making his case for the role of ensemble constraint in shaping the nature of improvisation. Since the former genres are more constrained by the "subject" of the piece (and the need to coordinate with other parts), they are less free to develop the open-ended style of improvisation that Powers argues is more linguistic in character (1980, 37–46). Powers places jazz improvisation on chord progressions nearer to the Javanese and Renaissance cases. Here the recurrent chord progression functions as the cantus firmus, in his thinking. In the modal jazz discussed here, fewer chord changes imply fewer ensemble constraints, and hence more expansive improvisation as Powers predicts. Nevertheless, I would argue that jazz improvisation generally is closer to the North Indian end of the improvisational spectrum than to musics characterized by a fixed subject. The mastery of melodic vocabulary (melody types) is a central component of jazz improvisation and requisite for the improviser with the goal of playing

fluently and freely over chord changes (Berliner 1994, 95–145). A harmonic progression defines a time-cycle as well as a tonal progression, functioning in a manner more analogous to *tala* (albeit with specified tonal areas) than to cantus firmus.

21. The bassists on "Africa" are Art Davis and Reggie Workman; on "India," Reggie Workman and Jimmy Garrison (Fujioka 1995, 166, 179).

22. On percussion patterns in mambo see Mauleón (1993, 206); on clave in early jazz see Chris Washburne (1996).

23. Fujioka's discography lists Abdul-Malik as playing the oud (1995, 179), but sympathetic strings of the tamboura resonate from the very first notes of the piece. I believe that it is a tamboura, but it might be an electrically enhanced oud which produced the effect of a tamboura. Abdul-Malik was known as both a bassist and oud player (Kernfeld 1988), but had been involved with concerts featuring Indian music as well (Abdul-Malik 1959).

24. Lynn Westendorf (1994) provides an excellent in-depth analysis of the version of "India" that appears on *Impressions* (Coltrane 1961b), and it includes a complete transcription of Coltrane's solos. She has identified several other North Indian musical devices utilized in the performance, including a *tihai.*

25. Ghana became independent in 1957. Sixteen African nations were admitted to the United Nations in 1960.

References

Abdul-Malik, Ahmed. 1959. "Sounds of Middle and Near East and Jazz." Concert handbill. Topics Files: New York Jazz Clubs. Institute for Jazz Studies, Rutgers University, Newark, N.J.

———. 1960a. "Oriental and Jazz: Sounds of the Middle and Near East." Concert handbill. Topics Files: New York Jazz Clubs. Institute for Jazz Studies. Rutgers University, Newark, N.J.

———. 1960b. *East Meets West: Musique of Ahmed Abdul-Malik.* RCA Victor LPM-2015.

———. 1962. "East Meets West." Concert handbill. Topics Files: New York Jazz Clubs. Institute for Jazz Studies, Rutgers University, Newark, N.J.

Aebersold, Jamey. n.d. *All "Bird."* A New Approach to Jazz Improvisation, vol. 6. New Albany, Ind: Jamey Aebersold.

Appiah, Kwame Anthony. 1992. *In My Father's House: Africa in the Philosophy of Culture.* New York: Oxford University Press.

Ballets Africains. n.d. Program. Topics Files: Africa. Institute for Jazz Studies, Rutgers University, Newark, N.J.

Baraka, Amiri (LeRoi Jones). 1963. *Blues People: Negro Music in White America.* New York: William and Morrow.

Basie, Count. 1939. "Dickie's Dream." Reissued on *The Essential Count Basie,* vol. 2. Columbia CK 40835.

Berliner, Paul F. 1994. *Thinking in Jazz: The Infinite Art of Improvisation.* Chicago: University of Chicago Press.

Blakey, Art. 1957. *Orgy in Rhythm.* Vols. 1 and 2. Blue Note BLP 1554–1555.

———. 1962. *The African Beat.* Blue Note BLP-4097 (BST 84097).

Butler, Judith. 1990. *Gender Trouble: Feminism and the Subversion of Identity.* New York: Routledge.

Bynum, Caroline. 1995. "Why All the Fuss about the Body? A Medievalist's Perspective." *Critical Inquiry* 22 (1):1–33.

Cerulli, Dom. 1958. "George Russell." *Down Beat* (May 29):15–16, 46.

Coleman, Ornette. 1959. "Lonely Woman." On *The Shape of Jazz to Come.* Atlantic SD 1317.

Coltrane, John. 1959. "Giant Steps." On *Giant Steps.* Atlantic SD 1311.

———. 1960. "My Favorite Things." On *My Favorite Things.* Atlantic SD 1361.

———. 1961a. "Africa." On *Africa Brass.* Impulse MCAD-42001.

———. 1961b. "India." On *Impressions.* Impulse AS-42. Recorded 3 November 1961.

———. 1961c. "India." On vol. 2 of *John Coltrane: The Collection.* MCA CCS CD 435. Recorded 5 November 1961. Also issued on *Coltrane "Live" at the Village Vanguard.* Impulse MCVI-23004-5.

Davis, Miles. 1958. *Milestones.* Columbia CK 40837.

———. 1959. *Kind of Blue.* Columbia CK40579.

———. 1964. *Miles in Berlin.* CBS/Sony CSCS 5147.

———. 1965. *Live at the Plugged Nickel.* Columbia C2 38266.

Davis, Miles, with Quincy Troupe. 1989. *Miles: The Autobiography.* New York: Simon and Schuster.

Derrida, Jacques. 1982. "Différance." In *Margins of Philosophy,* translated by Alan Bass, 1–27. Chicago: University of Chicago Press.

Du Bois, W. E. B. 1947. "The Freeing of India." *Crisis* 54 (October):301–304, 316.

Foucault, Michel. 1972. *The Archaeology of Knowledge and the Discourse on Language.* New York: Pantheon Books.

Fox, Richard, and Orin Starn, eds. 1997. *Between Resistance and Revolution: Culture and Social Protest.* New Brunswick: Rutgers University Press.

Fujioka, Yasuhiro. 1995. *John Coltrane: A Discography and Musical Biography.* Metuchen, N.J.: Scarecrow Press.

Gilroy, Paul. 1992. "Cultural Studies and Ethnic Absolutism." In *Cultural Studies,* edited by Lawrence Grossberg, Cary Nelson, and Paula A. Treichler, 187–98. New York: Routledge.

———. 1993. *The Black Atlantic: Modernity and Double Consciousness.* Cambridge: Harvard University Press.

———. 1994. "'After the Love Has Gone': Bio-Politics and Etho-Poetics in the Black Public Sphere." *Public Culture* 7(1):49–76.

Gridley, Mark C. 1994. *Jazz Styles: History and Analysis.* 4th ed. Englewood Cliffs, N.J.: Prentice Hall.

Gurdjieff, Georges Ivanovitch. 1973. *Beelzebub's Tales to His Grandson: An Objectively Impartial Criticism of the Life of Man.* New York: E. P. Dutton.

———. 1974. *Meetings With Remarkable Men.* New York: E. P. Dutton.

———. 1991. *Life Is Real Only Then, When "I Am."* New York: Viking.

Harrison, Max. 1983. "George Russell—Rational Anthems, Phase One." *Wire* (Spring):30–31.

Hentoff, Nat. 1958. "An Afternoon with Miles Davis." *Jazz Review* 1 (December):9–12.

Kapur, Sudarshan. 1992. *Raising Up a Prophet.* Boston: Beacon Press.

Kernfeld, Barry, ed. 1988. *The New Grove Dictionary of Jazz.* London: Macmillan.

Mauleón, Rebeca. 1993. *Salsa: Guidebook for Piano and Ensemble.* Petaluma, Calif. Sher Music.

Monson, Ingrid. 1997. "Abbey Lincoln's Straight Ahead: Jazz in the Era of the Civil

Rights Movement." In *Between Resistance and Revolution: Culture and Social Protest,* edited by Richard Fox and Orin Starn, 171–94. New Brunswick: Rutgers University Press.

Moore, James. 1991. *Gurdjieff: The Anatomy of a Myth.* Shaftesbury, England, and Rockport, Mass.: Element.

Nisenson, Eric. 1993. *Ascension: John Coltrane and His Quest.* New York: St. Martin's Press.

Porter, Lewis, and Michael Ullman. 1993. *Jazz: From Its Origins to the Present.* Englewood Cliffs, N.J.: Prentice Hall.

Powers, Harold S. 1980. "Language Models and Musical Analysis." *Ethnomusicology* 24:1–60.

Roach, Max. 1960. *We Insist! Freedom Now Suite.* Candid CCD 9002.

Russell, George A., comp. 1947. "Cubana Be/Cubana Bop." *Dizzy Gillespie: The Complete RCA Victor Recordings.* Bluebird 07863 66528–2.

———. 1953. *The Lydian Concept of Tonal Organization.* New York: Russ-Hix Publishing.

———. 1956. *The Jazz Workshop.* RCA Victor LPM 2534.

———. 1958. *New York, N.Y. and Jazz in the Space Age.* Decca MCAD-31371.

———. 1964. *The Lydian Chromatic Concept of Tonal Organization for Improvisation.* 1959. Reprint, with appendix, Cambridge, Mass.: Concept Publishing Company.

———. 1995. Interview by the author, Boston, Mass., 7 August.

Said, Edward W. 1978. *Orientalism.* New York: Pantheon Books.

Schuller, Gunther. 1986. *Musings—The Musical World of Gunther Schuller: A Collection of His Writings.* New York: Oxford University Press.

Spivak, Gayatri Chakravorty. 1988a. "Can the Subaltern Speak?" In *Marxist Interpretations of Literature and Culture: Limits, Frontiers, Boundaries,* edited by Lawrence Grossberg and Cary Nelson, 271–313. Urbana: University of Illinois Press.

———. 1988b. *In Other Words: Essays in Cultural Politics.* New York and London: Routledge.

———. 1990. "Poststructuralism, Marginality, Postcoloniality and Value." In *Literary Theory Today,* edited by Peter Collier and Helga Geyer-Ryan Collier, 219–44. Ithaca: Cornell University Press.

———. 1992. "Acting Bits/Identity Talk." *Critical Inquiry* 18 (Summer):770–803.

Stowe, David W. 1994. *Swing Changes: Big Band Jazz in New Deal America.* Cambridge: Harvard University Press.

Szwed, John F. 1997. *Space Is the Place: The Lives and Times of Sun Ra.* New York: Pantheon.

Tirro, Frank. 1993. *Jazz: A History.* New York: W. W. Norton.

Washburne, Christopher. 1996. "The Clave of Jazz: The Cuban Contribution to the Development of African-American Music." Paper presented at the annual meeting of the Society for Ethnomusicology, 31 October, Toronto.

Westendorf, Lynette. 1994. "Analyzing Free Jazz." Ph.D. thesis, University of Washington.

Weston, Randy. 1958. "Bantu Suite." On *New Faces at Newport.* Metrojazz 1005.

———. 1960. *Uhuru Africa.* Roulette R 65001.

CHAPTER EIGHT

Improvisation and Group Interaction in Italian Lyrical Singing

TULLIA MAGRINI

When dealing with a problematic term such as "improvisation," it is customary to look at its roots to understand its fundamental, original meaning. "Improvise" comes from the Latin *in* (= un) + *provideo* (= to see in advance, to foresee, to make provision for); *de* or *ex improviso,* or simply *improviso,* means "suddenly," "unexpectedly." The term conveys a negative sense, as Treitler observed (1991, 66), and suggests that what is improvised is to some extent unforeseeable. There are two main reasons for an event being considered unpredictable: the aleatory and unsystemic character of the event and/or a lack of knowledge and information on the part of people who will see, hear, or otherwise experience it.

The first condition hardly concerns many musical events included in the realm of improvisation. Considering the issue from the historical point of view, we find that one of the first works which refers to improvisation is an anonymous treatise of the thirteenth century on the art of "componere et proferre discantum ex improviso" (Ferand 1938, 133; 1957, 1102). The treatise teaches the rules for composing a *discantum* extemporarily: thus improvisation appears historically as a practice which has system. It is likely that the rules for improvising a *discantum* are not so different from the rules for writing it down: the difference lies more in notation than in the music itself. Further, the Renaissance distinction between the practices of singing a counterpoint *super librum* or *in cartella* (that is, precomposed) or *alla mente* (improvised) emphasizes the role of notation, not a difference of system of musical creation (Gallico 1984, 667).

In the world of improvisation studied by ethnomusicologists, musical events which are not the outcome of chance and which reveal systemic character are certainly prevalent. Actually, the main goal of researchers on improvisation has often been to unravel its systemic aspects (Nettl 1974, 19). Let me discuss, as a typical study of improvisation considered as a solo activity of professional or semiprofessional musicians, the outstanding research of Andreas Fridolin Weis Bentzon on the music of the Sardinian *launeddas* (Bentzon 1969). Playing this instrument, a directly blown triple clarinet, implies the use of circular breathing[1] as well as a particular way of composing *alla mente,* which is ruled by the aesthetic ideal of thematic continuity *(sonai a iskala).* The launeddas player employs predefined short musical entities (the *nodas* or *pikkiadas*), connecting them in groups according to two essential requirements: (1) except for the main noda, there should be no repetitions of the nodas in a group; and (2) there should be the least possible difference between nodas which succeed each other (60). The launeddas players are perfectly aware of the aesthetic and technical aspects of their improvisations and emphasize the role of the organization of thematic material over invention. When Bentzon asked Efisio Melis, a celebrated player, whether he would play some nodas which he had himself composed, he answered: "No, you cannot make new nodas, they have already been made, all of them—and I can play them all. But it is just as with poetry: you do not alter the words of the language, they remain always the same; what counts is the manner in which you put them together!" (77). The launeddas players judge the elegance of the overall structure as the essential feature of a good performance: "Each group should be well developed, no nodas should be repeated, and the principle of thematic continuity should not be broken" (76). The system is well known to launeddas players, who possess a technical terminology and can explain their way of making music. And one cannot avoid noting that this knowledge is connected to the specialized and professional (or semiprofessional) character of their activity. The skill of launeddas players is a result of their musical training in addition to their personal talent. The role of teachers is acknowledged,[2] so that along with the system, we know the heritage of personal styles of playing. Even so, performances have a degree of unpredictability, which results from the players' skill in creating intricate developments of the familiar main nodas of the *iskala* through a refined technique of variation and transformation. In practice, putting the nodas together "requires a degree of compositional genius, which is only possessed by a few" (60). The role of creativity cannot be overlooked when dealing with improvisation. The system of composition is always in the background and surely most important in determining the musical product. But the ever new interest of launeddas players' performances is due to their creative and innovative contributions.

Another theoretical condition of the unpredictability of an event lies, as I suggested, in the absence of knowledge and information on the part of the audience about what will happen. Actually, this condition is hardly relevant to improvisation, according to Edward T. Hall. In *Improvisation as an Acquired, Multilevel Process,* he states that "improvisation is viewed as a high context proposition" (1992, 230). Hall defines context as "the information that surrounds an event [which is] inextricably bound up with the meaning of that event." Given that "the elements that combine to produce a given meaning— events and context—occur in different proportions depending on the situation, but depending particularly on the culture," Hall maintains that "a high context (HC) communication or message is one in which most of the information is already known to the recipient, while very little is in the coded, explicit, transmitted part of the message or the music" (229–30).[3] Hall further adds that "with any HC system, the link to the audience is more binding (since there is more shared information) than with the . . . lower context forms" (231). Thus we can add that "communication . . . is in fact an invitation to participation [and] not simply . . . a transfer of knowledge from a place where it was to a place where it was not" (Ong 1977, 118).

The high context situation described by Hall seems well represented in the world of Italian lyrical singing, the typical extemporized vocal genre practiced throughout southern and central Italy. Let me give an example of this musical practice. At the night feast for the Madonna della Serra at Cetraro (a little village in the Calabrian coast in southern Italy) everybody is free to sing lyrical verses *alla cetrarese* (literally, in the manner of the Cetraro people), carrying out an extempore performance, irrespective of gender or musical skill (for examples of this practice see Magrini 1986, 1991). Singing is not meant here as a specialized or professional activity, and nobody is excluded from it, even if he or she is not particularly skilled: it is more a social activity than an aesthetic one. All Cetraro people share the same knowledge about carrying out such an extempore vocal performance; nevertheless, a performance is never repeated exactly. Shared knowledge does not mean that every aspect of singing is predetermined, but rather that everyone knows how to sing, interact with other performers, and evaluate the performances of others. It goes without saying that Cetraro singers have no formal musical training and no teacher and that their musical skill is entirely "acquired," as Hall uses the term, that is, "literally absorbed without the intervention of others or even conscious awareness" (Hall 1992, 231). Thus, in the performances of Cetraro people a particular set of conditions occurs: musical skill entirely acquired and shared by the community, a high context situation (most of the information is already known to all members of the village), and, finally, a certain degree of unpredictability of the musical event, which depends on the way information will be creatively worked out and communicated.

Distinctive Features of Italian Lyrical Singing

Various kinds of Italian lyrical singing share some basic features. The genre was studied first by nineteenth-century scholars of folklore, who documented verbal texts by asking the performers not to sing them but simply to dictate the words. The unitary character of Italian lyrical texts, notwithstanding inner formal differences, was maintained by many scholars (among others, D'Ancona 1906, 210): they share the same verse structure (the endecasyllable, or elevensyllable line); they deal generally with feelings, mainly with the love; and variants of these texts are found in different regions of Italy. Considered as a literary phenomenon, lyrical singing was viewed as one large repertory, typical of central and southern Italy (Sanga 1979, 16–17).

More recent ethnomusicological researchers have taken into consideration many other aspects of this repertory and have argued that lyrical singing does not seem to be endowed with such inner consistency when considered not as a literary phenomenon but rather as both musical and verbal performance practice (Magrini 1986, 1996a, 1996b). Lyrical singing is not based on what are generally termed songs, which can be described as musical objects with intimately connected and well-determined words and melody which may circulate from person to person and over large areas. On the contrary, lyrical singing is based on creative acts which involve the impromptu joining of words and music and which are performed according to particular customs. These practices are generally connected with small population groups, they form an essential part of the culture of their locality, and they are considered a strong symbol of cultural identity (Magrini 1986, 1989). In fact, every social group in the region has its own specific way of performing lyrical verses and maintains the distinctiveness of its musical practice in juxtaposition to those of its neighbors.

Considered as a whole, lyrical singing may best be studied as a system for bringing about musical actions rather than musical objects. The role of the performer's action is always more important than the immediate product of this action, which is actually short-lived. This way, the system stresses the importance of the music makers and their creative contribution.[4] But the music maker is not alone in making music. Actually, although it is generally monodic, lyrical singing is not usually performed by a single singer[5] in traditional practices, it is often sung by two or more persons in turn.[6] This is one of the most distinctive features of this kind of musical practice and distinguishes it from other musical genres of Italy. Indeed, I suggest that the characteristic of interactive performance among different subjects is a peculiar feature of the system of lyrical singing.

The interactive character of these musical practices (which is of course not exclusive to Italian lyrical singing) seems to me particularly significant, since it highlights the relational value of music making and its capacity to effect interpersonal relationships and represent the way they are conceived by social groups. This is a very important aspect of social life. As Anthony Seeger writes, "music and dance are part of what makes *social life* social and one of the ways in which groups of people create and re-create themselves and their images of others" (1987, xiv). According to this approach, we can delve more deeply into the social meaning of lyrical singing by considering the relational patterns it manifests and studying their social value. This approach takes into account similar perspectives developed in the fields of linguistics—in particular Schmidt's concept of *Kommunikative Handlungsspiele* (1974–76), based on Wittgenstein's *Sprachspiel*—and anthropological performance studies (e.g., Turner 1986; Tambiah 1985).

In conclusion, improvisation is studied here as an aspect of musical practices which share the following main features: (1) connection with the identity of social groups; (2) high context situation; (3) performers' musical competence entirely acquired; (4) interaction as a basic aspect of performance; and (5) polytextuality as the outcome of creative and interactive processes enacted in the course of performance.

A System for Making Music

In earlier publications I have tried to point out that any group practice in lyrical singing is based on shared knowledge and on a collective overall plan (GP, for "group plan") for making music (Magrini 1989, 1992a, b, 1993, 1996a). What a group wants to express through making music is embodied in its own GP. This involves the general organization of singing and suggests the essential guidelines of the group's creative and performative activity. GP originates from the whole body of knowledge about making music acquired by the group, and entails a range of possibilities that constitute the very foundation of the activity of musical production, that is, the elements of a system of making music which is open to various configurations. It must be stressed that this overall plan is a typical outcome of informal learning, that is, it "is acquired, non-linear, cooperative and not controlled by anyone except the group" (Hall 1992, 229). GP is a collective mental product related to the entire community, acquired rather than consciously learned, and it is the point of reference for anybody who wants to take part in group singing. It establishes the identity of a specific singing practice, within which individual musical actions are seen by group members as being undifferentiated. The existence of a shared GP is what determines the high context (HC) situation in which group improvisation may be accomplished. In this context participants can interact and relate to each other. One of the most important aspects of GP lies in establishing relational patterns among performers which embody the basic meanings of their specific musical practices.

Another important aspect of lyrical singing is the differentiation among the group members' performances, that is, the polytextuality inherent in these musical practices, which is the outcome not of chance but of the performers' individual creativity working within shared guidelines. In this context the musical outcome of one performance is not seen as something to store in memory in order to be preserved and recalled. Rather, it is considered the ephemeral result of a creative action, legitimized not by reference to memory but by the fact of working out a collective GP. This is a very important point, for it means that the musical identity of the group does not require that individual members stifle their creativity. The very act of partaking of GP is the determining factor that situates a musical activity within a given tradition; it is not merely a matter of paying homage to what has previously been created. In this process, individual skill in executing GP has a very important role. In fact, the individual renditions which occur in a collective performance show subjective aspects, although they are considered by the performers to be actualizations of the same singing practice. Each performer has his or her own way of singing; moreover, each may realize this individual manner in different ways, so that renditions never seem to be repeat performances of well defined and immutable musical products. To understand the subjective and ever changing aspect of individual renditions, we can turn to the concept of "play" (Hall 1992; see also Kaemmer 1993, 151–55). Play is an activity rooted in the limbic system of the brain and "is the device which not only permits all mammals to have fun, but gives them a means of mastering the skills needed for survival." Play is deeply involved in improvisation, because "one of the most effective ways of improvising performance is to have enough skill to be able to play with the system, to wed the music to your inherent playfulness. This is another way of demonstrating to yourself what you can do and where your natural limits are" (Hall 1992, 224). Making music within the GP system allows participants to test their creative skill and their competence in musical performance, that is, "playing with music." The "playful" attitude entails creativity, the basic component of improvisation, but individual creativity works within the guidelines of the GP, which determines the possibility of reciprocal communication, interaction, and exchange among the performers of a group improvisation. The group conceives itself as the sum of individuals, who are allowed to develop personal (although consistent) modes of expression within a common system of communication. According to this view, these group musical practices represent a field where the individual and social dimensions of music making are strictly bound together.

GP represents both the foundation in tradition and the basis of music-making principles for the group's creative activity, and entails intrinsic polytextuality: it lends itself to a range of uses and practices that are as varied as allowed by the creative impulses of the individual members of the group, as well as by the concrete opportunities for interaction that arise in the course of its life. It goes without saying that the relationship between group members and GP works in both directions, and in these terms GP is also the point of convergence for what is proposed by individual members through their performances. This dynamic character of performance has also been emphasized by Victor Turner: "To perform is thus to bring something about, to consummate something, or to '*carry out*' a play, order, or project. But in the 'carrying out,' I hold, something new may be generated. The performance transforms itself." He adds that "the 'flow' of action and interaction . . . may conduce to hitherto unprecedented insights and even generate new symbols and meanings, which may be incorporated into subsequent performances" (Turner 1982, 79). In these terms, it is perhaps possible to state a formula that establishes a dual relationship between the overall group plan (GP), its individual elaboration (gp_i), and its realization through time (gp_{it}):

$$GP \longleftrightarrow gp_i \longleftrightarrow gp_{it}$$

It may be worth pointing out that GP does not coincide with the term "model" widely employed in the literature on improvisation. This term has been used to mean many different things, as Bruno Nettl argues in the introduction to this book, but it has generally been dealt with as a uniquely musical concept which concerns melody, rhythm, form, and so on,[7] and does not take into consideration the social dimension of performance and its relational value, which are essential aspects of what I term GP.

By contrast, the concept of GP takes into account the complexity of music making and integrates it within a system of behavior, ideas, and practices that transcends the mere dimension of sound and reflects the deep values held by particular groups. Seen in this way, the tradition embodied in a particular GP becomes a living force, or the foundation of a system of social action: its main content is the opportunity given to group members, here and now, to shape and express their relationships within the group through musical performance. The relational pattern is an essential part of GP and deeply affects the ways performers behave in singing and the ways they employ words and music.

Singing for Madonna dell'Arco

As an example, I shall examine a practice of lyrical singing from Giugliano, a village in the Campania region, near Naples. First, it must be noted that this performance practice is connected with a religious feast. Singing is part of the complex devotional behavior of the people of Giugliano to honor the Madonna dell'Arco, whose feast occurs on Easter Monday. Groups of worshippers perform this kind of singing as the dance music for Madonna dell'Arco only during the week following Easter.

In this performance, three singers (two men and one woman) freely take turns singing, without regular alternation (see De Simone 1979). Singing is based on endecasyllable verses[8] deriving generally from traditional *canzoni* (texts in endecasyllables dealing with one topic, generally of lyrical content; singular, *canzone*),[9] but these are freely elaborated. That is, the performance does not involve the complete rendition of the full verbal text of a single canzone; rather, it freely employs fragments of different lengths coming from different canzoni. In our example, Raffaele, the first performer, begins singing the canzone marked "A"; Giuseppe, the second performer, continues the same text; then Antonietta performs a fragment of a new canzone, marked "B." Thus the series of individual renditions, continuing in the same manner, gives rise to a verbal sequence composed of fragments of ten canzoni (A–L) freely combined. The whole series of renditions has the form of an "interrupted speech" (Magrini 1986, 164–72), that is, a sort of incoherent dialogue made up of disjointed parts, occasionally connected by recurring words. Moreover, each performer may enrich the canzone fragment he/she is singing by inserting a series of octosyllabic verses, which is termed *barzelletta* (these verses are printed in italics below). The barzelletta has no fixed number of verses; it is a kind of joking or nonsense sometimes endowed with erotic nuances, differing in meter and generally contrasting the content of the endecasyllables of the canzoni.

The text of the performance follows; it is accompanied by schematic indications regarding the type of music on which each line is sung ("S" for melodic segment, "D" for dance music) and the type of elaboration represented by the verse structure, which is described following the text and translation.

Text	Music	Elaboration
Raffaele:		
A		
Oh cielo quanto sogn'àvte sti ffenés	S1	scheme b
oh cielo quanto sogn'àvete queste ffené	S2	
e comme song'ariose	D	
e comme song'arios	D	
e comme song'ariose	D	
e comme song'arios	D	
e comme song'ariose oi sti ffenesta	S3	
ce sta na nenna ca sempe s'affác	S1	scheme b
ce sta na nenna ca sempe s'affá	S2	
e m'arracqua li garofene	D	
e m'arracqua li garó	D	
e m'arracqua li garofene	D	
e m'arracqua li garó	D	
e m'arracqua li garuofene alli ttesta	S3	
nce sta na nenna ca sempe s'affác	S1	scheme b
uh nce sta na nenna ca sempe s'affá	S2	
e m'arracqua li garofene	D	
e m'arracqua li garó	D	
e m'arracqua li garuofene alli ttesta	S3	
Giuseppe:		
ce n'aggio ritto—menamméne unë—	S1	scheme a
ce n'aggio ritto—menamméne u—	S2	
essa me n'ha menatë nu rammaglietto	S3	
nu rammagliett'a mme mò nun m'abbás	S1	scheme a
nu rammagliett'a mme mò nun m'abbás	S2	
e ce voglio la padrona co tutt'e ttesta	S3	
Antonietta:		
B		
Tengo na mamma n'ata ué ne vulés	S1	scheme c
tengo na mamma n'ata ne vulé	S2	
x.1 e vuless'a mamma *e llena*	D	
vien te mòve Matalena	D	
nn'o tità ca chillo vène	D	
tira tira s'n'è venuto	D	

Text	Music	Elaboration
e 'o pantofol'e velluto	D	
e chella vàvra e chillu mussu	D	
e 'o garufaniello è rus	D	
chella vita dillicata	D	
me pareva na pupata	D	
picceré cu ss'uocchi a zennetiello tu m'ha ngannatë	S3	
vulesse a mamma r'o nennillu mi	S1	scheme a
vulesse a mamma r'o nennillu mi	S2	
e cu essa vulesse rirere e pazziare	S3	
nun l'aggiu visto n' aiere e nu og	S1	scheme c
nun l'aggiu visto n' aiere e nu oggë	S2	
x.2 e quinnece juorn' *e bbà*	D	
leta le'nu'pazzia'	D	
nu zumpo 'ncuollo te voglio fa'	D	
e quinnece juorne li ffanno rimane	S3	

Raffaele:

C

Text	Music	Elaboration
Anema santa r' o primmo marít	S1	scheme b
anema santa r' o primmo marí	S2	
e vieneme nzuonno a mme	D	
e vieneme nzuonno a mme	D	
e vieneme nzuonno a mme	D	
e vieneme nzuonno a mme	D	
e vieneme nzuonno a mme mò n'ata vota	S3	
chi me l'ha mannato sto mùgnulo friddë	S1	scheme c
chi me l'ha mannato sto mùgnulo frí	S2	
x.3 e d'ogni ssei' *mis'e bbà*	D	
vuo' veni' che bbiene a ffa'	D	
mannaggia ccà	D	
mannaggia llà	D	
mannaggi' 'a nàsceta 'e mammetà	D	
sott' 'o pont' 'e Matalune	D	
llà nce stan' 'e lampiune	D	
lampiun'e llampetelle	D	
'o tricchitracco int' 'a vunnella	D	
'o piglio 'mman' 'o pòso 'nterra	D	
'o faccio fa' Pulicenella	D	
e d'ogni ssei mise se avota na vota	S3	
—O figlio fi cuntèntate a stu ppoc	S1	scheme a
o figli fi cuntèntate a stu ppó	S2	

Text	Music	Elaboration
e so quinnice anne nu ll'aggiu truvatë—	S3	

Antonietta:
D

Addore re garuofene ca i sen	S1	scheme a
addore re garufene ca i sen	S2	
e chille nu sso garuofene e mmanco amenta	S3	
e chill'è nennillu mio	D	scheme d
e chill'è nennillu mi	D	
e chill'è nennillu mio ch'addore tante	S3	

Giuseppe:
E

Sera passavo e màmmeta te vatté	S1	scheme a
sera passavo e màmmeta te vatté	S2	
e nun te putiette nemmeno aiutade	S3	
si t'aiutavo màmmeta che ddicé	S1	scheme a
si t'aiutavo màmmeta che ddicé	S2	
—Chella m'è ffiglia e la voglio 'mparade—	S3	

Antonietta:
F

Uh Teresella va vòta li pin	S1	scheme a
uh Teressella va vòta li pi	S2	
e li pinte so arrevate allu Cavone	S3	
errano trenta e mmò so bbinticí	S1	scheme b
errano trenta e mmò so bbinticí	S2	
e cinche se ll'ha pigliate	D	
e cinche se ll'ha pigliate	D	
e cinche se ll'ha pigliate lu primm'amore	S3	

G

Juorne passaie pe mmiezze Casalë	S1	scheme f
juorno passaie pe mmiezze Casá	S2	
e ce steva nu pèr' e fiche carreco re prune	D	
e ce steva nu pèr' e fiche carreco re prune	D	
e sagliette ncoppa e li scutuliavo	D	
e sagliette ncoppa e li scutuliavo	D	
abbascio carevano tutte pere ammature	S3	
scenniette abbascio pe m'e gghi aruná	S1	scheme h
e scenniette abbascio pe m'e gghi aruná	D	

Text	Music	Elaboration
x.4 e d'ogni percuoco *e bbà*	D	
leta le' nu' pazzia'	D	
nu zumpo 'ncuollo te voglio fa'	D	
e d'ogni percuoco è nu ruotolo ll'unë	S3	
venette lu patrone r' e ccerase	S1	scheme g
e venette lu patrone r' e ccerá	D	
e ddice—Mariuncello	D	
e ddice—Mariuncellë	D	
e ddice—Mariuncello t'è rrubbato ll'uva—	S3	

H

Text	Music	Elaboration
Uh mamma mamma vatte a Luvisél	S1	scheme a
uh mamma mamma vatti a Luvisél	S2	
e ch'è piccerell' e l'ammore vo fare	S3	
si s'ammarita troppa picceré	S1	scheme h
e si s'ammarita troppa picceré	D	
x.5 e la croce è *bell'e bbà*	D	
leta le' nu' pazzia'	D	
nu zumpo 'ncuollo te voglio fa'	D	
e la croce è grossa e nun la pò purtade	S3	

Raffaele:

I

Text	Music	Elaboration
Tengo na passione uè si ve las	S1	scheme a
tengo na passione uè si ve là	S2	
e n'ata ce a tenghe si ve lasso e mmoro	S3	

L

Text	Music	Elaboration
Ih comme abballa bello o frate e a sò	S1	scheme b
ih comme abballa bello o frate e a sò	S2	
e li bboglio mmaretà	D	
e li bboglio mmaretà	D	
e li bboglio mmaretà	D	
e li bboglio mmaretà	D	
e li bboglio mmaretà a santa Lucia	S3	
ce voglio da' nu ricco marenaro	S1	scheme e
uh nce voglio da' nu ri	D	
uh nce voglio da' nu ri	D	
ce voglio da' nu ricche marenare	S3	
e chillo ca pigli' o pesce	D	scheme d
e chillo ca piglia pesce	D	

Text	Music	Elaboration
e chillo ca piglia pesce	D	
e chillo ca piglia pesce	D	
e chillo ca piglia pesce sera e mmatina[10]	S3	

Translation (without elaboration)

A

Heavens, how high these windows are!
And how airy these windows are!
There is a girl who always leans out
And waters the carnations in the flowerpots.

I told her: "Toss me one flower,"
She tossed me a little bunch.
A little bunch is not enough for me.
I want the girl with all the flowerpots.

B

I have a mother and would like another one,
And I would like my boyfriend's mother,
And I would like to laugh and play with her.
I saw her neither yesterday nor today
And tomorrow it's fifteen days since I have seen her.

C

O my first husband's blessed soul,
May I see you again in a dream!
Who sent me this man so cold,
That turns to me only every half year?
"O my daughter, be satisfied.
It's fifteen years since I have seen him."

D

I smell carnations
And it's neither carnations nor peppermint,
It's my boyfriend who smells so sweet.

E

Yesterday night I passed by and your mother was beating you up
And I could not help you.
Had I helped you, what would your mother have said?
"This is my daughter and I want to train her."

F

Uh, Terry, have the turkeys come back!
The turkeys have arrived at the Cavone valley.

They were thirty and now are twenty five.
My first love took five of them.

G

Once I went through Casale
And there was a fig tree full of plums.
I climbed up the tree and shook the plums
And ripe pears fell down.
I came down and gathered them
And each peach was as heavy as one *rotolo*.
The owner of cherries came
And told me: "Thief! You stole the grapes!"

H

O mother, O mother, beat up Louise,
Who is still a child and wants to make love.
If she gets married too young,
Then she cannot bear such a cross.

I

I am in anguish if I leave you,
And I am in anguish if I leave you and die.

L

How well brother and sister dance!
I want to marry them on St. Lucy's Day.
I want a rich sailor for them,
A sailor who catches fish day and night.

The singing is performed in the typical vocal style of lyrical singing, that is, in the high register, with rhythmic freedom, descending contour, and decoration. It is a style that provides a strong contrast to the dance rhythm accompaniment of flute, drums, castanets, and cymbals. The performance is arranged as a sequence of verbal/musical units. In most cases each verbal unit is based on a distich of endecasyllables and may be worked out in a variety of schemes, as noted in the example above.

(a) The simplest way to work out a distich is to repeat the first endecasyllable to get three lines, corresponding to three melodic segments which form the basic melodic unit. Example 8.1 demonstrates this approach.

nu rammagliett'a mme mò nun m'abbás	segment 1
nu rammagliett'a mme mò nun m'abbás	segment 2
e ce voglio la padrona co tutt'e ttesta[11]	segment 3

(b) This three-segment sequence may be enlarged by inserting, after the repetiton of the first endecasyllable, the double repetition of the first eight

Example 8.1. Note: In this and subsequent examples, the symbol 𝆑 indicates a slightly prolonged note, 𝆑 indicates a slightly shortened note, 𝆑 indicates a note slightly raised, and ♪ indicates a *coup de glotte*.

syllables[12] of the next endecasyllable, which is performed once or twice (ex. 8.2). The words so inserted in the three main lines are sung not in the previous vocal style but in the style of the dance accompaniment, with no melodic expansion but with strict rhythm and quick syllabic enunciation of the words.

Oh cielo quanto sogn'àvte sti ffenés	segment 1
oh cielo quanto sogn'àvete queste ffené	segment 2
e comme song'ariose	sung on dance rhythm
e comme song'arios	sung on dance rhythm
e comme song'ariose	sung on dance rhythm
e comme song'arios	sung on dance rhythm
e comme song'ariose oi sti ffenesta[13]	segment 3

(c) after the repetition of the first endecasyllable, the performer sings the first syllables of the following line and then inserts a barzelleta (verses in italics marked with an "x").[14] The barzelletta is sung on the dance rhythm and with rapid syllabic enunciation of the words. Finally, the second endecasyllable is performed on segment 3.[15] Example 8.3 demonstrates this approach.

Tengo na mamma n'ata ué ne vulés	segment 1
tengo na mamma n'ata ué ne vulé	segment 2
x.1 e vuless'a mamma e llena	sung on dance rhythm
vien te mòve Matalena	sung on dance rhythm
nnò tità ca chillo vène	sung on dance rhythm
tira tira s'nè venuto	sung on dance rhythm
e 'o pantofol'e velluto	sung on dance rhythm
e chella vàvra e chillu mussu	sung on dance rhythm
e 'o garufaniello è rus	sung on dance rhythm
chella vita dillicata	sung on dance rhythm
me pareva na pupata	sung on dance rhythm
picceré cy ss'uocchi a zennetiello tu m'ha ngannaté[16]	segment 3

Example 8.2

(d) The unit is based on one endecasyllable: the performer begins by singing the double repetition of the first eight syllables of the line, which is performed once or twice on the dance rhythm, then ends by singing the whole line of the melody of the third segment.

e chill'è nennillu mio	sung dance rhythm
e chill'è nennillu mi	sung on dance rhythm
e chill'è nennillu mio ch'addore tante[17]	segment 3

(e) The unit is based on one endecasyllable: the performer sings the endecasyllable on segment 1, then sings the double repetition of its first eight syllables on the dance rhythm, and ends with the repetition of the whole line on the melody of segment 3.

ce voglio da' nu ricco marenaro	segment 1
uh nce voglio da' nu ri	sung on dance rhythm
uh nce voglio da' nu ri	sung on dance rhythm
ce voglio da' nu ricche marenare[18]	segment 3

184 • *Tullia Magrini*

Example 8.3

(f) In this case, similar to (b) and (c) musically, new irregular verses are sung on the dance rhythm with a particular melody.

Juorne passaie pe mmiezze Casalë	segment 1
juorno passaie pe mmiezze Casá	segment 2
e ce steva nu pèr' e fiche carreco re prune	sung on dance rhythm
e ce steva nu pèr' e fiche carreco re prune	sung on dance rhythm
e sagliette ncoppa e li scutuliavo	sung on dance rhythm
e sagliette ncoppa e li scutuliavo	sung on dance rhythm
abbascio carevano tutte pere ammature[19]	segment 3

(g) The verbal text is organized like (b), but the repetition of the first endecasyllable is sung on the dance rhythm.

venette lu patrone r' e ccerase	segment 1
e venette lu patrone r' e ccerá	sung on dance rhythm

e ddice—Mariuncello	sung on dance rhythm
e ddice—Mariuncellë	sung on dance rhythm
e ddice—Mariuncello t'è rrubato ll'uva—[20]	segment 3

(h) The verbal text is organized like (c), but the repetition of the first endeca-syllable is sung on the dance rhythm.

scenniette abbascio pe m' e gghi aruná	segment 1
e scenniette abbascio pe m' e gghi aruná	sung on dance rhythm
x.4 e d'ogni percuoco *e bbà*	sung on dance rhythm
leta le' nu' pazzia'	sung on dance rhythm
nu zumpo 'ncuollo te voglio fa'	sung on dance rhythm
e d'ogni percuoco è nu ruotolo ll'unë[21]	segment 3

These eight examples represent different ways adopted by the performers to work out the verbal/musical units of their renditions. One can say that these different possibilities are contained in the GP, which does not prescribe a fixed scheme but leaves the performers free to find various ways of organizing their renditions. Considering the whole performance, it is apparent that each performer tries to work out his or her rendition in a personal way, by adopting and combining different ways of arranging the single units. Clearly, they are "playing," testing their skill at working out the singing in distinctive ways. Moreover, as the performance goes on each performer tries to propose new forms. Schemes (a), (b), and (c) can be considered the most common: the performers' skill lies not simply in working out and combining these schemes differently, but also in violating them, for example by cutting (d, e) or adding (f) lines, or by singing a line usually linked to a melodic segment on the dance music (g, h).[22] These forms appear only after rendition of the common schemes (a), (b), and (c), when the performance approaches its climax and the singers try to work out something new, more fully displaying their skill. These features are readily apparent in the following outline of the whole performance:

Raffaele	b b b
Giuseppe	a a
Antonietta	c[23] a c
Raffaele	b c a
Antonietta	a d
Giuseppe	a a
Antonietta	a b f h g a h
Raffaele	a b e d

It cannot be said that the singing here is ruled by a strict pattern which entails predetermined choices; rather, it is reasonable to suggest that the singing is developed within a general GP which makes available to the performers, some schemes which have already been tested, but which also allows the performers to modify these schemes in sheer creative play. What is important is the existence of a common point of reference which allows each performer to understand what the others are doing and to "play" with them, developing proper verbal and musical interaction.

In the performance of the Giugliano worshippers, a tendency to let individual creativity emerge is easily recognizable. This is true not only with reference to their ways of working out the form of their rendition, but also in terms of strictly melodic behavior. A basic common idea of the configuration of the three main melodic segments is shared by the performers, but Raffaele, Giuseppe, and Antonietta try to personalize them, and moreover, they often insert syllabic two- or three-tone dance melodies which modify the musical outcome. Comparing the transcriptions, it is easy to see that Giuseppe's (ex. 8.1) and Raffaele's (ex. 8.2) melodies are similar in many respects, but that they differ in modal choice, range, configuration and outline of the second melodic segment, organization of duration and accents, ornamentation, and other minor aspects; moreover, Raffaele inserts a short syllabic two-tone melody in regular dance rhythm between segment 2 and 3. The melody proposed by Antonietta (ex. 8.3) differs from the previous ones in range (raised by a sixth) and, above all, in its bimodal character. Antonietta sings melodic segments 1 and 2 on a Lydian pentachord (tonic = F), then employs the three-tone dance melody of the barzelletta to shift the tonic to G, and sings the third melodic segment in a non-Lydian mode (which is ambiguous because of the restricted range and the "blue" third degree), ending on G. It may be noteworthy that both Raffaele and Antonietta present something new and unexpected in the third segment— Raffaele uses F♯ instead of F, so that the Aeolian exachord of segments 1 and 2 changes into a Dorian mode;[24] and Antonietta performs a true modal *metabole* by changing the tonic too—so that their melodic behavior also confirms the general attitude toward "play" and "surprise."

We could examine more thoroughly the melodies performed by Raffaele, Giuseppe, and Antonietta and the way they change during the performance, but what seems to me more important here is to discern the general content of the GP which informs their singing. Its most important features seem to lie in the equal and convivial relation among performers, who freely take turns singing without any hierarchy among them. All interpreters have in principle an equal role in carrying out the performance, but interpreters who are particularly skilled (like Antonietta in this performance) are allowed to sing longer than the others. At the verbal level, they are free to sing the verses they want (it is not required that they repeat or go on with a given text), and a sort of symbolic (even if incoherent) dialogue among them is attained during the performance. Individual choices have been acknowledged also at the level of musical organization. Moreover, GP facilitates differentiation of the performers' successive renditions, at both formal and musical levels of organization. That is, it prompts the performers' skills at interacting with their partners by offering new inputs. The individual performer's creativity and skill in "playing" with music is stressed; therefore, the relationship of the singers appears convivial and rich in playfulness. Obviously, this style of singing is highly creative, since every performance, considered as a whole, gives rise to a new and different product: polytextuality is inherent to the system.

In the Giugliano worshippers' singing practice we can thus acknowledge a set of aspects contained in the GP:

> A proper occasion for singing (the worshippers dance for Madonna dell'-Arco, performed the week following Easter): singing is meant as a devotional act
>
> The interactive character of the performance within which singing is carried out: singing and dancing for Madonna dell'Arco is a group activity
>
> "Convivial" relationship among performers: all interpreters have a basically equal role in determining the verbal and musical outcome of the performance, which is the result of their creative and interactive behavior
>
> The production of ever renewed verbal texts in each performance, through free extempore combination of fragments coming generally from traditional canzoni and their elaboration through (whole or partial) repetitions of lines and insertion of barzellette
>
> The opportunity to "play" offered to performers—within their individual renditions—with contrasting meanings (lyrical lines/nonsense), poetic forms (endecasyllables/octosyllabic verses), melodic organizations (expanded melismatic melody/syllabic two- or three-tone melody), and rhythm (free rhythm/dance rhythm)
>
> Verbal interaction carrying out a symbolic dialogue among performers
>
> Musical interaction conceived as a sort of game, where individual creative skill is manifested in working out basic musical elements (three main melodic segments, regular dance melody) and providing new inputs
>
> Accompaniment of dance music supplied by flute, drum, and in the case examined, some idiophones *(castagnette, piatti),* which contrasts dramatically with the singing of endecasyllables but complements the performance of octosyllabic verses.

A well-organized improvised group performance like the one examined here requires that all performers share this GP, which contains the necessary information about performance mode and the types of interaction to enact through singing. In these terms, this is a high context improvisation.

Singing "Alla Verbicarese"

I shall briefly compare the previous performance with an example of the practice of lyrical singing in Verbicaro, a Calabrian village, with which I have dealt elsewhere (e.g., Magrini 1986, 1989, 1991). This practice is based on extempore renditions of predefined verbal texts (canzoni) according to the style of singing "alla verbicarese." Texts are equivalent as regards form—they employ the same verse—but not as concerns content: they may be either *canzoni d'amore* (songs of love) or *canzoni di sdegno* (songs of disdain). This difference in content reflects the former practice of using singing to make public the relationship between a man and a woman, that is, to facilitate the social control of these relationships. Several nights a week, a man had to serenade his fiancée with *canzoni d'amore*, sung in a group with his friends. If the relationship ended, he would sing *canzoni di sdegno*, and thus the entire village was informed of the scandal.

But lyrical singing in Verbicaro also occurs in a completely different situation, that is, the entertainment of men's groups. Here the musical performance acquires a different meaning and stresses the value of the collective relationship among men. These two kinds of occasions were the only ones available for men to sing "alla verbicarese," and this is an essential aspect of the GP on which this practice was based, which reflects the meaning of male lyrical singing at Verbicaro (Magrini 1986).

The survey of this performance practice allows us to recognize a relational pattern which gives structure to the musical performances. As regards the elaboration of lyrical texts, performances seem to represent a relationship of dependence, both with respect to the tradition of the group—in the sense that the verbal text of a canzone is inherited and cannot be changed—and with respect to the canonical performance practice of the canzone, since the performance takes place according to a rigorously hierarchical model. One of the singers acts as leader, the others as subordinate partners. The leader chooses the verbal text to be sung and leads the performance, and the others take turns in repeating his words. Consider the following example.

1. Palazzi frabbicat'in mienzo mare
   ed addove fu ligate lo prim'amore
2.   e ma mienzu mare
                    e mmienzu mare
   e duvi fi ligate lo prim'amore
3.   o mezzo mare
                    o mezzo mare
   dove fude legato lo sov'amore
4.   e mienzo mare
                    o mienzo mare
   ed addove fu llegata e lo primm'amore

1. e c'è na ragazza che porta bbandiera
   ia te portava fiaccolo d'amore
2.   e porta bbandiera
                    e porta bandiera
   e ia ti portava fiaccola d'amore

3.   e porta bandiera
                porta bandiera
        al petto porta fiaccole d'amore
4.   e porta bandera
                e porta la bandera
        e mpette portave di fioccole d'amore

1. e ma li tinia li doi rosi bianca
    alla centura na nocca d'argento
2.   e sa rosi bianca
                e si rosi bianca
        e m'alla cintura portava na nocca d'ora
3.   se rose bianca
                e se rose bianca
        alla centura na nocca d'argenta
4.   e rosi bianche
                doi rose bianca
        ed alla centura na nocca d'argenta

1. ed alla centura na nocca d'argenta
    e lu paradise che totti li santa
2.   e nocca d'argenta
                e o piccolina
        e ndavi nel paradise o di li sante
3.   e nocca d'argenta
                vacce vera sola
        e lo paradiso che tutti li santa
4.   e nocca d'argento
                e nocca d'argento
        e lo paraviso che totti li santa

Translation (without elaboration)
[There is a] palace built in the middle of the sea
where my first love was bound
There is a girl with a flag
I brought her torches of love
She had two white roses
And a silver belt-buckle
A silver belt-buckle
the paradise with all saints

Example of the elaboration of one distich:
1. There is a girl with a flag
    I brought you torches of love

2.   with a flag
                        with a flag
        I brought you torches of love
3.   with a flag
                        with a flag
        She has torches of love in her breast
4.   with a flag
                        with a flag
        She has torches of love in her breast.

The first performer, who acts as the leader in this performance, begins the song by proposing the first couplet of verses. Then, any person attending the musical event may join the performance, by singing in turn, one after the other, the repetition of the couplet reworked as an "answer." In "answers" the first hemistich of the first line is omitted and the second one is repeated twice; moreover, some slight variation may be carried out in words (see the example of elaboration, where "I brought you torches of love" is changed to "She has torches of love in her breast"). After three answers, in the case examined here, the performance goes on with the leader beginning a new couplet, and the same pattern of propositions and answers continues until the text is over. It should be noted that this kind of performance presents the text as an "uninterrupted speech": that is, one topic is developed from the beginning to the end.

This example shows a hierarchical pattern of verbal communication inside the group: each singer can use only the words proposed by the leader. In this sense, the performance is altogether redundant, and its meaning seems to reside especially in the socialization of the verbal content presented by the leader. The sense of creating a collective action by having all participants repeat the same words is predominant in this performance practice. The element of repetition is also evident in the group's concern with the integrity of the texts, as if the group had altogether delegated the function of expressing itself to the repetition of texts inherited from tradition. Tradition clearly offers the certainty of a prepackaged discourse which makes possible a form of communication within the group. But on the other hand, it sets a clear limitation on the development of new or additional expressive forms. As regards the strictly musical behavior, the different singers' renditions in Verbicaro's practice have something in common. The overall structure of the melody is bipartite, and the two main segments end on fixed degrees (the first segment on the second degree, the second segment on the tonic). Each segment (corresponding to one whole line or to the double repetition of one hemistich) has a descending outline. This is true for the melodies sung to the accompaniment of diatonic accordion (ex. 8.4) as well as for those sung to the accompaniment of bagpipe (ex. 8.5). But these are the only broad limits that must be respected when performing "alla verbicarese," and it is clear that they are not sufficient to build a model or an archetype.[25] Within these limits, singers try to manifest their skill in differentiating their renditions from the others. Of course, the melody is very short and theoretically does not offer many possibilities for differentiation. Nonetheless, differentiation is apparent in many parameters: register (middle or high), range (from a fifth to an eleventh), rhythm (completely free when the singing is accompanied by bagpipe, tendentially triple but markedly *rubato* when accompanied by diatonic accordion), form of melodic segments (sometimes clearly divided into two sections) and their extent (the melody may be expanded or contracted), arrangement of syllables, melismatic rate, type of ornamentation (for example, the specific type of ornamentation which imitates the bagpipe; see ex. 8.5), and modal organization (Magrini 1986, 1989). Even when four performers are singing together to the accompaniment of a diatonic accordion (which states the tonic, suggests the triple rhythm, and regularly alternates one chord on the dominant and one on the tonic, supplying a point of reference for melodic elaboration), they work out their melodies in a personal way (see ex. 8.4). It is clear that, while the first two performers insist on the dissonance provided by the fourth Lydian degree (E), the third performer insists on G in the attack and development of his melody, thus creating a strong new dissonance on the dominant chord (F) which gives his rendition a very particular character.[26] This suggestion is accepted by the fourth performer, who insists again on G.

To summarize, no hierarchical pattern can be observed as regards musical behavior. On the contrary, an equal, balanced, and cooperative relationship among the performers is manifested: each respects the dimension stated for the individual renditions but is free to work out the melody in a personal way, within broad general limits. Moreover, the individual performer "plays" with music while singing: he never repeats exactly "his" melody, but always changes some aspect of it. In exercising their creative skill, however, Verbicaro's performers do not act by chance; their performances must relate to a collective way of conceiving melody, which allows all of them to interact musically.

The main contents of Verbicaro's GP may be therefore sketched like this:

The proper occasion for singing (serenades in the past, men's group entertainment now), which reflects the male character of this musical practice

The interactive character of the performance (performers refuse to sing alone; at least two persons must take part in performance; the number of performers should not exceed fifteen, otherwise "there is too much confusion," as performers say)

Performances based on the extemporary rendition of predefined verbal texts (canzoni), which are inherited and cannot be changed; dependence on tradition and the need to base performance on a consistent text

A hierarchical pattern organizing the singers' participation in a performance (there is one leader and one or more partners)

Verbal interaction aimed at socializing the verbal content of one canzone ("proposals" and "answers")

Example 8.4

> Musical interaction aimed at establishing equal, balanced, and cooperative
> relations among performers
> Subjectivity manifested in musical behavior: performers may test their cre-
> ative skill in working out their melody and in "playing" with it, within
> some broad limits (bipartite overall structure of melody, main cadences
> on fixed degrees, and descending outline of melodic segments)
> Accompaniment supplied by diatonic accordion or bagpipe, which influence
> singers' musical behavior in different ways. (Magrini 1986, 197–224)

This GP determines the level of context but not the outcome of particular
performances. Many aspects remain unpredictable: the number of performers
who will take part (which will be known only after the beginning of the canzone, at the end of the first turn), the verbal text that will be sung and its
character (love or disdain), the type of instrumental accompaniment, the personal way of singing of the individual interpreters, the way they will "play"
with music on that occasion. These aspects embody the degree of improvisation of a given performance.

Example 8.4. *Continued*

Conclusion

Lyrical singing has often been considered simply as a kind of extempore practice entrusted to the whims of the performers, but I have tried here to show that
it is comprised of much more organized behavior, especially insofar as group
performance practices shared by a community are involved. Here, improvisation may have varying roles. The comparison of two different local practices
of lyrical singing shows that, even within the same musical genre, whose extemporized character is universally recognized, improvisation involves different aspects of the musical practice. In Verbicaro, improvisation does not concern the organization of the performance (which is strictly established) and
concerns the verbal text only to a small degree: the choice of a text for a particular rendition is extempore, and the technique of "answers" may lead to occasional variations of some words, but the text is essentially precomposed and
memorized. Thus, improvisation is found only in musical elaboration, where
it engenders a variety of melodies sharing some features (of which overall
structure is the most important, because it assures a balanced sequence of indi-

Example 8.5

vidual renditions), and where it is constantly renewed thanks to the performers' skill in "playing" with the melodies. To the contrary, in Giugliano improvisation importantly involves above all the performers' skill in interacting and carrying out a sort of game, a game strongly emphasizing subjective invention and the ability to offer innovation and provide surprises.

However, the aim of this essay is not simply to show the different degrees and types of improvisation involved in some practices of Italian lyrical singing. In addition, I want to point out that improvisation can be studied as an aspect of the behavior involved in musical performance, and that this kind of study is necessary to get a more comprehensive knowledge of the context in which improvisation is practiced and to realize its specific meaning. Improvisation is an aspect of musical behavior which belongs to a very wide and variegated range of musical practices. It always entails a degree of creativity carried out in an extemporized performance. But the conditions in which creativity is carried out may be very different among various practices, and they need to be examined from different perspectives. The case of Sardinian launeddas players mentioned at the beginning of this chapter is very different from the practices of group lyrical singing, where individual creativity is more strictly controlled because it is contained within an interactive process. In the latter case, improvisation is one aspect of a complex of musical behavior which is meant to activate and bring forth meaningful social relations. The behavior of the performers in Verbicaro emphasizes values such as male group cohesion and organization, socialization of verbal content, and equivalence of musical actions, while the behavior in Giugliano emphasizes differentiation, individualism, and the equal role of men and women in playing a collective game. I hope that the cases here examined are sufficient to show that Italian lyrical singing, to the extent that it is founded on interactive performance, turns out to be an important occasion to exhibit, by means of music making, a way of conceiving and enacting interpersonal relationships among individuals which pertains to the group and represents an important aspect of its social life.

Finally, I want to stress that the perspective of group musical practices such as those here examined may usefully suggest particular concepts which could help overcome the theoretical difficulties encountered when dealing with the superimposition of individual and social factors operating within the same phenomenon. The function of concepts such as "high context situation," "group overall plan," and "play" lies in emphasizing the existence of shared information, knowledge, and "know-how," which determine, at the social level, a particular set of conditions within which individual creative activity is enacted.

Notes

1. This technique enables the player "to keep up a constant and uninterrupted air-flow by puffing air into the instrument with the cheeks whilst inhaling through the nose" (Bentzon 1969, 26).

2. "The launeddas players' interest in the prestige of the school of playing in which they have been raised is evinced in the fact that they generally know the descent of their style in the form of a genealogy of masters and pupils" (Bentzon 1969, 88).

3. "A low context (LC) communication is just the opposite: the mass of the information is vested in the explicit code. . . . the emphasis is on the transmitted message apart from the context" (Hall 1992, 230).

4. A study of a number of performances of particular forms of lyrical singing carried out by the same interpreters has pointed out the uniqueness of each performance, that is, the impossibility of repeating it without changing something. What changes is connected to the particular form performed (Magrini and Bellosi 1982).

5. A notable exception is represented by the Sicilian cart drivers' songs, even if cart drivers too liked to sing together when they had the chance to spend some time together.

6. Sometimes it is possible to get an individual performance for the purpose of documentation; therefore individual performance are documented in many recordings. But the musical events which traditionally give occasion to the performance of lyrical singing, at least those so far studied, seem to be essentially collective and generally involve the participation of at least a small group of persons who take turns singing. Examples of group practices are provided in Magrini 1986, 1989, 1991.

7. I shall mention only two examples from the literature. Nettl argues that "each model, be it a tune, a theoretical construct, or a mode with typical melodic turns consists of a series of obligatory musical events which must be observed, either absolutely or with some sort of frequency, in order that the model remain intact" (Nettl 1974, 12); while the model is ambiguously defined by Lortat-Jacob, both as a sort of musical archetype, "composé d'un nombre d'éléments fini, entièrement mémorisés," and after some pages, as a set of rules and principles which "permet l'existence de différents formes" (Lortat-Jacob 1987, 46, 51).

8. The endecasyllable verse used in lyrical singing is not regular and may be worked out by cutting and adding syllables.

9. For a wide collection of texts of canzoni, see Cassetti and Imbriani 1968.

10. This performance ends with a different form of singing, named "voci a ffigliola" (DeSimone 1979, 34).

11. *Giuseppe:* A little bunch is not enough for me / A little bunch is not enough for me / I want the girl with all the flowerpots.

12. The number of syllables is not always regular.

13. *Raffaele:* Heavens, how high these windows are! / Heavens, how high these windows are / And how airy / And how airy / And how airy / And how airy / And how airy these windows are!

14. The elaboration of endecasyllable verses described in (a), (b), and (c) also occurs commonly in the singing of a dance named *Tammuriata* (performed with a drum, *tammorra*), widespread in the region of Naples (De Simone 1975; 1979, 16–17), while the musical elaboration in this performance is typical only of Giugliano's worshippers.

15. In this example, while the second line of the distich is expected ("And I would like my boyfriend's mother"), the performer sings a different irregular line on segment 3 ("Little girl, you deceived me with your roguish eyes").

16. *Antonietta:* I have a mother and would like another one / I have a mother and would like another one / x.1 And I would like a mother *e llene / vien te mòve Matalena / nnò tita ca chillo vène / tira tira s'nè venuto / e 'o pantofol'e velluto / e chella vavra e chillu mussu / e 'o garufaniell'è rus / chella vita dillicata / me pareva na pupat* / Little girl, you deceived me with your roguish eyes.

17. *Antonietta:* It's my boyfriend / It's my boyfriend / It's my boyfriend who smells so sweet.

18. *Rafaelle:* I want a rich sailor for them / Uh, I want a rich / Uh, I want a rich / I want a rich sailor for them.

19. *Antonietta:* Once I went through Casale / Once I went through Casale / And there was a fig tree full of plums / And there was a fig tree full of plums / I climbed up the tree and shook the plums / I climbed up the tree and shook the plums / And ripe pears fell down.

20. *Antonietta:* The owner of the cherries came / The owner of the cherries came / And told me: "Thief!" / And told me "Thief!" / And told me "Thief! You stole the grapes."

21. *Antonietta:* I came down and gathered them / I came down and gathered them / x.4. And each peach *e bbà / Leta le' nu' pazzia' / nu zumpo 'ncuollo te voglio fa'* / And each peace was as heavy as one rotolo.

22. This behavior is probably connected to what Pressing says about musical improvisation: "Novel actions are built primarily by distorting aspects of the existing ones" (Pressing 1988, 162).

23. See note 15.

24. It must be noticed that within the practice of Italian lyrical singing the tendency to modify modal setting while singing a tune is not rare. In some repertoires, this tendency is so marked and repeated in a number of performances that I suggested speaking of "modal mobility" as a peculiar feature of the musical practice. (Magrini and Bellosi 1982; see also Magrini 1992b).

25. This has been for a long time the main goal of many studies of oral musical traditions: "Studies of variability . . . ordinarily had as their central purpose the identification of the nature of *the* song or modal entity" (Nettl 1991, 3).

26. Of course, this feature is much more evident when listening to the performance than when reading the transcription.

References

Bentzon, Andreas Fridolin Weis. 1969. *The Launeddas: A Sardinian Folk-Music Instrument.* Copenhagen: Akademisk Forlag.

Casetti, Antonio, and Vittorio Imbriani. 1968. *Canti popolari delle provincie meridionali.* 1871–72. 2 vol. Reprint, Bologna: Forni.

D'Ancona, Alessandro. 1974. *La poesia popolare italiana.* 1906. Reprint, Bologna: Forni.

De Simone, Roberto. 1975. "Testo verbale e strutture musicali nei canti popolari." In *L'etnomusicologia in Italia,* edited by D. Carpitella, 151–58. Palermo: Flaccovio.

———. 1979. *La tradizione in Campania.* Seven LPs and booklet. EMI 164-18431/37.

Ferand, Ernst. 1938. *Die Improvisation in der Musik.* Zurich: Rhein Verlag.

———. 1957. "Improvisation." In *Die Musik in Geschichte und Gegenwart,* edited by F. Blume, vol. 6, 1093–135. Kassel: Bärenreiter.

Gallico, Claudio. 1984. "Polifonia e contrappunto." In *Dizionario enciclopedico universale della musica e dei musicisti,* edited by A. Basso, vol. 3, 662–79. Torino: Utet.

Hall, Edward T. 1992. "Improvisation as an Acquired, Multileveled Process." *Ethnomusicology* 36(2):223–35.

Kaemmer, John E. 1993. *Music in Human Life: Anthropological Perspectives on Music.* Austin: University of Texas Press.

Lortat-Jacob, Bernard, ed. 1987. *L'improvisation dans les musiques de tradition orale.* Paris: Selaf.

Magrini, Tullia. 1986. *Canti d'amore e di sdegno.* Milano: Franco Angeli.

———. 1989. "The Group Dimension in Traditional Music." *The World of Music* 31(2):52–78.

———. 1991. *Canti lirici della Calabria settentrionale.* LP with booklet. Albatros VPA 8505.

———. 1992a. "Lo studio del comportamento musicale come fondamento del processo analitico: Riflessioni sulla musica vocale di tradizione orale." *Analisi* 3(8):6–20.

———. 1992b. "La musica del Maggio." In *Il maggio drammatico: Una tradizione di teatro in musica,* edited by T. Magrini, 129–65. Bologna: Analisi.

———. 1993. "Analisi fra suono e uomo." In *Antropologia della musica e culture mediterranee,* edited by T. Magrini, 165–81. Bologna: Il Mulino.

———. 1996a. "Aspetti del canto monodico in Italia." In *Guida alla musica popolare in Italia. 1. Forme e strutture,* edited by R. Leydi, 103–60. Lucca: Libreria Musicale Italiana.

———. 1996b. "Italien. Volksmusik." In *Die Musik in Geschichte und Gegenwart,* edited by L. Finscher, vol. 4, 1282–306. Kassel: Bärenreiter Verlag.

Magrini, Tullia, and Giuseppe Bellosi. 1982. *Vi do la buonasera: Studi sul canto popolare in Romagna: il repertorio lirico.* Bologna: Clueb.

Nettl, Bruno. 1974. "Thoughts on Improvisation: A Comparative Approach." *The Musical Quarterly* 60(1):1–19.

———, ed. 1991. "New perspectives on improvisation." *The World of Music* 33(3).

Ong, Walter. 1977. *Interfaces of the World.* Ithaca: Cornell University Press.

Pressing, Jeff. 1988. "Improvisation: Methods and Models." In *Generative Processes in Music: The Psychology of Performance, Improvisation, and Composition*, 129–78. Oxford: Clarendon Press.

Sanga, Glauco. [1979]. *Il linguaggio del canto popolare*. Milano: Me/di Sviluppo and Giunti/Marzocco.

Schmidt, Siegfried J. 1974–76. *Pragmatik*. Vol. 1. *Interdisziplinäre Beiträge zur Erforschung der sprachlichen Kommunikation*. Vol. 2. *Zur Grundlegung einer expliziter Pragmatik*. Munich: Fink.

Seeger, Anthony. 1987. *Why Suyá Sing: A Musical Anthropology of an Amazonian People*. Cambridge: Cambridge University Press.

Tambiah, Stanley J. 1985. *Culture, Thought, and Social Action: An Anthropological Perspective*. Cambridge: Harvard University Press.

Treitler, Leo. 1991. "Medieval Improvisation." *The World of Music* 33(3):66–91.

Turner, Victor. 1982. *From Ritual to Theatre*. New York: PAJ Publications.

———. 1986. *The Anthropology of Performance*. New York: PAJ Publications.

CHAPTER NINE

Exploding the Belly: Improvisation in Cantonese Opera

SAU Y. CHAN

Chinese opera is a conglomeration of more than 350 genres; of these, Cantonese and Peking (or Beijing) opera are probably the best-known styles in China and overseas. Unlike Peking opera, which mainly employs Mandarin Chinese and which the Chinese government promotes as a "national" genre, Cantonese opera uses the Cantonese dialect[1] and hence is rated as a "regional" opera along with the other 350 styles. Peking opera, however, subsists only with government subsidies, while Cantonese opera is one of several regional styles that maintain their popularity without governmental support. Cantonese opera flourishes in Hong Kong, where it is one of the most traditional forms of performing arts and popular entertainment. Moreover, with increased migration from the territory to other parts of the world due to uncertainties surrounding Hong Kong's change of sovereignty in 1997, Cantonese opera is finding audiences in North American cities such as New York, San Francisco, Los Angeles, Toronto, and Vancouver, in European cities such as London and Paris, and in most major Southeast Asian cities.

The purpose of this chapter is to highlight the improvisatory practices within the performance of Cantonese opera. Following an introduction to the genre, including a considerable overview of the basic elements of its musical structure, I will cite a specific improvisatory performance from my fieldwork in order to describe the process of improvisation and the contexts in which it is learned and performed.

Cantonese Opera in Hong Kong

Employing the predominant Chinese dialect used in Hong Kong, Cantonese opera remains the most popular form of traditional entertainment in the territory. While some of its stylistic traits can be traced back to the Ming (A.D. 1368–1644) and Qing (1644–1911) dynasties, it was in the 1920s that the traditional stage dialect began to be replaced by Cantonese (Chan 1988, 14). During the 1930s, the genre reached its peak of popularity in Hong Kong, Macau, Guangzhou, and some Southeast Asian cities. As Hong Kong became the base for many established musicians and performers—and a melting pot of Chinese and Western cultures—Cantonese opera underwent a further localization with the incorporation of Western instruments such as saxophone, violin, trumpet, xylophone, steel guitar, and banjo in the accompanying ensemble. The genre has gradually evolved into a local style with a strong Hong Kong flavor, while it has constantly revitalized itself by responding to changes in public taste and competition from other forms of performing arts and entertainment.

In the 1980s, about thirty troupes staged an average combined total of four hundred to five hundred "days" of performances every year, some two-thirds within ritual contexts and the rest as theatrical, often commercial, productions (Chan 1988, 12). In the 1990s, an average of seven hundred days of performances have been staged annually, of which slightly less than half have been ritual performances. (Within a performing day, the performance customarily takes place in the evening; matinee operas are frequently scheduled in ritual series and sometimes in commercial productions. Hence, a day contains at least one and sometimes two operatic productions.)

Other than street performances in the Temple Street area of downtown Kowloon, Cantonese operas are invariably staged in theaters. Currently, only one movie theater stages Cantonese opera regularly on a commercial basis. With limited exceptions, performances staged in the various town halls in different parts of Hong Kong are also commercial in nature. The theaters in these contexts are physically permanent. For ritual performances, which are often organized by regional communities for the purpose of celebrating religious events, temporary theaters are built with bamboo, wood, and tin sheets. Expenses are rarely covered by charging admission; rather, donations are sought from members and friends of the communities. In this chapter, performances in both the cinema and town hall theaters are referred to as "commercial," whereas the temporary theater is referred to as "ritual" or "religious."

Commercial performances are often elegant, artistic, and sophisticated, and sometimes experimental; ritual series staged for the celebration of traditional festivals and birthdays of patron deities are usually dynamic, vernacular, lively, and full of comic episodes and improvisations. It is in these annual ritual events that many aspects of Cantonese customs can be observed and studied.

The Music of Cantonese Opera

The aural dimension of Cantonese opera can first be categorized into two components: a vocal component, consisting of speech and singing, and an instrumental component, consisting of percussive and melodic music. Vocal music in Cantonese opera is composed of three major families of melodic material: *ban hong* (literally "beat and melody"), *syt coeng* ("speech and singing") and *kuk pai* ("tunes with programmatic titles").

The *ban hong* family is used in a variety of regional operatic genres in China, including Peking opera (also known as Jing opera), which flourishes in northern China as well as major cities in other parts of the country, and Sae Coen opera, which is popular in the eastern coastal region of Guangdong Province. Though accommodating different styles, structures, and dramatic situations, a number of forms of *ban hong* share common names within the three operatic genres, which suggests that the three genres—Cantonese, Peking, and Sae Coen—may have some historical connections.

Rulan Chao Pian first translated the term *ban hong* as "aria type" (Pian 1972, 1975), and this translation was later adopted by Yung (1976, 1989) and Chan (1986, 1991). Liang (1985, 233) points out that since the *ban hong* family comprises forms that are rhythmically and melodically related, it is thus a "melo-rhythmic motivic type" of vocal music (see also Chan 1991, 14–15). In order to reflect the literal meaning and structural characteristics of the *ban hong* family, the present study translates the term as a "melo-rhythmic" type of vocal music.

Syt coeng is a family of traditional Chinese vocal music that is independent from opera. It is a kind of storytelling characterized by the alternate use of speech and singing. It is comprised of five genres of storytelling, all of which employ the Cantonese dialect, which were absorbed into Cantonese opera during the first decade of this century (Lai and Wong 1988, 77); since then, *syt coeng* (translated here as "sung narrative") has become an essential constituent of Cantonese operatic music.

Kuk pai, the third family of vocal music in Cantonese opera, is translated as "fixed tune" in Chan 1991 because such tunes have relatively identifiable preexistent or precomposed melodies. Taking into consideration the literal meaning of the term *kuk pai* ("tune title" or "tunes with titles") and the fact that most of the titles of these tunes are programmatic in nature, the present chapter translates the term as "programmatic tunes" (Chan 1991, 10).

Programmatic Tunes and Melo-Rhythmic Forms

The structure of the melo-rhythmic family of vocal music as used in Cantonese opera can be better understood in comparison with programmatic tunes. This writer estimates that there are about a hundred programmatic tunes and approximately thirty melo-rhythmic forms frequently employed in Cantonese opera. The following discussion covers musical elements such as melodic content and the verse structure of lyrics, as well as creative process.

Regarding the melodic content, each programmatic tune is identified by its preexistent or precomposed succession of pitches. When a scriptwriter creates a segment of vocal music in this style, he first chooses a tune, then sets the individual syllables of the text to individual notes or groups of notes. Since Cantonese dialect is a tonal language (i.e., different tonal inflections of the same phonetic syllable convey different meanings), the scriptwriter—now in the role of a composer (actually "text-setter")—must match the linguistic tonal contour of the syllables with the melodic contour of the succession of pitches in order to project the intended meaning (Yu 1994). Such vocal music is said to be in the style of *lou zi* ("displaying the syllables or words"), which is aesthetically desirable. Yet matching the two contours is not always the sufficient criterion for achieving the *lou zi* effect: the oral manner (the correct positioning of the tongue, teeth, and lips, and other factors) in which a singer enunciates the syllables, as well as his or her ability to add melodic ornaments to facilitate projection of the linguistic tones, also contribute to this effect. Needless to say, *lou zi* is an indispensable style in each of the various families of vocal music in Cantonese opera.

With respect to the textual structure of the lyrics, the number of syllables in each phrase and line, as well as the number of phrases and lines of each programmatic tune, is indefinite. In fact, the number and length of phrases and lines in a tune are jointly determined by its melodic structure and by the syntactic and semantic structure of its lyrics. The rhyming scheme is also flexibly observed in a programmatic tune: only some of the phrase- or line-ending syllables are required to rhyme with the predominant vowel (or compound vowels) within the operatic act or song.[2]

In contrast to programmatic tunes, each melo-rhythmic form has a strict structure in terms of the number of syllables, phrases, and lines, but its melodic content is more flexible. Within a fixed scheme of phrase- and line-ending notes, singers can introduce melodic notes that follow the tonal inflections of the individual syllables, as long as the notes follow the mode of the melo-rhythmic form. This practice is known as *ji zi heng hong* ("creating pitches by following the syllables") (Chan 1991, 186). In short, the melodic content of a particular melo-rhythmic form is subject to change when it is applied to a particular text. Thus a melo-rhythmic form, known as *ban sik* ("form of beat") in Cantonese, is identified not by its succession of notes but by the following five elements: (1) the text's verse structure; (2) the placement of the syllables within the pattern of pulse; (3) the phrase- and line-ending notes; (4) the *sin* (tuning and mode); and (5) the form of accompaniment (Yung 1989, 69–71; Chan 1991, 11).[3]

Speech Forms

Seven forms of speech used in Cantonese opera are identified by Chan (1991): versified speech, patter speech, plain speech, percussion speech, supported speech, rhymed speech, and comic rhymed speech (1991, 263). The structure of patter speech, plain speech, and supported speech will be discussed here in preparation for the detailed analysis of an improvisatory episode which will follow.

Plain speech is referred to as *hau bak* ("oral speech") in Cantonese. Structurally it resembles the daily speech that Cantonese use in nondramatic contexts. It is translated as "plain speech" in reference to the absence of constraints on the number of syllables, phrases, and lines, as well as on rhyme. In Cantonese opera performance, actors often use this form to facilitate their improvisation.

While plain speech is delivered in free rhythm and with no regular pulse, patter speech, referred to as *bak lam* ("white olive"),[4] is recited to steady pulses regulated by strokes played by the head percussionist on the large woodblock. A line of patter speech generally has five or seven structural syllables (excluding padding syllables added for elaborative and decorative purposes); three-syllable lines are only occasionally used. Lines are grouped into couplets, composed of the upper and lower lines, and the ending structural syllables of two lines must be on the oblique and even tones respectively.[5] Whether the ending syllable of the upper line rhymes is optional, but that of the lower line must follow the rhyme scheme of the operatic act or song. However, nonsense syllables, particles, and exclamations can be added to the ending structural syllables for the enrichment of expression.

Supported speech is referred to in Cantonese as *long ney bak* ("speech in sea waves"), indicating melodic music that has a wavelike contour. Theoretically, supported speech results from the addition of a melodic accompaniment to any form of speech; in practice, supported speech is often plain speech accompanied by melodic instrumental music. Aesthetically, the nuances created by the interface between the tonal contours of the speech and the melodic contours of the accompaniment provide an interesting effect (Chan 1990, 154, 168).

Vocal Improvisation in Cantonese Opera: An Introduction

In Happy Valley, a community on Hong Kong island with residents from a variety of social strata, a five-day series of Cantonese opera performances is usually held in the early days of the third or fourth lunar month at the temples of the Lord of the North and the Revered Tam for a joint celebration of the birthdays of these two deities.[6] This is one of about seventy Cantonese operatic performance series held annually in Hong Kong to highlight religious ritual activities. Unlike well rehearsed and script-oriented commercial theatrical productions presented as fine art, religious ritual performances often feature extensive use of improvisation. A typical extended improvisatory episode, as discussed in my previous study (Chan 1991, 177–180; 264–265), took place in the Happy Valley series in 1985. It remains a classic case for studying improvisation in Cantonese operatic music.

From 21 to 25 April (the second to sixth day of the third lunar month) of that year,[7] the Gem Lung (Golden Dragon) Cantonese Opera Company[8] was hired by the organizers of the joint temple festival to perform a five-day series. While these performances are usually held on a temporary stage facing the temples, organizers of this series staged the operas in a small auditorium in the junior employees clubhouse of the Hong Kong Royal Jockey Club.

In the evening of 24 April, Gem Lung's actors started the play *The Courtship of the Phoenix by the Side of Lake Peach Blossom* at 8 P.M. At around 11 P.M., when the major characters in the play were about to conclude the performance (by revealing which one had a secret affair with the princess), the comic role actor led the other actors into a long episode of improvisation. This consisted of a passage of patter speech, a passage of melo-rhythmic vocal music in the

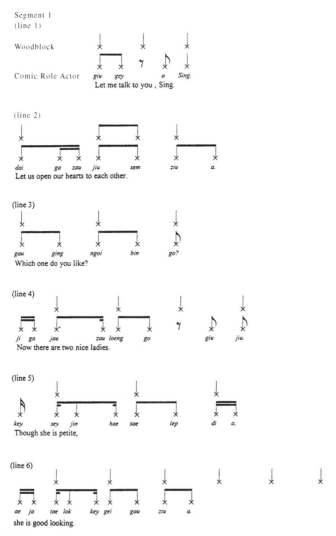

Example 9.1. Excerpts from patter speech passage.

moderate seven-syllable form, and another line of melo-rhythmic vocal music in free rhythm (known as "rolling flower"), with thirteen segments of plain speech interpolated at various points in the speech and vocal passages.

Examples 9.1 and 9.2 are excerpts from this improvisatory episode. Example 9.1 contains excerpts from the opening passage of patter speech, which has eight segments, each recited by an individual actor, totaling forty-four lines. Example 9.2 transcribes portions of the following passage of moderate seven-syllable melo-rhythmic form, which has six segments, each sung by an

Segment 7

Second Female Role

(line 1)

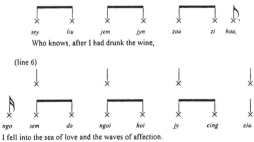

e   e,   ngo zi si sem   zok sey.

e, e, it was my selfish heart that caused trouble.

(plain speech segments 4 and 5. see ex. 9.3)

(line 2)

ngo   zoeng   na   sam   gang   goi wae ji   gang.

I changed the fifth hour to the third hour.

(line 3)   (line 4)

juk   hei   mong,   jy   ta   loi   tam   cing.

I planned,   to talk about love to him.

(plain speech segment 6. see ex. 9.3)

(line 5)

sey   liu   jem   jyn   zau   zi   hau,

Who knows, after I had drunk the wine,

(line 6)

ngo   sem   do   ngoi   hoi   jy   cing   ciu.

I fell into the sea of love and the waves of affection.

(plain speech segment 7. see ex. 9.3)

Example 9.1. *Continued*

Example 9.2. Excerpts from moderate seven-syllable passage.

individual actor, totaling twenty-seven lines; the last line is followed by a line of "rolling flower" in *bong zi* mode which concludes the whole improvisatory episode. The thirteen segments of plain speech in the episode are translated in example 9.3. These are scattered in various spots within the two passages. For example, plain speech segment 1 (recited by the comic role and third female role actors) takes place at the same time that the supporting male role actor recites the second line in patter speech segment 2. Similarly, plain speech segment 8 starts in the second segment of example 9.2, when the military role actor has just finished the first phrase of line 2.

Segment	Actor	English Translation
1	Comic role	You have no guts!
	Third female role	Don't be afraid!
2	Third female role	Don't you have anything to say?
3	Third female role	Say something! Please!
4	Military role	Speak up! Take your time!
5	Third female role	"Zi zi" heart?
	Second female role	Yes! I had a selfish heart.
	Third female role	What is a "zi zi" heart?
	Comic role	Ha! You had been troubled by your "si si" heart! You know how to say the word "si si heart"!
6	Military role	To change from three points [on the domino] to two points? You would certainly die if you were the banker in a game of dominoes.
	Comic role	Would it then become two and three points? You would die even if you were only the co-banker!
7	Comic role	Did your heart leap like drum-beats after you had drunk the wine?
	Second female role	My heart leaped and I laughed.
	Comic role	That is why I say you young girls' hearts [continues with patter speech]
8	Comic role	Hey, you bad guy.
	Military role	What? [I was going to say that the secret lover] could not avoid serious trouble. What are you trying to do?
	Comic role	You are no good, you laughed at me. You made an excuse to laugh at me.
	Military role	I was just imitating you.
	Comic role	I don't like it.
	Military role	[sings] Isn't it right?
	Comic role	This is what I don't like. You imitated the way we girls speak. Shame on you!
	Military role	My royal aunt!
	Comic role	What?
	Military role	My royal aunt, you are almost sixty years old!
	Comic role	Not yet!
	Military role	Do you still call yourself a girl?
	Comic role	I am still forty-something.
	Military role	Forty-something?
	Comic role	Look at me! I am all right except my chin is a bit rough.
	Military role	Your chin? It seems you have no chin!
	Comic role	No, only a bit rough. Don't you know why?
	Military role	Only a bit rough? All right!
9	Comic role	Who was your secret lover?
10	Comic role	Think! Think! Think! Think carefully!
11	Principal female role	Who did you drink your wine with? What did you do after drinking the wine?
	Military role	Think about it; see if you have any impression. Don't you have the slightest hint of an impression?
	Principal female role	It wasn't him?
	Military role	Think about it!

Example 9.3. Thirteen segments of plain speech.

	Principal female role	It wasn't him, it wasn't Gem Sing! Who would that be?
12	Second female role	It was you!
13	Second female role	It was definitely you!
	Military role	Ha! You are dead, it was you! What are you going to do?
	Third female role	Now you are the only one left, aren't you?

Example 9.3. *Continued*

Improvisatory Practices

When the actors who were involved in this improvisatory episode were interviewed the next day by this writer, they invariably said that the episode was added for the purpose of prolonging the performance. An examination of the script confirmed that the episode was not part of the original version of the play.

Men Coi-sing, the military role actor, and impresario of the troupe (ca. 1928–1988), explained that since the auditorium was in a residential area, the local police station prescribed that the evening performances conclude at 11 P.M. so residents would not be disturbed by the "loud" music. But the audience enjoyed the performance enormously, and festival organizers requested police approval for prolonging the performance by ten to fifteen minutes. The police notified the organizers at around 11 P.M. that the request was approved, and the actors were then asked to prolong the performance. As noted by Cen Zi-hung, the comic role actor (b. 1935) and Men Coi-sing, the addition of an episode to the performance through *bao tou* ("exploding one's belly") was the only means to realize prolongation. As they explained, Cantonese operas were performed without scripts before the 1930s. Actors were invariably required to *bao tou* during their performances. A good performance would depend on whether an actor had enough "stuff" in his belly. Thus, *bao tou* has a connotation similar to that of improvisation.

At the start of the improvisatory episode, the comic role actor signaled the accompanying musicians with a hand gesture, and another gesture was used right before the moderate seven-syllable form. As Cen explained the following day that these gestures are known as *sau jing* ("shadow of the hand"). The first gesture—stretching out four fingers and moving them up and down—is called *pok deng ngo* ("moth rushing to the lamp") and functions to cue the musicians and other actors for an improvised passage of patter speech. The second gesture—extending the index and middle fingers held together—is called *zung ban* (moderate pulse) and indicates a passage of melo-rhythmic vocal music in moderate pulse and the mode of *bong zi*.

The practice described by Cen is consistent with this writer's observations from 1985 to 1995 (though in more recent years improvisations often occur in more limited scope). During an actor's training, in addition to learning a large repertory of vocal and speech passages (i.e., the "stuff" to be applied during improvisation), one has to acquire two sets of sign language—hand shadow and gestic hint—to facilitate communication with musicians and actors. Hand shadows mainly involve only one hand and are used by actors to notify accompanists of the type of speech or vocal music they intend to employ and to indicate stage movements; they are direct communications between the actors and the head percussionist. Each hand shadow usually cues a particular percussion pattern, which functions to start a passage of speech or vocal music. Gestic hints are known as *jing tau* ("head of a shadow"), and along with oral signals, these are used by actors as well as musicians (especially the head melodic instrumentalist and head percussionist) to deliver a variety of messages (Chan 1991, 115–137). In short, a gestic hint or hand shadow is a marker of the beginning of *bao tou,* that is, of improvisation.

The Aural Dimension of Improvisation

PATTER SPEECH PASSAGE

As mentioned above, the comic role actor started the long improvisatory episode by signaling with the hand shadow "moth rushing to the lamp." After the percussion pattern indicated by this hand shadow was played, this actor started his segment of patter speech. As shown in table 9.1, after six lines (i.e., three couplets), he was followed by the principal male actor, who recited two lines, the principal female actor, who recited six lines, the supporting male role actor, who recited four lines, the military role actor, who recited eight lines, the third female role (also known as "second supporting female role") actor, who recited six lines, and the second female role (also known as "supporting female role") actor, who recited six lines. This was immediately followed by six lines of patter speech by the comic role actor, who then gave the hand shadow signaling moderate pulse; after the percussion and melodic introductions, he started the passage in the moderate seven-syllable form of melo-rhythmic vocal music shown in example 9.2.

In this improvisatory episode, Cen Zi-hung, an experienced actor in the comic role, played a key part in the overall improvisatory process. According to many informants, actors in the comic role are usually the ones who initiate improvisations.

As described above, lines of patter speech often have seven or five structural syllables; three-syllable lines are rare. But as shown in table 9.1, the number of structural syllables within this improvisatory passage of patter speech was treated flexibly by each of the actors involved in the improvisation. Among the forty-four lines, eight have three syllables, fourteen have five syllables, and fifteen have seven syllables. Lines having four and six syllables provide contrast to the prevalent structure. The four lines that have more than seven syllables all occur at the end of a segment: tradition requires an actor to repeat the last three syllables of the ending line of a segment in order to signal its conclusion, so the next actor can start his turn at the right moment. Occasionally, however, some actors repeat more than the standard three syllables. An example of this is found in line 8 of the military role actor's segment in table

Table 9.1. Analysis of patter speech passage

Segment	Role	Lines	No. of Woodblock Strokes	No. of Structural Syllables
1	Comic	1	3	4
		2	3	5
		3	3	5
		4	4	6
		5	3	5
		6	3	5
2	1st male	1	4	7
		2	4	7
3	1st female	1	3	5
		2	4	7
		3	5	5
		4	3	5
		5	3	5
		6	6	8
4	2nd male	1	4	7
		2	6	7
		3	4	7
		4	7	10
5	Military	1	5	5
		2	3	5
		3	4	7
		4	3	5
		5	2	3
		6	2	3
		7	4	7
		8	7	12
6	3rd female	1	6	7
		2	4	7
		3	3	5
		4	4	7
		5	4	7
		6	6	10
7	2nd female	1	8	6
		2	4	7
		3	2	3
		4	3	5
		5	4	7
		6	4	7
8	Comic	1	2	3
		2	3	5
		3	2	3
		4	2	3
		5	2	3
		6	2	3

9.1. While structurally there are seven syllables in this line, the military role actor repeated the last five syllables, creating an unusually long line of twelve syllables.

Yet in this particular episode of improvisation, not every actor followed the performance practice of repeating syllables in an ending line, and irregularities resulted. In segment 1, line 6, of example 9.1, when the comic role actor failed to observe this practice, other actors could not connect immediately and three woodblock strokes were played with no speech recited. Similarly, at the end of segment 2 (table 9.1), when the principal male actor failed to repeat the ending syllables of this segment, the principal female actor could only connect after the gap of one woodblock stroke. Such discontinuities are considered unsatisfactory in the tradition. Since the 1930s, as script-oriented performance has become more dominant, younger actors often fail to understand the functional significance of repeating ending syllables. Though older actors have all acquired skill in this practice, they are often less sensitive in recalling it in contemporary script-oriented performances. In example 9.1, another discontinuity occurs in the supporting female actor's segment. This actor was reluctant to recite her patter speech, probably due to inadequate training in improvisation.

MODERATE SEVEN-SYLLABLE PASSAGE

As mentioned earlier, five elements are responsible for defining a form of melo-rhythmic vocal music in Cantonese opera, namely, the accompaniment, the verse structure, the cadential notes, the mode, and the syllable placement pattern. Example 9.4 illustrates that the syllable placement patterns used in the twenty-seven lines of melo-rhythmic form in this episode more or less follow the patterns prescribed by tradition.[9] Since the accompanists followed the traditional performance practice in a relatively strict manner during the actors' improvisatory singing, and since the conventional pentatonic mode of *bong zi* is used throughout the twenty-seven lines,[10] the following discussion will specifically focus on the verse structure and the cadential notes.

Verse Structure Compared to the patter speech passage that had just been improvised by the same actors, this singing passage contains less material that deviates from the structure stipulated by tradition. In other words, the actors were more fluent in handling this improvisatory passage, probably because the preceding passage provided an adequate warm-up.

Example 9.4 arranges the twenty-seven lines of melo-rhythmic form, using the number of woodblock strokes to show the time duration of each line. The order of the woodblock strokes is represented by Roman numerals; the order of the seven structural syllables in each line is represented by Arabic numerals.

In segment 2, the military role actor's first attempt to recite a second line was interrupted by the comic role actor's plain speech, which resulted in an incomplete line containing only five syllables. This line is thus not counted

Example 9.4. Structural syllable placement in moderate seven-syllable passage.

among the twenty-seven lines. In segment 3, sung by the supporting male role actor, the first line contains only three syllables, probably due to the actor's inadequate preparation in improvising his segment. According to informants who are singers trained in the tradition, this line deviates from the traditional structure and is considered irregular. Aside from these cases, the remaining twenty-six lines follow the verse structure of the moderate seven-syllable form. The rhyme scheme was followed as well, with each actor ending his or her lines with syllables containing the compound vowel "iu."

Cadential Notes   The tradition stipulates that female and male characters follow different schemes of cadential notes in melo-rhythmic vocal forms in the *bong zi* mode. Upper lines sung by female characters end on C, and lower lines end on G; upper and lower lines sung by male characters end on D and C,

line 4

Segment 3
Supporting
male role
line 1

line 2

line 3

line 4

Segment 4
Principal
female role
line 1

line 2

line 3

Example 9.4. *Continued*

respectively. Among the actors and characters who participated in this improvisatory passage, male characters were played by actors of the principal male role, the supporting male role, and the military role; female characters were played by actors of the comic, principal female, second female, and third female roles.[11] As shown in example 9.4, all lines follow this cadential-note scheme except line 1 of segment 2.

Line 1 of segment 2 is a lower line, judging from the linguistic tone of the ending syllable (i.e., the syllable *ciu* is sung in the lower even tone in this context). Since the military role actor was playing a male character in the opera, this line should end on the note C according to the scheme described above. The actor, however, chose G as the cadential note, which is the note that a female character would use. This immediately aroused strong reactions from the comic role and other actors, and the military role actor's next line was

Example 9.4. *Continued*

interrupted by the comic role actor's plain speech. This self-explanatory dialogue between the two actors can be found in segment 8 of example 9.3.

It is uncertain whether the military role actor mistakenly ended his lower
line on G instead of C. In the ensuing dialogue, however, he claimed that in
fact he intended to imitate the singing of the comic role actor, a male actor
portraying a female character in the play. In the same dialogue, the comic role
actor used the fact of his impersonation of a female to arouse laughter from
the audience (by saying that he was all right except his chin was a bit rough).
This is one of numerous examples in which actors use gender as the subject of
their improvisations, which are often warmly received by the audience.

The plain speech segment cited above is also a good illustration of an improvisatory chain reaction. Triggered by the motif of "chin," the military role
actor accused the comic role actor of having no chin, alluding to a popular
Cantonese notion that only ghosts have no chins.

Example 9.4. *Continued*

PLAIN SPEECH SEGMENTS

In addition to using plain speech to elaborate their improvisations, actors also speak to prompt other actors to continue the improvisation. For example, the plain speech line by the third female role actor in segment 3 of example 9.3 was intended to remind the second female to respond to the principal female's patter speech segment. When the second female role actor still had no reaction, the military role actor started his segment of patter speech.

As mentioned above, among the actors involved in this episode, the actor in the second female role showed the most reluctance in improvising; several segments of plain speech found in example 9.3 were hence intended to help her. For example, in her segment of patter speech (segment 7), she could barely continue to improvise after her first patter speech line. Recognizing this, the third female and comic role actors used plain speech (segment 5) to cover for her (see exx. 9.1 and 9.3). In this segment of plain speech, her slight inaccuracy in pronouncing the word *zi si sem* (*zi si* means "selfish," *sem* means "heart") became another motif for improvisation. After the plain speech, the second female role actor successfully recited another five lines of patter speech, though two of them failed to rhyme correctly. Having warmed up, however, this actress was highly fluent in improvisatory singing following the patter speech passage.

According to many actors, although improvisational skill is essential for the performance of Cantonese opera, actors seldom acquire it from their teachers. Most of the comic role actors currently active in Hong Kong told this writer that they learned improvisation from watching and imitating their idols' performances (also see Bailey 1980, 15–16). In fact, actors are often forced to develop improvisational skills during actual performance; the case of the second female role actor discussed here seems to be an example of this.[12]

Conclusion

As a form of mass entertainment which has developed from religious and ritual contexts, Chinese opera has a rich and strong tradition of improvisation. Unlike Peking opera, which is heavily dominated by government officials and intellectuals and hence has been purified by "artistic refinement," Cantonese opera staged in ritual contexts still exemplifies this improvisatory tradition.

Improvisation in Cantonese opera serves to coordinate the stylistic elements (i.e., "building blocks," in Nettl's words; see Nettl 1974, 13) of the genre and gives the performances a sense of spontaneity; it also solves problems that occur during a performance. But while Cantonese opera is booming in Hong Kong, improvisation within the genre is declining since Hong Kong is still dominated by Westernization. The improvisation which I have cited and discussed in this chapter may be just the remnant of a once vital and strong tradition.

Notes

I would like to thank Professors John Larry Witzleben and Michael E. McClellan for their suggestions in revising this paper. I wish also to thank Tsui Ying-fai for the artistic preparation of the musical examples.

1. With only a few exceptions, Romanizations used throughout this paper are according to the Cantonese dialect and based on Wong Lik's system; see Chan 1991, xv.

2. In creating a Cantonese operatic act or piece of operatic song, the scriptwriter has to choose a predominant vowel or compound vowel, known as *wen* (rhyme) in Cantonese. In vocal music, all lines of the melo-rhythmic and singing narrative families must conclude in syllables that rhyme with this vowel or compound vowel; lines in programmatic tunes rhyme flexibly. However syllables with a vowel (or compound vowel) that sounds similar to the chosen rhyme are also acceptable as line endings.

3. It is beyond the scope of this paper to discuss these five elements in detail. Sung narratives are also organized in terms of such elements.

4. Some informants speculate that patter speech was originally recited by hawkers selling white olives.

5. For the tonal aspects of Cantonese dialect, see Chan 1991, 187. For convenience of reference, tones other than the upper and lower even tones are collectively termed "oblique." Even tones have descending tonal inflections and thus create an effect of resolution; they are known as *ping sing* ("stable tones") in Cantonese. Oblique tones include rising, level and abruptly-ending tonal inflections and create an effect of suspense; they are known as *zek sing* ("tilting tones") in Cantonese.

6. Most of the religious ritual operatic performance series held in Hong Kong celebrate one particular religious event or the birthday of one particular deity. Yet, probably due to the limitation of resources, organizers of this series intend to celebrate the birthdays of both deities. The birthdays of the Lord of the North and the Revered Tam are observed on the third day of the third month and the eighth day of the fourth month, respectively; the yearly performance series are held during the early days of the third and fourth month alternately.

7. In my previous study (Chan 1991) of this improvisatory episode, I mistakenly

reported that 24 April was the last day within the performance series (see Chan 1991, 34, 178).

8. In Hong Kong, Cantonese opera troupes are often known as *keik tyn* (drama or opera group) and seldom explicitly as *jyt keik tyn* (Cantonese opera group).

9. The seven structural syllables within a line of the moderate seven-syllable form can be placed in a number of different patterns; this will be discussed in a future paper.

10. As shown in example 9.4, among the 317 notes found in the twenty-seven lines, the three notes that show relative prominence are C (84 occurrences), G (56 occurrences), and E (84 occurrences). Taking into consideration that C and G are both cadential notes, they are considered the important notes in the mode. However, among these two notes, it is difficult to determine which one is more important, though the note C receives more emphasis. This will be further discussed in the paragraphs on cadential notes.

11. In this performance of the play, actors of the principal female, second female, and third female roles were women; actors of the comic, military, principal, and supporting male roles were men. One could note the relationship among actor, role type, and character in a play: male and female roles are usually played by male and female actors and they portray male and female characters, respectively; comic and military roles often portray male characters and are usually both played by male actors, who are also occasionally required to impersonate female characters.

12. This actress, Gwok Fung-ji (b. 1954), has become a principal female actor in the 1990s.

References

Bailey, Derek. 1980. *Improvisation: Its Nature and Practice in Music.* London: Moorland Publishing.

Chan, Sau Y. 1986. "Improvisation in Cantonese Operatic Music." Ph.D. dissertation, University of Pittsburgh.

———. 1988. *A Study of Cantonese Opera in Hong Kong* (in Chinese). Vol. 1. Hong Kong: Wide Angle Press.

———. 1990. *A Study of Cantonese Opera in Hong Kong* (in Chinese). Vol. 2. Hong Kong: Chinese University of Hong Kong, Chinese Opera Research Project.

———. 1991. *Improvisation in a Ritual Context: The Music of Cantonese Opera.* Hong Kong: Chinese University Press.

Lai, Bak-goeng, and Wong, Geing-ming. 1988. *History of Cantonese Opera* (in Chinese). Beijing: Chinese Theatre Press.

Liang, David Mingyue. 1985. *Music of the Billion: An Introduction to Chinese Musical Culture.* New York: Heinrichshofen Edition.

Nettl, Bruno. 1974. "Thoughts on Improvisation: A Comparative Approach." *Musical Quarterly* 60:1–19.

Pian, Rulan Chao. 1972. "Text Setting with the Shipi Animated Aria." In *Words and Music: The Scholars' View,* edited by Laurence Berman, 237–70. Cambridge: Harvard University Press.

———. 1975. "Aria Structure Patterns in the Peking Opera." In *Chinese and Japanese Music-Dramas,* edited by J. I. Crump and W. P. Malm, 65–89. Ann Arbor: University of Michigan, Center for Chinese Studies.

Yu, Siuwah. 1994. "Creativity in Musical Adaptation: A Hakka Zither Melody in a Cantonese Opera." In *Themes and Variations: Writings on Music in Honor of Rulan Chao Pian,* edited by B. Yung and J. Lam, 111–44. Cambridge: Department of Music, Harvard University; Hong Kong: Chinese University of Hong Kong, Institute of Chinese Studies.

Yung, Bell. 1976. "The Music of Cantonese Opera." Ph.D. dissertation, Harvard University.

———. 1989. *Cantonese Opera: Performance as Creative Process.* Cambridge: Cambridge University Press.

Chapter Ten

Melodic Improvisation in Karṇāṭak Music: The Manifestations of Rāga

T. Viswanathan and Jody Cormack

Rāga is the foundation of melodic composition and improvisation in South Indian music. Yet attempts to describe or define it often fall short. Some fall back on the near romantic quality of historical classification relating rāga to time of day, emotion, and so on. Others rely on the dense scholarship of Indian music theory and its weighty terminology. Furthermore, because different rā-gas can share melodic material, definitions which exclude knowledge gained through practical experience can leave both the trained and the average listener mystified.

Unfortunately there is no shortcut to understanding rāga. Theory tells us that rāga is made up of pitch and microtones, scale, and specific ornaments. Tradition tells us that rāga phrases emerge from composition and performance practice. Analysis tells us that although a musician adheres to these basic "rules" of rāga in performance, there is yet another level of rules dictated by context. That is, every rāga changes slightly depending on the form in which it is performed. For the listener to decipher the intricacies of rāga, or for the performer to comprehend what is fixed within what is flexible, an awareness must be developed from persistent listening and practice. By using analysis as a vehicle we can get some sense of the subtle effects of form on rāga. What must eventually come through a process of absorption for the listener and performer can thus be illustrated by examining rāga in more than one environment—in this case, two Karṇāṭak (South Indian) improvisatory forms from the art music tradition.[1]

Ālāpana and *svara kalpana* are two among five improvisatory forms performed in Karṇāṭak music.[2] *Ālāpana* can be described as melodic improvisation in free rhythm, using syllables of no meaningful significance, set within the framework of a single rāga (melody type). *Svara kalpana* is the improvisation of melodic/rhythmic passages using *svaras* (sol-fa syllables), taking place within the *tāḷa* (metrical cycle) of a composition.[3] Both of these can be visualized on a continuum where, in the context of the other improvisatory forms of the system,[4] they range from those which least involve *tāḷa* to those which involve it the most. *Ālāpana* would thus fall in the former category, and *svara kalpana* closest to the latter.

Insofar as each improvisatory form has a structure that is uniquely its own, and formulas and procedures for its performance that are equally individual, it is logical that something as elemental as rāga would in turn behave according to its context. From this viewpoint we can discuss rāga in *ālāpana* and *svara kalpana.*

Rāga

Powers's work on rāga is arguably the most succinct and thorough to date. In part, he defines rāga as both a "particularized scale" and a "generalized melody." Regarding this he says: "A rāga is more specific than a scale, for any number of rāgas can share a single collection of pitches. Yet a rāga is less specific than a tune, for any number of tunes can share the same rāgas" (1984, 328).

Another way of looking at rāga is as "a ready-made 'system' of formulas," a "total melodic 'tool-kit' which contains all of the pitch materials . . . the performer will use" (Reck 1983, 91–92). This system of formulas distinguishes the melodic character of a rāga from any other, and is traditionally defined as *lakṣana*—the grammar or "theory" particular to a rāga. It includes scale, the treatment of individual tones (how they may be ornamented, stressed or not, elongated, shortened, and so forth), phrases, and shape (*svarūpa* or "gestalt" of the rāga as a whole). A music student learns most aspects of the *rāga lakṣana* and masters the techniques of improvisatory forms through an extended process of musical absorption. Ultimately, this process translates into an instinctive understanding of the architecture and the rules of each form. For *ālāpana* and *svara kalpana,* these are roughly presented as follows.

ĀLĀPANA

Ālāpana precedes the composition and is therefore performed without drum accompaniment. An *ālāpana* can be very short (one or two minutes), long (fifteen minutes to half an hour), or any length in between. Several factors influence the musician's choice of length, such as the pacing of the concert, the scope a particular rāga may have for development, the composition about to follow, the singer's mood and vocal condition, and the response of the audience. Every *ālāpana* follows a common contour and may be broken down into a series of broad developmental sections. The average *ālāpana* begins by exploring the rāga around the tonic *(sa).* It systematically rises through the middle octave *(madhya sthāyi),* stressing the important *svaras* of the rāga along the way, then gradually builds up to the octave tonic *(tāra sthāyi ṡa).* There,

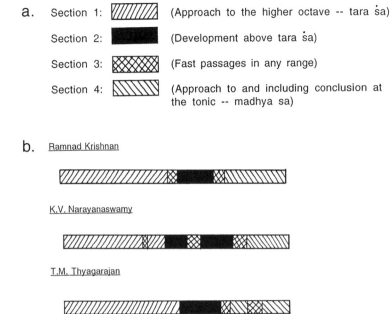

Figure 10.1. *a, Ālāpana* sections; *b,* three *ālāpana* performances.

higher octave development takes place. Once this has occurred, the rāga may continue its development over a span of approximately two octaves in fast passages called *brikka*. A rapid descent back toward the tonic *sa* follows where, in a relaxed and slower tempo, the *ālāpana* resolves on the tonic. The sections may be distinguished as shown in figure 10.1a.

There is no fixed rule or standard to determine the relative length of each of these sections, and certainly there is no formal indication of transition from one section to another—no sudden break in the rate of notes or melodic development. Graphic representations of *ālāpana* performances by three eminent musicians shown in figure 10.1b conform to this proposed four-section format, albeit with variations in proportion and sequence (see Viswanathan 1974, 188).

SVARA KALPANA

Svara kalpana assumes not only the intricacies of rāga, but adds many of the complexities of the *tāḷa* tradition as well. It is the "forming" or "fashioning" *(kalpana)* of solfege syllables or notes *(svaras)* which are either sung or articulated instrumentally at a chosen point within a composition. Alternated between a solo performer and a melodic accompanist, each completed turn (or "round") of *kalpana svaras* ends on a particular pitch *(svara)* in the rāga and at a specific place *(iḍam)* in the *tāḷa* cycle. The *iḍam* is where a phrase from a line of text in the composition begins. Sung or played instrumentally, the phrase acts as a refrain.

Unlike *ālāpana,* which may be described as a form in which rāga builds stepwise to peak at and above the octave and then quickly descends to conclude on the tonic, *svara kalpana* builds by the gradual lengthening of successive rounds. It also builds by a change of speed (where it is doubled or quadrupled), by the expansion of range (within the pitch limitations of the rāga scale), and by a buildup of rhythmic activity, and often complexity, as it nears conclusion. Any of these elements may be used depending on the type of composition within which the *svara kalpana* is set, its placement in the program, the *tāḷa,* the restrictions of the rāga, and the performance habits, mood, and abilities of the artist.

The sequence of events possible for a *svara kalpana,* as well as a delineation of the major structural options available, is shown in figure 10.2.[5] At the top of the figure is an abstracted *tāḷa* cycle with an arrow connecting the beginning (which is the first *tāḷa* count or *sama*) to the end (also *sama*). The slow tempo *(vilambita kāla)* and fast tempo *(madhyama kāla)* sections start as short rounds near the end of the cycle, and gravitate outward to the left as the rounds lengthen, where they finally span the whole cycle as extended rounds. The beginning of each round is marked with a number, the end with an asterisk (indicating a return to the refrain line, or *eḍuppu*).[6] The lines shown here are merely representative of the many rounds of *svaras* possible in a performance. A *korappu* (represented here by an upside-down staircase configuration) is the gradual reduction (by halves) of *kalpana* (improvised) *svaras,* normally in a statement-and-response exchange between the soloist and melodic accompanist. The fermatas represent briefly held *svaras* which signal the end of the soloist's (or accompanist's) turn. The final cadence marks the climax of the entire *svara kalpana* performance, which resolves with a last restatement of the refrain phrase. This is represented in figure 10.2 as contrasting lines, since cadential patterns vary so greatly in size, shape, and content.

A clear distinction between *ālāpana* and *svara kalpana* is evident from these brief and general descriptions. Many details of the consistencies and the variables in each have not been discussed. Nonetheless obvious differences between the two forms can be seen. In large part this is due to the metered environment of the one and the absence of meter in the other. Closer examination will show several of the ways basic rāga principles can be expressed.

Scale

At its most basic level, a rāga is defined by its scale. *Kāmbhōji* is one of the oldest rāgas still in use in Karṇāṭak music,[7] and continues to be among the most popular. Musicians today consider it a *rakti* rāga, or a rāga which has a particular "feeling" or "emotion" *(bhāva)* attached to it. Such rāgas generally predate the nineteenth century and, having so established themselves in com-

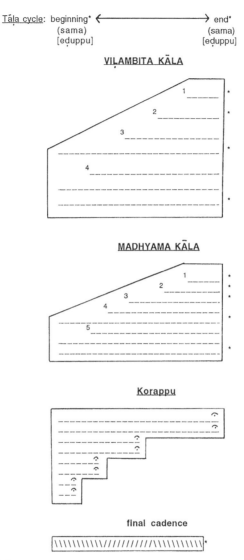

Figure 10.2. *Svara kalpana* sequence.

positions over a long historical period, rely more on characteristic phrases and ornamentation than the more scalar and less phrase-dependent rāgas of recent times. *Kāmbhōji* is thus an accessible and appropriate choice for analysis and discussion. *Kāmbhōji* is made up of the following pitches:

$$C\ D\ E\ F\ G\ A\ C' - C'\ Bb\ A\ G\ F\ E\ D\ C^9$$

The corresponding *svara* (solfege) syllable for each note would be:

sa ri ga ma pa dha śa – śa ni^b dha pa ma ga ri sa[10]

Svara (Pitch)

Every rāga has certain pitches that have specific functions. At the *svara* level, these function tones are a rāga's second most fundamental identifying features.

Reck observes, "Each composition, each composer, each performing tradition, and each performing musician (perhaps on different occasions) may present a slightly different picture of the characteristics of [a] rāga" (1983, 210)—and indeed this testifies to the dynamic life of performed rāga. The frequent occurrence of certain function tones relates to the inherent rules of the rāga. These tones can also reflect the structure of the forms (that is, *ālāpana* and *svara kalpana*) within which they occur, as well as the performer's own musical habits.

The primary function tones of a rāga are its *amsa svaras* or "predominant tones" (equated with *jīva svaras* or "soul tones"), *graha svaras* ("initial tones" of composed sections or improvised phrases and sections), *nyasa svaras* ("final tones" of phrases and sections of a composition or improvisation), and *dīrgha svaras* ("elongated" or "sustained" tones).

For each category of function tones discussed in *ālāpana* and *svara kalpana,* example 10.1 shows the four most prominent *svaras,* presented left to right, in order of their appearance. The differences (and the similarities) in relation to the employment of function tones in *ālāpana* and *svara kalpana* were gathered from a broad assortment of improvisations in both forms.[11] *Svaras* were individually added, averaged, and compared. It is important to remember that the conclusions reached cannot be taken as absolute, since there is always room for individual expression and creativity. In *svara kalpana,* for example, a musician may opt for a refrain line starting on the octave tonic *śa* instead of the fifth

a. Amsa Svaras for Kambhoji Alapana

dha   pa   śa   ma

b. Amsa Svaras for Kambhoji Svara Kalpana

dha   pa   ma   ni

Example 10.1. *Amsa svaras.*

degree *pa* ordinarily taken. The result is greater emphasis on notes performed in the middle and higher octaves. The predominance of certain function tones is thus influenced by the beginning pitch of the refrain line (the *eḍuppu svara*) and its location in the octave.

The slight difference between the two improvisatory forms regarding predominant tones (involving *ṣa* in *ālāpana* and *ni* in *svara kalpana*) can best be explained from the viewpoint of performance convention. As *ālāpana* phrases approach the higher octave, they either weave around, sustain, begin with, or end on the octave tonic *ṣa*. Vocalists particularly make use of this *svara* since it is in a strong area of their vocal range. In *kāmbhōji svara kalpana*, musicians often prefer certain phrases beginning with or stressing *ni*. Some common examples are *ni–dha–pa–dha—ma* and versions of it, such as those shown in example 10.2 Musicians also consider these phrases "emotional" *(rakti)* phrases.

The initial tone or *graha svara* of an improvised phrase is more easily identified in *ālāpana*, where each phrase or group of phrases is marked by a pause, than it is in *svara kalpana*, where pulsed melodic phrases tend to blend. *Graha svara* in *svara kalpana* describes more accurately the opening pitch of a section, specifically the tone beginning a round of *svaras*. The preference for the fifth degree *pa* as an initial tone in *ālāpana* (see ex. 10.3) reflects the ease with which one tunes to the fifth degree expressed by the drone. *Dha* is preferred in *kāmbhōji svara kalpana* because it is considered an important "soul tone" of the rāga, and as such communicates the emotional aspect of the rāga at the outset of a round.

Example 10.2. Common phrases in *kāmbhōji svara kalpana.*

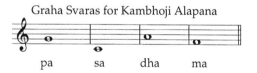

Example 10.3. *Graha svaras.*

Ending tones or *nyāsa svaras* in *ālāpana* and *svara kalpana* must be looked at other than by statistical comparison. Although individual phrases will end on a variety of *svaras* in *ālāpana*, the improvisation as a whole ends on the tonic *(sa)*. Ending tones in *svara kalpana* phrases are generally determined by the first note of the refrain line. Each round of improvised *svaras* then ends on the note above or below that pitch.

Dīrgha svaras (shown in ex. 10.4 are sustained notes that by definition emphasize a *svara*'s importance. The fifth degree *pa* and tonic/octave-tonic *sa* are *dīrgha svaras* in any performance of *kāmbhōji ālāpana*, since they are traditional settling points for resting and tuning with the drone. In *kāmbhōji, dha* is a prominent sustained tone for both improvisatory forms. In *svara kalpana* especially, it provides a break from the constant pulse of *tāḷa*.

Gamaka (Ornamentation)

Although *svaras* constitute the basic unit of musical meaning within the vocabulary of *ālāpana* and *svara kalpana,* they derive their color and individuality from *gamaka* or "ornamentation." A *svara* can be properly defined only when the ornament traditionally associated with it is considered. For example, the *svara ga* (E) in *kāmbhōji* is treated very differently from *ga* in *kalyāṇi rāga,*[12] as example 10.5 shows. The *kāmbhōji ga*s are ornamented with a momentary flick to a higher tone at the end of the principal tone (*ga* to *ma* [F]). In *kalyāṇi rāga,* the sustained *ga* has an ornament that is successively stressed from above. Each *ma* (not the sharped *ma* of the rāga scale) comes down to a prolonged *ga*.

The characteristics of an ornament can vary according to tempo, duration of the note being ornamented, and improvisatory form. In *ālāpana* and *svara kalpana, gamakas* are particularly sensitive to tempo.

Kampita ("oscillating" *gamaka*) is an ornament that is often found in the slower tempos of *ālāpana* and *svara kalpana.* Because it is an oscillation, a sustained *kampita* is used less often in a faster tempo, since it is awkward to

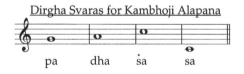

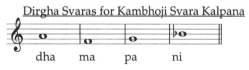

Example 10.4. *Dirgha svaras.*

g   g   g   r   s   (kāmbhōji)

g   ,   ,   (kalyāṇi)

Example 10.5. *Gamaka.*

r   ,   ,   ,   d   p   d   p   m   g   ,   m   g   r   ,   s

Example 10.6. *Kampita.*

r   ,   d   p   d   p   m   g   m   g   r   s

Example 10.7. *Kampita* in faster tempo.

perform. Example 10.6 shows a sustained, oscillated *ri* as part of a characteristic *kāmbhōji* phrase.

Ri is treated differently in faster-tempo *svara kalpana,* since sustained *ri*s (as they might be expressed in the rāga phrase in ex. 10.6) are generally considered ineffective in the pulsed environment of the form. By shortening the oscillation, the phrase in example 10.7 would be a more likely candidate for a faster-tempo *svara kalpana.*

Other ornaments common to both forms are likewise sensitive to tempo. *Odukkal* (stressed from below on successive, non-repeated notes; ex. 10.8) ornaments only faster-tempo notes in *ālāpana* and *svara kalpana.*

Ullāsita, the "sliding" *gamaka,* is most effectively used as an ascending ornament for *ni* in *ālāpana* and *svara kalpana* (ex. 10.9), though the power of the phrase is best realized at a slower tempo.

Finally, some ornaments will more typically occur in one improvisational form than in another, regardless of the rāga. The combination of tempo and rhythmic framework can be a factor in the frequent presence of an ornament

Example 10.8. *Odukkal.*

Example 10.9. *Ullāsita.*

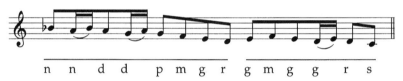

Example 10.10. *Sphurita.*

like *sphurita* (stressed from below on the second of successively repeated notes, ex. 10.10), which is very common in *svara kalpana.*

Sañcāra (Phrase)

Regardless of how essential they are, *svaras* and *gamakas* do not in themselves define a rāga; they become musically meaningful only in the larger context of phrases which, when strung together, constitute the *svarūpa*—the "totality" or "gestalt" of the rāga.

Generally, each rāga has its own characteristic phrases *(rāga-chāya sañcāras)* which can appear regularly in compositions, and which produce instant recognition in an audience.[13] There are also phrases which have become "characteristic" because of their pervasive use in improvisation, though they are not necessarily used in compositions. These phrases may be found in either *ālāpana* or *svara kalpana* (an example in *kāmbhōji* would be *ni–dha–pa*), or they may be especially typical of one rāga form (as mentioned previously with the *kāmbhōji* phrase *ni–dha–pa–dha-ma* or any variation on it).

At the outset of an *ālāpana,* every musician will draw upon certain characteristic phrases which clearly identify the rāga. In *kāmbhōji,* these might include the four phrases shown in example 10.11.

However, meter in *svara kalpana* will usually direct rāga away from the frequent employment of identifying phrases that are typical in *ālāpana.* As a result, there is a difference in the kinds of opening phrases a musician may use.[14] The phrases shown in example 10.11 would not therefore successfully

r , , d p d p m g m g r , s

ṡ , s n d p d , , ṡ

d m g , , p d , , ṡ

m , g , s , s p. d , s

Example 10.11. Four characteristic phrases in *rāga kāmbhōji*.

initiate a *svara kalpana*. Since the first note of the refrain influences both the general pitch area of the *kalpana svaras* preceding it and the direction in which those *svaras* move, phrases concluding on the octave tonic or tonic *sa* could not accomodate a midrange refrain note such as *pa* or *dha*. Svara kalpana is more likely to open with an appropriate scalar phrase, like the three shown in example 10.12.

Meter in *svara kalpana* can also affect rāga-identifying phrases. Such phrases must either be reinterpreted to fit into the rhythmic context, or omitted altogether and replaced with phrases more suited to the staccato-like demands of the form. In either case, certain ornaments would be abbreviated or left out. An illustration of this can be seen in examples 10.13–14, the first of which shows a characteristic phrase with ornaments that could appear in *ālāpana* or slow-tempo *svara kalpana*.

When that same phrase is performed in faster-tempo *svara kalpana,* it changes. One could conceive it as an entirely different phrase, or as a variation. Hence, the original *ālāpana* phrase is abbreviated to the point where it includes simple ornaments on one or two notes (ex. 10.14).

Meter can also alter a phrase's emotional meaning *(bhāva).* The highly orna-

Example 10.12. Opening phrases in *svara kalpana.*

Example 10.13. Characteristic phrase with ornaments.

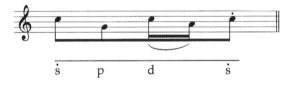

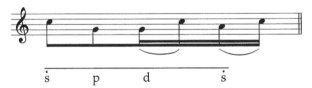

Example 10.14. Related phrase with simplified ornaments.

mented, prolonged *ri* (D) in the characteristic *kāmbhōji* phrase in example 10.15 gives that phrase its "soul" *(jīva).*

If the same characteristic phrase is used in *svara kalpana,* the musician ignores the emotional aspect of that phrase and converts it by filling the prolonged *ri* in with *ga* (E) and *ma* (F), as example 10.16 shows.

s   r   ,   ,   ,   m   g   s

Example 10.15. Ornamented *ri* in characteristic *kāmbhōji* phrase.

s   ,   r   g   m   m   g   s   ,

Example 10.16. Ornamented *ri* in *kāmbhōji svara kalpana.*

The articulation of the notes in this way creates a different feeling from the original *ālāpana* phrase. Because of the extent to which a characteristic (or rāga-identifying) phrase can change, some rāgas are thus considered more appropriate for *ālāpana* than for *svara kalpana.* This is especially true when rāgas are identified by a predominance of slow phrases with many elongated tones.

Thus, the canonical elements of *kāmbhōji rāga*—from the basic *svara* level, to ornamentation, to phrase—have been examined as they behave in *ālāpana* and *svara kalpana.* Rāga, as one of the primary elements of a Karṇāṭak musician's improvisation, can change in different contexts. Here, meter has figured largely in the subtle but distinctive expression of the rāga and its treatment in each form. When musicians perform an *ālāpana, svara kalpana,* or any of the other melodic improvisatory forms in the system, they exhibit sensitivity to both the consistencies and the differences that describe rāga. For them, there is no mystery involved—this is a skill that is learned over many years. A broad system of rules has been absorbed and used like a blueprint for molding the edifice of each improvisatory form. The ability to be conversant and creative with rāga, then, is ultimately what defines the Karṇāṭak musician's art.

Notes

1. The Karṇāṭak musical system is one which is confined geographically to the regions of South India including Andhra Pradesh, Karnātaka, Kerala, and Tamil Nadu. The Hindustāni music system dominates the rest of the states to the north.

2. The idea of improvisation in Karṇāṭak (and Hindustāni) music can be put in historical context where a distinction is made between the free elaboration of a rāga (melody) independent of a composition *(anibaddha),* and the elaboration of a rāga confined within the limits of *tāḷa* (metrical cycle) being attached to a composition *(nibaddha).* *Anibaddha* and *nibaddha* ultimately come from the concept of *ālāpti,* which can be interpreted as "that which is elaborated" (i.e., improvised). *Ālāpti* is discussed at length in the thirteenth-century treatise *Saṅgīta-Ratnākara* by Sārṅgadeva.

3. Brown defines *tāḷa* very concisely as "a metrical cycle of given length *(āvarta),* consisting of a number of durational units of equal size *(akṣara* or *akṣarakala),* which

are grouped into one or more subdivisional sections of variable size *(anga)*" (1965, 6–7).

4. *Tānam* is pulsed rhythmic improvisation characterized by a stereotyped series of rhythmic permutations of twos and threes. *Niraval* is essentially extempore melodic variation on a line of text from a given composition, where each word of the text generally remains fixed within its original place in the *tāla* cycle. Like *svara kalpana, niraval* returns to a refrain, in this case a simple restatement of the beginning of the line selected for elaboration. *Tani āvartanam* is the solo percussion improvisation occurring after the main composition of the concert.

5. For a comprehensive look at both the major and minor structural possibilities of *svara kalpana,* see Cormack 1992 (195–220).

6. The *eduppu* is the point where music "takes off" in the *tāla* cycle. It is essentially the same as *idam,* but is the more vernacular of the two.

7. *Kāmbhōji rāga* first appeared as *pan takkēsi* in the South Indian *tevaram* hymns of the seventh to ninth centuries (Viswanathan 1974, 76).

8. The pitch frequency used for the tonic will vary according to the performer's vocal range or instrument (for example C for men, G for women, D-sharp for violin, G for a small flute). Once the tonic pitch is established, it will remain the same for every item rendered in performance—what Powers calls the "system tonic" (1980, 429–30). Here, C has been taken as the tonic to simplify the reader's understanding of the scale.

9. Musical examples presented in the traditional Indian system of *svara* (solfege) notation are indicated in Roman script. This is a form in which they appear as often as they might in Hindi, Bengali, Tamil, or Telegu. Each *svara* syllable respectively corresponds to the tonic through the seventh degree of the scale. In the musical examples, they are abbreviated as *s r g m p d n.* Dots above the *svaras* indicate the higher octave, and dots below, the lower octave.

In addition to the *svara* syllables, commas mark each pulse or inner time unit of the note. Single or double horizontal lines above a *svara* represent halving or quartering of the inner time unit. Melodic ornaments *(gamakas)* related to any *svara* assume these same time values.

10. This data was obtained from performances of distinguished Karnatak musicians. Included are K. V. Narayanaswamy, T. M. Thyagarajan, Ramnad Krishnan, T. Brinda, M. L. Vasanta Kumari for *ālāpana,* and K. V. Narayanaswamy, Voleti Venkatesvarulu, T. N. Krishnan, N. Ramani, G. N. Balasubramaniam, and T. Viswanathan for *svara kalpana.*

11. *Kalyāni rāga:* C D E F# G A B C–C B A G F# E D C.

12. The exception to rāgas that are identified by *rāga-chāya sañcāra* are those which have been in existence only for the last fifty to one hundred years. These rāgas were created on the basis of scale and not phrase.

13. Also, initial establishment of the rāga is not as critical in *svara kalpana,* since that would already have been accomplished in the *ālāpana* and composition.

References

Brown, Robert E. 1965. "The Mrdanga: A Study of Drumming in South India." Ph.D. thesis, University of California at Los Angeles.

Cormack, Josepha A. 1992. "Svara Kalpana: Melodic/Rhythmic Improvisation in Karnatak Music." Ph.D. thesis, Wesleyan University.

Powers, Harold S. 1980. "Mode." In *The New Grove Dictionary of Music and Musicians,* edited by Stanley Sadie, vol. 12, 376–450. London: Macmillan.

—————. 1984. "Musical Art and Esoteric Theism: Muttuswami Dikshitar's *Anandabhairavi Kirtanams* on Siva and Sakti at Tirivarur." In *Discourses on Siva: Proceedings of a Symposium on the Nature of Religious Imagery,* edited by Michael W. Meister. Philadelphia: University of Pennsylvania Press.

Reck, David. 1983. "A Musician's Tool-Kit: A Study of Five Performances by Thirugokarnam Ramachandra Iyer." Ph.D. thesis, Wesleyan University.

Viswanathan, Tanjore. 1974. "Raga Alapana in South Indian Music." Ph.D. thesis, Wesleyan University.

STUDIES OF INDIVIDUAL ARTISTS

CHAPTER ELEVEN

Setting the Stage: Clara Schumann's Preludes

VALERIE WOODRING GOERTZEN

Late in her life, Clara Schumann (1819–96) notated a series of preludes to represent those she had improvised publicly and privately during her more than sixty-year career. These preludes constitute unusually direct evidence of the practice of improvising introductions to piano pieces, a practice carried over to the piano from lute and harpsichord music in the eighteenth century and continued into the twentieth (Goertzen 1996). Schumann's preludes are of particular interest given their author's stature as a performing artist of the first rank, her gifts as a composer, and her role in winning public acceptance of a serious repertory for piano. During the years 1828–91, Schumann concertized widely in Europe, including Russia and the British Isles (Reich 1985, 275–78), and came to be recognized as a champion of the music of Chopin, Mendelssohn, Henselt, Robert Schumann, and Brahms, as well as that of Beethoven and Bach. She was acclaimed as one of the greatest improvisers of her time ("Liszt in Wien" 1838; Litzmann 1902, 201–2).

Schumann's preludes, which she wrote out at her daughters' request, are preserved in three sources: an autograph (Staatsbibliothek zu Berlin Preußischer Kulturbesitz, Musikabteilung ms. autogr. 9), a copyist's manuscript of the same items (Robert-Schumann-Haus, Zwickau, Nr. 7486, 5), and an autograph containing just four of the preludes (Robert-Schumann-Haus, Nr. 11514-A1). The pieces were never published. The Berlin autograph carries the following note by the Schumanns' daughter, Marie, dated 1929:

> In the last year of her life, our mother, at our request, wrote out the exercises she played before her scales, with which she began her practice daily, as well as a few preludes of the kind she was in the habit of improvising before the pieces, quite freely on the spur of the moment; she also did this publicly, and one could get an idea of her frame of mind from the way in which the harmonies flowed to her.
>
> Now, of course, she maintained that it was not possible for her to capture this type of free improvisation on paper, but she finally gave in to our requests, and these small preludes came into being.[1]

An entry in Schumann's diary suggests that the manuscript was written in October 1895 or shortly thereafter (Litzmann 1908, 601).

In improvising preludes, Schumann engaged in a practice that was well established before her birth. Dozens of collections were published beginning in the late 1760s for amateurs to memorize or use as models for constructing original preludes for harpsichord or piano; further guidelines were given in instruction books by Hummel (1828), Czerny (1983 [1829] and 1839), Kalkbrenner (1970 [1849]), and others. A prelude was a means of trying out an instrument, warming up, focusing the mind of the performer, establishing the key, and displaying technical skill. It could be used to draw the audience's attention and to adapt a given piece to a particular situation or audience (Goertzen 1996). In a small didactic book entitled *Klavier und Gesang* (*Piano and Song*) published in 1853, Schumann's father, Friedrich Wieck, recommended preluding on practical grounds, advice that stemmed no doubt from many miserable experiences with inadequate instruments during their concert tours:

> Before beginning a piece, play a few fluent arpeggios and some decent passages or scales, *piano* and *forte,* up and down the keyboard—but none of the stupid stunts I have heard from many a virtuoso—in order to make certain that the piano in its condition of the moment will not put any unanticipated difficulties in your way. . . . And test the inevitable pedal! A rattling, squeaking, snarling pedal is a pianistic horror. (Wieck 1988, 113)

Wieck's studies, published in 1875, include examples of short preludes to be practiced in every key and used as introductions to or transitions between scales or pieces (Wieck ca. 1980, 41).

Improvisation in Clara Wieck's Training

Friedrich Wieck intended that Clara would become a celebrated pianist; every aspect of her life was directed toward this goal from age five onwards. Until about 1840 Wieck owned a *Piano-Fabrik*—a store where he sold and evidently also serviced pianos mainly of Viennese makers Conrad Graf and Andreas Stein—as well as a music lending library (Wieck 1988, 3; Meichsner 1875, 25). But he hoped to gain renown as a teacher through his daughter's successes.[2]

Wieck's *Klavier und Gesang* is constructed as a series of vignettes, several of them conversations between himself, portrayed as "DAS"—*Der alte Schulmeister* (the old schoolmaster)—and students, parents, or amateur musicians. Although it does not offer a systematic account of his teaching techniques, it clearly outlines his principal concerns: (1) the cultivation of a beautiful singing tone (hence the title of the book), (2) the learning of theory and harmony from the first lessons, (3) the tailoring of teaching methods to accommodate student's individual needs and abilities, and (4) the need to avoid overtaxing the student with long practice sessions.[3] He described his approach as allied with the school of Field, which he considered to stand in opposition to the mechanical Viennese school. Although he recognized frivolousness and empty virtuosity in the new French music of the 1830s, he also recognized in it the extension of Field's ability to make the piano sing (see his review of Chopin's Opus 2, quoted in Joss 1902, 124–25). Upon hearing Kalkbrenner play in 1833, Wieck pronounced him the principal representative of *complete* playing, combining a singing tone with mechanical mastery of the instrument (Joss 1902, 143–44). If Wieck should die, he instructed, his daughter was to study only with Kalkbrenner (Wieck 1912, 11).

The young Clara did not learn to read music in her first year of study. Her father sought instead to develop her touch and tone together with her knowledge of harmony and rhythm without the distraction of written notes. She played by rote the small pieces he taught her, learned to play cadential progressions in all the keys and to transpose, and began to improvise (Reich 1985, 44, 290; Wieck 1988, 11–18). In Wieck's essay on elementary instruction in piano playing, which he claimed reflected the method he used in teaching his daughters, he suggested letting the student invent small exercises in the cadences, employing the common chords of a key "in ever new figurations and passages" (Wieck 1988, 17). He illustrated several means of fleshing out chordal progressions in his *Studies* (ca. 1980, 36–38). Clara's training in improvisation continued with her study of Czerny's newly published *Systematic Introduction to Improvisation on the Pianoforte,* Op. 200, around 1830, which enabled her to improvise on given themes (Litzmann 1902, 26; Czerny's publication is discussed in Goertzen 1996). In February 1837, Wieck reported that his daughter was taking counterpoint lessons with Siegfried Dehn in Berlin in order to learn to create circle canons and fugues, a skill that would be of great help to her in improvising (Wieck 1968, 58).[4] Other components of her training were the study of voice, violin, score reading, orchestration, composition, theory and harmony, and French and English, as well as frequent visits to the opera, participation in performances in her home in Leipzig, and regular exercise in the fresh air (see also Reich 1985, 44–45).

Improvisation, then, was a fundamental part of Clara's study of the piano throughout her years of training, a means of developing both technical mastery of the instrument and understanding of the musical styles of her day. Wieck encouraged this facet of her training also as a method of creating compositions that she could perform and publish, because it allowed her to display her individual technique and creativity, and because it was expected of a virtuoso. Early nineteenth-century audiences took great pleasure in witnessing the creation of fantasies and variation sets, often on themes from operas in vogue, and the embellishment of existing compositions through preludes, cadenzas, and ornamentation. Allowing audiences to be privy to an artist's creative impulses (or to believe they were), even as these were acted upon, played to the public's preoccupation with fashion, originality, and technical facility, as well as to the Romantic conception of music as essentially elusive (Plantinga 1967, 16–23; Wangermée 1970). Improvisation was so highly regarded that pianists who lacked training in the art resorted to memorizing preludes in instruction manuals and published sets; they could pretend to supply these "off the cuff," in imitation of the gestures of accomplished artists (Czerny 1839, 3:119, 123).

Improvisation in Clara Wieck's Early Programs

From 1830 to 1838 Clara toured with her father first in Germany, then in Paris and Vienna. Her concert repertory in these years consisted largely of variation sets, rondos, arrangements, and other showpieces reflecting the popular taste of the day,[5] though she studied many more serious compositions (Litzmann 1908, 615–24; Reich 1985, 260–64). Improvisations were a regular feature of her private performances. Among documented instances are improvisations on given themes at Kapellmeister Reissiger's (a teacher of Clara's) and before Princess Louise in Dresden in March 1830, at the Weimar Court in October 1831, and at Koch's in Erfurt later that month (Wieck 1968, 22, 29, 35; Litzmann 1902, 19, 30). Concerning Clara's performance at Reissiger's, Wieck boasted to his wife: "No one could believe that she could compose, since that has never been true of girls of her age, and when she improvised on a given theme, all were beside themselves" (Wieck 1968, 27). On another occasion he claimed, "Clara, as a girl, already has an advantage over all the female pianists in the world, in that she can improvise (*frei phantasieren*)" (Kleefeld 1910, 7). Even if one assumes a degree of exaggeration in this and other accounts by Wieck of his daughter's successes, it is clear that her improvisational abilities were exceptional, and not just by comparison with those of other women. An article appearing in the *Neue Zeitschrift für Musik* in 1838 comparing attributes of several top pianists ranked the nineteen-year-old Clara Wieck's improvisational skills as second only to Liszt's ("Liszt in Wien" 1838; portions quoted in Litzmann 1902, 201–2).

According to the collection of approximately thirteen hundred printed and handwritten programs for Clara's concerts which is preserved in the archive of the Robert-Schumann-Haus, she programmed extended improvisations rarely, and only in her early concerts. In Gotha on 31 October 1831, her free fantasy on "Einsam bin ich nicht allein" served as a prelude to the final piece on the program—Herz's Variations, Opus 20, on this theme with quartet accompaniment (Program Collection #10). Her decision to close the first half of her concert in Paris on 9 April 1832 with an improvisation on given themes (PC #18; Meichsner 1875, 64) was a bow to the French taste for display pieces based on vocal music (see Reich 1985, 263; Plantinga 1967, 16–23).

After Clara returned to Germany from Paris in 1832, her programs grew more serious, incorporating more short works of Chopin (she had performed his variations on "La ci darem la mano," Opus 2, in 1831) and, in time, of Mendelssohn, Bach, Robert Schumann, Henselt, and herself. She used improvisation to fit these unfamiliar and in some cases distinctly non-showy pieces into concert situations. The first half of her concert in Plauen in April 1834 closed with two Grand Etudes of Chopin, with free introductions played by Clara (PC #41); her other performances of Chopin etudes around this time also may have had introductions. By the later 1830s, Clara's programs usually included a group of three or four short pieces, which constituted one number on the printed program and was performed as a continuous unit, with transitions connecting one piece with the next. Her second soirée given in Berlin on 1 March 1837, for example, featured a Bach fugue, a new *Song without Words* of Mendelssohn (from manuscript), and a mazurka and etude by Chopin, pieces which a reviewer described as "following directly one after another and introduced by short preludes based on the themes of the solo pieces" ("Berlin, im April" 1837, 257; PC). A review of her concerts in Vienna the following December speaks of "suites" of small pieces which "demonstrate the pianist's intention to show the individuality of each master, to represent him, his innermost being with understanding and feeling, and from a full soul" ("Berlin, im April" 1837, 257).[6] Concerts in Prague in November 1837 included groups of pieces that a reviewer for the *Neue Zeitschrift* described as "mosaics" of smaller compositions by several masters ("Clara Wieck in Prag" 1838, 6). Clara's preluding was not confined, however, to these short pieces. The Prague reviewer lamented her failure to play an extended free fantasy in these words: "That she could have done so is proved not only by her compositions and her performance of works of other composers, but also by the often surprisingly beautiful preludes with which she always prepared the public for the next composition" (7). A Dresden reviewer reported in the same month that Clara preluded before *most* of her pieces ("Aus Dresden" 1838, 201).

Clara's preludes and interludes helped to provide a context for the short pieces, which the public was unaccustomed to hearing in concerts and even resisted. Each piece was supported by the others in the group, and the resulting number on the program was comparable to the more usual showpieces in length and perhaps also in level of variety.[7] The approach met with success in some quarters: audiences demanded that pieces be repeated, either immediately or at a subsequent concert (Schumann and Schumann 1984, 58, 79). But Clara's serious programming was also criticized. Josef Fischoff, a conservatory teacher in Vienna and co-worker on Robert Schumann's paper, reported to Robert in 1838 that Clara was the first to play fugues and etudes in public in Vienna, and that audiences were prejudiced against this, having made up their minds ahead of time and through intrigues (Litzmann 1902, 200–201). A review from Hamburg the previous year criticized her program as too serious on the whole and singled out her selection from Mendelssohn's *Songs without Words* as particularly unsuitable for a concert (cited in Klassen 1990, 263).[8] Clara would continue to come up against complaints of this sort for many years, for instance on a second visit to Vienna in 1846–47, and in England and Pest in the 1850s ("Konzert-Salon" 1847; Litzmann 1905, 401). She gave a great deal of thought to the matter of finding a comfortable balance between her own tastes and those of her public (e.g., Schumann and Schumann 1987, 750; see also Reich 1985, 260–65).[9]

Clara's Programming of Robert's Works

Clara took particular care in programming works of Robert Schumann, of which she was the main proponent. The public found his music difficult, even aggravating, and neither Clara nor Robert could afford to have their careers jeopardized through incautious programming.[10] She played a few of Robert's most accessible pieces in Leipzig and during her tours with Wieck in the 1830s, among them the Toccata (beginning in September 1834), selections from the *Paganini Caprices* and *Etudes Symphoniques* (August 1837), and from the *Fantasiestücke* (August 1838) (PC; see also Schoppe 1978). She also played his works in private gatherings in Prague, Dresden, Vienna, Nürnberg, and other cities (Schumann and Schumann 1984, 44, 45, 77, 89–90, 108; 1987, 353). In Paris in 1839, where in her view the public was less knowledgeable about music than in Germany, she played Robert's pieces, including most of *Carnaval,* only for groups of connoisseurs (1987, 454, 469, 537, 566). After returning to Germany she offered more serious programs, including more works of Robert (whom she married in 1840): the Concerto, Piano Quintet, other chamber works with piano, and a few solo pieces. But it was only after her husband's confinement at Endenich in 1854 that Clara began to play selected pieces from his piano cycles on a regular basis (Reich 1985, 265–75; Struck 1989, 294).[11]

Still Clara was obliged to proceed cautiously. In 1856 she noted the existence of a real public for her husband's music in Vienna, but characterized the English public as "dreadfully behind the times," accepting only Mendelssohn from among the newer composers (Litzmann 1913, 1:134); at least one reviewer urged her to accept the fact that Robert's works would never succeed in England ("Londoner Briefe" 1856). Yet Clara noted a marked change in English attitudes during her visit in 1865 and wrote of a vogue for Robert's works in Paris in 1862 and in Russia in 1864 (Schoppe 1978, 21; Litzmann 1908, 116, 151).[12] By breaking the ice with some of the small pieces, then gradually introducing the larger piano works as well as chamber and orchestral works in her concerts, Clara played a crucial role in establishing a performance tradition for Robert Schumann's compositions in Europe, one carried forward by Rubinstein, Tausig, Brahms, and others (Schoppe 1978).

The Notated Preludes

When examining Schumann's preludes, one must bear in mind that she intended the notated versions as an indication of her improvisations, not as authoritative readings that were essentially fixed. In her diary she commented on the difficulty of writing out the preludes: "I would like to write out the preludes that I play [literally, make] before the scales, but it is so difficult because I do it differently every time, just as it occurs to me at the piano" (Litzmann 1908, 601).[13] The fact that the three sources transmitting the preludes agree closely does not argue against this. The copy and the Zwickau autograph were both made from the Berlin autograph, probably for use by the Schumanns' daughters.[14]

An inventory of the contents of the Berlin autograph appears as table 11.1.[15] The preludes are arranged in two groups, corresponding to the two types of preludes Marie Schumann mentions in her explanatory note—exercises and introductions. The seven exercises, notated in pencil, are separated from the remaining preludes, notated in ink, by three blank pages (i.e., the remainder of the bifolium containing just the last two measures of the seventh exercise on its first recto; these pages are represented by a dotted line in table 11.1). The exercises are ordered by key according to the circle of fifths, with the relative minor following each major key; the blank pages suggest that Schumann in-

Table 11.1. Contents of Clara Schumann's prelude collection

Title	Key	Meter	No. of Measures	Comments
Nr.1	C	C	40	right hand study
Nr.2	a	C	28	left hand study (a pair with Nr.1)
Nr.3	G	C	24	right hand study
Nr.4	e	C	32	left hand study
Nr.5	D	C	20	right hand study (similar to Nr.4)
Nr.6	b	C	16	left hand study
[Nr.7]	A	12/8	8	right hand study
- - - - -				
Nr.1 Andante. Ad libitum	C	C	15	with descending tag
Nr.2 Andante	f	2/4	35	for F-Minor Sonata
Nr.3 Allegro	E	2/4	37	
Nr.4 Andante	E♭	3/4	31	
Nr.5 Maëstoso	d	C	23	with unbarred beginning
Vorspiel zu "des Abends"	D♭	6/8	16	
Frei	G	C	16	
Frei. Allegro	A♭	C	17	mm. 6–9a rewritten on separate sheet
Vorspiel zu Aufschwung. Leidenschaftlich.	f	6/8	23	13 mm. with shorter ending
Vorspiel zu Schlummerlied. Andante.	E♭	6/8	20	
Allegretto	E♭	C	12	
- - - - -				
Einfache Praeludien	C	C	15	chordal
für Schüler (2)	A♭	C	15	chordal

Source: Staatsbibliothek zu Berlin Preußischer Kulturbesitz, Musikabteilung ms. autogr. 9.

tended to continue in this pattern to more distant keys.[16] Each exercise is constructed using a repeated figure in one hand accompanied by chords in the other; the odd-numbered studies are for the right hand, the even-numbered ones for the left (see ex. 11.1 for the opening of Number 4). The harmony is structured in four-bar units in all but the last prelude, in 12/8, where the units are a single bar. The progressions include secondary dominants and diminished seventh chords; suspensions and anticipations are used in several to strengthen the dominant in the final cadence. This first group of preludes is for warming up, strengthening the hands, developing an even touch, and solidifying harmonic progressions that were the basis for improvisation.[17]

The "Einfache Praeludien für Schüler" listed at the foot of table 11.1 are two progressions of fifteen chords each, one in C major and one in A-flat, notated on the verso of the last leaf of the autograph. These progressions could be fleshed out to produce technical exercises resembling those in Schumann's first group (though they would be longer if the four-bar scheme were followed). The exercises and the "Einfache Praeludien" both stem from Wieck's teaching of technique and harmony through improvisation. His *Piano Studies,* prepared by Marie Wieck, present shorter "Accordpraeludien" (chordal preludes) together with simple exercises based on them (Wieck ca. 1980, 36–40). Czerny's *Systematic Introduction* offers further examples of preludes based on simple progressions (1983, 7–11).[18]

Schumann's second group of preludes consists of eleven introductions of the sort she improvised in private and public circumstances. These preludes vary in length, tempo, meter, and character, and are not ordered by key (see table 11.1).[19] Although the preludes contain some brilliant passages, they are not primarily display pieces.[20] And although the preludes are richer and more varied than those in collections published for amateur use during Schumann's lifetime, they resemble those sets in characteristic ways. They are short—most of them between two and five lines long—and present several melodic or rhythmic ideas in turn; these are elaborated upon by means of sequential figures and progressions before breaking off to give way to another idea. This flexible structure, which accommodates the expansion or compression of materials at the pianist's discretion, is usual in published preludes for piano. Also typical is the prolongation of dominant harmony in the final section by means of pedal point (Goertzen 1996, 312–15).[21] The first half of Schumann's C-major prelude is given as example 11.2.

Among Schumann's set are introductions to four pieces by Robert Schumann: "Des Abends" and "Aufschwung" from *Fantasiestücke,* Opus 12, "Schlummerlied" from *Albumblätter,* Opus 124, and the slow movement of the F-minor Sonata.[22] The remaining preludes exhibit only general correspondences with pieces she is known to have studied or performed (see Litzmann 1908, 615–24; Süsskind 1977, 26, 35–36, 79–81, 147–49, 207–10, 228–33). Instead they exemplify an essentially abstract improvisatory mode of playing,

Example 11.1. Clara Schumann, Prelude in E Minor, beginning. (Staatsbibliothek zu Berlin Preußischer Kulturbesitz, Musikabteilung ms. autogr. 9. Used by permission.)

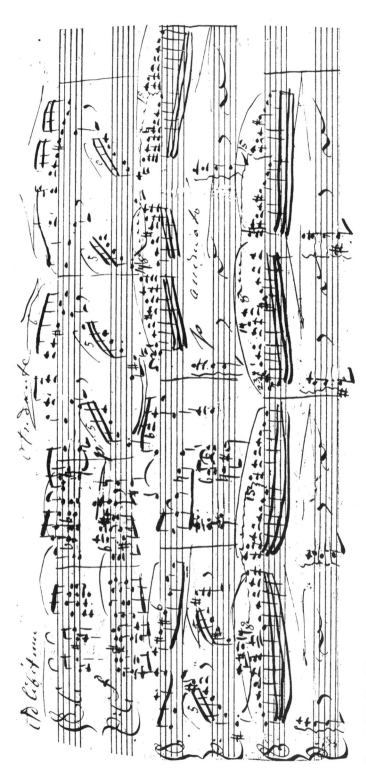

Example 11.2. Clara Schumann, Prelude in C Major, beginning. (Staatsbibliothek zu Berlin Preußischer Kulturbesitz, Musikabteilung ms. autogr. 9. Used by permission.)

with only occasional bits of melody, and one can only speculate about the pieces they introduced.[23] A sense of temporal freedom is conveyed through indications such as "frei" and "ad libitum," fluctuations of tempo, irregular groupings of notes, and, in the D-minor prelude, the inclusion of an unbarred passage. Like her exercises, Schumann's introductory preludes reflect the chordal approach taught by her father and by Czerny in his *Systematic Introduction.* Unadorned chordal progressions appear, as well as progressions embellished through octave displacement, arpeggios, scale passages, triplets, and other figures.

The Preludes to Robert's Pieces

"Des Abends," "Aufschwung," and "Schlummerlied" were among the pieces by Robert that Clara performed in public most frequently and kept in her repertory to the end. In a letter to Robert in March 1838, she named "Aufschwung" and "Des Abends" as among her favorite pieces in his new *Fantasiestücke,* a set which both Clara and Robert considered to be more accessible to the public than, for example, *Carnaval* (Schumann and Schumann 1984, 108; 1987, 367, 414). "Schlummerlied," which Robert presented to her and their infant daughter, Marie, as a Christmas gift in 1841,[24] was one of the "old favorites" Schumann was playing in October 1895, shortly before she wrote out her collection of preludes (Litzmann 1908, 601).

Each of these three pieces she almost always programmed within a group of three. Schumann's program collection, which covers her public concerts and soirées but not, of course, her playing in less formal surroundings at home or with friends, documents an early performance of "Des Abends" (composed in 1837) at Dorpat in 1844 on her Russian tour with Robert, and sixty-five additional performances between 1854 and 1880 in every country she toured.[25] From 1854 to 1871 she played the piece several times a year nearly every year, as many as nine times a year in the mid- to late fifties.

In more than two-thirds of the documented performances of "Des Abends," the piece either preceded or followed "Traumeswirren," number 7 of Opus 12. In a letter of February 1838, Robert himself referred to these pieces as a possible pair, further warning that "In der Nacht" (Opus 12, no. 5) was probably too long for concert use (Litzmann 1902, 184; Schumann and Schumann 1984, 105). The third piece of the group, usually in last position, might also be by Robert—for example, the D-Minor Romance from Opus 32, "Jagdlied" from *Waldszenen* (Opus 82), or in fact "In der Nacht" or another piece from Opus 12. Other works rounding out the group included Mendelssohn's *Songs without Words* and *Rondo capriccio* (Opus 14), Chopin's A-flat Impromptu and etudes, Heller's *Saltarello,* Weber's Rondo from the C-Major Sonata, Scarlatti's *Tempo di ballo,* Bach's Gavotte, and a piece from Kirchner's *Albumblätter.* From the 1860s on, Schumann's concerts often included two groups of short pieces. Then in the early 1870s she programmed four and five pieces from Opus 12 together (PC #938, 1017).

"Schlummerlied" is named in eighty-four of the concert programs from 1855 to 1887. (Litzmann 1908, 620, and Reich 1985, 269, list the piece in Schumann's repertory from 1854.) In more than half of its appearances it is the first of a group of pieces. Works programmed with it included Bach's Gavotte in D Minor, Mendelssohn's *Rondo capriccio,* one or more of the *Songs without Words,* Chopin's C-sharp Minor Impromptu, and Robert Schumann's "Jagd-lied," "Traumeswirren," "Aufschwung," and D-Minor Romance. Schumann also chose "Schlummerlied" as an encore in at least two London concerts (added by hand to PC #392 and 1273).

The program collection documents thirty-one performances of "Auf-schwung" between 1859 and 1879, plus an additional one in 1887. None of these took place in France or Russia, though Schumann very likely played the piece privately in these countries.[26] More often than not, the piece was pro-grammed as the first of a group of three; in nearly half of the performances, it either followed or directly preceded "Warum?" (Opus 12, no. 3). Its other most frequent companion pieces were Chopin's Waltz in A-flat, the Scherzo from Weber's A-flat Sonata, and Robert Schumann's "Des Abends," "Traumeswir-ren," "Schlummerlied," and F-Major Novelette.

By including preludes to these three pieces in her collection, Schumann transmitted versions of introductions to pieces that she especially loved, that she had performed in numerous public concerts, and that she often played as the first of a group. (Although "Des Abends" led off a group in only about 20 percent of her documented performances of it, this piece is, of course, the first number in Opus 12.) Her less formal performances featured similar groupings of short pieces and afforded further opportunities for preluding.

The situation with Robert's F-Minor Sonata (Opus 14, composed in 1836) is very different. There is no record of a public performance by Clara Schu-mann either of the Sonata as a whole or of its slow movement, which was based on an unidentified theme of hers and entitled "Quasi Variazioni, Andantino de Clara Wieck" (concerning the Sonata see Reich 1985, 231–32; Roessner 1975, 98–130).[27] Schumann noted in her diary for 12 October 1853, just a few weeks after the publication of the four-movement version of the work as "Grande Sonate pour le pianoforte," that she had performed the Sonata as part of a musical program at her home (Litzmann 1905, 282–83). Although she wrote that she played Robert's F-Minor Sonata ("Ich spielte erst Roberts F-moll-Sonate"), Litzmann listed only the Variation movement and the second Scherzo (composed for Opus 14 but not included in either published version) as in her repertory, assigning the Variation movement to the year 1871 (Litz-mann 1908, 623–24), perhaps working from evidence in diaries that no longer survive. Thus it seems that Schumann used a prelude resembling her notated one in F minor primarily, and perhaps exclusively, in private circumstances. She may have introduced the Variation movement in this way as early as 1836 and, especially if Litzmann's repertory list is correct, even after 1871.

Each of the preludes to works of Robert Schumann begins by introducing the main theme of its corresponding piece and continues with materials derived from this theme. The songlike melody of "Schlummerlied," which Robert accompanied with a syncopated rocking figure (ex. 11.3b), is set by Clara as the top voice of a simple homophonic texture (ex. 11.3a). The melody is allowed to wander in the middle of the second phrase, which is left unresolved in a deceptive cadence in measures 8–9. There is an ascent from tonic to dominant in a sequential passage in measures 9–13, based on a half-step motive and upper neighbor figure from measures 3–4. The final segment of the prelude presents another reworking of the main theme, which descends this time to the tonic with the help of secondary dominants. The prolonged dominant harmony in measures 17–18 underscores another reference to the melody of measure 3.

Although Clara reinterprets Robert's materials somewhat, her main concern is to set the key and mood for this little lullaby and to acquaint the listener with its melody.[28] Such a prelude would have been of obvious advantage on the dozens of occasions when "Schlummerlied" was programmed as the first of a group of pieces. Following the blustery "Jagdlied," also in E-flat, the prelude would have effected a change of character. Where "Schlummerlied" followed works in distant keys (e.g., Chopin's C-sharp Minor Impromptu, Mendelssohn's *Rondo capriccio* [in E] or Bach's D-Minor Gavotte), a harmonic reorientation would have been needed more urgently. It is very possible that Schumann moved away from the tonality of one piece in her improvisation before embarking on what she notated as the prelude to the next, creating a transition resembling those described by reviewers of her early concerts.[29] Where "Schlummerlied" was played as an encore, a brief prelude might have served as an announcement of the piece to come.

In the prelude to "Aufschwung" (ex. 11.4a), which Clara Schumann marked *Leidenschaftlich* (passionately), she incorporates two principal themes from the piece. The opening motive (ex. 11.4b) is first carried upward sequentially. Following a series of descending chords that come to rest on F minor, the material of the second section of Robert's piece (mm. 16 ff, ex. 11.4c) is presented, and its half-step figure is developed using diminished seventh chords. A brief enharmonic change from D-flat major to C-sharp minor is followed by movement again to F minor and a reappearance of the main theme over tonic six-four; a forceful authentic cadence confirms F minor as the tonic.[30] Schumann also provided an alternative, shorter ending for this prelude, which carries the piece's second theme upward, outlining an F-minor arpeggio; this version omits the less stable middle section and the return of the opening melody.

The establishment of a clear tonal frame of reference in both versions of this prelude greatly affects the way "Aufschwung" is heard. The piece plays on an ambiguity between A-flat major and F minor as tonal center, and it is only in the fourth and final appearance of the main theme, in the last two measures of the piece, that the principal melody turns abruptly and surprisingly toward F

Example 11.3. *a*, Clara Schumann, Prelude to "Schlummerlied." (Staatsbibliothek zu Berlin Preußischer Kulturbesitz, Musikabteilung ms. autogr. 9. Used by permission.) *b*, Robert Schumann, "Schlummerlied," beginning. (From *Robert Schumann's Werke*, edited by Clara Schumann [Leipzig: Breitkopf & Härtel, 1879], series 7, vol. 6, p. 93. Used by permission of Breitkopf & Härtel, Wiesbaden.)

b.

Example 11.3. *Continued*

minor. Evidently Schumann judged that her audiences needed help coping with
the tonal structure of "Aufschwung." And it was, of course, in her best interest
to ensure that the closing measures of the piece had a welcome, not perplexing
effect. She did not go so far as to present Robert's entire melody with the
conclusion in F minor, however, which would have preempted the "soaring"
consequent phrase (mm. 5–6) and also lessened the impact of the ending too
much.

A version of this prelude would have served well in the many performances
in which "Aufschwung" was the first of a group of pieces. As far as key relationships were concerned, "Aufschwung" would have followed "Schlummerlied," "Traumeswirren," or the F-Major Novelette fairly well, and Chopin's
Waltz in A-flat, the Scherzo from Weber's A-flat Sonata, and of course "Des
Abends" very smoothly. Thus in the programs that included "Aufschwung," it
would seem that introducing themes and clarifying tonality in this piece were
more important than effecting a smooth harmonic transition from the preceding piece.

Schumann's F-minor prelude is a miniature fantasy based on ideas drawn
from the Variation movement of Opus 14. It begins with a somewhat simplified
version of the theme (ex. 11.5a), then leads by means of sequence to a passage
based on a figure from Variation 4 (ex. 11.5b). After taking up a figure from
Variation 2 (ex. 11.5c), the prelude closes with a series of arpeggios.[31] The
addition of the prelude to the Variation movement, which begins directly with
the theme, creates a design that was common in notated and non-notated music
of the period.

One might ask why Schumann's preludes to Robert's pieces elaborate on
materials drawn from these pieces, whereas the remaining notated preludes are
more general, built of figures and progressions that were proper to a given
character or perhaps key. In practice she may have used both approaches in
introducing pieces by various composers. But it may be that Schumann be-

Example 11.4. *a,* Clara Schumann, Prelude to "Aufschwung." (Staatsbibliothek zu Berlin Preußischer Kulturbesitz, Musikabteilung ms. autogr. 9. Used by permission.) *b,* Robert Schumann, "Aufschwung," beginning. *c,* Robert Schumann, "Aufschwung," mm. 16 ff. (From *Robert Schumann's Werke,* edited by Clara Schumann [Leipzig: Breitkopf & Härtel, 1879], series 7, vol. 2, p. 84. Used by permission of Breitkopf & Härtel, Wiesbaden.)

lieved her audiences needed fairly direct preparation for her husband's works, especially in her early performances of them, and for this reason designed introduction built around principal themes. Such a consideration also seems to have motivated her incorporation of themes into preludes to unfamiliar works of Bach, Mendelssohn, and Chopin in the late 1830s. In her preludes to Rob-

Example 11.5. Clara Schumann, Prelude in F Minor, excerpts. (Staatsbibliothek zu Berlin Preußischer Kulturbesitz, Musikabteilung ms. autogr. 9. Used by permission.)

ert's pieces, moreover, Schumann found the opportunity to build on her husband's music, just as she did in many of her more formal compositions (and as
he did on hers—see Klassen 1990; Cai 1989, 56–60; Reich 1985, 231–49).

Reviews and concert programs referring specifically to Schumann's preluding beyond the 1830s have not been found. Yet there is ample evidence to
suggest that she continued to improvise preludes in concerts even after Robert's
pieces were well established (by the 1860s) and the format of a group of short
pieces was set. Nearly all of her documented public performances of "Schlummerlied" and the two pieces from Opus 12 were given after the mid-1850s, and
she continued to perform these pieces into the 1880s. Although Schumann is
known to have composed only a couple of formal, notated pieces after Robert's
death in 1856,[32] improvisation was part of her music making throughout her
life. Concert reports refer to her addition of embellishments to Beethoven's E-
flat Concerto in 1844 ("Leipzig" 1844) and to Chopin's Impromptu in C-sharp
Minor in 1871 ("Berichte" 1871). Eugenie Schumann's reminiscences tell of

254 • *Valerie Woodring Goertzen*

her mother's lengthy improvisations played in private of an evening (Schumann 1927, 96–97), and Schumann's diary notes that she began her daily practice sessions with improvised preludes in the 1890s (Litzmann 1908, 601; see also Schumann 1927, 17). Moreover, Marie Schumann's note to the Berlin autograph of the preludes implies that her mother improvised before pieces even late in her life. That the practice of supplying preludes and interludes in performance was still current in Europe in the early 1870s is clear from the writings of the American pianist, Amy Fay (S. Margaret W. McCarthy, personal communication, 1991; McCarthy 1995, 161). As late as 1912, Marie Wieck commented on the appropriateness of modest transitional preludes:

> I ally myself with the artists who introduce their pieces with preludes that are not too long. Clara played only a few nice chords before her pieces. On the other hand, Bülow and the others improvised not only on the upcoming piece, but also on the preceding one, so that they were a long time getting past the prelude. Nevertheless, I do not mean to suggest that one should go to an unrelated key without any transition. (Wieck 1912, 348)

Schumann's collection exemplifies two categories of nineteenth-century preludes—exercises and introductions.[33] Her preludes of both types are grounded in the training she received in improvisation from her earliest lessons. In her early concerts, Clara Wieck preluded to display her improvisational skills and technique: preluding, like composing and improvising on given themes, was expected of concertizing pianists. When she began to incorporate short pieces of Chopin, Mendelssohn, Henselt, and Bach into her concerts in the 1830s, she wove these together with improvised preludes and interludes to create a structure roughly on the scale of the usual showpieces. Each small piece was supported by those surrounding it, and the improvised segments helped lessen the newness of the pieces and were of interest themselves. In this way, her preludes played a role in the development of what came to be the conventional recital format—a work by Bach or Scarlatti, a sonata or comparable work, and one or more groups of short pieces. Schumann played programs of this kind, without assisting artists, in Russia in 1844 and elsewhere in later years (Reich 1985, 269).

In preludes to the pieces of Robert, Schumann sought to help audiences find a way into his individual musical language. With the exception of the F-Minor Sonata, which she reserved for herself and those close to her, the pieces for which she notated introductions were among those she performed most often—in many countries and over a span of several decades. They were among the earliest of Robert's pieces to become widely known, and helped to lay the groundwork for the gradual acceptance of his oeuvre as a whole. For Schumann, such preludes were also a means of responding in her own medium to Robert's music while leaving his musical texts intact.

In the preludes—particularly the introductory preludes—one recognizes the creative outlet Schumann found in improvisation. Here she could put her talent and training to work in the medium in which she was most at home, without having the results subjected to intense scrutiny by reviewers and the public, and without the inevitable comparison with the music of Robert. On many occasions Clara Schumann expressed insecurity about her abilities as a composer (Cai 1989; Reich 1985, 228–31). But she seems to have had no doubts about her ability to improvise. That came easily to her, so much so that Robert felt it necessary to channel her creative energies to notated works: "One word of advice, *don't improvise too much;* too much gets away that could be put to better use. Resolve always to get everything down on paper right away" (Schumann and Schumann 1984, 307).[34] In notating sample preludes toward the end of her life, Clara Schumann endeavored to document an improvisatory practice that for decades had provided an outlet for self-expression and a means of furthering her artistic ideals.

Notes

Research on this project was funded by a travel grant from the Deutscher Akademischer Austauschdienst. I am indebted to Bernhard Appel and the staff of the Robert-Schumann-Forschungsstelle in Düsseldorf, to Joseph Kruse and Inge Hermstrüwer at the Heinrich-Heine-Institut, and to Gerd Nauhaus and his staff at the Robert-Schumann-Haus, Zwickau, for their generous assistance during my visit. I wish to thank Wolfgang Goldhan for providing me with a microfilm of the Berlin manuscript, and Nancy Reich for her guidance and suggestions. I presented an early version of this paper at the 1993 national meeting of the American Musicological Society in Montreal.

1. Interlaken, Feb. 1929. Marie Schumann: Erläuterung zu den Niederschriften in diesem Buch: In ihrem letzten Lebensjahre schrieb unsre Mutter auf unser Bitten die Uebungen nieder wie sie sie in ihre Tonleitern, mit denen sie täglich ihr Studium begann, einflocht, sowie einige Vorspiele, wie sie sie vor den Stücken zu improvisieren pflegte, ganz frei dem Moment hingegeben; auch öffentlich tat sie dies u. man konnte aus der Art wie ihr die Harmonien zuströmten, ermessen wie sie disponiert war.

Nun meinte sie zwar es sei ihr nicht möglich diese Art von freiem Phantasieren festzuhalten, doch gab sie endlich unsere Bitten nach und so entstanden diese kleinen Vorspiele. (All translations are by the author unless otherwise noted.)

2. Wieck also trained Clara's half-sisters Marie and Cäcilie as concert pianists. Clara's mother, Marianne Tromlitz, an accomplished soprano and pianist, left Wieck before Clara's fifth birthday (Reich 1985, 32–37).

3. Points 2 and 3 may show the influence of the system of Johann Bernhard Logier, which was popular in Germany at the time (Reich 1985, 289). Much of Wieck's approach was clearly individual, however.

4. Clara and Robert Schumann studied counterpoint together in the mid-1840s; Clara's *III Praeludien und Fugen,* Op. 16, were among the outgrowths of this study.

5. Wieck considered the study of salon pieces useful for the technical exercise they afforded, as well as for their value as crowd-pleasers (Wieck 1988, 40, 99–100).

6. According to the printed programs, the short pieces played on December 14 were Henselt's "Wenn ich ein Vöglein wär," Chopin's Nocturne in F-sharp Major and Arpeg-

gio Etude no. 11, and Henselt's Andante und Allegro; on December 21 they were Bach's Prelude and Fugue in C-sharp Major and Chopin's Mazurka in F-sharp Minor and Etude no. 5 in G-flat. The review notes that the difficult fugue of Bach and the bagatelles of Chopin and Henselt were repeated by demand ("Wien. Musikal. Chronik" 1838). I am grateful to Camilla Cai for rechecking these programs in Zwickau.

7. Whether the fact that Clara was female made her performance of these short pieces more acceptable to the public is a question that warrants investigation. Kallberg discusses the association of the nocturne and other (but not all) categories of short pieces with the feminine (Kallberg 1996; see also Kallberg 1992).

8. In December 1837 Clara remarked in a letter to Robert that Mendelssohn's *Songs without Words* lay untouched in music shops in Vienna (Litzmann 1902, 157).

9. During visits to England from the 1860s through the 1880s, she tried out works on her host, Arthur Burnand, whom she regarded as a reliable barometer of English taste (Litzmann 1908, 255).

10. They discussed these matters extensively—see Litzmann 1902 and Reich 1985, 271–72.

11. Cycles of character pieces generally were not performed in their entirety at this time, nor were song cycles. Reich notes that Robert Schumann never heard his piano cycles performed in public (1985, 269).

12. Robert's works enjoyed some success in Russia even in 1844, during the Schumanns' visit (Shitomirski 1961, 23–25).

13. "Gern schrieb ich mal meine Präludien, die ich immer vor den Tonleitern mache, auf, aber es ist so schwer, weil ich sie immer wieder anders mache, wie es mir eben gerade am Clavier einfällt." The English translation by Hadow (". . . it is too difficult as I always alter them just as it strikes me at the moment"; Litzmann 1913, 2:433) gives the false impression that the preludes had prototypes from which she diverged in daily use.

14. An annotation in the Zwickau copy identifies it as a gift from the estate of their grandson, Ferdinand Schumann, in 1954.

15. In the Zwickau copy, the "Einfache Praeludien" are positioned between the exercises and the introductions. The "Praeludium" in Staatsbibliothek zu Berlin Mus. ms. 8, cited in Reich 1985, 305, is an F-minor version of a prelude in F-sharp minor owned by the Sächsische Landesbibliothek in Dresden (Mus. Sch. 267); it is paired there with a fugue and dated 8 June 1845. The F-minor prelude has been recorded by Josef DeBeenhouwer (Partridge 1129–2).

16. The third leaf was cut off, apparently in the course of notating the preludes.

17. See, for example, Kalkbrenner's treatise (1970). The reminiscences of Eugenie Schumann recall her mother's playing of scales and passagework in a grand manner (Schumann 1927, 17).

18. Schumann used Czerny's works in her own teaching, and published *Fingerübungen und Studien aus Carl Czerny's grosser Pianoforte-Schule, Op. 500* (Hamburg: Cranz, [1880]), actually prepared largely by Marie Schumann (see Reich 1985, 256; and Schumann and Brahms 1971, 219–20).

19. Again, the presence of several blank pages suggests that Schumann left room to notate additional preludes. The introductions run through folio 10r; 10v–14r are blank with the exception of a single D-minor chord on 11r. The "Einfache Praeludien" are notated on the first system of folio 14v.

20. Schumann criticized Anton Rubinstein's preluding in 1857: "It seemed to me so inartistic to wander up and down the piano in sixths and thirds" (Litzmann 1908, 19–20).

21. In spirit her introductory preludes recall those of J. B. Cramer's unbarred preludes (*Twenty-six Preludes or Short Introductions in the Principal Major and Minor Keys for the Piano Forte,* London: Chappel [*sic*] and Co. and Clementi and Co., [1818]), though Schumann's are more lush and overtly expressive.

22. The F-minor prelude is not so identified in the manuscript, but the connection is obvious; a note in the Zwickau copy in a hand other than Clara Schumann's also connects it with the Andante of the Sonata.

23. The C-major prelude, Nr. 1 (ex. 11.2), which ends with a descending tag in tiny note heads, would seem of a suitable length and weight to introduce Beethoven's "Waldstein" Sonata, a work that Schumann performed many times from 1842 onwards (Süsskind 1977, 228; Litzmann 1908, 618). Czerny warned against lengthy preludes before Beethoven sonatas, but supplied a prelude to the last movement of the Waldstein in his Opus 61 (Czerny 1983, 18, 25n).

The D-minor prelude, Nr. 5, is similar in register, texture, and character to the Bach Chaconne (from BWV 1004), performed by Schumann from 1844 (Süsskind 1977, 147). It begins with an unbarred passage that may hearken back to an older style— Czerny related preludes of this kind to Bach (1983, 23). Several preludes in the collection seem to match well with more than one piece in Schumann's repertory.

24. Autograph inscription (Sächische Landesbibliothek Dresden). See also Schumann 1982, 716n, and Schumann and Schumann 1993, 124. "Schlummerlied" was published as no. 16 of *Albumblätter* in 1854.

25. Several other programs cite an unidentified "Fantasiestück." Clara Wieck played at least some of Opus 12 privately for Liszt in Vienna in 1838 (Litzmann 1902, 188; Schumann and Schumann 1984, 112).

26. References to private performances of Robert's works in Paris appear in Schumann and Schumann 1987, 469, 537, 566. On 25 February 1839, Clara wrote Robert from Paris: "You are entirely right that I always prefer to play some of your *Fantasiestücke* before playing *Carnaval* (Schumann and Schumann 1987, 414).

27. Brahms appears to have given the first public performance of the Sonata in Vienna in January 1863, in the three-movement version published in 1836 as "Concert sans orchestre pour le pianoforte" ("Wien" 1863; see also Schumann 1982, 808n; and Hofmann and Keil 1982, 20).

28. Acquaintance with the melody is of even greater advantage in "Des Abends," which is more complex rhythmically (see Goertzen 1996, 320–22).

29. Josef Hofmann's Golden Jubilee Concert, played in New York in November 1937, included a modulatory transition between Chopin's "Minute" Waltz and G-Minor Ballade (recorded on Columbia KL 4929).

30. Czerny recommended the use of enharmonic modulations in closing formulas in his *Systematic Introduction* (1983, 15).

31. Robert Schumann reordered the variations before publication; in his original manuscript, however, the material of the variation published as no. 2 preceded that of the one published as no. 4 (Roessner 1975, 110).

32. A B-Minor Romance is dated Christmas 1856. A March in E-flat Major, composed for friends' golden wedding anniversary in 1879 and containing references to Robert's works, is recorded on Partridge 1129-2 (see Nauhaus 1990).

33. The prelude paired with a fugue, which Schumann also composed, is a category of introductory prelude; the independent prelude is a separate type (see Goertzen 1996).

34. He gave similar advice in his *Musikalische Haus-und Lebens-Regeln* (Schumann 1859, vii).

References

"Aus Dresden." 1838. *Neue Zeitschrift für Musik* 9, no. 50 (21 December):201.

"Berichte. Nachrichten und Bemerkungen." 1871. *Allgemeine musikalische Zeitung* (Neue Folge) 6, no. 9 (1 March):140.

"Berlin, im April." 1837. *Allgemeine musikalische Zeitung* 39, no. 16 (19 April):257–58.

Cai, Camilla. 1989. "A Woman Must Not Desire to Compose." *Piano Quarterly* 37 (Spring):55–61.

"Clara Wieck in Prag." 1838. *Neue Zeitschrift für Musik* 8, no. 1 (2 January):3–4; 8, no. 2 (5 January):6–7.

Czerny, Carl. 1839. *Complete Theoretical and Practical Piano Forte School,* Op. 500. 3 vols. Translated by J. H. Hamilton. London: R. Cocks & Co.

———. [1880]. *Fingerübungen und Studien aus Carl Czerny's grosser Pianoforte-Schule, Op. 500.* Edited by Clara Schumann. Hamburg: Cranz.

———. 1983. *A Systematic Introduction to Improvisation on the Pianoforte* (Systematische Anleitung zum Fantasieren auf dem Pianoforte). [1829]. Translated and edited by Alice L. Mitchell. New York and London: Longman.

Goertzen, Valerie Woodring. 1996. "By Way of Introduction: Preluding by Eighteenth- and Early Nineteenth-Century Pianists." *Journal of Musicology* 14 (Summer): 299–337.

Hofmann, Kurt and Siegmar Keil. 1982. *Robert Schumann: Thematisches Verzeichnis sämtlicher im Druck erschienenen musikalischen Werke.* 5th ed. Hamburg: J. Schuberth & Co.

Hummel, Johann Nepomuk. [1828]. *Ausführliche theoretisch-practische Anweisung zum Piano-Forte-Spiel.* Vienna: Tobias Haslinger.

Joss, Victor. 1902. *Der Musikpädagoge Friedrich Wieck und seine Familie.* Dresden: Oscar Damm.

Kalkbrenner, Frédéric. 1970. *Traité d'harmonie du pianiste,* Op. 185. [1849]. Reprint, Amsterdam: A. J. Heuwekemeyer.

Kallberg, Jeffrey. 1992. "Small 'Forms': In Defence of the Prelude." In *The Cambridge Companion to Chopin,* edited by Jim Samson, 124–44. Cambridge: Cambridge University Press.

———. 1996. *Chopin at the Boundaries: Sex, History, and Musical Genre.* Cambridge and London: Harvard University Press.

Klassen, Janina. 1990. *Clara Wieck-Schumann: Die Virtuosin als Komponistin.* Kieler Schriften zur Musikwissenschaft 37. Kassel: Bärenreiter.

Kleefeld, Wilhelm. 1910. *Clara Schumann.* Bielefeld and Leipzig: Volhagen & Klasing.

"Konzert-Salon. Drittes Konzert der Frau Clara Schumann, geb. Wieck, den 1. Jänner." 1847. *Wiener Allgemeine musikalische Zeitung* 7, no. 2 (5 January):6–7.

"Leipzig." 1842. *Allgemeine musikalische Zeitung* 44, no. 2 (5 January):18–19.

"Leipzig, den 6. Dezember 1844." 1844. *Allgemeine musikalische Zeitung* 46, no. 50 (11 December):842–44.

"Liszt in Wien." 1838. *Neue Zeitschrift für Musik* 8, no. 34 (27 April):135–36.

Litzmann, Berthold. 1902–1908. *Clara Schumann: Ein Künstlerleben nach Tagebüchern und Briefen.* 3 vols. Leipzig: Breitkopf & Härtel.

———. 1913. *Clara Schumann: An Artist's Life.* 2 vols. Translated by Grace E. Hadow. London: Macmillan & Co.

"Londoner Briefe." 1856. *Niederrheinische Musik-Zeitung* 4, no. 28 (12 July):224.

McCarthy, S. Margaret W. 1995. *Amy Fay: America's Notable Woman of Music.* Warren, Mich.: Harmonie Park Press.

Meichsner, A. v. 1875. *Friedrich Wieck und seine beiden Töchter Clara Schumann, geb. Wieck, u. Marie Wieck.* Leipzig: Heinrich Matthes.

Nauhaus, Gerd. 1990. Notes to *Clara Schumann, Complete Works for Piano,* vol. 1. Partridge 1129–2.

Plantinga, Leon B. 1967. *Schumann as Critic.* New Haven and London: Yale University Press.

Program Collection (PC). *Die große Programm-Sammlung Clara Schumanns (eigene Konzerte).* Robert-Schumann-Haus, Zwickau, No. 10463.

Reich, Nancy B. 1985. *Clara Schumann: The Artist and the Woman.* Ithaca and London: Cornell University Press.

Roessner, Linda Correll. 1975. "The Autograph of Schumann's Piano Sonata in F Minor, Opus 14." *Musical Quarterly* 61 (January):98–130.

Schoppe, Martin. 1978. "Schumann-Interpretation Clara Schumanns (Tageskritik und Konzertbericht)." In *3. Schumann-Tage des Bezirkes Karl-Marx-Stadt, 1978.* Zwickau: Robert-Schumann-Gesellschaft.

Schumann, Clara, and Johannes Brahms. 1971. *Letters of Clara Schumann and Johannes Brahms, 1853–1896.* 2 vols. Edited by Berthold Litzmann. Translated by Grace Hadow. 1927. Reprint, New York: Vienna House.

Schumann, Clara, and Robert Schumann. 1984, 1987. *Clara und Robert Schumann: Briefwechsel, Kritische Gesamtausgabe.* 2 vols. Edited by Eva Weissweiler with Susanna Ludwig. Basel and Frankfurt am Main: Stroemfeld/Roter Stern.

———. 1993. *The Marriage Diaries of Robert and Clara Schumann from Their Wedding Day through the Russia Trip.* Edited by Gerd Nauhaus. Translated by Peter Ostwald. Boston: Northeastern University Press.

Schumann, Eugenie. 1927. *Memoirs.* Translated by Marie Busch. London: William Heinemann, Ltd.

Schumann, Robert. 1859. *Musikalische Haus- und Lebens-Regeln.* Leipzig and New York: J. Schuberth and Co.

———. 1982. *Robert Schumann Tagebücher, Band III: Haushaltbücher, Teil 2, 1847–1856.* Edited by Gerd Nauhaus. Leipzig: VEB Deutscher Verlag für Musik.

Shitomirski, Daniel Wladimirowitsch. 1961. "Schumann in Rußland." In *Sammelbände der Robert-Schumann-Gesellschaft,* 19–46. Leipzig: Deutscher Verlag für Musik.

Struck, Michael. 1989. Review of *Clara und Robert Schumann: Briefwechsel, Kritische Gesamtausgabe, Band II: 1839,* edited by Eva Weissweiler with Susanna Ludwig. *Die Musikforschung* 42 (July–September):291–95.

Süsskind, Pamela Gertrude. 1977. *Clara Wieck Schumann as Pianist and Composer: A Study of Her Life and Works.* Ph.D. dissertation, University of California at Berkeley.

Wangermée, Robert. 1970. "Tradition et innovation dans la virtuosité romantique." *Acta Musicologica* 42 (January–June):5–32.

Wieck, Friedrich. 1968. *Friedrich Wieck Briefe aus den Jahren 1830–1838.* Edited by Käthe Walch-Schumann. Beiträge zur Rheinischen Musikgeschichte 74. Cologne: Arno Volk-Verlag, 1968.

————. 1988. *Piano and Song: Didactic and Polemical (Klavier und Gesang: Didaktisches und Polemisches).* 1853. Translated and edited by Henry Pleasants. Monographs in Musicology no. 9. Stuyvesant, N.Y.: Pendragon Press.

————. ca. 1980. *Piano Studies.* Edited by Marie Wieck. [1875]. Reprint, Melville, N.Y.: Belwin Mills.

Wieck, Marie. 1912. *Aus dem Kreise Wieck-Schumann.* Dresden and Leipzig: E. Piersons.

"Wien. Musikal. Chronik dess 4. Quartals." 1838. *Allgemeine musikalische Zeitung* 40, no. 10 (7 March):164–65.

"Wien." 1863. *Signale für die musikalische Welt* 21, no. 4 (15 January):56.

CHAPTER TWELVE

A Sense of the Possible: Miles Davis and the Semiotics of Improvised Performance

CHRIS SMITH

My greatest tribute to Miles would just be to be aware.

—Keith Jarrett

Between 1949 and his death in 1992, Miles Davis was one of the most influential figures in Black American music. His musical innovations, performance conduct, and public persona excited extensive comment, imitation, and castigation. Moreover, a vast majority of the important jazz musicians and bandleaders who came after Miles either went through his band or otherwise came under his tutelage, and virtually all of these individuals have cited their time with Miles as crucial to their musical development.[1] Yet the specific nature and details of his influence have proven remarkably resistant to analysis.

In this paper, I argue that Miles Davis's particular genius was centered in an ability to construct and manipulate improvisational possibilities, selecting and combining compositions, players, musical styles, and other performance parameters. Specifically, my goal is to explore Miles's manipulation of what Eero Tarasti described as "cultural semiotic" or "the 'possible' world of [a performance's] community" (Tarasti 1987, 167). This cultural semiotic, which in Miles's approach was manifested as a unique "sense of the possible," is recognizable in the symbolic techniques which he developed for leading and shaping improvised performance.[2]

The following anecdote is a classic illustration of the ambiguity inherent in Miles's procedures, and of their resistance to traditional communicative analysis: "For 'Aida' [1980], he told [bassist Marcus] Miller to play an F and G vamp, but when Miller stuck resolutely to the chords, Davis stopped the band. 'Is that all you gonna play?' he asked. 'I heard you was *bad.* You ain't playin' shit.' So Miller filled in his vamp ornately on the next take, and Davis stopped the band again. 'What are you playin'?' he asked Miller. 'Just play F and G and shut up'" (Chambers 1987, 303–4).

Miles's technical vocabulary was not arbitrary or sadistic, but it was subtle and complex, and for this reason has proven resistant to conventional identification and analysis. In fact the subtlety and ambiguity were intentional, Miles's preferred mode of musical interaction being dependent upon the invocation of a very particular kind of attention from his players. I suggest the following:

(1) Miles's artistic interest was the creation and manipulation of a symbolic "ritual space."[3]

(2) Miles enacted this semiotic environment because he believed that certain musical objects (performances, improvised compositions, etc.) and musical processes could only come out of a richly ambiguous symbolic experience.

(3) Miles intentionally supplied, withheld, and distorted performance information because of a quality of attention that such an environment evoked from his players, some of whom nevertheless recognized his motives and the dynamic perspectives from which they derived: "Miles is a boxer, and he thinks like a boxer when he talks. If the other person is someone who might pick up on what he's doing, it'll be like parrying" (Keith Jarrett, quoted in Keepnews 1987, 96).

(4) Moreover, his techniques for creating this ritual space were intentional, consistent, and susceptible to analysis, as Miles himself acknowledged: "What we did on *Bitches Brew* you couldn't ever write down for an orchestra to play. That's why I didn't write it all out, *not because I didn't know what I wanted;* [but because] I knew that what I wanted would come out of a process and not some prearranged stuff" (Davis and Troupe 1991, 300. Emphasis added).

What Miles bequeathed his colleagues and musicians was an enhanced ability to create and respond in a symbolic interpretive space, dedicated to the enactment of what has been described as the "experiential possibility of music [as] a vivid and continuous present" (Kapferer 1986, 198). With this insight, we can view Miles Davis's improvisational procedures through the lens of contemporary performance theory.[4]

Miles wanted a quality of attentive musical flexibility that would lift his players to the level of co-composing interpreters; that would encourage them to respond to the improvisational moment with his own alert flexibility. Communicating in an intentionally ambiguous and nonverbal fashion meant that Miles's players were forced to engage with him by interpreting what they thought such communication demanded.[5] As Miles explained: "See, if you put a musician in a place where he has to do something different from what he does all the time, then he can do that—but he's got to think differently in order to do it. He has to use his imagination, be more creative, more innovative; he's got to take more risks. . . . So then he'll be freer, will expect things differently, will anticipate and know something different is coming down. . . . Because then anything can happen, and that's where great art and music happens" (Davis and Troupe 1991, 220).

Of course there is a paradox here: the semiotic techniques Miles used to create the improvisational environment (ambiguity, visual and sonic cues, etc.) often had the secondary effect of centering the players' attention upon him.[6] So there is an implicit tension between Miles's decentering actions and the players' learned and habitual attention, which was itself heightened by these actions.[7] Thus Miles was obliged to manipulate the ambiguity still further; as his players became familiar with certain cuing techniques, he constantly replaced those techniques. As a result, subtle sonic and visual gestures took on layers of associational meanings, in turn demanding further responses. But, as Schieffelin acknowledges, this is a profoundly involving and fertile space in which to create performances: "[Such an] experience of inconclusiveness and imbalance gives people little choice but to make their own moves of creative imagination if they are to make sense of the performance and arrive at a meaningful account of what is happening. In so doing . . . they complete the construction of its reality" (Schieffelin 1985, 721).

So the deliberate incompleteness of Miles's directions was itself the element which, through the attention and response it elicited, enacted the completion of the creative process. Record producer Teo Macero described Miles's impact on his musicians in the studio this way:

> [His] influence was so potent and so strong every time they went in [the studio] that [they] couldn't afford to screw around . . . and, in fact, none of the musicians do. When they're in the studio it's like God coming—"Oh, oh, oh, here he comes." They stop talking, they tend to business and they listen, and when he stops, they stop. When he tells the drummer to play, the drummer plays. When he tells the guitar players to play, they play and they play until he stops them. . . . *They got more out of him than they have given to him.* He is the teacher. He's the one who's sort of pulling the string. (Chambers 1987, 159; emphasis added)

Such a process could only come from interaction within a ritual space that took the participants out of their usual mode of perceiving, interpreting, and reacting.[8]

Symbolic Vocabularies

In analyzing the technical means by which Miles made the music react to the improvisational context,[9] I choose to focus on visual and sonic evidence[10] from two phases of his career, the so-called second great quintet[11] and the post-retirement bands.[12]

The first performance excerpt examined (on audio tape) comes from 1967, and features Miles, saxophonist Wayne Shorter, pianist Herbie Hancock, bassist Ron Carter, and drummer Tony Williams (Davis 1986). This quintet developed a performance style based on a modal[13] repertoire, sparsity, and highly flexible rhythmic, dynamic, and textural juxtapositions, as well as extensive and very sophisticated interaction. Their musical communication was marked by its complexity and immediacy and by the degree to which it appeared almost instinctive. Visual cues between players were extremely subtle, almost invisible to outsiders, and contrasting performances from one night to the next showed that the shifts, contrasts, and juxtapositions were not precomposed, yet were accomplished with a cohesion as seamless as if they had been carefully rehearsed.

This group interaction was a product of a sophisticated mode of hearing and interpreting performance cues developed by this group of players. In the following description, therefore, the most important performance cues are sonic: small, highly *significant* bits of musical information which the players use to instruct and forewarn one another of impending shifts, and to comment on musical events as they occur.

The sequence opens with a drum solo by Tony Williams in a style influenced by free jazz, emphasizing polyrhythms, interaction with the horn players, and a rejection of the traditional time-keeping role. The solo sets up the opening theme statement of "Gingerbread Boy" (1964), a twisting chromatic line played twice in unison by trumpet and tenor saxophone.

The solos open with four trumpet choruses.[14] The accompaniment is similar to that used for the composed melodic theme, or "head": drums are furiously interactive; piano offers sparse, carefully ambiguous modal voicings; and double bass retains the outline of the composed bass line and its implicit tonalities. Although the texture and rhythm are broken up, subdivided, and altered, the duration of each tonal center (the "underlying tempo") remains essentially the same. Hence the tune's form itself is essentially, though loosely, retained.

Under Herbie Hancock's piano solo, the rhythmic groove quickly mutates and breaks down. Together, pianist, bassist, and drummer cue one another into a looser, less beat-oriented feel. The tonal durations[15] remain approximately the same, and the underlying tempo remains essentially constant, but the impressionistic texture is more radically explored; Williams continues a furious but largely free rhythmic commentary.

Approximately halfway through the third chorus of the piano solo, on an octave scale passage that specifically outlines a Phrygian mode, Hancock drastically slows the internal rhythm of the melodic line, thus bringing the tempo to a complete standstill.

Seizing the opportunity, Miles enters with a descending C minor scale in a radically different key, tempo, and rhythmic feel, as shown in example 12.1. By the fifth beat (that is, the second measure in the new 4/4 meter), bassist Ron Carter responds to Miles's cue, identifies and adjusts to the new key, tempo, and groove, and begins playing steady quarter-note lines in C minor under Miles's new solo; Williams joins him.

In the next 48 beats, Miles conveys a lot of information, all of it consistent and musically interpretable to his players, and to which they respond: (1) Miles clearly subdivides the rhythm to yield twelve bars of 4/4 accented time. Williams joins him in this. (2) In the first, fifth, and eighth bars he clearly outlines the chords of a C-minor blues. Hancock follows harmonic suit. (3) As a pickup to bar 12 (the last of the form), Miles plays a descending figure (3b–4b–G), with a slowed "fall-off" from the last pitch, effectively cuing a held chord to which the whole ensemble then joins in.

Over this held chord, Miles plays the opening figure of a new tune, the 6/8

Example 12.1. Solo implying C-minor blues, Miles Davis, "Gingerbread Man," 1967 (from Davis 1986). All transcriptions by the author.

Figure 12.1. Miles plays the opening figure of "Footprints" (from Davis 1986).

C-minor blues "Footprints" (1964). By the repeat of the four-bar phrase (measure five of the blues form), Shorter has recognized the tune, and waiting for a musically appropriate entrance point, he joins Miles with the new tune's harmonized saxophone part (ex. 12.2). The rhythm section retains characteristics of the earlier rubato, but shifts smoothly to the new tune's key and tonal centers.

Then, under the repeat of the melody, Williams sets up a new groove which drives toward the solos. As the first soloist, Miles plays four choruses, but leaves his improvisation unresolved, ceasing to play at an unexpected point before the end of the fourth chorus. Wayne Shorter emphasizes the intentionality of this pause by delaying his entrance until measure seven of the next chorus.

Under Shorter's continuing solo, the rhythm section begins to dismantle the groove: the accompaniment becomes sparser and more interactive and conversational. Tonal durations are retained, but they are concealed or even left unplayed. Shorter responds with a solo that becomes progressively more disjunct, speech-oriented, and nonlinear.

By the fourth chorus, the tonalities, while maintained, are barely implied. Tonal, rhythmic, and tempo ambiguity are foregrounded; drums do not play. Shorter ends his eighth chorus with a melodic phrase which closely recalls the original melody, and which marks the entrance of the piano solo (ex. 12.3).

The rhythm section retains the consistent tonal durations under Hancock's first chorus; however, he quickly takes radical steps to override the harmonic continuity. He plays a harmonized phrase in the eighth and ninth measures of his first chorus which echoes the melody and fits the chord progression. But then he plays it again, and a third time. This carefully chosen figure so clearly

Example 12.2. Cuing the melody, Miles Davis and Wayne Shorter, "Footprints," 1967 (from Davis 1986).

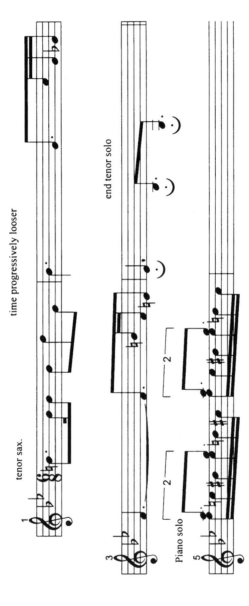

Example 12.3. Conclusion of tenor solo, Wayne Shorter and Herbie Hancock, "Footprints," 1967 (from Davis 1986).

outlines the underlying harmony that when Hancock repeats it, bassist Carter follows, breaking the tune's sequential chord progression.

In jazz common practice, what Hancock and Carter have just done is really quite radical: by removing the unvarying succession and consistent durations of the tune's tonal centers, in essence they have stopped the form in its tracks. This forces a different sort of interaction, in which, rather than *leading* the sequential and rhythmically repetitive progression of chords, the accompanists shift harmony only *after* Hancock does, essentially following his lead. Hancock completes the chorus and continues to a second and third, but the durational pause he has signalled to his bandmates allows his note choices, rather than specific temporal durations, to dictate when the tonality shifts.

By the third chorus, Carter has relinquished any propulsive or harmonizing function at all: he is simply bowing a sustained bass note figure. Williams has suspended the drum part almost entirely, playing only very occasional, nonrhythmic commentary on cymbals. Gradually Hancock slows and quiets his solo, coming to a virtual rhythmic standstill, poised over Carter's sustained pedal (shown in ex. 12.4).

Then Hancock plays a cue in the original tonality and rhythm—an octave motif which unmistakably recalls the head—and Miles and Shorter enter on the top of the melody (ex. 12.5) They play the head twice through and end with a collectively improvised coda over the bass's repetitive figure. Here, where jazz common practice might end the piece, the rhythm section holds the tonic chord. In soloistic "cadenza fashion," Miles plays an ascending D Phrygian line (ex. 12.6), holding a fermata—first on a high G and then on a high (chromatic) Ab—and cuing a rubato on a Bb-Ab trill. As the band enters on the new rubato, Miles plays a quick two-bar motive (ex. 12.7) quoting the end of "The Theme," a bebop standard which all players recognize; they join Miles for the set-closer's final cadence.

There is very subtle sonic communication going on here, as is evidenced by the frequency and minimalist nature of the cues which players share with one another. The presence in Miles's band members of the extraordinary aural attention necessary to recognize and react creatively to these cues as they pass "on the fly" is powerful evidence in favor of Miles's choice to limit directions to his players in ways which actually stimulate creativity.

Signifying Intimacy

By the mid-1980s, in contrast to the various '60s bands' emphasis on sonic interplay, Miles's repertoire of visual signals had grown enormously. This was partly a result of the larger performance spaces and higher volumes the band was utilizing, in which larger and more visible gestures were effective, and partly the result of an apparent relaxation of Miles's earlier aversion to interacting with the audience. However, the gestural results had become tightly interwoven and both sonically and visually highly significant: "In one adven-

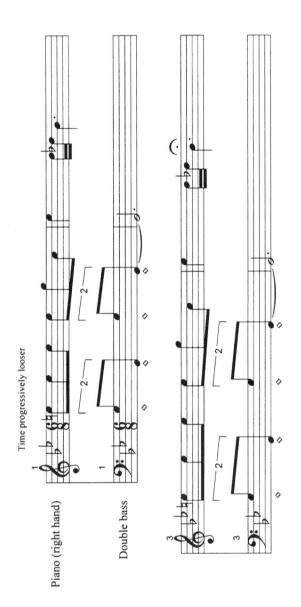

Example 12.4. Excerpt from piano solo, Herbie Hancock and Ron Carter, "Footprints," 1967 (from Davis 1986).

271

Example 12.5. Piano cuing the melody, Herbie Hancock, Miles Davis, and Wayne Shorter, "Footprints," 1967 (from Davis 1986).

Example 12.6. Trumpet cadenza, Miles Davis, "Footprints," 1967 (from Davis 1986).

Example 12.7. Quoting "The Theme," Miles Davis, "Footprints," 1967 (from Davis 1986).

turesome exchange with [Kenny] Garrett, [Miles] reached out and put his hand on the saxophonist's chest; Garrett immediately stopped playing, and the pause proved an eloquent accent on the rhythm" (Goodman 1989, 12).[16]

The first example of an integrated sonic/visual cue recurs in several performances of the Michael Jackson tune "Human Nature." In one example performance, recorded at the 1986 New Orleans Jazz and Heritage Festival (Davis 1986), Miles's arrangement opens with a syncopated chordal figure played by keyboards over the 2/4 groove (ex. 12.8), and this is succeeded by the A theme of the piece (ex. 12.9), played with trumpet as the top voice, which is repeated. The B theme moves into a higher register, incorporates more syncopation, and is framed by a more lush and sustained chordal accompaniment (ex. 12.10). As it begins, Miles steps close to soprano saxophonist Bob Berg; hunched over, heads almost touching, instruments parallel and pointed at the floor, the two play the line together (fig. 12.2).

This is a highly affective gesture because in American culture, and especially perhaps in the sometimes hypermasculine arena of jazz performance, such a close posture signals unusual intimacy; moreover, the intentionality of the gesture is confirmed by the way in which it has been recognized and framed by the video's editors. The "intimacy cue" is also reflected in the melodic unison of trumpet and soprano sax, the first time this texture has been employed in the piece.

In a version of the same tune recorded in Paris in 1989 (Davis 1990), the signifying behavior has been repeated and enhanced. This time it is "lead bass" player Foley (Joseph "Foley" McCreary, who goes by the single nickname) who stands close to Miles, playing an improvised, arpeggiated countermelody which closely follows the trumpet lines. The rehearsed, intentional, and "signifying" nature of this visual behavior is made clear when Miles moves: as he walks to stage left, Foley moves with him, maintaining the close posture, shadowing Miles physically as his bass line shadows Miles's part musically (shown in fig. 12.3).

It should be reiterated here that this behavior, in its visual, repeated, "intentional" aspects, is *not* solely directed at signifying to the audience. In the ritual environment which Miles created among his players, close physical and musical proximity on his part commanded even greater attention on theirs.

Signifying Humor

An example of sonic and visual "signifying humor" comes during the 1989 concert's version of "Amandla" (Davis 1990). In the midst of a sequence of call-and-response solo exchanges between Miles and flutist Kenny Garrett, Miles plays a simple blues figure and inadvertently cracks a note in the middle of it. Garrett immediately repeats the line, mimicking it exactly, even to the cracked note (see ex. 12.11). Miles punches him gently in the chest, and Garrett, laughing, momentarily stops playing (see fig. 12.4). The comic aspects of

Synth.

Synth. and bass

Example 12.8. Introduction to "Human Nature," Miles Davis band, 1986 (from Davis 1986).

tpt.

Synth. and bass

Example 12.9. A theme of "Human Nature," Miles Davis band, 1986 (from Davis 1986).

tpt. and soprano sax.

synth. and bass

Example 12.10. B theme of "Human Nature," Miles Davis band, 1986 (from Davis 1986).

Figure 12.2. Miles Davis and saxophonist Bob Berg play the harmonized B section of "Human Nature" in intimate physical proximity (from Davis 1986).

Figure 12.3. Bassist Joseph "Foley" McCreary follows Miles Davis physically and musically while playing "Human Nature" (from Davis 1990).

Swing 16th-notes ("New Jack" groove)

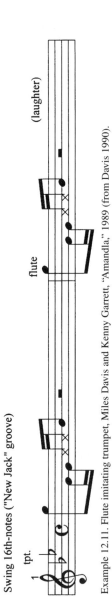

Example 12.11. Flute imitating trumpet, Miles Davis and Kenny Garrett, "Amandla," 1989 (from Davis 1990).

Figure 12.4. Davis punches flutist Kenny Garrett in the chest after Garrett plays an imitation of Miles's cracked note during "Amandla" (from Davis 1990).

Kenny's literal interpretation of Miles's unintentional "wrong" note are clearly dependent on insider knowledge, deriving meaning from and shaped by the signifying environment in which the two are operating.

Signifying Failure

The conscious and constructed nature of these signifying vocabularies is additionally demonstrated by Miles's reaction when they seem to have failed. Late in the Paris concert's version of "Tutu" (Davis 1990), Miles is soloing and has moved back center stage, and he has cued Foley downstage with him. They stand facing each other, Foley watching him closely: it appears that Miles is about to initiate another call-and-response duet. But the bent-over posture, and perhaps Miles's earlier don/doff choreography, has left his signature sunglasses perched precariously on his nose; as he bends into his first phrase, they fall off. Foley is so attentive that he catches the glasses as they fall and hands them back to Miles, who immediately stops playing (see fig. 12.5). Almost instantly, without any other further signal, Foley turns to head back to his usual station, and Miles stops playing, walking upstage toward the drumset.

Now, more is going on here than simply the adverse reaction of a performer to a moment of onstage chaos. The metaphorical weight of the sunglasses, the degree to which they quite literally represent a personal mask for Miles, has been established earlier in this concert: when Miles wants his players to look directly at him to start a tune or when he wants to acknowledge the audience after a tune, he removes his glasses. But during solos they stay on, implanting

Figure 12.5. When Miles Davis drops his sunglasses while playing the song "Tutu," bassist Joseph "Foley" McCreary catches them (from Davis 1990).

the message that Miles is playing the notes first of all for himself. Thus, when the mask quite literally falls off his face, he reacts by acknowledging a moment of failure and aborting the solo.

Signifying Music

I would like to conclude this exploration of Miles's sonic and visual vocabulary of the 1980s with two examples of cuing in which sonic, musical, and behavioral aspects are integrated, and indeed become part of the expressive fabric. The first example is from the Paris concert's version of "New Blues" (Davis 1990). In the arrangement of the tune, provision is made for Miles to cue the rhythm section to double-time, lending intensity and giving the sensation that the tune itself is moving twice as fast. Toward the end of bass player Foley's lengthy solo, which follows the general outline of a crescendo, Miles plays the simple descending figure which cues the double-time section.

Then, glaring at drummer Ricky Wellman over the masking sunglasses, Miles hits the cue again, reinforcing its intensity by playing it on trumpet with one hand and keyboard with the other. As Wellman picks up the double-time, Miles nods abruptly at him, with an emphatic hand gesture (see fig. 12.6). The sheer force of this cue virtually demands an intensified response. Even we, who unlike Ricky Wellman are distanced from the gesture by time and intervening electronic media, can feel Miles's kinesthetic communicative intensity.[17]

The second example comes from the Paris concert's version of "Amandla" (Davis 1990): Toward the end of his first solo, Miles is standing at extreme stage right, facing into the large speaker columns that flank the stage. He turns back toward center, walking from the left of the video frame toward the right, the camera panning with him. As he passes the keyboard station, Miles turns slightly toward Kei Akagi, raises his horn for a moment, and plays a final

Figure 12.6. Miles cues drummer Ricky Wellman for double-time section of "New Blues" (from Davis 1990).

seven-note phrase. At this cue, Akagi begins his keyboard solo, spinning out variations based on an exact repetition of the improvised melodic idea with which Miles signalled him (see ex. 12.12).

Akagi is obviously listening hard and responding to what he hears, but the implications travel further: the keyboardist not only begins with Miles's last phrase, but constructs his entire solo using that phrase as his thematic material. Thus Miles has supplied an integrated visual/sonic cue which directs not only the start but also the motivic content of the keyboard solo. An entirely new compositional section has grown out of the interaction of the players' attention and Miles's improvised material in this ritual space.

The mutual interaction and "shared sense of the now" was considerably more complex and centralized in Miles Davis's band than is the case·with most performing musical ensembles. Of course, focus on the improvisational "now" is to some extent a mandatory aspect of every performance situation: even in fully notated music, a conductor needs attentive response from the orchestra. But such focus is particularly essential in a musical genre such as jazz, which so directly foregrounds improvisational practices.

Conclusions
Miles made his musical process especially dependent upon ambivalent ritual space, by setting up performance situations which demanded unique improvisational attention. He brought it into the studio, made it the main topic of musi-

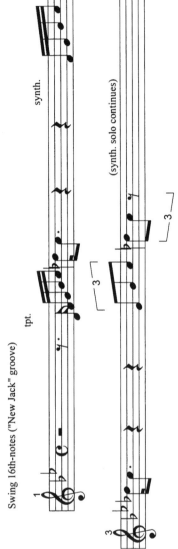

Swing 16th-notes ("New Jack" groove)

tpt.

synth.

(synth. solo continues)

Example 12.12. Trumpet motif used for synthesizer solo, Miles Davis and Kei Akagi, "New Blues," 1989 (from Davis 1990).

cal discourse, and developed virtuosic skills in the subtle art of manipulating signs in the service of performance.

Most profoundly, Miles developed a basic musical building block out of a heightened sensitivity to the interaction of all signifying elements: players, tunes, performance parameters, and cues.[18] The interactive process was allowed to take place because Miles recognized its centrality and understood the means of its creation, and he was willing to tailor standard jazz practices sufficiently to permit, indeed to demand, that it occur.

I have suggested that Miles Davis's artistic interest was in the creation and manipulation of a ritual space, in which gestures could be endowed with symbolic power sufficient to form a functionally communicative, and hence musical, vocabulary. The intentional ambiguity of this vocabulary and the perceptual frame in which it was employed made it more potent in impact, but also more resistant to conventional analysis. Yet the techniques, their method, and their results can with the right tools be recognized and analyzed.

Finally, I have suggested that Miles utilized these techniques because the musical experiences which resulted could only come out of a process which was intimately engaged with the improvisational "now." Kapferer put it this way: "Art and ritual share potentially one fundamental quality in common: the Particular and the Universal are brought together and transformed in the process. . . . The Universal 'is given a focus, an experiential content, in the immediacy of the individual's situation'" (Kapferer 1986, 191, quoting Natanson).

Miles's performance tradition emphasized orality and the transmission of information and artistic insight from individual to individual. His position in that tradition and his personality, talents, and artistic interests impelled him to pursue a uniquely individual solution to the problems and the experiential possibilities of improvised performance. Miles deployed these techniques specifically in order to highlight the interplay of musical procedures and the communicative moment, resulting in the sense of heightened creative possibility which is common to all ritual behaviors.[19]

It was this "sense of the possible" which profoundly influenced generations of jazz musicians who played with Miles.[20] It is no coincidence that, in paying tribute to Miles's influence, these players uniformly allude not to issues of technical or compositional approach but, more profoundly, to a way of hearing and responding, and encouraging others to do the same; to the cultivation of a unique capacity for attention. This allows us to situate Miles's approach and his role as leader in the broader context of ritual performance.[21]

Miles Davis came from an African-American performance tradition which focused on individual expression of communal feeling, empathic interaction among participants, and creative response to shifting contexts. The ritual music space that he constructed offered a literal, experiential manifestation of this model. Music educator Christopher Small calls it "that ideal society, those relations between human beings, that can enable each one to feel, in a literal sense, in tune with all the others and with the world" (Small 1988, 483). This potent legacy is manifested again and again, in the music he initiated, performed, and recorded, in anecdotes and reminiscences about him by his players, and in musical endeavors inspired and influenced by him. Miles emphasized and constructed a specific ritual performance context. And the behavior he demanded within that space evoked a centered, focused sensitivity to the enormous creative possibilities of the ever precious, ever fleeting, present moment.

Notes

This paper is a revised version of an article that appeared in *The Drama Review* 39, no. 3 (Fall 1995). The epigraph is from Doerschuk 1987 (66).

1. In this paper I will follow the convention of referring to Miles Davis by his given name only. Within the jazz community, certain artists are named in "shorthand fashion": "Monk" (Thelonius Sphere Monk); "Bird" (Charlie "Yardbird" Parker); "Dizzy" (John Birks "Dizzy" Gillespie). In its own way, it is a gesture of respect.

2. The term "improvisation" is utilized here with a limited definition, the one which is most commonly intended in jazz terminology. In this construction, "improvisation" connotes musical procedures that depend upon the selection, sequencing, and juxtaposition of musical elements, which selection is done in the moment by the players. It does not necessarily mean the spontaneous composition of completely new material, a process more often referred to in jazz as "free improvisation." Preexistent material may include chord sequences, favorite motivic/melodic ideas, quotations, common-practice conventions of accompaniment or arrangement (familiar introductions, endings, accompaniment patterns, etc.), in addition to new materials. But the specific selection and combination is improvised in the moment, and is a response to the specific performance situation.

3. Specifically I employ this definition of "ritual": "a code or system of rites . . . any practice done or regularly repeated in a set precise manner so as to satisfy one's sense of fitness and *often felt to have a symbolic or quasi-symbolic significance*" (*Webster's New International Dictionary*, 3d ed. Emphasis added).

4. "Performance [constructs a social reality] by socially constructing a situation in which the participants experience symbolic meanings as part of the process of what they are already doing" (Schieffelin 1985, 709).

5. Keyboardist Chick Corea described this process: "With Miles, there was never any sitting down and discussing the music: 'Hey, I'd like you to play a little more of this or that.' No instructions, no analytical conversation. There were grunts, glances, smiles, and no smiles. Miles communicated, but not on a logical or analytical level" (Lyons 1983, 261). Corea played with Miles in 1969 and 1970, at the end of the first style period to be discussed ahead.

6. Comments from keyboardist Adam Holtzman, who worked with Miles in the second style period we will examine, confirm this: "He keeps you watching him, keeps you on your toes, so you don't just become a player in the band, playing a tune. He doesn't want you to think you know what's going to happen" (in Dery and Doerschuk 1987, 82–85).

7. In most interview situations, musicians who have played with Miles have shown a marked propensity to avoid analytical language and simply to tell stories about him.

Few are willing to say "Miles is this way or that way," or "I think Miles meant this or that." Rather, almost all prefer to relate anecdotes, often focusing on Miles's ambiguous behavior, and usually replete with imitations of his gravelly whisper. Players from Miles's ensembles from the 1950s to the '80s—including drummer Jimmy Cobb, keyboardist Herbie Hancock, producer Teo Macero, bassist Dave Holland, and guitarist Mike Stern—all have pet Miles anecdotes, complete with vocal imitations.

8. "Art forms provide protected situations, categorized by high walls of excited insulation, in which 'disorientation' or the 'discontinuity of experience' can be savored. . . . Art thus permits humans to experience chaos symbolically and without danger; it provides the novelty which is necessary to break up old orientations" (Hanna 1979, 68).

9. Jay D. Dobbins's discussion of ritual symbols is particularly relevant here: "The building blocks . . . of ritual . . . are symbols. Symbols are simply articles, gestures, spaces, or times that—in a ritual context and by convention—stand for something else. . . . More important than a definition of symbol is its dynamic or function, which explains how ordinary articles and gestures are believed to achieve extraordinary results. . . . Hence, there is a latent ambiguity about symbol, and this ambiguity allows the ritual symbol to be open to many meanings, or to be *multivocal*" (Dobbin 1986, 99).

10. I regard the video and audio sources employed in this study as historical documents, not as omniscient or comprehensive records of "all that occurred." The process of recording video or audiotape is necessarily selective: in "framing" certain elements or events, others are ignored or lost. My analysis proceeds with this selectivity in mind. However, in this respect audiovisual material is no different than manuscript scores, letters, or descriptions–all of which, as records of events, are equally selective and incomplete.

11. This group was dubbed the "second great quintet" in hindsight to distinguish it from the so-called "first great quintet/sextet" of 1956 to 1960, which included saxophonists John Coltrane and Cannonball Adderley, pianists Red Garland or Bill Evans, double bassist Paul Chambers, and drummer Philly Joe Jones.

12. These groups tended to have much more flexible personnel rosters. Miles formed particularly close playing relationships with drummers Al Foster and Ricky Wellman, keyboardist Adam Holtzman, bass guitarists Darryl Jones and Joseph "Foley" McCreary, and saxophonist Kenny Garrett. These players in particular tended to remain in contact with Miles over lengthier periods of time than other band members of the period.

13. The term "modal," in jazz parlance, refers to a composition or improvisation built on scales other than those of common-practice European diatonic music. In the West, most listeners associate certain modes with certain ethnic musics: the Phrygian mode with flamenco, the Dorian mode with Celtic folk musics, etc. In jazz improvisational practice, these modes offered a range of tonal colors and an escape from bebop's dense and frequently changing chord progressions.

14. "Chorus", in jazz parlance, refers to a single repeat of the sequence of chords (often twelve, sixteen, or thirty-two measures) which accompany the composition's melody. The term itself derives from the fact that jazz musicians often opt to improvise on the chord progression of a song's chorus only, leaving out the verse. In practice, jazz musicians tend to conceive and assign solo durations in terms of multiples of choruses ("I'll take two choruses; you take four," etc.).

15. By "tonal durations," I mean a musical situation in which a chord's duration may

be fixed (that is, it may last for a relatively consistent length of time), but the usual rhythmic matrix of regular and even beats has somehow been altered.

16. It is worth noting in this performance instance not only the interaction of a visual cue (Miles placing his hand on Garrett's chest) and its sonic result (Garrett momentarily ceasing to play), but also the particular connotations that gesture invokes. In the context of a jazz band onstage, Miles laying his hand over Garrett's heart is an extremely intimate gesture, carrying implications we shall explore in later examples from the '80s bands.

17. That the physicality of such a response is a real phenomenon is consistent with ideas from dance theory: "Motion has the strongest visual appeal to attention, for it implies a change in the conditions of the environment which may require reaction" (Hanna 1979, 68).

18. One of the skills of the great jazz bandleaders was their ability to create great ensembles and ensemble approaches simply via selection of players. This is why jazz critics and historians tend to speak of the "first great quintet" and "second great quintet" in language which conflates the individual personalities, the individual approaches, the bandleader's vision, and the historical results. In this context Duke Ellington, Art Blakey, Jelly Roll Morton, and Charles Mingus may be cited, among others.

19. "Any meaningful activity is a conjunction of preexisting constraints (or rules, or structures, or laws, or myths) with the present, the unpredictable, particular *now*" (Becker 1979, 213).

20. John Coltrane, Cannonball Adderley, Herbie Hancock, Wayne Shorter, Joe Zawinul, Chick Corea, John McLaughlin, and many others went on to important and influental careers as bandleaders.

21. "One of the most important skills [of the ritual's director] was the ability . . . to control the focus of everyone's attention and maintain the right unity of mood throughout the performance" (Schieffelin 1985, 713).

References

Becker, A. L. 1979. "Text-Building, Epistemology, and Aesthetics in Javanese Shadow Theater." In *The Imagination of Reality*. Norwood, N.J.: Ablex.

Chambers, Jack. 1987. *Milestones: The Music and Times of Miles Davis*. Toronto: University of Toronto Press.

Davis, Miles. 1986. *Miles Ahead: A Tribute to Miles Davis*. Directed by Mark Obenhaus. Produced by Obenhaus Films, Yvonne B. Smith, Chrisann Verges, and Edward Gray. First aired 17 October on WNET, New York, a segment of *Great Performances*. Obenhaus Films. 120 min. Unreleased videocassette.

———. 1990. *Miles in Paris*. Directed by Frank Cassenti. Produced by Hubert Niogret. Trumpet Production. Burbank, Calif.: Warner Reprise Video. 60 min. Videocassette.

Davis, Miles, with Quincy Troupe. 1991. *Miles: the Autobiography*. New York: Simon and Schuster.

Dery, Mark, and Bob Doerschuk. 1987. "Miles Davis: His Keyboardists Present— Bobby Irving and Adam Holzman." *Keyboard Magazine* 13 (October):82–88.

Dobbin, Jay D. 1986. *The Jombee Dance of Montserrat: A Study of Trance Ritual in the West Indies*. Columbus: Ohio State University Press.

Doerschuk, Bob. 1987. "Miles Davis: the Picasso of Invisible Art." *Keyboard Magazine* 13 (October):67–77, 80–81.

Goodman, Fred. 1989. "Master Class in Times Square." *Rolling Stone* no. 544 (26 January):12.

Hanna, Judith Lynne. 1979. *To Dance is Human: A Theory of Nonverbal Communication.* Austin: University of Texas Press.

Kapferer, Bruce. 1986. "Performance and the Structuring of Meaning and Experience." In *The Anthropology of Experience,* edited by Victor Turner and Edward E. Bruner, 188–203. Urbana: University of Illinois Press.

Keepnews, Orrin. 1987. "Miles Davis: His Keyboardists Past." *Keyboard Magazine* 12 (October):96.

Lyons, Len. 1983. *The Great Jazz Pianists: Speaking of Their Lives and Music.* New York: William Morrow.

Schieffelin, Edward L. 1985. "Performance and the Cultural Construction of Reality." *American Ethnologist* 12, no. 4: 707–24.

Small, Christopher. 1988. *Music of the Common Tongue: Survival and Celebration in Afro-American Music.* New York: Riverrun.

Tarasti, Eero. 1987. "On the Modalities of Opera." *Semiotica: Journal of the International Association for Semiotic Studies* 66, no. 1:167.

CHAPTER THIRTEEN

The Improvisation of Louis Armstrong

LAWRENCE GUSHEE

Some of the first generation of New Orleans jazz musicians who moved to Chicago between 1918 and 1925 went beyond the inherent limits of their local style, taking not only a significant but an essential role in the formation of the dominant jazz style of the 1930s. It was sometimes unspectacular so far as the general public was concerned, as with a legion of string bassists; sometimes mediated and indirect, as with the inspiration Jimmy Noone gave Benny Goodman and Jimmy Dorsey, and which they in turn passed on; and sometimes so early and special as to be easily forgotten, as with Joe Oliver's talking cornet.

Against this background, Louis Armstrong's achievement is incomparable. The direct impact of his example on trumpeters—indeed, on all jazz players and singers—was unmatched in its time (approximately 1925 to 1935), as was his eventual rise to world recognition and the durability of his art. Although always a New Orleans musician in the bone, he grew with the music as it developed nationally, learning something from each situation in which he found himself, and teaching a generation of jazz musicians how to do it. He became indispensable in the way summed up by pianist Art Hodes: "Jazz is not—never has been—a one man show. But if I had to vote for one representative for jazz, that one would have to be Louis Armstrong" ("Roses for Satchmo" 1970, 16).

* * *

There is nothing in Armstrong's early upbringing or musical experience to explain his genius—nor is there in any artist's biography—but there is much to explain his competence and professional versatility. His first public performances as an eleven-year-old were as a street singer, something not typical for jazz musicians, from New Orleans or elsewhere.[1] Before Armstrong was a cornetist, he was an entertainer; small wonder, then, that his international stardom rested on his extrovert singing personality, something of which he, in contrast to many critics, was never ashamed. Perhaps his mugging and jiving ("Uncle Tomming," so far as many were concerned) were of a piece with this early seasoning as a street performer, no doubt drawing on eighty years of minstrel show stereotypes.[2]

So far as his early cornet experience goes, Armstrong played about every kind of music that was available to a Negro musician in New Orleans at that time, with the exception of theater pit orchestras (of which there was but one). He played in honky-tonk trios, in high- (Tom Anderson's) and low-class (Pete Lala's) cabarets, at society dances, central city and suburban dance halls, with street bands, and on the Streckfus excursion boats—in short, for every social or economic class, black or white. This intensive six-year period of apprenticeship was not untypical, and it went hand-in-hand with whatever time he devoted to study of the cornet as such, or to learning note reading and harmony.

Armstrong left no doubt whatever that Joe Oliver was his "main man"; not only was Armstrong inspired by Oliver, but the older man taught him important things about cornet playing and musicianship. Most important of all, perhaps, he restrained Armstrong's tendency to abandon the melody, to make variations which were too free.

> That's the first thing Joe Oliver told me when he listened to me play. . . . He used to come around the honky tonks where I was playing in the early teens [sic]. "Where's that lead?" I'd play eight bars and I was gone . . . clarinet things; nothing but figurations and things like that, like what the cats called bop later; that was just figuration to us in the early days. Running all over a horn. Joe would say, "Where's that lead?" and I'd say "What lead?" "You play some lead on that horn, let the people know what you're playing." (Morgenstern 1965; see also Pleasants 1974)

If Joe Oliver insisted on staying close to the lead, in what sense was he as "creative" as Armstrong repeatedly insisted? First of all, he played wonderful breaks—and much of what Armstrong plays are seemingly limitless realizations of a basic dominant seventh break. Second, Oliver's music embodies a kind of ethic of variation, in which, ideally, no note is played automatically. Even the most inconsequential motif is shaped, and any repetition is varied. It is this "ethic" which, applied thoroughly and with ingenuity, can make those paraphrases of Armstrong's which stick close to the melody—and which are therefore uninteresting to melodic and harmonic analysis—deeply satisfying to hear.[3]

Oliver showed a further concern for Armstrong that can justly be described as paternal (without requiring us to see Armstrong as "needing a father"), inviting him home, passing on his old cornet to him. Armstrong often said that he tried to play just like Oliver, and there is little doubt that his extraordinary blues playing (including the rare instances in which he used one of Oliver's favorite devices, the plunger mute in conjunction with a pixie mute) stems directly from Oliver, the Oliver who was so spectacularly adept at blues, far outclassing any of the older New Orleans players of whose style we have some tangible evidence (Freddie Keppard, Mutt Carey, Bunk Johnson, or Ernest Coycault).[4]

It's not easy to identify models other than Joe Oliver, not least because of the absence of phonograph recordings that would back up a claim of influence.

For example, Armstrong is said by many to have had much in common with his near-contemporary, Buddy Petit, and had many good things to say about his playing, perhaps even admitting to a major influence.[5] Indeed, so many competent musical witnesses testify to resemblances that we would be foolish to reject the evidence. What can't be determined, of course, is which aspects of his style parallel Petit's, and how "major" the influence was.

It was Willie "Bunk" Johnson who was offered, and who offered himself, as the major teacher of Armstrong, a claim which, on the basis of Johnson's recordings of 1942–47 as well as his reputation as a notorious liar, has struck most critics as of little merit. Collier is particularly skeptical, contending that "what Louis actually believed we do not know" (1983, 60). In a little-known interview from 1949, however, Armstrong clearly distinguishes between Johnson, someone admired from afar, and Oliver, who assumed an active and concerned role in his apprenticeship:

> Whenever ol' Bunk came by, I'd leave my corner [where he was selling newspapers] and follow the wagon. . . . He'd let me carry his horn when he wasn't playin', and it was a big thing for me. . . . I never knew a man that could get the tone, or the phrasing, like Bunk. He was a young man then. . . . Bunk was my idol, but Oliver used to come over to the honky tonk where I played and sit in. He'd show me things you know. He had some ideas. I think he was a little more alive musically than Bunk. Everything I did, I tried to do it like Oliver. (Jones 1949)[6]

There were other musicians who taught the young Armstrong something about note reading and the theory of music. The first of these appears to have been saxophonist and mellophonist Dave Jones, who worked with him on the Streckfus boats, "a fine musician with a soft mellow tone and a great ability to improvise" (Armstrong 1955, 182). Armstrong could already "spell," that is, slowly decipher a written part, but could not play at sight, something he admired in Fate Marable (the leader for Streckfus) and his musicians and wished to learn: "Kid Ory's band could catch on to a tune quickly, and once they had it no one could outplay them. But I wanted to do more than fake the music all the time, because there is more to music than just playing one style" (1955, 182). Jones taught him to sight-read, wrote Armstrong, well enough that he could read "everything he [Marable] put before me." If "everything" consisted only of the cornet parts from stock arrangements of the current hits, this wouldn't have been very difficult, and certainly not as difficult as the Fletcher Henderson arrangements that are said to have given him so much trouble in 1924. On the other hand, Armstrong might have been reading very little in the preceding two years and consequently merely rusty when he joined Henderson.[7]

From the testimony of New Orleans contemporaries, there is no doubt that by 1922, young Armstrong was one of the best young cornetists in the city.

Perhaps he was not as far ahead of his competitors in swing and imagination as he was to be after the seasoning of two years of steady work with Oliver in Chicago and the year with Henderson in New York; but there is no reason to doubt that his style was fixed in its essentials.[8]

* * *

When Armstrong arrived in Chicago in the summer of 1922, the leading trumpeters on the South Side besides Joe Oliver were Freddie Keppard, Joe Sudler, and Bobby Williams. Listeners were also taking note of the featured soloist with Vassar's orchestra, Tommy Ladnier from Mandeville, Louisiana, across Lake Pontchartrain from New Orleans, where he is said to have taken cornet lessons from Bunk Johnson. Ladnier had arrived in Chicago some four or five years earlier and had played briefly in St. Louis. An impressive sample of his playing from this period survives in the excellent recording of "Play That Thing" made by Ollie Powers' orchestra in the fall of 1923.[9]

Over the next two years, Ladnier recorded extensively in small bands, and at approximately the same time as Armstrong, made the move to a large eastern band playing from written arrangements, Sam Wooding's, with which he made an extensive European tour. Eventually he was to be a featured soloist with Fletcher Henderson's band two years after Armstrong's departure. After a second trip to Europe, Ladnier dropped out of the big band life, and the paths of the two men diverged. Subsequent to his swan song, the famous Mezzrow-Ladnier recording session organized by Hugues Panassié, he died miserably in 1939.

To understand something about where Armstrong was going by 1924 or 1925, you only need compare the two musicians, most directly perhaps on two performances of "Shanghai Shuffle," one by Armstrong with Fletcher Henderson, the other by Ladnier with Sam Wooding.[10] Ladnier seems a true, if slightly swingier, disciple of Joe Oliver; his solo, however, lacks the overall coherence of Armstrong's.[11] It's also instructive to listen to the solos with Isham Jones' orchestra of young Louis Panico, said to have taken wa-wa lessons from Joe Oliver. They are musically interesting, but lack the tonal warmth and swinging momentum that never seem to be absent in Armstrong's playing.[12]

When Oliver sent for Armstrong in the summer of 1922, he had only recently returned from an apparently not very successful year in California to a Chicago rather different from 1919, when at least three or four New Orleans bands of more or less standard makeup (violin, cornet, clarinet, trombone and rhythm of string bass, guitar, piano, and drums) had dominated the South Side music scene. A year or two later, the concept of a dance band as composed of sections, as well as featuring the novel timbres of hooting saxophones and intensively percussive banjo, had been widely popularized by the recordings of Paul Whiteman. By 1922, Whiteman had thickened his brass section by the addition of a second cornet, something heard in many other dance bands, a fashion which was beginning to be followed even in New Orleans. Perhaps Joe

Oliver, in sending for Armstrong, was also following fashion; perhaps he was asked to do so by the management of Lincoln Gardens; and perhaps he wanted to ease the burden on himself. Whatever the case, Armstrong arrived prepared to play second, and perhaps not minding at all: exempt from the obligation of carrying the melodic lead, the second cornet had much more freedom to explore harmony and counterrhythms.[13]

Whatever Oliver's motives, the thickening of the texture created by the additional part has much to do with the monumental impact the Oliver band's 1923–24 recordings have had on most critics and attentive listeners. To be sure, it's also a matter of enrichment and excitement, often from the way in which Armstrong appears to capitalize on the differences between their two styles. Although much of his phrasing follows Oliver with uncanny exactitude, in the spaces left by Oliver there is a constant presence of another musical personality, one with a different sense of time and a different vibrato.[14] At any rate, Oliver's band was almost the last large New Orleans–style band to hold down a major job in Chicago; in the later 1920s, the tradition could be maintained only by quartets and quintets. To the extent that Oliver's band was a traditional New Orleans band in its relative deemphasis on solos, it was regressive and an obstacle to Armstrong's career, at a time when bands all over the country were beginning to give a good deal of space to hot soloists, including trumpeters.

Lil Armstrong, who joined the Oliver band a few months after Armstrong and married him in February 1924, described her role in Armstrong's career on several occasions. According to one of her accounts—which Louis himself appears to have accepted—Oliver said to Lil, "As long as little Louis is with me he can't hurt me." This led her to recognize Louis' great talent—I find it curious that she did not recognize it at once—and she proceeded to convince him that he would have to leave the Oliver band in order to advance his career. According to Meryman (1971, 35) she also kept him from returning to Oliver in 1926.

Lil apparently also played a crucial role in furthering Louis' musical education. None of her biographies fail to mention youthful musical studies at Fisk University before she moved to Chicago in 1917, and her classical musical aspirations continued throughout the 1920s—she is even reported as playing Scriabin and Chopin in a 1929 concert. The evidence of her skill as a tunesmith lies before us in dozens of tunes recorded by Louis between 1926 and 1928; her abilities as a leader are witnessed by the universally and deservedly highly regarded series of recordings made under the names of the New Orleans Bootblacks and the New Orleans Wanderers in 1926.

During the time they were part of the Oliver band, the two Armstrongs apparently spent some of their free hours playing classical or light classical duets, and Lil is credited with instructing Louis in music theory, no doubt harmony. Armstrong may have been referring to that time when he wrote that "as a kid it just came natural. I never was one for going on and on about the changes of

Weather Bird Rag

By Louis Armstrong

Example 13.1. "Weather Bird Rag." (Transcribed from Copyright Deposit E561680, 14 April 1923.)

Example 13.1. *Continued*

a tune, if I've got my horn in my hand then let's go, all I want to do is hear that chord. I started to go through all that business of studying them big chords and harmonies way back, but then I found out I'd been playing them all the time" (Jones and Chilton 1971, 215). How much Lil helped Louis in writing tunes is uncertain. Beside the statement from Preston Jackson that she would write them down as fast as Louis would play them (Shapiro and Hentoff 1966, 102), we can observe that some of the early tunes submitted for copyright in 1923 and 1924 are in Louis' hand, some in Lil's.

We should in any event consider the group of tunes sent in for copyright by Louis Armstrong during the Oliver years, most notably "Cornet Chop Suey," "Weather Bird Rag," "I Am in the Barrel, Who Don't Like It" (or "Yes, I'm in the Barrel"), "Coal Cart Blues," and "Drop That Sack."[15] With the exception of "Coal Cart Blues," they are all in Armstrong's hand. First of all, it's surprising that they were set down on paper to begin with; second, that some of them existed two to three years before they were recorded with the Hot Five; third, that they are so close to the versions which were recorded; and finally, that they show as many harmonic traits associated with Armstrong's improvising style as they do.[16]

Our view of Armstrong's interests and abilities has to be modified in the light of some of these compositions. "Weather Bird Rag" (ex. 13.1), for instance, should no longer be ascribed to Joe Oliver, who presumably either purchased the rights to it, or simply exercised the rights of a band leader when it was recorded in 1923—in a melodically simplified version, let it be said. The 1928 duet recording with Earl Hines, then, is no longer a much elaborated version of a piece from the Oliver repertory—much less a "one-time affair," as it is termed by Godwin (1975, 414)—but a belated recording of one of Armstrong's own pieces in a version considerably closer to the original. As a rag, the piece is quite unconventional, with all three strains in the same key and with few of the rhythmic figures characteristic of the genre. Viewed positively, the tune has a great deal of forward, propulsive movement, signaled at the outset by the lengthy upbeat figure, and carried through by the mid-measure articulation of the first three phrases (mm. 2, 4, and 7) and the well-crafted melodic shape, climaxing in measure 12. From the harmonic point of view, there is much interest in the ingenious way Armstrong has of deriving melody from the chords, as in measure 3, with the elaboration of the subdominant E-flat triad; measures 43–44, which play around with the dominant F seventh; and measures 45–46, functioning as a kind of turnaround, many years before we might expect to find one.[17]

We can only guess about some of the sources of Armstrong's melodic inspiration. Certainly the opening of "Weather Bird Rag" sounds a lot like the very popular "Hiawatha" of 1903, and the trio resembles the famous "Eccentric Rag" of J. Russell Robinson, said to have been part of the Oliver repertory. Such connections should be no cause for surprise; a large number of the "original" tunes by New Orleans musicians are adaptations of well-known popular favorites, sometimes drawing on the earlier tune more or less directly ("Ory's Creole Trombone" and Clarence Wiley's "Car-Balick-Acid Rag-time" from 1901), sometimes simplifying and modifying the original ("At the Jazz Band Ball" and Chris Smith's famous "Ballin' the Jack"), sometimes identifiable only through a shared harmonic progression (as "Muskrat Ramble" may draw on "Maple Leaf Rag").

Of the other copyright submissions, the lead sheet of "Cornet Chop Suey" (ex. 13.2) (originally designated as a cornet part) is the most interesting, not only because so much of the recorded performance is seen to have been fixed on paper, but because of the small differences between the written version of January 1924 and the recorded performance of February 1926. These changes are especially noticeable in the first measures of the verse and of the chorus, and result in improved melodies, in the first instance by smoothing out the line, in the second by making it more angular. Also interesting are the inaccuracies of rhythmic notation,[18] such as the incorrect quarter rest in the first measure of the chorus, which reveal the articulation Armstrong had in mind.

The first two copyrighted tunes in which Armstrong had a hand were registered as by Louis Armstrong and Lillian Hardin. These are "New Orleans Cut-Out" (which, ascribed to Oliver, was recorded as "New Orleans Stomp") and "Coal Cart Blues," recorded with Clarence Williams two years after it was sent to Washington. The two melodies have strong points of resemblance, for instance the harmonic progression I–vi underlying the first strain of "New Orleans Stomp" and the second strain of "Coal Cart Blues." More notable than that, however, is the very prominent use made of melodic outlining of the tonic diminished seventh. In fact, it is an important feature of all of the early tunes, and may reveal Armstrong striving for a degree of harmonic sophistication.[19]

Example 13.2. "Cornet Chop Suey." (Copyright Deposit E580818, 18 January 1924.)

Armstrong was producing these copyrighted tunes at the same time Sidney Bechet was producing a substantial number in New York, where they were published under the aegis of Clarence Williams.[20] Like Armstrong, Bechet appears to have stopped writing tunes after an initial spurt of activity. Nonetheless, it is remarkable that the two New Orleans musicians regarded as the most creative improvisers also expressed their creativity in writing at the onset of their national and international careers.[21]

* * *

Armstrong's year-long stay in New York with Fletcher Henderson's band (October 1924 to October 1925) exposed him to a higher technical level of musicianship than he had previously known.[22] And despite the likelihood that Henderson would have preferred to hire as his new third trumpet Joe Smith— regarded by some to this day as Armstrong's artistic equal—Armstrong was amply capable of astonishing some of the rising young cornetists of the East Coast (for example, Rex Stewart), and doubtless other musicians (Coleman Hawkins is often cited). The charm and the challenge wore off in a matter of months: there is evidence that Armstrong eventually became bored with little more than brief eight- and sixteen-measure solos, and displeased at the lack of professional discipline in some of his fellow band members. Still, the freshness and vitality of those short solos in the context of the often rather drab and plodding Henderson arrangements of the time has led to the elevation of the episode in jazz history as a climactic turning point. But we must always ask whether the sequence of events as staked out by recordings truthfully represents an artist's development.[23]

In a very detailed discussion, informed by admiration and insight, of Armstrong's solos with the Henderson band, Gunther Schuller (1968, 90–95) offers a picture of a burgeoning and expanding talent who had already been moving away from his New Orleans musical style. The central idea is that over a six-year period Armstrong built his personal style around tiny phrase cells (Schuller also hears this in every great jazz artist). One should add that Schuller believes that in New Orleans only paraphrase or, as he terms it, "referential improvisation" was practiced. This is in contrast to the direction of the future, improvisation on chord progressions, in the development of which Armstrong was to play such a major role. One should note, somewhat in anticipation, that Schuller shares the prejudice of the majority of writers on Armstrong, namely, that the popular songs Louis played after 1929 are sentimental trash, only redeemed by the transformations achieved by improvisation on chord progressions.

This idea of the hegemony of paraphrase in the New Orleans style appears to be founded on the older practice of such as Joe Oliver, not on that which much evidence suggests was prevalent among younger players coming up after 1915. It's clear that a trumpeter of the same age as Armstrong could be conservative: Tommy Ladnier is a case in point. (This may be because he came to

Chicago in 1917 as a youthful disciple of Bunk Johnson and escaped the influence of such as Rena, Petit, Armstrong.) If, however, we pay close attention to the excellent Lee Collins (later one of the replacements for Armstrong hired by Joe Oliver), as he sounded in 1924 in a band under Jelly Roll Morton's direction,[24] we can hear some of the same figures and mannerisms as in Armstrong—chords being run, a strong and expressive vibrato, and a bold musical imagination. An alternative to Schuller's view, then, is that Armstrong had already constructed a coherent personal style out of common-property New Orleans jazz trumpet playing of the post–World War I years, and was not limited to melodic paraphrase. Indeed, when we listen to the arabesque of Sidney Bechet's first recorded solos in 1923, we may well surmise that New Orleans players born around 1900 had already by the early 1920s added other kinds of variation technique to that of the most obvious, melodic paraphrase.

Schuller's detailed analyses of three Armstrong solos from recordings with the Henderson band draw attention to his ability to recast or dislocate the rhythmic structure of the popular song, both by upbeats and by extensions at the end of a phrase. These Tin Pan Alley songs, just as those he began to play after 1929, require transformation, Schuller seems to believe. My ears hear and my eyes see, however, that all three examples—as vigorous and expressive as they are in the Henderson context—are still paraphrases in depending for their overall melodic progression on the pitches of the original song, embedding them, to be sure, in figuration. If the tune is well crafted so will be the solo, all things being equal. The surrounding of these nuclear pitches with elaborate prefixes and suffixes or their ingenious rhythmic placement can make structural repetitions into fresh musical events, but it doesn't support the general thesis of "cellular construction."

Perhaps a middle ground can be found in making far more emphatic the importance of the break in the formation of Armstrong's style. As Schuller observes, "Long a tradition in the New Orleans style, these breaks were what every interested listener waited for" (1968, 79). Of the four phrase-cells offered by Schuller as the foundation stones of Armstrong's style, three are in fact breaks. In my view, then, the Armstrong solos with Henderson, rather than meek but pregnant foreshadowings of a chordal improvisational style, are paraphrases larded with ambitious and well-integrated breaks.[25]

The concept of an orderly development in Armstrong's style from the Oliver band through the stint with Henderson also receives little support from his playing in the two other principal recorded contexts during this first New York period. If he sounds a bit stiff and tentative in some of the Henderson recordings, as Schuller would have it, this is certainly not the case in the nearly thirty recorded appearances with Clarence Williams's Blue Five and the Red Onion Jazz Babies. The most successful of these are the ones with Sidney Bechet, which show a spontaneity and energy surely in large part due to the challenge of Bechet's playing. Armstrong also goes well beyond the limits of playing either a second part, as with Oliver, or a rather straight paraphrase, as with Henderson—and this in a more traditional New Orleans context than with either Oliver or Henderson. He stays dramatically above G on "Pickin' On Your Baby," plays around with ambitious and abstract octave leaps on "I'm a Little Blackbird," and creates remarkably free and unpredictable background figures on "Mandy, Make Up Your Mind."[26]

Listening to Armstrong's many blues accompaniments of this period, especially those for Maggie Jones, further illuminates the question of stylistic development and consistency. Armstrong can sometimes be restrained and traditional, using Oliver's muting technique (as on "Poorhouse Blues" or "Thunderstorm Blues"); incompetent or confused, as in "If I Lose, Let Me Lose," a song with an unusual structure; or baroque and virtuosic, as in "Screamin' the Blues" and "Good Time Flat Blues."

The informal studio session organized by Perry Bradford that produced "I Ain't Gonna Play No Second Fiddle" (anecdote has it that the issued recording was to the players a trial run) also shows a more mature and exploratory Armstrong than many critics lead us to expect. Is it Armstrong who will change over the years to come, or is it the musical world around him, the context (to the demands of which he seems as a rule very sensitive)?

* * *

Armstrong returned to Chicago to play first trumpet and have featured billing in his wife's band at the Dreamland, back on the South Side. Whether a long-term record contract with the Okeh Company was already seriously under discussion before Armstrong's return to Chicago is not known, but very quickly after arriving he embarked on a two-year-long series of recordings under his own name. After the first nine releases, of which only two feature Armstrong's singing, there came a succession of twelve or fifteen on which he sings. All of these appeared in the Okeh 8000 "race" series, which, although not readily available outside of record stores and mail-order firms catering to Afro-Americans, were nonetheless heard by black and white musicians all over the country. During this period, Armstrong was playing in Carroll Dickerson's eleven-piece orchestra at the black-and-tan Sunset Cafe (he had left Lil's band at the Dreamland after a few months) and in Erskine Tate's even larger Vendome Theater orchestra. For most of 1927, Armstrong was billed as the leader of the Sunset orchestra—Dickerson had been fired for drinking—with Earl Hines as musical director.

At the end of the year the Sunset closed, and after an ill-fated excursion into dance hall management with Hines, Zutty Singleton, and Lil, Armstrong opened with a new Dickerson orchestra at the Savoy Ballroom. His eighteen Okeh recordings of 1928 are with a six- or seven-piece band drawn from this orchestra and called variously Louis Armstrong and his Hot Five, Savoy Ballroom Five, or even Louis Armstrong and his Orchestra. In these recordings many critics have heard Armstrong's greatest achievement, even while conventionally bewailing the allegedly inadequate musicianship of several musicians in the band.

The most extreme claims are made for the recordings of the Hot Five and Hot Seven: that they "revolutionized" jazz, or "turned it around." Schuller, often impatient with what he perceives as technical inadequacy, is remarkable in his standoffishness, especially with respect to the Armstrong–Ory–Dodds–St. Cyr Hot Five, although he also calls the series as a whole "one of the most remarkable long-term recording projects in the history of jazz."[27] Despite his reserve concerning artistic merit, he grants that the discs "not only made Armstrong an international name, but probably contributed more than any other single group of recordings to making jazz famous and a music to be taken seriously" (Schuller 1968, 98). More recently, James Lincoln Collier has asserted unequivocally that these are "the most important set of recordings of twentieth-century improvised music," and that "all across the United States musicians were enthralled by what Armstrong was doing, and they all wanted to do the same" (1983, 169).

It's difficult to imagine how one would actually demonstrate such sweeping propositions, and certainly Schuller and Collier don't attempt to do so. But I feel obliged to raise the question here, since the veneration of the Hot Fives and Sevens often goes hand-in-hand with rejection of the popular song performances of 1929–33, and a corresponding neglect of their widespread influence at home and abroad.

The first question that might be examined is that of repertory. We can begin with the observation that the influence of the Original Dixieland Jazz Band can be demonstrated by the rapid passage of perhaps a dozen of their tunes into the then forming body of jazz "standards." Bix Beiderbecke showed his roots by choosing to record their "At the Jazz Band Ball" and "Ostrich Walk," among other tunes. Jelly Roll Morton's impact can be measured in part by the standard status rapidly attained by "Milenberg Joys"—mediated to be sure by the recording by the New Orleans Rhythm Kings—and "King Porter Stomp." Furthermore, many of his tunes were made available (as those of the Original Dixieland Jazz Band had been earlier) in the form of orchestrations from Melrose Brothers Music Company. If musicians all across the United States wanted to do the same as Armstrong on the Hot Five recordings, one might expect to find some significant number of recordings or orchestrations of the Hot Five/Seven repertory in the decade 1926–1936. Failing that, one might hope for a good many instances of replication or imitation of Armstrong's solos, as we have, for example, for Beiderbecke's and Trumbauer's "Singin' the Blues." (As in Benny Carter's arrangement, recorded by Fletcher Henderson's band in 1931). Surely there can't be many such instances, since those critics who most strongly assert the influence of these records cite none.[28] Against this are the many performances of the post-1929 pop tunes which feature would-be facsimiles of Armstrong solos, and the fact that an astounding number of the standard jam session tunes of the 1930s were first recorded by Armstrong.[29]

The second feature that might have been imitated, the ensemble performance style, would have been difficult to copy, given the richly idiosyncratic timbres and somewhat antiquated rhythmic styles of Johnny Dodds and Kid Ory. If the recordings made in New York in 1926 under the leadership of Thomas Morris are such attempts, then they are also a measure of the difficulty of achieving the goal. That leaves us with Armstrong's performance style, in general (the vibrato, the manner of syncopating) and in particular (the storehouse of licks and formulas). The subject calls for an orderly approach that would go beyond the common-sense perception that a lot of musicians in the late 1920s were beginning to adopt the rhythmic phrasing that so immediately identified Armstrong's manner. The danger lies in attributing too much to Armstrong. For example, when Collier states that in the collection of cornet breaks published by Melrose in 1927 (see Armstrong 1951), "Characteristically, [Armstrong] bobs and weaves, constantly shifting direction, frequently in sawtoothed patterns" (Collier 1983, 178), he's describing one of the most salient features of the style associated with Bix Beiderbecke, as well as Miff Mole and Frank Trumbauer.[30]

My belief is that Armstrong's influence increases gradually, until by 1930–31 it's virtually a tidal wave; but that the earliest recordings made an impact primarily on the young Chicago musicians to whom they were most readily accessible. All the same, when they went to hear Armstrong in the flesh, those same musicians wouldn't have heard the somewhat antiquated New Orleans chamber music of the first set of Hot Fives, but in all likelihood the bravura Armstrong big band style.

By all accounts, little or no rehearsal was required for the recordings of 1925–26; all members of the group had worked together at one time or another in New Orleans and Chicago. Minimal rehearsal did not always result in sterling performances, and these Hot Fives are replete with instances in which another company with another market might have demanded another take. Eliminating alternate takes and keeping to a minimal instrumentation kept costs at a minimum, and it may also be that the use of a small band, common enough in the studios of producers of music for the "race market" at this time, made the task of the recording engineer easier.[31] In any event, considering that the first twenty-five Hot Fives were recorded acoustically—electrical recording, although available since early 1925, was not used by Okeh in Chicago until the end of 1926—their fidelity is exceptionally high, and Armstrong's playing and singing has very great "presence." Perhaps, as in the case of the Original Dixieland Jazz Band's recordings of eight or nine years previously, some important part of their impact is due to Armstrong's "phonogenic" sound.

Nevertheless, one is struck by how little solo playing by Armstrong there is in this earliest series, and how much by clarinetist Dodds. This modesty—of

Example 13.3. "Big Butter and Egg Man." *a,* Unadorned melody (mm. 9–12). *b,* Embedded melody (indicated by plus signs) with overshooting at both ends and rhythmic diminution (4th chorus, mm. 8–11). Louis Armstrong, recorded 16 November 1926 (Okeh 8423).

style, range, tone, and assertiveness, as well as in the amount of solo space claimed—is less in evidence on the last tune recorded at an otherwise unimpressive (even catastrophic) recording session in June 1926, "Sweet Little Papa," a prefiguration of the "Ding Dong Daddy" type. Five months later, there is a big change in Armstrong; his high range is more under control, he's working harder, and (consequently, I imagine) the band is better. "Big Butter and Egg Man" is the best-known and most highly regarded of these recordings. Its relatively slow chord changes possibly permit a degree of linear integration not previously achieved on record, and it presents particularly effective uses of Armstrong's practice of displacing phrases an octave down, and of embedding the pitches of the original melody in a long descending line with both prefix and suffix, as example 13.3 shows. Nonetheless, the solo is as much a paraphrase as ever in its structural outline.

About this time, Armstrong had also switched to and begun to master the trumpet. This was, according to his own account, to go along with James Tate, the first trumpet of the Vendome Theater orchestra.[32] It is more important that on this job he began to play much of the light classical repertory, standard overtures and the like, in addition to being featured as a jazz soloist.[33] The two extant recordings of Armstrong with Erskine Tate's orchestra feature the jazz soloist, albeit a rather hysterical one without a strong sense of form. Armstrong's first electrical recording date in his own name also casts him in this bravura role; that even he had technical growing pains, with a mind that was moving faster than his lips and fingers, can be heard on "Wild Man Blues."[34]

Even though Armstrong was still recording with the old gang, he had by now become so assertive—or was permitted to be by the men in the recording studio—that the entire texture and meaning of the records changes. "Alligator Crawl," recorded three days after "Wild Man Blues," can in retrospect be heard to be headed towards the "West End Blues" of a year later. (The same might be said of the somewhat later "Savoy Blues.") At the same session came what to many is the most important "classic" solo of 1927, "Potato Head Blues."

Before I had a chance to examine the lead sheet of this tune submitted for copyright in Lil Armstrong's hand, I wrote in an early draft of the essay that it

Example 13.4. "Potato Head Blues." (Copyright Deposit E67895, 26 November 1927.)

was difficult to know how much of this performance was composed, predetermined statement, how much paraphrase, and how much creation of new melody. I further stated, "[One assumes that] the theme is the same kind of thing as a bebop 'head,' i.e., Armstrong's elaborate and relatively fixed melody or 'line' over a well-worn chord progression." If Lil's hastily written lead sheet has any authority, however, we have to conclude that the simple lead is not stated by Armstrong until the final chorus, and the characteristic rhythms of the verse are quite absent.[35] I'm still inclined to give credence to my first reaction, before the recovery of the lead sheet, comparing Armstrong's line to a bebop "head." A good candidate for the source tune would be Ferd Morton's "Froggy Moore," alias "Frog-I-More Rag," which was given so powerful a reading by Joe Oliver's band in 1923. And we are also fortunate to have a solo of Armstrong's on that tune (ex. 13.5), as recorded for the Melrose publication of 1927, *Fifty Hot Choruses of Armstrong* (see Armstrong 1951).

The question of harmonic models arises again with another of his famous solos of the period, from "Hotter Than That."[36] The harmonic model here appears to be the trio strain of "Tiger Rag," or rather its version in E-flat, "Milenberg Joys," which was to the twenties what "I Got Rhythm" was to be to the thirties and forties.[37] "Struttin' with Some Barbecue" also follows "Tiger Rag" closely in its last half, but in the first half it takes a turn to the supertonic minor chord (C minor in the key of B-flat), which it has in common with many other tunes of this period, in particular "Potato Head Blues." What we have is a cluster of closely related tunes, in which the same structural principles clearly govern Armstrong's classic solos: organization into four-bar phrases at a time when many musicians could barely handle one or two bars; rather close parallelism of both pitch and contour between successive phrases, frequently starting high and ending low for the first two, with the third one ending higher; and often a very strong degree progression, with stressed pitches comprising a descending scale.[38]

The perplexity expressed above concerning the difference between the carelessly notated lead sheet of "Potato Head Blues" and the recorded performance of the tune is matched by perplexity of a different sort in the presence of the lead sheet of "Savoy Blues" (ex. 13.6), of which Edward "Kid" Ory is the copyright holder. If the copyright deposit of "Muskrat Ramble" is in his hand, as seems likely, then certainly "Savoy Blues" is not. If it were, the careful and amazingly complete sketch of the recording, tantamount to an arrangement, would radically alter our notion of the kind of musician Ory was. In any event, it is difficult to know what to make of the situation. My guess would be that the lead sheet was made as the first step of the conversion of the recorded performance into an orchestration. It could also be that "Savoy Blues" existed as a big band arrangement for the Carroll Dickerson band, but was recorded by the Hot Seven in a reduced version. Either situation would make sense of the cues, such as "Brass trio break," "Banjo or guitar solo," and "Cornet solo ad lib." The most shocking possibility would be that the entire performance was planned at the level of detail represented in the lead sheet—which is actually more like a short score. Whatever the case, contrary to Collier, who regards this as a "classic New Orleans number" (1983, 185), it seems to me that with the recording of "Savoy Blues," Armstrong definitively breaks with the

FROG - I - MORE RAG

By
FERD "JELLY ROLL" MORTON

Example 13.5. "Frog-I-More Rag" (transcription of Armstrong solo; from Armstrong 1951 [37]).

New Orleans ensemble style. Everything in the performance serves as a setting for his deeply affecting solo.[39]

In these last recordings with the old Hot Five, Armstrong had found an adequate foil in Lonnie Johnson, an astounding instance of a major blues artist more than able to hold his own in a jazz context.[40] The recordings of 1928 with pianist Earl Hines show an Armstrong more flexible and adventurous in phrasing, not just in anticipations and delays, but in his cutting entire phrases

Example 13.6. "Savoy Blues." (Copyright Deposit E687646, 9 April 1928.)

afloat from the beat. In this Hines was perhaps his model.[41]

These eighteen titles recorded in 1928 by the contingent from Dickerson's Savoy Ballroom Orchestra have been justly appreciated by many, perhaps most notably by Gunther Schuller (1968) and Richard Hadlock (1965). Of all the titles, "West End Blues" has attained the rank of a supreme jazz classic. Just appraisals aside, there has been relatively little attempt to explain, insofar as such things can be explained, how this masterpiece came about and what led up to it.[42] Was it a number featured by Dickerson's big band at the Savoy Ball-room? (At least one person reports hearing it as such.) Was it the only such extended cadenza that Armstrong played at this time?

Nearly equally admired is the tour de force of the Hines-Armstrong duet performance of *Weather Bird*.[43] Schuller understands it as a spontaneous cre-ation, even though it also strikes him as having the cohesiveness of a "con-sciously premeditated composition" (1968, 126). Collier does not commit him-self, and generally regards the recording as less of an instance of masterful "interplay" than previous writers (1983, 191). The evidence of the lead sheet from King Oliver's Creole Band days indicates that the piece is Armstrong's, and shows highly original features, particularly in phrasing, which drop out of Oliver's orchestral version. The degree to which what is played is represented in writing is reminiscent of "Cornet Chop Suey," with the spice contributed from some intense moments of empathy of two mature talents, and the new way of playing without an obtrusively stated beat.

So far as the group of recordings as a whole is concerned, J. R. Taylor, in his comprehensive liner notes to the major reissue of these 1928 recordings, sees an important change in musical texture resulting from a change in policy by executives of the Okeh record label: "Henceforth, Armstrong would record more intricate and 'up-to-date' arrangements; he would take more of his reper-tory from Tin Pan Alley, and less from indigenous New Orleans favorites" (Taylor 1975). It is well known, however—or should be—that two groups of white jazzmen recording in New York at this time were listened to by most U.S. jazz musicians, black and white: these groups were led by Frank Trum-bauer and Red Nichols. If a progressive, sophisticated influence *at this time* is sought, then this is the music to attend to.[44] What I hear in many moments of Armstrong's "Fireworks," "Skip the Gutter," "Sugar Foot Strut," and "Knee Drops" are echoes of Vic Berton, Arthur Schutt, Fud Livingston, and yes, even Nichols himself . . . to be sure, with a very heavy South Side Chicago accent.

Now, for commercial Tin Pan Alley–Broadway material, we should listen to the accompaniments provided by Armstrong for Lillie Delk Christian. They represent, shall we say, the club date Armstrong, relaxed and horsing around somewhat at the expense of a singer who must have been more notable for her looks than her voice. But there are at least three things that bear noticing: the modernity or timelessness of the accompanying quartet, where much of what the Savoy Ballroom Five does is distinctly of its period; second, the degree to which Armstrong is, once again, responsive to another major soloist, in this case Jimmy Noone, emulating him in extraordinary low-register playing and very fluid scales;[45] and finally, how much difference up-to-date popular song material makes. In fact, two of Armstrong's finest recordings of the 1929–34 period, "Sweethearts on Parade" and "I Can't Give You Anything But Love," are not merely anticipated, but prefigured. Armstrong, once again, was prepared to do what was needed to fit into a new musical environment without any stumbling or hesitation.[46]

Considering how much importance is attributed to Armstrong's second move to New York, in the spring of 1929, and the subsequent redirection of his recording career which turned him into a major performer of mainstream popular songs, it is vexing that the details of his managing and booking remain obscure. The times at which Tommy Rockwell and Johnny Collins became directly involved with Armstrong's business seem to be known only approximately, although it was Rockwell who brought Armstrong to New York.[47] We would also like to be clear about the 1931 incidents in which gangster interests attempted to pressure either Armstrong or his management (or both). The biography by Jones and Chilton gives some of this story (1971, 118–22; although as a prank of fate, the crucial passage is marred by drastic errors of typesetting!), the upshot of which may have been to keep Armstrong out of New York, and perhaps even to convince him to travel and stay in Europe. Collier appears to subscribe to this idea but can provide no additional information on the tangled relationships that may have existed between Rockwell, Collins, and various criminal gang interests (1983, 225 ff.).

After an initial period of jobbing around New York, Armstrong spent about a year in the east, with New York as his base of operations. He was backed as a solo attraction by at least three different bands (Dickerson's, Luis Russell's, and one which eventually was to be Mills' Blue Rhythm Band), with all of which he recorded. He then spent nine months in Los Angeles, at Frank Sebastian's Cotton Club, in front of two orchestras, one led by Leon Elkins, the other by Les Hite. From April 1931 to April 1932, he toured with a group organized and under the musical direction of trumpeter and arranger Zilner Randolph. Another brief engagement in Los Angeles intervened before his departure for four months of appearances in England.[48]

Armstrong had been the last major star to join the stable of Okeh recording artists prior to the company's collapse in 1932. On his return from England he began recording with the Victor company. For the first session in December, he was accompanied by the Chick Webb band, then subsequently by a new band organized for him by Zilner Randolph. In July 1933, he left again for Europe, where he was to remain for eighteen months, appearing in England and extensively on the Continent. There was only one European recording session, the results of which were not distributed in this country, and thus an effective two-and-a-half-year gap between the last Victor session and the first one for Decca in October 1935. This startling discontinuity in the recording career of an artist who since 1924 had never been absent from the studios for longer than six months was matched by nearly six months of layoff from performing after his return from Europe in early 1935. Armstrong put it this way on one occasion: "When I come back to America I didn't blow the horn for about six months. I'd thrown it out of my mind. Couldn't go no further with all them shysters yiping at me" (Jones and Chilton 1971, 159). This may be an allusion to a support suit filed by Lil Armstrong. Damage to his lip—which had already forced him to rest for months in Europe—has also been cited as a (or the) cause.

At this point, Armstrong began to be managed by Joe Glaser, who had been one of the managers of the Sunset Cafe in Chicago when Armstrong played there. It may be that Glaser had been associated with Rockwell in the Irving Mills organization at some time; certainly he was part of the Rockwell-O'Keefe agency. Glaser had considerable success in dealing with black performers and jazz musicians. (At his death his firm, Associated Booking Corporation, was said to have over one thousand clients of all complexions.) I assume that Glaser was responsible for Armstrong's Decca record contract (Decca was managed by Jack Kapp, another Chicagoan from the twenties), which lasted for over a decade. Under the Decca contract Armstrong recorded profusely: approximately 125 titles in the eight years before the 1942 recording ban, often with other musicians under contract to Decca, such as the Casa Loma Orchestra or the Mills Brothers. It is striking that a sizeable number are remakes of earlier successes of the 1929–32 period; equally striking that very few, if any, of the contemporary pop tunes entered into either the jazzman's or the gigging dance musician's standard repertory in the way the earlier tunes had.[49]

Corresponding with the move to New York and a pop tune repertory in 1929, there is a change of the critical guard. One group of critics (including Schuller and Collier) places Armstrong's peak somewhere between 1926 and 1928; they either disparage his later work or find it inconsequential and nothing new. On the other hand, a second group, while finding the Chicago recordings fine enough, is more interested in and more sympathetic to his later career; concomitantly, they are as a rule little interested in his New Orleans background. Among such critics, one should name Hugues Panassié, John Chilton, Albert McCarthy, and from the technical point of view especially, André Hodeir. The first three provide useful critical surveys of Armstrong's later recordings.

The bases for either outright rejection of or at least disappointment in the 1929–32 period are several and deserve some discussion. First, there is in some writers a general hostility to Tin Pan Alley and its "commercial" product, often with strong ideological overtones. Second, the bands which accompany Armstrong, including their soloists and arrangers, are felt to range from incompetent to mediocre. Third, Armstrong's grandstanding (if not Uncle Tomming) and increasing reliance on formulas and quotations is deplored. It's as if Armstrong failed to measure up to the greatness of his own art as demonstrated just a few years earlier.

On the first point, Louis, as a true son of New Orleans, would want both to give people what they wanted and to keep up to date ("moldy-fig" purism is not a musician's doctrine). On the second point, Armstrong appears to have verged on irresponsibility when it came to selecting and rehearsing bands. The result was certainly unevenness; nonetheless, some of the backup bands are more than satisfactory. As to the final point, some of Armstrong's playing—particularly when taken out of the theatrical context—strikes most listeners today as hysterical or tasteless. "Some" here, however, means now and then, not most of the time. Alongside the most overblown and "tasteless" Armstrong we can hear the most austere, the most reflective and thoughtful.[50]

Armstrong had this to say about some of the things he was doing during this period:

> But I wasn't thinking about nothing in those days. Just idling away all day and blasting all night. Just trying to please the musicians. And they the ones with passes, ain't putting out nothing. Those cats would bring their sandwiches, sit there and catch four more shows a day. . . . And the audience, the ordinary public, thought I was a maniac or something, running amuck. I was only standing on my head, blowing my brains out, to please the musicians. I forgot about the audience—and it didn't do me no good.
>
> See, I think when I commenced to put a little showmanship in with the music, people appreciated me better. Always used to play one number after another. . . . So I found out, the main thing is live for that audience, live for the public. If the people ain't sick of it, I ain't. . . . I do that song "Hello, Dolly!" the same way every night 'cause that's the way the people like it. And even back in the old days it was like that—when everybody was supposed to be improvising. Who knows who's improvising? All trumpet players can hear what you play and they can play the same notes. . . . And always, once you got a certain solo that fit in the tune, and that's it, you keep it. Only vary it two or three notes every time you play it—specially if the record was a hit. (Meryman 1971, 40–43)

Certainly, he was still going overboard on his first English tour. Max Jones describes his impression, at a concert at the London Palladium, of "an image of the man out front—a lithe, smallish but power-packed figure prowling the stage restlessly, menacingly almost, and growling and gesticulating when he was not playing, singing or talking into the microphone. . . . Each tune was climaxed with outbursts of prodigious bravura trumpet. . . . I remember doubting if he was in full control of himself (Jones and Chilton 1971, 136).[51]

The change to the new kind of song was of major importance, not merely because Armstrong had now entered the mainstream of U.S. popular music, but because these songs were of a structural type different from most of those he had been accustomed to playing in the past. First, the break, so basic an

Mahogany Hall Stomp

Example 13.7. "Mahogany Hall Stomp." Louis Armstrong, recorded March 1929 (Okeh 8680).

event in all jazz up to that point, became inappropriate. These new AABA songs were in one respect more repetitious than the ABAC or similar 32-bar forms of yesteryear, since the initial eight-measure section is heard three times. This in turn often entailed a higher degree of contrast between the A section and the B section (or "bridge"). Where Armstrong's response to the slowly

[all ahead of beat]

Tag

Example 13.7. *Continued*

changing chords of the 32-bar long forms, such as "Tiger Rag" or other ABAC types, was to become a virtuoso at making long four-bar or even eight-bar phrases, the new frame pushed him in the direction of a more concise, less luxuriant style in which rhythmic permutation plays a larger role. The beautifully-crafted windings through dominant seventh chords became less common by far.[52]

Perhaps the new kind of song once again accentuated a tendency already present in Armstrong's playing. In the recording of "Mahogany Hall Stomp" made just before his turn to the pop song, the last two ensemble choruses are masterly rhythmic variations of Armstrong's first solo chorus (ex. 13.7).[53] Particularly obvious here is a use of the sixth, major seventh, and ninth of the prevailing harmony which seems more studied and self-conscious than before. Almost from the beginning, Armstrong had used such pitches in a manner that seemed entirely natural, in distinction to such "advanced" trumpeters as Beiderbecke and Nichols. It's not beyond the realm of possibility that he had begun to listen to them and take them seriously, thereby becoming more ingenious and less predictable in his choice of chord tones.

Some of his performances around this time abandon any simple or even relatively complex paraphrase, relying instead on the creation of quite brief and readily recognizable motifs, often with a strongly melodic character of their own. Although these may sometimes outline a harmony, it is very rare for Armstrong to indulge in arpeggiation of the sort that his great near-contemporary Coleman Hawkins was bringing to a fine art. The third chorus of his performance of "Lonesome Road" (ex. 13.8) can serve as an example.

The Lonesome Road

Example 13.8. "The Lonesome Road." Louis Armstrong, recorded 6 November 1931 (Okeh 41538).

In this solo, one feature is not at all new: the parallelism of the first and the second eight measures. Each of the four subphrases of the first eight measures occurs in the same order, but with considerable alteration and displacement, in the second eight. What is new is the conciseness and the distance from the tune. Measures 5 and 6, for example, are replaced by what was to be a swing era cliché. Louis also shows considerable sensitivity to the difference between a first and a second ending, using the bare fifth in addition to a strongly directional tag in measures 13–16.[54]

Armstrong, then, creates new melody of an allusively motivic sort, in con-

Example 13.9. "I Got Rhythm" (last chorus, mm. 1–12, with 3-bar pickup). Louis Armstrong, recorded 6 November 1931 (Okeh 41534).

trast to the expansive festoons of earlier years. Sometimes he indulges in pure rhythmic invention, as at the start of his solo from "Georgia On My Mind." Here the old "ethic of variation" is most emphatically audible—as it had been also in the subtle rhythmic differentiations of the tiresome three-note motifs of "Twelfth Street Rag" and "Savoy Blues." Finally it was possible for him at this time to cut himself loose completely from the tune, as he does in "I Got Rhythm" (ex. 13.9).[55]

With this new, few-noted style Armstrong was as able to "tell a story" as he had been, and he was able to make it last longer. His four famous choruses on "I'm a Ding Dong Daddy from Dumas" (ex. 13.10) can serve as a more-than-adequate illustration of how it was done. First of all, he uses the simplest over-all plan in the book, that of starting in a lower range and then in successive choruses raising the level. In addition, however, the initial motif of measures 1–2 (which worries the minor third and puts in stark relief the semitone) is reused in the first six measures of the second chorus, with its slithering around A, G-sharp, and G. This then serves as the first motif of the third chorus. The technique of also using a long-held tone in the final one or two measures of a chorus to link it to the next one is perhaps a bit obvious and certainly very easy to overdo, but it clearly serves Armstrong well in "telling his story." The final chorus is a reprise of the first, but considerably altered in rhythm and in shorter phrases.[56]

In his *Hommes et problèmes du jazz* (1954), André Hodeir offered for the first time a well-founded, technically competent, and forcefully expressed analysis of Armstrong's procedures of this later period; the context was a general theory of improvisation that still has great value. In his view Armstrong is perhaps the most brilliant representative of the first of the two pathways of jazz improvisation: the interpretation of a preexisting melody in the form of paraphrase. Hodeir recognized, nonetheless, that this first path could result, "in the most favorable instances, in a kind of transfiguration [or transformation],

Example 13.10. "I'm a Ding Dong Daddy from Dumas." *a,* Melody, as played by saxes. *b,* Trumpet solo. Louis Armstrong, recorded 21 July 1930 (Okeh 41442).

Example 13.10. *Continued*

from the inside, of material often lacking any melodic interest in its own right.[57]

Hodeir, however, was an evolutionist who saw a kind of inevitable logic in the direction jazz style was to take: away from paraphrase to free variation on a given harmonic progression.[58] Where Schuller saw too much of the "progressive" in Armstrong, Hodeir saw too little. I hope my readers will listen attentively to the Armstrong of 1929–32 for a freedom with respect to the melody not incomparable in principle to that found in the work of Lester Young.

One recent author who tussles with the question of Armstrong's approach to improvisation has suggested with some reserve that he may have used a procedure called the "correlated chorus": "play two measures, then two related, making four measures, on which you played another four measures related to the first four, and so on ad infinitum to the end of the chorus (Collier 1983,

132).[59] Collier's reserve is understandable, inasmuch as Armstrong's true mastery was in welding together parallel four-measure units, not in the creation of antecedent-consequent constructions. The explanation for coherence in Armstrong's choruses, taken as a unit, is to be found, in my opinion, in his careful attention to strong melodic patterns (often scales) in the overall contour—a lesson learned from Armstrong by many other skilled jazz soloists.[60]

When it comes to solos of more than one chorus in length, Collier subscribes—this time unhesitatingly—to an explanation Armstrong himself is said to have provided: "On the first chorus I plays the melody, on the second chorus I plays the melody around the melody, and on the third chorus I routines." Collier unpacks the verb "to routine" in several hundred apt words, but does not do the same for the notion of playing a melody around the melody, which is susceptible of more than one interpretation (1983, 287). He doesn't pose the further question: why should such a procedure make for continuity? I would propose a possible answer: that this three chorus scheme is a kind of large ABA' structure, two relatively simple sections framing a complex one. Furthermore, the "routining" chorus can use some of the material of the first one, albeit in transposed or otherwise altered form. This I take to be the case with the "Ding Dong Daddy" solo.[61]

A few words are in order concerning Armstrong as an improviser in situations when multiple takes have survived from the same recording session.[62] Over the years a kind of romantic idealism has taken shape with respect to jazz solos—call it the jam session esthetic—according to which the heat of inspiration produces solos which are each time new, original, spontaneous, and surprising. Armstrong, however, often came under fire for repeating himself, both in repertory as well as in the solos developed for individual tunes. To be sure, he seems to have chosen this course quite deliberately, to judge from the lengthy quotation cited above (p. 313).

The second and third takes of "Between the Devil and the Deep Blue Sea,"[63] recorded in January 1932 when the song was quite new, show that the main outlines of his solo, including the chief pitches of the opening motif, were clearly in mind, but the detail is very different, and also the overall character. Take 2 is rather slow, but perhaps the tempo enabled Armstrong to bring out arabesques in sixteenth notes of a very "modern" sort. This solo is consequently packed with ideas, really too many of them. On the next take the tempo is a notch faster and Armstrong creates a half chorus which is more economical, better balanced, and more thoughtfully shaped, placing his sixteenth notes to maximum effect instead of sowing them prodigally throughout the initial sixteen measures. (Still, it's take 2 I prefer!) Both solos are quite distant from the melody, something which may have been facilitated by its construction on the I–vi–ii–V chord sequence, the greatest of clichés by 1940, but in 1930 relatively fresh.[64]

There are also two takes of "Star Dust" from the same period, which are often cited for imagination and originality.[65] Here Armstrong stays much closer to the tune than with "Between the Devil and the Deep Blue Sea," although these two takes differ substantially in the placement of explicit return to the melody. And although the "Star Dust" performances are more dramatic in their plan, the amount of material not traceable to Hoagy Carmichael's song is relatively small—except, that is, in the vocal chorus of take 3, famous, perhaps even notorious, for the extent of the "destruction" of the melody. Since some of the same departures appear virtually identical in the next take, it's reasonable to assume that they were part of the routine—although perhaps only blocked in, as it were. It's notable that in take 3, after a definitely unstraight vocal chorus, the trumpet chorus is rather close to the melody, whereas the inverse occurs in the next take.[66]

Armstrong's technical equipment, his musical memory, harmonic sense, and freedom with the beat were such that he could easily produce successive realizations of the same tune that fit any reasonable listener's definition of improvisation. Whether Armstrong thought of them that way is another question entirely. And the studious critic may have yet other views.

All this question of definition aside, I think that attentive hearing of the best of Armstrong's recordings of this period (often cited are "Blue Again," "Sweethearts on Parade," "If I Could Be with You," "I've Got the World on a String," "Confessin'," and among the up-tempo tunes, "Laughin' Louie," especially for its spectacular cadenza) reveals a control of musical structure beyond that of his earlier recordings—or perhaps it's that the popular song obliged or allowed that control to emerge with greater clarity. And no doubt the difference between the New Orleans ensemble and the emerging swing band made a good deal of difference. Armstrong's recordings prior to 1929 had taught many players such things as licks, breaks, ways of managing certain kinds of harmonies, and so forth. His work from 1929 onward was more forward-looking and was a kind of primer for jazz soloing in the context of the swing band.

* * *

In a brief and interesting section on black brass players of the '20s, Gunther Schuller devoted special attention to Johnny Dunn and Jabbo Smith, two trumpeters often neglected in jazz histories, although highly regarded and influential in their day (1968, 207–14). Perhaps he overrates their esthetic or artistic stature; nonetheless, he forces us to remember that Armstrong had locked horns with Dunn on several occasions in New York and Chicago, and viewed Jabbo Smith, especially, as significant competition.[67]

The two dozen or so young black trumpeters remembered by jazz history as active in New York City between 1925 and 1930 responded to Armstrong himself in varying degree, sometimes by deliberate choice, sometimes probably by osmosis. And even if Armstrong's style in its concrete particulars affected some of them little, his example spurred them on by showing what a trumpet was capable of. As Doc Cheatham put it:

> The first trumpet player I liked was Louis Panico! Of course, what he was doing was a lot of funny stuff. Then came Johnny Dunn, and I liked the first recording of his I heard. After that I saw Joe Smith . . . but I don't think I would have continued on cornet if I hadn't heard Louis Armstrong. . . . [A]fter hearing Louis Armstrong, Joe Oliver and all those trumpet players from Louisiana in Chicago, I saw something very different and interesting in the trumpet. . . . But my trumpet style didn't come from just one player. I had too many influences, and I liked the ones who could play lead trumpet. (Dance 1979, 309–10)

This is the pattern, with differences, we see in Roy Eldridge, who tells us of his liking for Red Nichols ("not because it was clean, but because it was different"), for Rex Stewart and Bobby Stark, and particularly Joe Smith (Dance 1979, 149). In early 1928 he had also heard St. Louis trumpet players who had come under Armstrong's influence, but he did not actually hear Armstrong in person until 1931 in New York. At that point, the twenty-year-old Eldridge learned to do Armstrong well enough, as subsequent recordings demonstrate, but kept the fast style he had already developed. Eldridge's musical inheritance was multiple, but our seemingly innate desire for simplicity has led to a single-stranded jazz trumpet lineage, one even promulgated by trumpeters themselves in moments of piety. Thus Dizzy Gillespie: "I know that I came through Roy Eldridge, a follower of Louis Armstrong" (1979, 295).[68]

The coexistence of competing and to some extent incompatible concepts of rhythmic and melodic shape was, in fact, a major difficulty for many young trumpeters around 1930; it blurred their vision of style. So with Louis Metcalf, born in St. Louis in 1905. On his recordings of 1929 with Luis Russell's orchestra, he has a marvelously full sound and is beginning to reach for the stratosphere. At his best in ensemble, Metcalf could not come near Armstrong in swing and rhythmic continuity. Metcalf's borrowings from Bix Beiderbecke were not well assimilated, and they fight against those from Armstrong, not to speak of a residue of inflexible Johnny Dunn-isms.

Metcalf eventually did arrive at a coherent style, less dramatically perhaps than Henry "Red" Allen, a trumpeter of force, flexibility, and subtle imagination. In Allen's 1929 recordings under his own name and with Luis Russell's group, his imitations of Armstrong are gauche, and what is original in his playing often fails, for example, his last solo appearance on "Jersey Lightning." Very rapidly, however, he converted his mannerisms (a very rapid trill, a special kind of crescendo, and a more eccentric and original repertory of rhythms and phrases than Armstrong's) into style and imbued them with a nervous intensity very much his own.[69]

* * *

After his return to the American scene in 1935, Armstrong more and more shared the fate of other highly influential jazz players, who found that their once trail-blazing style had become old hat to critics and customers alike. It is widely agreed that his playing was less spectacular, if no less imaginative, and his vocal mannerisms could verge on self-parody. Armstrong, however, did find supporters for this later, less athletic and more economical style,[70] and he found new audiences for his voice and stage personality with songs ranging from "Blueberry Hill" and "Someday" to "Mack the Knife" and "Hello, Dolly." Careful listeners could find much to praise in individual performances between 1935 and 1960, both those which repeated and surpassed successes from the twenties—his 1938 "Struttin' with Some Barbecue" or the 1957 "King of the Zulus"—or those which reached out in new directions—the Columbia LP devoted to W. C. Handy tunes or the collaborations with the Dukes of Dixieland.

Armstrong, to be sure, had never been an organizer of or composer-arranger for orchestra,[71] so that path to further musical development was not open to him; nevertheless, he kept working, very hard indeed for someone who often said he just wanted to have a good time in music. With the coming of bebop, Armstrong became fair game for music reporters who could count on him for querulous or downright contemptuous opinions of the new jazz. He had, after all, staked his entire career after 1935 on giving the public and his record company what they wanted.

Mostly, Armstrong seemed imperturbable and indestructible. Perhaps in a different time or place, or with a different musical upbringing, he would have done something really new after 1932, and continued to be part of jazz history seen journalistically as a succession of innovations. The fact is that for all art in which the acquisition of a consistent personal style and technique are primary, there is a kind of built-in limit which is rarely or never gone beyond, and thus an inevitable end to innovation so far as the individual is concerned.

It is the contention of this essay that Armstrong ripened early, was particularly fortunate in learning to balance his fancy figuration with a sober respect for the "lead," and that without consciously making "career decisions," he did many of the right things at the right place, perhaps with some strategic nudging from his managers.[72] The unfolding of his work is perhaps as much a product of expanding opportunities and a taste for many kinds of music, as it was of wider conceptual horizons.

Louis Armstrong was a great musical artist; of all jazz players he has had the broadest and longest appeal and success, and as a player he was integral and consistently vital from beginning to end of the nearly five decades of his national and international career. He was not the only jazz trumpeter of his time to move people to laughter and tears and to inspire other musicians to seek their own freedom—Joe Smith and Bix Beiderbecke are two cases in point, and there were other trumpeters who were adventurous, even reckless, if unfinished when compared with Armstrong, Smith, and Beiderbecke, and who might have provided models for virtuosity and eccentric personal expression: we might remember Bobby Stark, Jabbo Smith, and Red Allen. So that if by some mischance Armstrong had skidded off the road and out of our lives when he was driving to New York in 1929, the history of the jazz trumpet would not have come to an end. It is even possible that the kind of on-the-beat but off-the-phrase trumpeting, rather nervous and not a little abstract, which was beginning to be heard before 1930 might have resulted in a Roy Eldridge not too unlike the Eldridge to whom Dizzy Gillespie listened so intently.

So far as Armstrong's total achievement is concerned, however, it seems unlikely that any other jazz musician at the time would have been able to step into his shoes. Who else had the combination of technical prowess, experience in entertaining, links to a New Orleans tradition emphasizing melodic playing and catering to the demands of a public, a certain docility in assuming the stage darky's traditional role, a broadness of taste extending well beyond the confines of jazz, and finally, the iron lip and demonic energy he had prior to 1934 which held it all together? Parts of Armstrong could be and were studied, borrowed, and imitated, and they can be heard re-echoing down to our own day, but perhaps only one player of the thirties, Bunny Berigan, even came close to meeting his larger challenge.

It may be that Armstrong's Louisiana swing—not his sole property by any means, but beautifully exemplified in all his playing—was his most significant contribution to the direction jazz (including the hot dance music of the big bands) was to take, and an indispensable leaven to the heavy-footed on-the-beat playing of midwestern and eastern bands and the tiresome backbeat of Kansas City. And the swing was expressed with finesse and grace.

In the long run, the specific technical inspiration of an Art Tatum or Coleman —Hawkins may have been of greater importance in determining the direction jazz was to take in the later 1930s and 1940s. Neither one of them could ever be the popular favorite Armstrong had been; and both had more difficulty than Armstrong ever seems to have had in achieving an expression poised between lyric simplicity and luxuriant musical play. That expression was never cold or sour, and even at its most melodramatic or sentimental was informed by a relatively unselfconscious but nonetheless active thought, a sculptural plastic sensibility which decisively raised the expectations we have of jazz music, past, present, or future.

Note on Recordings

Information on the original issues of recordings discussed in the chapter is available in Rust 1978.

Louis Armstrong

Early Louis Armstrong recordings can be found on *Louis Armstrong and King Oliver,* Milestone MCD-47017-2, covering 1923–24, and the three-CD *Complete Louis Armstrong with Fletcher Henderson, 1924–1925,* Forte Record Productions F-3800 1–3. The CD series, *The Complete Louis Armstrong and the Singers,* on King Jazz (as well as a similar set from Affinity) compiles his 1920s accompaniments: his recordings with Perry Bradford are on vol. 2 (KJ 140FS), and those with Lillie Delk Christian are on vol. 4 (KJ 6142); see also *Maggie Jones, Aug. 1923–April 1925,* Document DOCD

5348. His 1924 recordings under Clarence Williams are on the LP *Louis Armstrong and Sidney Bechet,* Smithsonian Collections R026; chronological CD sets of Clarence Williams' recordings which include this material are available on several labels.

Virtually all the recordings under Armstrong's name mentioned in the text through 1931 are available on vols. 1–7 of Columbia's *Louis Armstrong Collection* (CK44049-44253-44422-45142-46148-46996-48828), including all the recordings used for musical examples in this chapter; other labels are also issuing chronological series which include this material. Recordings from the 1930s can be found on the CD *Stardust,* Portrait RK 44093, including "Between the Devil and the Deep Blue Sea," "Stardust," "Georgia on My Mind," and others; the LP *Louis Armstrong in the Thirties,* Alamac QSR 2401, which includes the 1932 soundtrack recordings of "Shine" and "You Rascal You"; and *The Complete RCA Victor Recordings,* BMG Classics 09026-68682-2, which includes "I've Got the World on a String" and two takes of "Laughin' Louie." Later recordings mentioned in the chapter can be found on *Louis Armstrong Plays W. C. Handy,* Columbia Jazz Masterpieces CJT-40242, *"Satchmo" and the Dukes of Dixieland,* 2 vols., Blue Moon CD 3071 and 3073, and *Louis Armstrong's "Hello, Dolly!"* MCA MCAD-538.

Other Artists

The LP *New Orleans Horns: Freddie Keppard and Tommy Ladnier,* Milestones M-2014, includes Ladnier's solo on "Play That Thing," as does the CD *"Play That Thing": Quintessential Tommy Ladnier,* King Jazz 170FS; Ladnier's "Shanghai Shuffle" is on the LP *Sam Wooding and His Chocolate Dandies,* Biograph BLP 12025. CD compilations of Freddie Keppard in the '20s are available on King Jazz and EPM. The Jelly Roll Morton recordings with Lee Collins are on *Jelly Roll Morton, vol. 2, 1924–26,* Media MJCD20.

Thomas Morris's 1926 sessions have been reissued on *New York Horns, 1924–29,* Musiques Archives Documents 151022. For Bix Beiderbecke (including recordings with Frank Trumbauer) see *Singin' the Blues,* Columbia CK 45450, and *At the Jazz Band Ball,* Columbia CK 46175. Red Nichols' work is available on *The Rhythm of the Day,* ASV CD AJA 5025.

Johnny Dodds's 1926 session with Armstrong is available on *Johnny Dodds, 1926–1940, pt. 1,* Affinity CD AFS 1023-3, and *Johnny Dodds, 1926–1928,* JSP CD 319, both of which include the New Orleans Bootblacks and New Orleans Wanderers sessions with Lil Armstrong. Sidney Bechet's 1923 recordings have been issued as volume one of the *Sidney Bechet: Complete Edition,* Media MJCD5, and on *Sidney Bechet 1923–36,* Classics 583. Red Allen's 1929 recordings can be found on chronological CD series on Classics and JSP; his recordings with Luis Russell (including "Jersey Lightning") are on *Luis Russell and His Orchestra, 1926–29,* Classics 588.

Notes

The present essay was originally written for inclusion in an anthology planned by the late Martin Williams as a successor to that compiled by Nat Hentoff and Albert McCarthy in 1959. The original project was redefined as a college textbook, for which my Armstrong essay would have been too detailed; as matters turned out, however, the textbook project was never realized. The Note on Recordings was assembled by Curtis Black.

1. This may have been in part a function of where Armstrong lived. Freddie Keppard was another early cornetist who, like Armstrong, lived a few blocks from Canal Street, and he is said to have entertained tourists on the streets.

2. An obscure point in Armstrong's biography is how much, or whether, he sang once he had become a professional cornetist, and before he began to sing on the recordings of the Hot Five. There are indications, for example, that he sang during the two years he worked for Joe Oliver in Chicago.

3. This is not to say that only Oliver of all New Orleans players espoused this "ethic." For example, Freddie Keppard in his few recordings takes a similar approach.

4. Of all aspects of Armstrong's playing, his blues are the most formulaic—this is not intended pejoratively—something which stems not only from the intrinsic nature of blues modality but also from the early age at which he probably learned to play the blues. It seems likely that much of what he played in his first professional job with the piano-drum-cornet trio at Matranga's was blues, based on a very limited repertory of standard phrases. (Cf. Collier 1983, 61.)

5. "Perhaps," because the crucial passage in Armstrong 1947 is garbled. For a recent synthesis of Petit's brief career and a juxtaposition of reactions by contemporaries to his playing see de Donder 1983.

6. Despite its length and seriousness, Collier's book is not thoroughly documented, so it's not possible to know whether this 1949 interview by Will Jones from a Minneapolis newspaper was known to him. It should be kept in mind that Armstrong was highly disapproving of musicians who drank to excess, and may have been reluctant for that reason to grant any significant influence from Johnson, who was known for his alcoholism.

7. Armstrong 1936 gives important credit for expanding his technical and theoretical horizons to another man working for Marable, cornetist Joe Howard, and others have cited clarinetist Sam Dutrey as well.

8. This is amply confirmed by his sound and phrasing in the recordings with Oliver—unless there were some reason to believe that he drastically altered his style at Oliver's behest. But in any event, one is hard-pressed to cite many instances of a major jazz performer altering essential features of his style past his early twenties. Perhaps Coleman Hawkins would be an example.

9. The discographies list six takes of this tune, four of which were supposedly issued; four takes are included on the recent CD, *Play That Thing*. See Note on Recordings.

10. See Note on Recordings for information on reissues.

11. Armstrong, not especially prone to making judgements in print concerning his fellow musicians, accurately, if somewhat curtly, describes Ladnier's strengths and weaknesses: "I thought he was a good blues man, good shout man, but he didn't have no range. A trumpet player should have a range he's sure of" (Armstrong 1950, 22).

12. Many of these solos were transcribed from the recordings and published by Panico himself in his remarkable book, *The Novelty Cornetist* (1924). Such comparisons can, of course, be extended to other important white musicians of the period 1924–26, such as Muggsy Spanier and Bix Beiderbecke.

13. The conversion of Oliver's band to a more cosmopolitan type of ensemble took place over a three-year period. He first dropped the violin, by firing James Palao in

California in 1921, and at the same time experimented with the temporary addition of a saxophonist. The guitar, which although normal in New Orleans was not part of U.S. dance orchestras in general, was readily replaced by the tenor banjo, so much more favored by acoustic recording technology. Although Oliver dabbles in saxophones in the 1923–24 recordings, he would have been held back by the relative inexperience and perhaps reluctance in doubling of clarinetist Johnny Dodds. Once Dodds left, Oliver appears to have moved to reed players, at first a pair, then three, who were comfortable with the saxophone.

14. For an excellent exposé of Armstrong's manner of seconding Oliver, see Schuller 1968, 84.

15. Herewith the basic details of copyright: "Cornet Chop Suey" (E580818, 18 January 1924), "Weather Bird Rag" (E561680, 14 April 1923), "I Am in the Barrel, Who Don't Like It?" (E577785, 8 December 1923), "Coal Cart Blues" (E574625, 3 November 1923), "Drop That Sack" (E577784, 8 December 1923), all as unpublished compositions.

16. Collier 1983, along with other earlier and less comprehensive works, appears not to have looked into the question of copyrights. Although some of the lead sheets of Armstrong's early pieces deposited for copyright were in the catalogued collection of the Music Division of the Library of Congress and physically located in its stacks, most of them were still in storage arranged by copyright registration number at the Library's warehouse in Landover, Maryland, in June of 1986, at which time the writer, with the kind assistance of Wayne Shirley, was permitted to remove them from the storage boxes and bring them back to the Music Division, where they now are.

17. A similar passage in "Cornet Chop Suey" as performed with the Hot Five prompted the remark in the transcriptions made by Lee Castle and originally published in 1947 (most recently available in Schiff 1975), "The two bars before [G] form a good pattern and can be used often."

18. These, by the way, make it seem more likely to me that Armstrong was not simply copying from a draft made by Lil.

19. Both "Coal Cart Blues" and "New Orleans Cut-Out" are copyrighted jointly by Armstrong and Lillian Hardin, leaving room for the argument that "sophisticated touches" are attributable to Lil's formal education in music theory. I see no way to rule this out absolutely.

20. Of course, some or all of Armstrong's compositions may have been conceived earlier; and there is some possibility that he was creating original tunes as early as his entry into Kid Ory's band in 1918. At least, he claimed this to be the case with the tune which became known in the form published by and ascribed to Clarence Williams and Armand J. Piron as "Sister Kate."

21. Bechet, four years Armstrong's senior, left New Orleans five years before Armstrong did, with the touring vaudeville act of Bruce & Bruce, and then, as is well known, went to Europe in 1919 with the Southern Syncopated Orchestra. On his return to New York in 1922, he was highly touted by the influential and respected Will Marion Cook as one of the most promising young composers.

22. Armstrong's ears, receptive as always to a wide variety of music, were greatly impressed by trumpeters outside the jazz tradition, such as B. A. Rolfe, then a featured soloist with Vincent Lopez's orchestra. (Cf. Collier 1983, 147.) Collier's belief that

Rolfe was the inspiration for Armstrong's exploitation of the high trumpet register is problematic: there is evidence that young contemporaries of Armstrong in New Orleans, such as Kid Rena, also were exploring the stratosphere.

23. Also to be kept in mind is the degree to which the Henderson orchestra recorded material from the Tin Pan Alley publishers in relatively straightforward form. The interest of publishers is to keep the melody as intact as possible: that is what they sold. I find it reasonable to think that Armstrong's more abstract flights of fancy would have been discouraged.

24. This band recorded four tunes for the Autograph label, "Fishtail Blues," "High Society," "Weary Blues," and "Tiger Rag." Apart from the first, which Collins claimed as his own piece, the tunes are common repertory items without composer credit on the record label, something highly unusual for Morton's recordings.

25. This was one way he could follow Joe Oliver's teaching on maintaining the lead at all times, while indulging his own taste for figuration. Armstrong's concept of the break can, by the way, be conveniently studied in the collection of over a hundred breaks in various keys published by the Melrose Music Company in 1927 and currently available in a reprint (Armstrong 1951).

26. Although Armstrong's work on several of these recordings has been widely known, particularly the two versions of "Cake Walking Babies," the records as a group have not been the object of much study, perhaps due to the lack of a comprehensive microgroove reissue until the excellent set released in 1978 by the Smithsonian Collection, with highly informative annotation by Lewis Porter.

27. Schuller's phrase "recording project" is perhaps a bit overdrawn; it's as if the recording executives of Okeh were present-day arts bureaucrats—presumably with ample government subvention—rather than businessmen hoping to turn a profit by meeting the taste of urban black record buyers for hot dance music.

28. Collier observes that in 1927 Armstrong was "sufficiently celebrated for the Melrose Music Company to issue transcriptions of his solos" (1983, 178). But none of these were transcriptions from the commercially issued recordings, rather they were specially recorded by Armstrong in accordance with the list of Melrose orchestrations. Perhaps it was because those Hot Five/Seven tunes which were copyrighted were held by the Consolidated Music Publishing Company, which I take to have been a shadow company set up by Okeh to recapture the mechanical royalties they would have had to pay otherwise.

29. This is not to deny that to many of the first wave of hot jazz collectors the Hot Fives, were the very essence of jazz. The late William Russell, for instance, is said to have been converted to jazz by them and concentrated his first collecting energies on acquiring all the early recordings made by Armstrong. Furthermore, many of the first collectors' reissues which began to appear in 1938 were of the Hot Fives, and Sevens, a role which Columbia records took over when they began their own reissue series in the 1940s.

30. Dapogny recognizes this: "Further, although Armstrong did not introduce 9ths, 13ths and chromaticisms into jazz harmony, he used them so systematically and with such effective placing that his choice of pitch sounded completely fresh" (1980, 601). He does not observe that one of the major differences in style between Armstrong and what for simplicity's sake we might call the Trumbauer school is that Armstrong is far more likely to play arpeggios moving in one direction than to play "saw-tooth" patterns.

31. Collier states that "ruined takes were simply scraped off the wax drum to clear a fresh surface. As a consequence, unhappily, no alternate takes of the Hot Fives exist" (1983, 170). No document is cited in support of this—not to speak of the implausibility of the "wax drum."

32. Hadlock hears Armstrong playing trumpet even in New York, at the Perry Bradford recording session of November 1925. I can hear what he means (Hadlock 1985, 23; cf. Collier 1983, 162).

33. Joshua Berrett (1992) has argued effectively for the importance of Italian and French opera as a component of Armstrong's style in general, and as the source of certain often-employed phrases, such as the one from the famous Quartet from *Rigoletto,* over Maddalena's words, "Ah, ah! Rido ben di core." This dates back to Armstrong's early youth in New Orleans, but was reinforced by his tenure in Erskine Tate's orchestra. Some of the turns of phrase for which Berrett finds a possible origin in opera could well come from cornet or trumpet exercises or etudes, themselves inspired by opera if not actually borrowing motifs from the repertory.

34. A slightly earlier version recorded under Johnny Dodds's leadership for Vocalion does not have these problems. On it Louis plays very well, but conservatively. The same is true of "Weary Blues," also extant in two versions.

35. The carelessness of the writing, as well as the submission for copyright six months after the date of recording, speaks against taking this lead sheet with the same seriousness as those for "Cornet Chop Suey" or "Savoy Blues."

36. For a transcription of portions of Armstrong's part and an interesting discussion in a place one might not think to look, see Austin 1966, 280–83. Another transcription is in Schiff 1975.

37. Also following this pattern, but in C, is "Knee Drops," recorded in 1928. Composed apparently by Lil Armstrong, it lacks the long four-bar phrases of all of Armstrong's themes. "Symphonic Raps," recorded the same year with Carroll Dickerson's orchestra, is a version in F of this chord progression.

38. For a discussion of "Potato Head Blues" and "Struttin' with Some Barbecue" from a different perspective, see Caffey 1975.

39. Collier, who devotes a great deal of space to this recording, provides no information concerning the significance of the title. He attributes the merits of the performance in its "several strains, breaks, and set figures for various instruments" to Ory's excellence as a writer of traditional New Orleans tunes, "although once again we cannot be sure how much he took from the common stock of music" (1983, 186). Actually, for the two other tunes he cites as evidence of Ory's skill, rather more can be asserted. Much of "Ory's Creole Trombone" is drawn from Clarence Wiley's "Car-Balick-Acid Rag-time"; and a case can be made for the partial derivation of "Muskrat Ramble"—claimed, not completely implausibly, as a work of Armstrong's—from "Maple Leaf Rag."

40. Perhaps it was a matter of Johnson's background as an urban musician (from New Orleans) rather than a rural bluesman.

41. With some possible encouragement from marijuana? It has been said that Armstrong began to use the drug at about this time. It is also conceivable that some of the "demonic" excesses of the next six years or so were also facilitated by it. This is the opinion, for example, of John Hammond (1977, 106).

42. Schuller (1968) places it in the American popular cornet tradition, which he sees

as the source for the opening cadenza. Collier (1983, 197), perhaps borrowing from Porter 1981, traces the ending of the introduction back to the blues accompaniment to Margaret Johnson's "Changeable Daddy of Mine," and further surmises that "the entire introduction was a version of something he had developed over time as a display piece for use in the theaters and cabarets," with nonetheless sufficient spontaneous elements that it can qualify as an improvisation. Collier also cites the evidence substantiating both prior rehearsal as well as several takes in the recording studio. Berrett 1992 lists seven Armstrong recordings between 1924 and 1932 that use the "Changeable Daddy" lick. To his list could be added an instance from the Melrose break collection, namely the third of the four G-seventh breaks (Armstrong 1951, 18). The larger picture is the as yet unwritten history of the use of sequential figures, sometimes chromatically descending, in jazz of the early twenties.

43. For a valuable transcription of both piano and trumpet parts, see Godwin 1975 (415–22).

44. This music was "commercial" only in the sense that their place with the Okeh and Brunswick record labels was secure and well-publicized, and that as white jazz musicians active in New York, they were extremely visible and well-paid. Their recordings sold in the several thousands, not the hundred thousands typical of successful recordings by the major dance orchestras.

45. There is also a considerable amount of chordal arpeggiation, perhaps as close to "running changes" as Louis gets—as if the accompanist's role released him from the responsibility both of hewing to the lead, as well as making a big production of his performance.

46. Collier spends little time with these performances, although he recognizes that the group achieved "an easy rollicking swing that anticipates the feeling that small jazz groups of the next decade would have" (1983, 190).

47. Rockwell had become general manager of Okeh records in 1926, then moved to the Brunswick label as A. and R. head two years later. In 1930 he became associated with Irving Mills, and eventually founded his own agency with F. C. O'Keefe, which eventually became the powerful General Artists Corporation. Although cognizant of the importance of management, Collier was not able to go further than this: "Precisely what kind of arrangement [Rockwell] made with Louis we do not know, but there was apparently a written contract of some sort because later on, when Armstrong signed with another manager, he had to make a cash settlement with Rockwell" (1983, 204). According to Collier and others the precise circumstances for Armstrong going to New York were that Rockwell had arranged for him a solo appearance in early March at the Savoy Ballroom.

48. The Los Angeles engagements made possible the beginning of Armstrong's film career; he was to appear in over thirty commercial films during his lifetime. Collier appears to believe that the first two of these films were made in New York (1983, 230). Apart from that, however, his judgement that Armstrong was "at his showy worst" seems wrong to me. The 1932 soundtrack version of "I'll Be Glad When You're Dead, You Rascal You" (from *Rhapsody in Black and Blue*) seems to me excellent, and recorded with a presence missing from the 1931 Okeh recording.

49. The degree to which this is true (for the tunes recorded for Okeh, not those for Victor) is one of the strongest testimonies to the impact of his playing of the 1929–32 period on musicians.

50. One surely has to reckon with the increasing dominance of his vocal personality.

Happy, natural, and spontaneous in essence, it was strongly laced with a flair for melo-drama which some listeners have found out of proportion to the character of the song, for example, in "I Can't Give You Anything But Love." We never hear something like the sober, even sardonic, vocalism of the 1941 "Do You Call That a Buddy."

51. More of this "demonic" Armstrong comes through on the 1932 soundtrack per-formances of "Shine" and "I'll Be Glad When You're Dead, You Rascal You" than on the studio recordings made for Okeh.

52. Many of the new songs were also of a different harmonic type (already foreshad-owed in "A Monday Date" and "Big Butter and Egg Man") with a more rapidly chang-ing ii7–V7–I chord sequence predominating. Perhaps this did not entail so much change, as Armstrong had already in his playing shown that he thought of the ii7 chord as a constant companion of the V7. In any event, this appears to have been a direction followed by many musicians independently.

53. In *Down Beat* (9 July 1970), clarinetist Bob Wilber published a transcription of the three solo choruses, little different from mine, and characterized them as succes-sively melodic, tonal, and rhythmic.

54. The last measure seems to be one of Armstrong's very rare errors of harmony, as opposed to errors of execution. The phrase should clearly go to G, the tonic.

55. Or at least to my ears, which have been ready enough to hear paraphrase in practically all of Armstrong's work before 1929. It may be that the rhythmic and me-lodic simplicity of this example is in part occasioned by the context; Armstrong is playing a kind of on-the-beat counterpoint to the off-the-beat sax riffs. Collier, it should be noted, places the move away from paraphrase considerably earlier, by 1927 (1983, 181).

56. The song requires a break in measures 9–12 of each sixteen measure chorus, that is, in a different position than the breaks of ragtime-derived tunes, and this elicits a different strategy from Armstrong. On this recording it sounds as though Armstrong begins with a thought borrowed from the preceding tenor saxophone soloist.

57. The meat of his discussion of Armstrong compares two performances of "I Can't Give You Anything But Love," one from 1929, the other from 1938. In the second of these, Hodeir understands Armstrong to have developed to his artistic peak, revealing his mastery of a kind of amplified paraphrase, as opposed to paraphrase functioning as statement.

58. His principal example is Lester Young's 1945 Aladdin recording of "All the Things You Are," in which the melody has entirely disappeared. The evolutionary view, to be sure, is shared by many, notably James Lincoln Collier.

59. The words are those of a friend of Bix Beiderbecke's, Esten Spurrier, as originally reported by Sudhalter and Evans (1974, 100). Spurrier said that he and Bix credited Armstrong as the originator of this procedure.

60. Hadlock touches on this matter with respect to a change he detects in Armstrong's style with the 1928 recording of "Squeeze Me": "His ideas come faster and in more tightly packed bundles now; rather than conceiving his solos as single chorus-length ideas, he begins constructing a chain of four-bar and even two-bar thematic units, each a miniature chorus unto itself but an essential link to the next unit and a logical part of the whole solo as well" (1965, 38).

61. For an extended discussion of the question of continuity in a multichorus solo by Lester Young see Gushee 1981.

62. In noteworthy contrast to certain other players and orchestras, there are very few

alternate takes of Armstrong's playing available, due perhaps to a policy of the Okeh label to destroy alternates, or in the case of the Hot Fives, to the ability of the musicians to produce acceptable recordings without any alternates being made. However, some of the alternates of the post-1929 recordings are due to the making of a wholly instrumental version of a tune which Armstrong sings, for distribution in non-English speaking countries—which did not necessarily take place. For example, volume 6 of the Columbia series, *St. Louis Blues,* offers two versions of "I Ain't Got Nobody" and "Dallas Blues," and three of "St. Louis Blues."

63. Both were reissued on the important collection *Louis Armstrong, V.S.O.P.* (Columbia Special Products JEE-22019), now available as the CD *Stardust* (see Note on Recordings). Neither take was the one originally issued.

64. Collier chooses to emphasize the points of similarity between the two songs for which multiple takes exist, and treats "Between the Devil and the Deep Blue Sea" as one performance. He too is struck by the "arabesques" in sixteenth notes, writing, "once again we see how Armstrong's musical imagination could lead him into devices quite remote from his usual style" (1983, 246). I would suggest that Armstrong was experimenting with a new tune. Collier's idea that comparison of the multiple takes give us "an opportunity to see how Armstrong's solos tended to change over time," should be understood in the light of the fact that the takes were made at the same recording session, not separated by days or weeks.

65. These are given in the liner notes of *V.S.O.P.* as takes 3 and 4, although Rust 1978 mentions only 1, 2, and 4, all of which were evidently originally issued.

66. The nature of the relationship between Armstrong as vocalist and Armstrong as instrumentalist has yet to be elucidated. (By this I do not mean the investigation of the physiological conditions requiring therapy that afflicted him both as trumpeter and as singer. These are discussed at some length in Collier 1983.)

67. This is not to say that Armstrong had not learned from trumpeters outside the black jazz fraternity. His admiration for the lead trumpeter with Sam Lanin in 1925, Vic D'Ippolito, and for Vincent Lopez's soloist, B. A. Rolfe, is a matter of record (Jones and Chilton 1971, 216).

68. Although later Gillespie talks about Jabbo Smith as a collateral branch descended, like Armstrong, from Joe Oliver, he does not link him to Eldridge (Gillespie 1979, 491).

69. Unfortunately for prospects of broad appeal for his style, Allen had trouble learning from Armstrong how to remain lyrically simple throughout a solo, or how to use obvious degree progressions to unite long time spans. The trumpeter who most eclectically learned from Allen and from Armstrong, not to mention Beiderbecke and Nichols, was Bunny Berigan, for whom Armstrong was to express great admiration.

70. Collier 1983 would trace the economy of style to the damage Armstrong did to his embouchure, both through excessive pressure in playing, as well as in destructive attempts at self-treatment. Perhaps the cause matters less than the effect.

71. Berrett draws attention to the Armstrong with "more than eighty compositions to his credit" (1929, 239), but apart from the jazz instrumentals from the Oliver years and the shared credits with Lil from 1926–28, none have proved memorable. Also, the matter of copyright ownership for a famous band leader is always problematic, given the common practice of shared credit between the actual creator of a tune and the leader of the band he happens to have been working in. It is nonetheless important to understand

that Armstrong was both capable of and interested in setting down his musical ideas in writing.

72. One would include Lil Armstrong in this group. I find the interpretation of Collier 1983—that Armstrong constantly sought surrogate fathers—unacceptable in the use he makes of it to explain an artist's work, and in general prefer to look for forces from the musical-social context rather than from psychic wounds.

References

Armstrong, Louis. 1947. "Louis Armstrong, Who Tells You about Storyville, Where the Blues Were Born." *True; The Man's Magazine* 21, no. 126 (November), 100–105.

———. 1951. *Louis Armstrong's 44 Trumpet Solos and 125 Jazz Breaks*. No. E8465a. New York: Charles Hansen. A reprint of two 1927 Melrose Company publications.

———. 1936. *Swing That Music*. London and New York: Longmans, Green.

———. 1950. "Louis on the Spot." *The Record Changer* (July–August): 23–24, 44.

———. 1955. *Satchmo*. Englewood Cliffs N.J.: Prentice-Hall.

Austin, William W. 1966. *Music in the 20th Century*. New York: W. W. Norton.

Bechet, Sidney. 1960. *Treat It Gentle*. New York: Hill and Wang.

Berrett, Joshua. 1992. "Louis Armstrong and Opera." *Musical Quarterly* 76:216–40.

Caffey, H. David. 1975. "The Musical Style of Louis Armstrong." *Journal of Jazz Studies* 3:72–96.

Collier, James Lincoln. 1983. *Louis Armstrong: an American Genius*. New York: Oxford University Press.

Dance, Stanley. 1974. *The World of Swing*. New York: Da Capo. New York: Charles Scribner's Sons.

Dapogny, James. 1980. "Louis Armstrong." In *The New Grove Dictionary of Music and Musicians,* edited by Stanley Sadie. London: Macmillan.

de Donder, Jempi. 1983. "My Buddy: An Attempt to Find Buddy Petit." *Footnote* (February–March): 24–34; (April–May): 4–13.

Gillespie, Dizzy, with Al Fraser. 1979. *To Be or Not to Bop*. Garden City, N.Y.: Doubleday.

Godwin, Joscelyn, ed. 1975. *Schirmer Scores: A Repertory of Western Music*. New York: Schirmer Books.

Gushee, Lawrence. 1981. "Lester Young's 'Shoeshine Boy.'" In *Report of the Twelfth Congress of the International Musicological Society, Berkeley 1977,* edited by Daniel Heartz and Bonnie Wade, 151–69. Kassel: Bärenreiter.

Hadlock, Richard. 1965. *Jazz Masters of the Twenties*. New York: Macmillan.

Hammond, John. 1977. *John Hammond on Record: An Autobiography*. New York: Summit Books.

Hodeir, André. 1954. *Hommes et problèmes du jazz*. Paris: Au Portulan.

Jones, Max, and John Chilton. 1971. *Louis: The Louis Armstrong Story*. Boston: Little, Brown.

Jones, Will. 1949. "Interview with Louis Armstrong." *Minneapolis Tribune,* 20 July.

Meryman, Richard. 1971. *Louis Armstrong—A Self-Portrait*. New York: Eakins Press.

Morgenstern, Dan. 1965. "Yesterday, Today and Tomorrow: An Interview with Louis Armstrong," *Down Beat,* 15 July, 15 ff.

Panico, Louis. 1924. *The Novelty Cornetist*. Chicago: Louis Panico.

Pleasants, Henry. 1974. *The Great American Popular Singers.* New York: Simon and Schuster.

Porter, Lewis. 1981. Liner notes for the LP, *Louis Armstrong and Sidney Bechet in New York, 1923–1925.* The Smithsonian Collection R 026.

"Roses for Satchmo." 1970. *Downbeat,* 9 July, 15–19.

Rust, Brian. 1978. *Jazz Records, 1897–1942.* 4th ed. New Rochelle N.Y.: Arlington House.

Schiff, Ronny, ed. 1975. *Louis Armstrong: A Jazz Master.* Melville N.Y.: MCA Music. No. U549.

Schuller, Gunther. 1968. *Early Jazz.* New York: Oxford University Press.

Shapiro, Nat, and Nat Hentoff, eds. 1966. *Hear Me Talkin' to Ya.* 1955. Reprint, New York: Dover.

Sudhalter, Richard M., and Philip R. Evans. 1974. *Bix: Man and Legend.* New Rochelle N.Y.: Arlington House.

Taylor, J. R. 1975. Liner notes for the LP, *Louis Armstrong and Earl Hines, 1928.* Smithsonian Collection R 002.

CHAPTER FOURTEEN

Keeping It Going: Terms, Practices, and Processes of Improvisation in Hindustānī Instrumental Music

STEPHEN SLAWEK

A discussion of improvisation in Indian art music could follow any of a large number of directions. The traditions of Hindustānī and Karnātāk music are so vast that even a direct, descriptive study of their genres would take several volumes. Hence, in a chapter of this scope, it is necessary to delimit the topic at hand to a very narrow focus. Here, I will discuss processes of improvisation idiomatic to North Indian plucked stringed instruments, focusing specifically on the music of the sitar, sarod, and *vicitra vīṇā*. Furthermore, I will center my discussion on aspects of the creative process to reveal some of the approaches individual musicians have taken in interpreting certain codified procedures of improvised performance practice such as *ālāp, joṛ, gat vistār* and *tihāī*. This discussion, then, focuses on syntagmatic aspects of the musical tradition,[1] and does so at the risk of leading the reader to draw the false conclusion that the paradigmatic components of the tradition, particularly *rāga,* are of less than integral importance in the process of creating improvisations.[2] The essence of Indian music is *rāga,* a modal construct that serves as the basis of melodic composition. Any improvisation in Indian music is of value only insofar as it advances the aesthetic impact of the *rāga* being performed. The *rāga*-essence is made manifest through improvised performance and in the form of precomposed, relatively stable compositions (*bandiś* in vocal music; *gat* in instrumental music). In the following discussion of syntagmatic improvisational models in Hindustānī instrumental music, we should not lose sight of the fact that we are skirting this most musically significant aspect of performance practice.

I am reminded of an evening during my first trip to India to study the sitar. In early March, 1972, I accompanied my first sitar instructor, Dr. Lalmani Misra, on a trip to Calcutta where he, I, and one other American student of his were to give a series of performances. One evening during this trip, we were invited to dinner at the home of Jnan Prakash Ghosh, a noted tabla player, teacher, and generally well-rounded musician. During after-dinner conversation, we talked about how important it was to practice a plentitude of traditional exercises, to learn the great diversity of *rāgas* that are central to the tradition; to have command over several *tāla* (rhythmic cycles); to have a great variety of *tān* (improvised passages) at one's disposal, and to be able to ornament phrases in various ways. We marveled at the complexities of the music and at the ineffable nature of improvisation in Indian music, where detailed models of grammar provide guidelines for winding one's way from beginning to end of a performed item, but in reality, a musician is free to do whatever comes to mind at the moment (so long as it doesn't "break the *rāga* or *tāla*") and often doesn't know what may come to mind next. Then Mr. Ghosh said something that was to stick with me until today: while mastery of all the various components of the tradition was certainly important, what was most essential in the process of performance was "to keep it going."

Keeping it going means that something has to be there to do next. And since what is there is not concrete or written down, it must be something remembered and reproduced intact on the spot, or something created extemporaneously by recombining stored musical information in a new way that is appropriate to the musical situation of the moment. The activity of improvisation in Indian music can be viewed as a dialectical process of creativity that is fueled by these two distinct, but overlapping, kinds of musical materials; thus, improvisations may be characterized by the place they occupy in this dialectic—that is, by their degree of fixity or flexibility. For instance, an improvisation created by variation of a phrase of a *gat* could be considered as having greater fixity since its model was a precomposed piece; one created by melodic peregrinations over three octaves held together by a recurring rhythmic figure would be situated near the flexible side of the musical continuum, since it is only the rhythmic character that gives the impression of preconditioning, while the melodic contours are only loosely predetermined by the constraints of the *rāga*. The point I wish to make here, however, is that the resultant improvisations are not the products of only one or the other of these types of musical sources. Rather, they are a combination of the two within a dynamic, dialectical musical creative process.

It may help at this point to clarify some notions that exist in literature on improvisation and composition as they pertain to Hindustānī music. Specifically, I wish to argue against equating the concepts of precomposition and improvisation with notions of musical fixity and flexibility, respectively. In reality, there can be flexibility of performance built into a precomposed piece of music, and there can exist fixed items of music within an improvisation. Nettl (1974) has demonstrated quite convincingly that there is no clear dividing line between improvised and precomposed music and that creative aspects similar to the compositional processes of the Western art music tradition exist in improvisatory traditions.[3] Here, what I especially wish to note is that much of what occurs in a performance of Hindustānī music—which, I would contend, is essentially improvised from start to finish—is actually "fixed" music (one might alternately say memorized) in the sense that the performer has practiced and rehearsed those exact melodic or rhythmic phrases hundreds, if not thousands, of times before. What makes the performance improvisatory is that there is freedom to construct the performance as it unfolds—the succession of events is only loosely predetermined.

Keeping it going, having something ready to throw into the musical mix at the next opportunity, must also be understood, at least in regards to Indian instrumental music, as a concerted effort by both the soloist and the accompanist, usually a tabla player. Neuman presents abundant information about various aspects of soloist-accompanist relationships in the classical music of North India, in general characterizing the accompanist's position as subordinate to the soloist in various ways (1980, 136–44; cf. Kippen 1988, 52). It is important to keep in mind that some musicians who specialize in tabla would view their position as superior if they were to be paired with certain soloists. There is in Hindustānī music a recognition of musical accomplishment; and a value that can be translated into a sociomusical positioning of status is definitely placed on accomplishment. Thus, an accomplished tabla accompanist would have greater flexibility and control over the course of a performance when paired with a comparatively less accomplished soloist than when accompanying a musician of equal or higher caliber.

In contemporary practice, most instrumental soloists—*sitāriyā, sarodiyā,* etc.—prefer the accompaniment of seasoned tabla virtuosos who have the ability to insert impromptu rhythmic gyrations at the shortest musical notice. A brief flourish by the drummer during the instrumental equivalent of a vocalist taking a quick breath maintains the flow of the performance, keeping it going, filling in the gaps to approach what Henderson has dubbed the ideal of a saturation aesthetic (personal communication).[4]

Keeping it going is also assisted by an involved audience. Racy's "ecstatic feedback" model for improvisation in Arabic music can be applied fruitfully to Hindustānī music as well, where musicians crave ongoing audience approval in the form of verbalizations of praise, bodily gestures, and facial expressions of rapture.[5] Hindustānī music performance practice fits well with Racy's theoretical model of a social-aesthetic complex which emphasizes the operative components of the musical process, in contrast to the Western model of creativity "that leads to the emergence of aesthetic works that are valuable in themselves . . . imbued with an objective, universal, and transcendental aesthetic value" (1991, 9). In this model, inspiration is linked to a specific ecstatic condition "which in turn owes to: the artist's own physical and emotional state; input from the accompanying musicians; possible inexplicable outside controls; and, above all, an educated and responsive audience" (10). Positive responses from an educated audience have many tangible effects. The psychological ramifications could include the removal of inhibiting fears from the performer's psyche as well as the gratification of the performer's ego, allowing the creative process to flow more easily. Positive audience response serves to validate the course the performer has chosen, creating a kind of musical inertia. This could possibly lead the soloist to incorporate into subsequent creations aspects of a musical idea that has received a positive response on an earlier occasion.

A metaphysical explanation for improvisatory music making in Hindustānī music would stress the removal of encumbrances and inhibitions to the creative act so as to allow for what occurs naturally in the human life process. The variety of blockages to the natural flow of music could range from impediments provided by the technical requirements of an instrument to nervousness created by anxiety over one's appeal to an audience. Rigorous, concentrated practice under the guidance of a master is the prescribed remedy for the first obstacle; control over one's own psyche is necessary to remove the second obstacle. Any number of other obstacles, some within the performer's control, some beyond, can intervene to keep a musician from reaching his or her creative peak during performance: a quirky sound system, a crying baby or some other inappropriate noise from the audience that breaks one's inner concentration, or possibly physical tiredness caused by the grind of a concert tour. But what I wish to point out here is the belief among Indian artists that as long as the context is prepared correctly, the music will happen. Context, in this sense, extends beyond the performance venue to include, at least by implication, the years of training and practice that go into an individual's preparation for a performing career.

When the performer is free of all inhibitions, an estatic state of effortless creativity ensues. It is here that some common ground may be found underlying both improvisational performance and ritual, in that both processes can lead to altered states of consciousness. Tambiah (1985) successfully employs information theory in a performative approach to the study of ritual that has several points of similarity to the present study. In particular, his assertion that the "horizontal relations and connections dynamically act upon one another to constitute the *vertical* dimension by which higher-level integration is achieved" (145) is especially consonant with my initial observation that it is through the syntagmatic elements of a performance that the paradigmatic aspects *(rāga* and *tāla)* are manifested. Tambiah continues, stating that "the second sense in which I see ritual as performative is as a dramatic actualization whose distinctive structure including its stereotypy and redundancy has something to do with the production of a sense of heightened and intensified and fused communication," whose objective is some kind of elevated, altered state of consciousness.

I am reminded of encouragement I received from one of my favorite accompanists, Ishwar Lal Misra, who assured me often that I need only "let go" and follow the flow of a rhythmic/melodic pattern and it would come out automatically every time at the correct point in the *tāla* cycle (if only it were so easy!); or of Ravi Shankar, who speaks of losing awareness of the strings of his instrument (and, therefore, the physical effort required in playing the instrument) when he attains his creative peak in improvising. At that point his sitar is no longer an external medium for producing music, but a fused part of his body, and the act of creating music is more a release of inner energy than an activity requiring conscious effort.[6] In this sense, there is a cathartic quality to improvisation in North Indian music. Catharsis is facilitated by syntagmatic aspects of the performed "text," such as the typical spiraling acceleration of tempo that occurs in many traditions of performance practice, or the common procedure of extending improvisatory flights in length and towards the "flexible" side of the above-mentioned dialectic as the performance develops. Both practices tend to create greater musical tension and add drama to the performance, as well as a growing sense of exaltation as each miniature drama is resolved in a musically acceptable manner. Such practices, in my opinion, are related to the beliefs of spirituality that pervade the Indian tradition of classical music. They can be compared to the exercises of an adept at yoga, who goes about his pursuit of spiritual enlightenment by following a pragmatic path of rigorous adherence to a regimen of physical and mental exercises. In the same way, a musician is trained rigorously, practicing a musical yoga of exercises and performed music that is pragmatically expected to lead both the musician and listeners to a higher spiritual plane.

Not all performances, nor all performers, reach the same level of catharsis. Those who reach extreme levels of intensity, primarily by increasing tempo to the point of a spatial blur and/or pushing the volume of their tone production to their voice's or instrument's musical limit (and, in the case of some instrumentalists, beyond), are often singled out for damaging the essence of the tradition—sacrificing the heart of the tradition, *rāga,* at the altar of speed. Nevertheless, whether the catharsis is mild and sweet, possibly resulting from an exquisite rendition of the subtleties of a *rāga,* or intense and exhausting, the result of following complex rhythmical gyrations at incredible tempos, a value is certainly placed upon music's ability to provide an elevating experience for those who play or listen to it.

* * *

It is apparent from the foregoing discussion that a Hindustānī musician has a multitude of choices to make before and during the rendition of a *rāga.* Some choices are to be made purely at the discretion of the soloist (choice of *rāga,* genre and *tāla,* setting and changing tempo, etc.); others are made by the soloist in "musical consultation" with the accompanist as the performance progresses (i.e., as the musical dialogue between soloist and accompanist develops, the actions of one surely influence those of the other). Still others may be the result of responding to audience feedback. Given the freedom of expression found in the tradition of Hindustānī music, it is not surprising that different interpretations of the ways of keeping things going have evolved within the tradition. It is well known that the Indian art traditions are broad, complex systems of music making that contain, as part of their transmission process, extended vocabularies of musical terminology—what Western musicologists generally refer to as a "music theory." Ethnomusicology would be inclined to view this descriptive vocabulary as an "ethnotheory," a body of indigenous discourse that serves to explain existent musical practices.

Having examined some of the less tangible forces at work in the course of the improvisational performance of Hindustānī music, I wish now to turn to the variety of creative musical technologies that exists among performers, but which gets masked over by a theoretical terminology that appears to imply a certain degree of standardization or uniformity of practice and concept. To do this, I propose to examine various approaches to the musical creative process at three different levels: the broad structures of ālāp and the *Masitkhānī*, or *vilambit, gat;* the internal rhythmic structure of *jor;* and the narrowly conceived structure of *tihāī*.[7] In doing so, I will compare actual performance practices of recognized authorities in the Hindustānī musical world, and I will utilize a mixture of descriptive, transcriptive and analytical procedures.

Ālāp

Rāga-ālāp is one of the oldest musical practices extant in Indian classical music. It has been shown that the broad outlines of modern instrumental performance practice of *ālāp* are commensurate with descriptions of *rāga-ālāp* found in the thirteenth-century musicological treatise by Śārṅgadeva, *Saṅgītaratnākara* (see Powers 1981, 9:110–112; Shringy and Sharma 1989, 199–200; and Widdess 1981, 155–59).[8] Then, as now, the basic manner of performing *ālāp* proceeded as an unpulsed, ametrical, free-flowing exploration of the melodic potential of a particular *rāga*. The *ālāp* was subdivided by Śārṅgadeva into four subsections that were defined by goal tones and relative tessitura, with the general plan of construction following an expanding range reaching into higher pitch areas as the *ālāp* progressed. Śārṅgadeva briefly describes an ensuing section of *rāga* elaboration making use of conventional patterns *(sthāya)* and artful melodic constructions; it is possible that this is the precursor of the modern *jor* and *nom tom*. While several varieties of *ālāp* exist today, musicians view the *ālāp* associated with the archaic vocal genre *dhrupad* as the lineal descendent of the ancient *rāga-ālāp*.

Beyond the few remaining vocal musicians who have maintained the *dhrupad* genre, the solo *ālāp* tradition of the *dhrupad* style has been most tenaciously adhered to in Hindustānī instrumental music. With the ascendence of the modern khayāl style, vocal musicians have moved away from performing an extensive, unaccompanied *ālāp,* replacing this aspect of performance with *ālāp*-like improvisations within the context of the barā khayāl bandiś set to a repeating *tāla* cycle (in which case, it is variously called *ālāpcārī, vistār* or *barhat*). Within plucked stringed instrument traditions, those claiming a direct connection to the *bīnkār* tradition, supposedly extending to Misri Singh, son-in-law of the legendary sixteenth-century musician Tansen, proclaim knowledge of the original manner of *ālāp* performance. Included among these musicians would be members of the Maihar *gharānā* (disciples and grand disciples of Ustad Allauddin Khan), the Gwalior *gharānā* (descendants of Ustad Hafiz Ali Khan), the sitar *gharānā* (stylistic school) of Mushtaq Ali Khan, whose principle disciple is Professor Devbrata Chaudhuri of Delhi University, and the few remaining musicians—the most senior being Ustad Asad Ali Khan—who specialize on the *bīn* (a stick zither with two large gourd resonators; also known as *rudra vīṇa*).[9] A different concept of *ālāp* is found among followers of the Imdādkhānī *gharānā*, including such noted musicians as Ustad Vilayat Khan and his brother Imrat Khan, their sons and other related musicians such as Ustad Rais Khan and Budhaditya Mukherjee. A comparison of the conceptualizations of *ālāp* performance practice held by these two schools of instrumentalists will illuminate differences in cognitive and generative processes at a relatively broad level of terminological specificity.

The *bīnkār* approach to *ālāp* has been elaborated in detail by Vimalakant Roy Chaudhury in his *Bharatiya Sangeet Kosh* (1975, 11–14).[10] I have also elicited parallel descriptions of the components of a full-blown *ālāp* from both Ustad Ali Akbar Khan and Pandit Ravi Shankar. Aside from a few minor discrepanies, the three explanations are relatively consonant with each other. The value these individuals place on this knowledge is very high, and there is a tendency to give purposefully incomplete explanations of the various stages of *ālāp* development. When I asked Professor Devbrata Chaudhuri if he would be willing to compare his knowledge of the *bīnkār ālāp* style with my own, obtained through repeated interviewing of Pandit Ravi Shankar, Chaudhuri refused, stating that his guru passed on this information to him only after twenty years of devoted study. I pointed out that I had been privileged with the information from my guru only after fifteen years of study, and we left it at that!

The conceptualization of *ālāp* by musicians who claim a *bīnkār* base to their knowledge has notably more components than that of the Imdādkhānī *gharānā* musicians. Typically, the list goes something to the effect of *vilambit* (including the *sthāyī, antarā, sañcārī, ābhoga*—or, according to some, *ābhoga, sañcārī*),[11] *madhya* (the beginning of *jor*), *drut* (conclusion of *jor*), *śuddh jhālā, thonk jhālā*, and various archaic practices including *laṛī, laṛ lapeṭ, tār paran,* and *guthāv*. Explanations of the last four items vary, but in general they are mostly concerned with rapid stroking patterns—some imitating rhythms of the *pakhāvaj* (the drum that normally accompanies *dhrupad*) and procedures for combining these with melodic figures (e.g., *guthāv* refers to the process of stringing flowers on a garland; thus, a *guthāv* strings together clusters of melodic figures, possibly sharing a similar rhythmic pattern).[12] Contemporary practice has drifted from differentiating between all of these component sections of an *ālāp,* but vestiges of the archaic approach to melodic improvisation in *ālāp* seem to influence the improvisations of today's instrumentalists who claim a connection to a *bīnkār* heritage.

The stellar musicians of the Imdādkhānī *gharānā* have a different and comparatively simplified approach to *ālāp* structure. They are aware of the *sthāyī, antarā, sañcārī, ābhoga* concept, but it is not foremost in their minds. For example, both Budhaditya Mukherjee and Shujaat Khan described their concept of *ālāp* as consisting of four major sections: *ālāp* proper, *jor, ulṭā jhālā,*[13] and *tān.* Shujaat Khan added that the *ālāp* proper contained the traditional four subsections of *sthāyī, antarā, sañcārī,* and *ābhoga,* and that in his conception, what follows the nonpulsed section—which I refer to here as the *ālāp* proper—should not be considered part of the *ālāp.* His explanation of these subsections was largely similar to Ravi Shankar's; according to both, the *sthāyī* contained most of the expansive development and occupies up to 85 percent of the *ālāp* proper's performance time, and the *antarā* moves to the upper-octave tonic. Shujaat's explanation differed from Ravi Shankar's in details of the last two sections. According to Shujaat, the *sañcārī* dips back down in a return to tonic, and the *ābhoga* revisits the entire range in a fast sweep. I have not been given the liberty of reporting the exact musical details of these sections as described by Shankar; however, I can note that their order was reversed in Shankar's explanation, and the defining characteristics of the sections had more to do with particular ornamentation procedures and rhythmic pacing than with ambitus and tessitura, although these too came into play in determining the character of the subsections.

The range of ornamentation employed by those who claim a *bīnkār* origin in *ālāp* performance is much more restricted than for those who do not. The explanation offered by Ravi Shankar is that the *ālāp* must reflect the constraints of *dhrupad* performance; rapid mordents, trills, and acciacaturas are to be avoided in the *ālāp,* as these ornaments are indicative not of *dhrupad* performance, but of *khayāl* and *ṭhumrī.* Such distinctions are not maintained by the majority of contemporary instrumentalists. So, while the *ālāp* form originally associated with *dhrupad* is maintaining its status as an independent genre in North Indian instrumental music (i.e., in contrast to its dependent status in *khayāl,* where it has been incorporated within the *baṛā khayāl*), it is rapidly losing its stylistic character as an expression of a *dhrupad* aesthetic, and is acquiring the romantic expressiveness of *khayāl* performance practice, especially in the hands of the Imdādkhānī *gharānā* musicians.

Jor

A variety of approaches to *jor,* the pulsed section of the *ālāp,* are presently practiced in Hindustānī instrumental music. Transcriptions of excerpts from *jors* by Pandit Ravi Shankar, the late Dr. Lalmani Misra, and Shujaat Khan are included here (exx. 14.1–3) to elucidate what I view to be basic differences in the cognition of *jor* performance practice. Additionally, an analysis of tempo changes throughout the *jor* sections of performances by Ravi Shankar, Ali Akbar Khan, Lalmani Misra, and Shujaat Khan are provided in table 14.1. In

Example 14.1. Ravi Shankar, *Rāga Mālkauns, joṛ*. (Transcribed from *Ravi Shankar: Sounds of the Sitar*, Beat Goes On Records BGOCD171; originally released on World Pacific WPS-21434.)

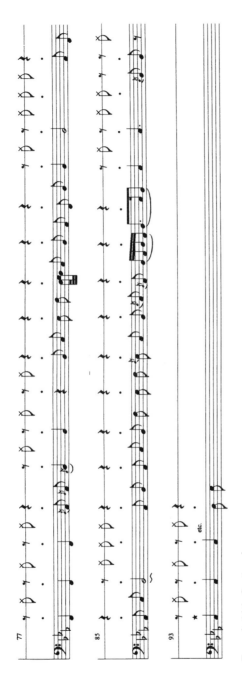

Example 14.1. *Continued*

345

Example 14.2. Lalmani Misra, *Rāga Mālkauns, joṛ*. (Transcribed from the author's recording of a live performance, August 1974.)

Example 14.3. Shujaat Khan, *Rāga Bāgeśrī, jor*. (Transcribed from the author's recording of a live performance, 5 May 1995.)

347

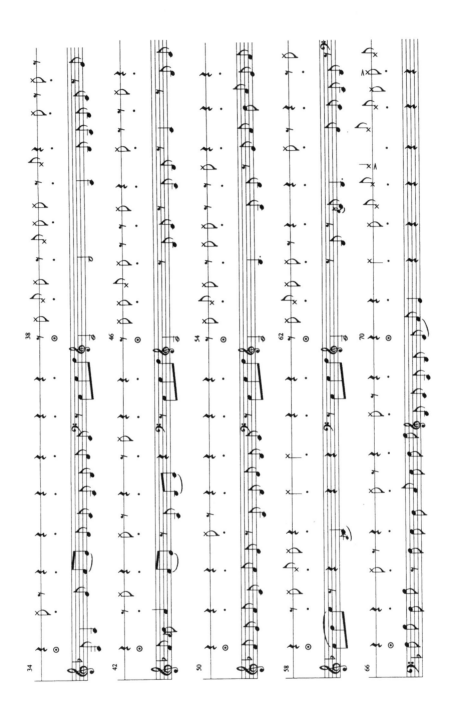

348

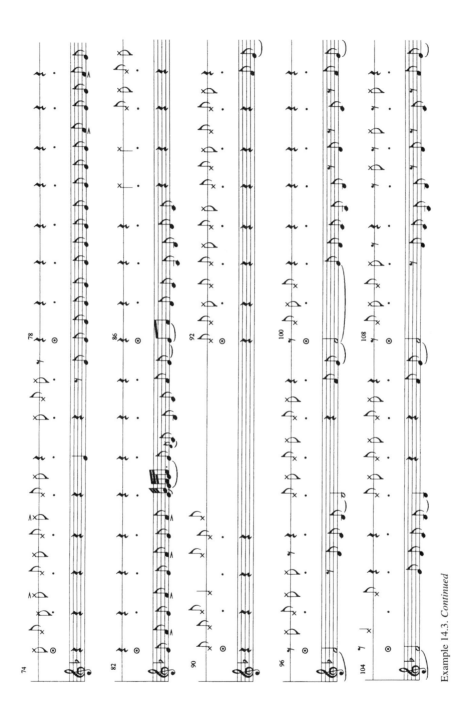

Example 14.3. Continued

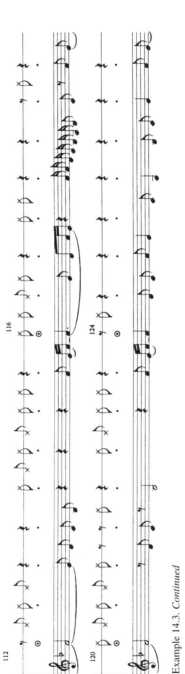

Example 14.3. Continued

the transcriptions, I have collapsed the pitches produced on the side drone strings (the *cikārī*) and on melodic strings serving a drone function into single notes with an "x" as the notehead, separating these onto a separate single-lined staff. The *cikārī* is notated with a downward pointing stem. Drone notes sounded by other strings are shown with upward pointing stems. Pulsation is indicated by the dots between the single-lined staff and the normal staff. Stars indicate cadential points ending sections in the Ravi Shankar performance. Numbers at the left and center above each system refer to groups of paired pulsation units which I refer to here as pseudo-measures (i.e., two pulsations equal one pseudo-measure). Circled dots in the Shujaat Khan performance indicate the first pulse of a repeating pattern of beats.

While the majority of *jor* performances will share a great deal in common, there are some differences in the creative process of improvising *jor* that are particularly telling of the way musicians must be thinking in order to construct musical phrases. The starting point of any conventional *jor* on a stringed instrument is the alternation of strokes on playing strings with strokes on the *cikārī* drone strings. Here, I will refer to such a unit—one stroke on a melody string followed by one on the *cikārī*—as the basic pulsation unit (b.p.u.). Some musicians use this unit as the primary structuring device governing rhythm in improvising melodic phrases within the *jor*.[14] The pulsation is not ordered into a higher level of rhythmic complexity. One common strategy for playing *jor* in this way is to allow the repeated articulation of a pedal tone (often the tonic pitch played on the second, or *jodī*, string) in alternation with the drone to serve as a musical space of relative repose between episodes of melodic extemporization played on the melody strings with a continuous inward stroking at a pace equivalent to that of the basic pulsation unit's strokes. Often, these melodic excursions are begun with repeated stroking on one pitch, followed by a contoured phrase. This phrase is often ended with a virtuosic *mīnd* (on sitar, producing several notes after one stroke by pulling the string across the fret) that is allowed to die out before the basic alternation stroking is continued. Musicians whose *jor*s make abundant use of this method would include Professor Debu Chaudhuri, Budhāditya Mukherjee, the late Lalmani Misra, and the late Nikhil Banerjee. A passage exemplifying this kind of construction can be found in example 14.3 in pseudo-measure 76–88.

Ravi Shankar has developed a systematic, highly structured procedure for performing *jor*. The rhythmic balance and overall organic plan revealed in his *jor* improvisations are striking in comparison with performers who adopt the approach described above. Within his *jor* (ex. 14.1), one often finds metricity existing throughout large sections, often of quadruple meter. On some occasions, I have observed him elevate this rhythmic regularity to the level of *tāla*, particularly *cautāla*, a *tāla* associated with the medieval *dhrupad* genre. In doing so, Shankar is demonstrating the authenticity of his style, as confining a

Table 14.1. Tempo analysis of four *joṛ* performances

Ravi Shankar (sitar), *Rāga Mālkauns*

{0:00–0:13   begins at 60 b.p.u.:
0:13–0:41   66 b.p.u.:
0:41–1:22   68 b.p.u.:
1:22–2:01   68 b.p.u.:
2:01–2:42}   70 b.p.u. (bass register):
2:42–2:52   72 b.p.u.:
2:52–3:43   76 b.p.u. (middle register):
3:43–4:33   77–80 b.p.u. (middle register):
4:33–5:22   80–84 b.p.u. (*antarā* and upper register):
5:22–5:54   80–84 b.p.u.:
5:54–6:14   94–100 b.p.u. (middle register and below):
6:14–6:48   96–102 b.p.u. (ranging from low to high):
6:48–7:39   106–112 b.p.u.:
7:39–8:42   110–118 b.p.u. *ulṭā jhālā* and *śuddh jhālā:*
8:42–9:20   110–118 b.p.u. *śuddh jhālā* and *ulṭā jhālā:*
9:20–10:33   124–128 b.p.u. end of *jhālā*

Ali Akbar Khan (sarod), *Rāga Bāgeśrī Kānadā*

0:00–1:13   begins at 54 b.p.u., ends at 62 b.p.u.:
1:13–2:44   63–70 b.p.u., dwells in lower octave:
2:44–4:10   74–80, then 80–88, dwells in middle octave;
4:10–9:46   this lengthy section, starting at 105 b.p.u., has several subsections, each
   one displaying a marked increase in tempo (115; 130; 150; 160; 175; 200),
   and centering on continuous 'da' stroking with closing melismas:
9:46–10:44   transition to *da-ra* stroking at 230 b.p.u.:
10:44–11:55   approximately halves b.p.u. to 130 to accommodate rapid *da-ra* stroking
   and *thoṅk jhālā* (effectively producing a density four times the b.p.u.):
11:55–12:33   b.p.u. rises to 160, rapid *da-ra* stroking and other, more complex patterns:
12:33–15:14   b.p.u. rises to 170–175, begins with continuous *da* stroking, then doubles
   to rapid *da-ra* stroking, reaching saturation density.

Lalmani Misra (*vicitra vīṇā*), *Rāga Mālkauns*

{0:00–2:30}   78–85 b.p.u.:
2:30–3:04   85–100 b.p.u.:
3:04–3:40   112–122 b.p.u. (*da* stroking sometimes pushed the b.p.u. to 128):
3:40–4:22   135 b.p.u., increases towards the end to 158:
4:22–7:09   starts at 95 b.p.u., doubles density of stroking do *bol tān* (i.e., improvisations making use of varied stroke patterns); increases to about 115 for
   most of the section; pushes tempo to 128 b.p.u.:
7:09–9:35   115–125 b.p.u., *jhālā* with *bol tān*

Shujaat Khan (sitar), *Rāga Bāgeśrī*

0:00–0:46   92–104 b.p.u.:
{0:46–1:29   100 to 113 b.p.u.,
1:29–2:44   fluctuates widely between 115 and 150 b.p.u.;
2:44–4:11}   fluctuates between 155 and 184:
4:11–5:17   cuts b.p.u. in half momentarily to 86, then more than doubles to 185–200
   includes *gamak tān* and other *tāns* played with *da-ra* stroking:
5:17–8:38   105 b.p.u.; 130 b.p.u. for *śuddh jhālā;* 140–156 b.p.u. for *tāns,* first short,
   then of increasing length, returning to bursts of *jhālā* in between each *tān:*
8:38–9:09   145 b.p.u. complex, varied stroking patterns using a lot of *cikārī:*

Table 14.1. *Continued*

9:09–9:50	130–135 b.p.u. for *ulṭa jhālā* (actual stroke density is 4 × 138, creating a saturation effect):
9:50–11:07	fluctuates between 105 and 120 for *tāns*.

Sources: Data are from performances recorded in concert by the author, except Shankar's *Mālkauns,* which is from *Sounds of the Sitar,* Beat Goes On Records BGOCD 171.

Note: Times given indicate beginnings and endings of sections. Tempo value is given in basic pulsation units (b.p.u.'s) per minute; one b.p.u. equals one set of alternating strokes on the melody and drone strings. Semicolons indicate subsections, and colons indicate rhythmic figures which end sections. Brackets indicate sections transcribed in examples 14.1–3.

jor to a *tāla,* according to many musicians, was a performance practice of *bīnkārs* in the past.

In contrast to the many musicians using liberal amounts of rubato in *jor,* Shankar eschews such tempo variation, employing tempo to indicate the progression of formal structure, with well-defined accelerations, indicating forward movement and usually occurring between subsections of the *jor.* The similarity of tempo gradations seen in the performances of Ali Akbar Khan and Ravi Shankar (see table 14.1) is a good indication of stylistic similarity deriving from *gharānā* affiliation. The use of tempo to demarcate sections (as marked off by a short rhythmic figure indicating closure of a section; see ex. 14.1 pseudo-measures 5–6, 21–22, 45–46, 67–68, 91–92) is clearly evident in the *jors* of both of these musicians. In addition, tempo changes always advance the tempo to higher values.[15] This unidirectional treatment of tempo change results in rhythm assuming a clear structural importance in the *jor* of these musicians, who can be regarded as representative of the Maihar *gharānā* in general. An extended *jor* by Shankar will often begin in a slow tempo (50–60 b.p.u.'s per minute). Melodic phrases will incorporate *mīnḍ* profusely. During this slow section, Shankar usually dips into the lower register of his sitar (as in ex. 14.1, pseudo-measures 49–93). Upon returning to the middle register, Shankar will then increase the tempo in gradations that conform closely to the formal sectioning of the *jor.* Occasionally, he will vary this approach slightly by beginning more slowly than usual in order to allow for a more expansive elaboration of the bass register. Upon returning to the middle register, he will then abruptly double the tempo, reaching the density of basic alternation stroking that most other sitarists begin with. Sectioning of the *jor* by such dramatic manipulations of tempo is yet another indication of the fundamental importance Shankar and other Maihar *gharānā* musicians have placed on rhythmics *(layakārī)* in their music, evidence of their adherence to the ideal of a *dhrupad* aesthetic, at least in their approach to *ālāp.*

Another noticeable feature of Shankar's *jor* is the control exerted over stroke density. The bulk of the section would be constituted with phrase building using a steady stroke pattern of regular note values equivalent to those constituting the basic pulsation rate. Internal organization of melodic phrases accentuates the pulsation unit by the occasional incorporation of odd-numbered groupings, throwing the accent off the beat and, eventually, back on the beat (see ex. 14.1, pseudo-measures 11–12).

By developing the feature of periodicity in his *jor,* Shankar has created a background that colors his melodic improvisations with greater rhythmic significance. For example, one technique he favors in generating melody amounts to a kind of subtractive diminution. A phrase is repeated, then continually varied in repetition by deleting notes from its end. A brief example of this technique can be seen in pseudo-measures 32–39 in example 14.1. The process may continue until a minimally acceptable melodic fragment remains; otherwise he ends the process as he pleases. Either way, the periodicity of *jor* rhythm remains to allow for an emphatic cadence at the conclusion of the process. Thus, in Shankar's *jor,* one finds rhythmic periodicity being employed in order to heighten the sense of return at the end of improvisatory excursions.

The metrical periodicity that Ravi Shankar has perfected reaches a level of rhythmic confinement that surpasses the requirements most other North Indian instrumentalists seek to meet in their *jor* melodies. That his rhythmic precision is purposeful is revealed by the kinesthetic manner in which Shankar ensures the continuation of the quadruple measure. He has devised a special way of tapping his foot to keep a measure of four: toe down, heel up, heel down, toe up.[16] Other instrumentalists tend not to tap their feet, at least not in this manner, as a rhythmic marker in *jor.* A strong sense of the elemental *laya* (rhythm) is continuously present in Shankar's style, reflecting the *jor*'s origin in the archaic *dhrupad* genre. The overall effect of his *jor* style is one of restraint and balance, achieved in large measure by the clockwork rhythm and the graduated tempo changes linked to major sections of form. By eschewing technical display in the *jor,* the essential qualities of the *rāga* appear to retain precedence over virtuosic display in the performances of this senior representative of the Maihar *gharānā.*

It is readily apparent that a clock-like periodicity is present in Shankar's *jor* that cannot be located in Misra's approach to *jor* performance (ex. 14.2). This can easily be seen if Misra's *jor* is divided into pseudo-measures of two basic pulsation units. A regularity is maintained for the first twenty pseudo-measures, but in the twenty-first, one basic pulsation unit is lost. Then Misra reestablishes the two-b.p.u. pattern, but it crosses over the imaginary barlines in pseudo-measures 22–29. A span of rhythmic ambiguity follows, continuing through the thirty-fifth pseudo-measure, and an extra drone beat is inserted in the thirty-sixth, where the two-b.p.u. pattern is again reinstated. This last articulation effectively inverts the arsis/thesis patterning of the basic pulsation unit. Listeners who may have been keeping a steady pulsation by lightly clapping or tapping a finger would have to make an adjustment at that point. It would be a mistake, however, to view this as a musical faux pas. Rather than demanding rigorous rhythmic regularity, Dr. Misra stressed a more relaxed approach to creating *jor* melodies, incorporating occasional passages of rhythmic ambiguity, then allowing the beat to reemerge in a way that, according to the kind of systematic analysis I have imposed here, would contradict the initial patterning of the basic pulsation unit. The aural effect of such strategies in the course of performance was actually quite pleasing.

An examination of tempo manipulation in Misra's and Shujaat Khan's *jor* (see table 14.1) reveals that tempo does not play an important role in maintaining the momentum of form in these performances. Here, in my view, the musicians retain relatively loose constraints on tempo changes. This flexibility allows for adjustments in tempo through rapid acceleration or deceleration in order to accommodate the particular variety of improvisation launched by the artist. Improvisations emphasizing repeated articulations of one pitch often tend to speed up, as it is relatively easy technically to accomplish this. On the other hand, much more difficult scalar runs are often preceded by a deceleration of tempo. In this case, form appears to be subordinate to technique in the creative thinking of the musicians.

Musicians of the Imdādkhānī *gharānā* perform *jor* in a way that differs markedly from the procedures described above. One feature of their approach is a pronounced tempo rubato effect. A common approach to phrase construction found here is to begin with continuous stroking on one pitch at double the density of the underlying pulsation unit, then gradually increase the tempo of the stroking as the phrase expands outward from the beginning pitch, until a climax is reached with a virtuosic flourish combining various left-hand articulation techniques, especially pulling the wire, to produce a rapid run of pitches with one stroke. At this point, the tempo is pulled back before the pulsation is begun again. Musicians of this *gharānā* are prone to substitute rapid vamp patterns for the basic pulsation unit. These consist of groups of strokes at double the basic density alternating between the *cikārī* drone and the first or second wire, which, in this instance, would serve a secondary drone function. These vamp patterns are similar in effect to the stroking patterns of the *jhālā,* the high speed section of *ālāp* (and often a conclusion to a *drut gat*) that alternates strokes on melody strings with groups of strokes on the *cikārī* drone strings. Here, however, the vamping would give way to melodic phrases of some sort or another. The alternation of lengthy periods of repose, during which drone stroking is maintained, with outbursts of intense melodic activity is strongly suggestive of the manner in which k̲h̲ayāl singers take a few moments to catch their breaths before vollying forth with cascades of *tāns*. The overall effect of the Imdādkhānī *gharānā's* approach to *jor* is one of lyrical sweetness combined with an abundant variety of virtuosic technical display. In many respects, one can say that this *gharānā* has overlaid both *ālāp* and *jor,* formal units originating in the *dhrupad* genre, with all the accoutrements of the k̲h̲ayāl genre.

Recursiveness is not absent from the *joṛs* of the Imdādkhānī *gharānā* instrumentalists, it is just attained through different means. In general, the *joṛ* section in this *gharānā*'s style, as stated above, is relatively free flowing. As represented in the playing of Shujaat Khan, an implied periodicity occurs more than occasionally, but it is not rigidly maintained. In example 14.3, a pattern four pseudo-measures in length carries through most of the excerpt, but there is a lapse in the regularity of this pattern after pseudo-measure 90. Furthermore, the implicit periodicity of melodic construction that is visible in this transcription is heavily masked when actually listening to Khan's playing because of his liberal use of acceleration and deceleration. It appears that this musician prizes the freedom to respond to the flow of his melody during the moment of creation more than he desires a clearly apparent metrical periodicity (see table 14.1).

In the excerpt contained in example 14.3, one can see that Shujaat Khan achieves recursiveness by introducing a catchphrase *(pakaḍ)* that, in some ways, can be viewed as a pseudo-*mukhṛā* (*mukhṛā* refers to the beginning part of a *gat* that serves also as an important point of return). Such a catchphrase occurs at the very outset of this example and is returned to after extensive flights of creativity (see pseudo-measures 5, 9, 13, 21, 29, 37, 45, 53, 61). Drone vamping (pseudo-measures 71–76), a melodic phrase built on continuous plectrum stroking (pseudo-measures 78–87), and a second passage of drone vamping (pseudo-measures 88–94) intervene before a second theme appears at pseudo-measures 95–103. Khan then subjects this theme to a few variations and, eventually, interpolates a series of virtuosic *tāns* (the first in the series appears at pseudo-measure 118), returning to the theme as he would return to the *mukhṛā* of a *gat*. The remainder of his *joṛ* in *Rāga Bāgeśrī* consisted primarily of virtuosic vamp patterns interspersed with a variety of *tāns,* sections of *jhālā,* and a final section of *tāns,* thus conforming in practice to his concept of *ālāp-joṛ* structure as outlined above.

Vilambit Gat

Another broad form of Hindustānī instrumental music that has been conceptualized in differing ways would be the slow *(vilambit) gat,* still referred to by some musicians as the *Masitkhānī gat.* Allyn Miner relates that the late Ustad Mushtaq Ali Khan, an important twentieth-century figure in the Jaipur Senia lineage of sitarists, spoke of a developmental sequence in elaborating the *gat* that included five phases: *gatkārī, mukhṛā, fikra, toḍā* and *layakārī.* Of these terms, *fikra* is one that I had not previously encountered. However, it is interesting to examine because it illuminates the kinds of coincidences of cross-referencing that occur between the highly verbal discourse of speaking about music and the highly variegated discourse of actual musical practices. To begin with, Miner describes *fikra* as "short, quick series of note permutations normally included in types of *tans*" (1993, 200). She also provides Mushtaq Ali Khan's explanation of *fikra* as "short, spontaneously composed phrases inserted into the *gat*," as well as Umar Khan's description: "the first, short, progressive rhythmic and melodic variations within the phrases of the gat" (201). Examples of *fikra* played by Umar Khan, however, are similar to rhythmic variations of the basic slow *gat* structure played by other musicians, including my own teachers, but left untermed. A variant interpretation of the significance of *fikra* as a defining term for music was offered to me by Pandit Ravi Shankar. He said a *fikra* could be anything; that the term, in essence, simply denotes any kind of improvisatory phrase. This interpretation appears to contradict those reported by Miner in that *fikra,* in Shankar's usage, has no significance relative to the overall plan of performance.

Miner provides other varieties of realizing the elaboration of a slow *gat,* and I have provided an analysis of yet another approach, the "modern" system of *vilambit gat vistār* developed and popularized by Pandit Ravi Shankar (Slawek 1987). Shankar's model for structuring the *vilambit gat* consists of two major sections, what I have termed *rāga*-oriented and *layakārī*-oriented. The first broad section recapitulates the kind of expansive, developmental procedure common in *ālāp*. This section concludes with the *antarā* section of the *gat* composition.

The second section gradually develops more regular rhythmic pacing in the improvisations and moves toward a greater density of articulations in mathematically precise manipulations of the rhythm. In simplest terms, the density of articulations moves through multiples of the basic pulse. A typical procedure would be to move from one-and-a-half times the basic pulse (three articulations in two beats) to two, three, four, five, six, seven, eight, and possibly nine and even twelve times the basic pulse. In order to allow for the latter stages, it is necessary to maintain a relatively slow tempo throughout the bulk of the performance of the *gat*. This approach to structuring improvisation in the *vilambit gat* can be found in several of Shankar's recordings, but it is not the only approach he has used.[17] An alternate course I have heard him take would be to start at a relatively faster tempo, move directly into improvisations at four, then six, then eight times the basic pulse. At this point, there might be an abrupt increase in tempo and a return to four times the basic pulse (with the quicker tempo, density remains relatively constant). Sometimes the basic tempo is pushed to the point that the *vilambit gat* enters the tempo range of a *madhya laya gat* (medium-tempo gat). Ustad Ali Akbar Khan employs similar developmental strategies in his approach to the *vilambit gat,* and, in general, these formal plans can be viewed as distinctive of Maihar *gharānā* musicians.

Lalmani Misra ordered his *vilambit gat* development slightly differently. The first, *rāga*-oriented section was similar, but in the *layakārī*-oriented section, he would often start in four times the basic pulse, then move to double that density and then gradually increase tempo while changing *layakārī* from eight times the basic pulse to seven, six, five, and back to four times the basic pulse, but now at a much faster tempo.

The existence of variant approaches to slow *gat* development in North Indian music once again reminds us that uniformity of music cognition in performance practice does not necessarily follow uniformity in music terminological practices. Such flexibility in the musical realization of formal concepts shared throughout the tradition both illuminates the nature of the musical tradition and raises questions of musicological methodology. We are faced with a multiplicity of understandings at the outset as a basic characteristic of the musical system. A musicological epistemology that seeks to elucidate elemental meanings in this tradition may thus be doomed to failure from the start. A more fruitful course for musicology to follow in elaborating such an improvisatory tradition might be to focus on the relational processes that engage its practitioners in sociomusical action that is layered with multiple meanings and results.

Tihāī

It has often been remarked that the most difficult part of improvising music is ending an improvisation in a way that is fitting to both the improvisation itself and the music that is to follow. The analogy has been made to flying—that landing is the most difficult and riskiest part of aeronautics. A conventional device for ending improvisations in Hindustānī music is the *tihāī,* a thrice-played figure that either elides with the first beat *(sam)* of the *tāla* cycle or concludes before the beginning of the *mukhṛā,* the section of a *gat* that precedes and cadences upon the *sam.* As the *tihāī* is essentially a rhythmic device, it would be expected—and it is the case—that musicians who have devoted more of their intellectual and physical energies to exploring the realm of *tāla* in Indian music would make greater and more varied use of *tihāī*s than those who have not. The *tihāī* is a special part of the repertory of tabla players, who memorize hundreds of fixed *tihāī*s in order to be able to end improvisations with one starting at any point within the *tāla* cycle and reaching the designated point of arrival.[18] Students of stringed instruments are often encouraged by their gurus to learn tabla in order to improve their rhythmic abilities in general, but also specifically to enhance their skills in concluding improvisations with *tihāī*s.

The *tihāī* concept has been manipulated, transformed, and inflated in various ways. For instance, a *cakkardār tihāī* is one whose internally repeated unit is a *tihāī* in itself. A more complex musical form of *cakkardār tihāī* is the *farmaiśī tihāī.* It is structured in such a way that the end of the first part of the internal *tihāī* falls on the *sam* in the first of its three articulations, the end of the second part of the internal *tihāī* falls on *sam* during the second articulation, and the end of the third part of the internal *tihāī* falls on *sam* during the third playthrough, concluding the entire *farmaiśī.* The spontaneous creation of such complex units of music during the act of performance is very difficult, if not impossible. Their inclusion in a performance, while possibly not preplanned, would most certainly fall near the "fixity" side of the dialectic I proposed at the beginning of this essay.

Table 14.2. Two *Farmaiśī Tihāī* formulas

Tīn-tāla

	1	2	3	4	5	6	7	8	9	10	11	12	13	14	15	16
marker	X				2				O				3			
Formula 1																
	[1	2	3	4	5	6	7	8	9	10	11	12	(1	2	3	4
	5)	(1	2	3	4	5)	(1	2	3	4	5)]	[1	2	3	4	5
	6	7	8	9	10	11	12	(1	2	3	4	5)	(1	2	3	4
	5)	(1	2	3	4	5)]	[1	2	3	4	5	6	7	8	9	10
	11	12	(1	2	3	4	5)	(1	2	3	4	5)	(1	2	3	4
	5]															
Formula 2																
	1	2	3	4	{1	2	3	4	5	6	7	8	9	[(1	2	3
	4	1	1	2	3	4	1	1	2	3	4)	1	1	2	(1	2
	3	4	1	1	2	3	4	1	1	2	3	4)	1	1	2	(1
	2	3	4	1	1	2	3	4	1	1	2	3	4)]}	1	{1	2
	3	4	5	6	7	8	9	[(1	2	3	4	1	1	2	3	4
	1	1	2	3	4)	1	1	2	(1	2	3	4	1	1	2	3
	4	1	1	2	3	4)	1	1	2	(1	2	3	4	1	1	2
	3	4	1	1	2	3	4)]}	1	{1	2	3	4	5	6	7	8
	9	[(1	2	3	4	1	1	2	3	4	1	1	2	3	4)	1
	1	2	(1	2	3	4	1	1	2	3	4	1	1	2	3	4)
	1	1	2	(1	2	3	4	1	1	2	3	4	1	1	2	3
	4)]}															

Note. The top line shows the traditional division of the sixteen beats of *tīn-tāla* (shown in the second line) into four groups, where X stands for the first beat (*sam*), indicated with a clap; 2 stands for the first beat of the second group, also indicated with a clap; O indicates the third group, indicated with a wave (known as *khali*); and 3 indicates the first beat of the last group, indicated with a clap.

If not totally prepared and memorized, a *farmaiśī tihāī* most certainly would be based upon a prefabricated structure. For example in *tīn-tāla*, the formula 3[12 + 3(5)] generates the *farmaiśī tihāī* shown as formula 1 in table 14.2. Another, more involuted *farmaiśī tihāī* in *tīn-tāla* taught to me by Ravi Shankar (formula 2 in table 14.2) condenses to the following expression: 4 + 2{9 + 2[3(4+1) + 2] + 2(4 + 1) + 4 + 1} + 9 + 2[3(4+1) + 2] + 2(4 + 1) + 4. In reading both expressions, the number 3 indicates the number of repetitions of quantities of beats, represented by other numbers inside brackets or parentheses. In the second expression, the number 2 represents a quantity of beats unless it immediately precedes some kind of left bracket or parenthesis, when it indicates repetition. Working through the arithmetic of the second formula shows this expression resolves to a total of 177 beats. Thus, the *farmaiśī tihāī* occupies a total of eleven full cycles of *tīn-tāla* (totaling 176 beats), and resolves on the *sam* of the twelfth cycle, totaling 177 beats in all. That tabla players, stringed instrumentalists, and vocalists alike could use such a formula to construct a pre-fixed unit to include in a performance is revealing of the degree to which the various components of the musical tradition are interlinked in the syntagmatic realm. Whether or not an individual chooses to do so is another matter altogether, with the choice depending on one's own capabilities and aesthetic preferences.

The following excerpts from discussions with Shujaat Khan and Ravi Shankar reveal an interesting contrast in the way these two musicians conceptualize improvisation and *tihāī* construction:

> SS: Say you are playing a slow *gat* and you want to make up a *tihāī*. What goes through your mind?
>
> SK: I don't. I don't like *tihāī*s. Sometimes, a fixed *tihāī*—I play one or two sometimes. Otherwise, I like *āmad*s [approaches to *mukhṛā,* usually without *tihāī*] better. How beautifully, without effort, and without people realizing, without your being able to see the brainwork, how beautifully you can end your improvisation and come back into the *mukhṛā*. I enjoy that very much. And sometimes there is an *upaj* [improvised] *tihāī* that comes out also, whether it is fast or slow or whatever. But basically, I am more impressed by, [and] I try and always come back to, not the *sam,* but the *mukhṛā* of the *gat.* So I, as in most other cases, am not really qualified to answer that one. But, if I would have to, I would think that it just comes. I'm sorry, Steve, I just have never thought of this. You see a space and you imagine the rest of the space before where you want to get and break it into three parts and choose a phrase. How big is the phrase that you would break it into three parts.
>
> SS: So when you see the space you think in terms of the number of beats?
>
> SK: No. Never look at the beats. Never! It is more the circle that is in my mind, not the one, two, three, four, but the whole sixteen—even if it is a slow *gat.* As soon as it starts, for me, I can basically picture the whole circle, so if I'm at five or seven and, say, I want to start into a *tihāī,* it seems like a nice phrase, immediately I can picture it as the rest of the clock and divide that into three parts, whatever phrase I might want. It is not the beats. If . . . I am concentrating and thinking of that, I am sure it is not the beats. . . . I don't think of it in numbers; it is more just a picture. (Khan 1995)

Ravi Shankar has said that improvisations should flow naturally, whether with or against the rhythm, and that if a *tihāī* is used, it should grow from the improvisation, not appear to be a calculated appendage; but he has also noted the importance of calculated precision, as well as a conscious awareness of the beat in manipulating rhythmic placement:

> I feel I have a lot of improvising capacity. It is not a question of pride, but of confidence. . . . But, I feel myself as doing so that when each line, when I play it, it will be different, it won't be exactly the same. So I have always loved this exploring, always new touches,—a little cut [grace note], or a little *bol* [stroke] difference, or eating up one *mātrā* here and adding it there—all that. But it is not a *bandiś* way of doing it, it is spontaneous. But there is a calculation behind it. It has to have that. Can't be without that.
>
> As far as improvising is concerned—the concept of newness, or compos-

ing a *gat* on the spot, or *toḍās*—the criterion of improvisation is that it shouldn't sound like a hit-and-run policy.[19] [He then, in Hindi, describes the wrong approach to take.] *Liyā, āyā to āyā, nahī̃ āyā to. Chalo,* again try *kar rahe usko tihāī khūb māñjh rahe hāĩ. Ayā nahī̃ phir.* [Take (a stab at improvising something), if it comes it comes, if not, so what. (They will) go on, again trying the same *tihāī* over and over even if it doesn't come to *sam.*] You see, otherwise it is *bandiś* [i.e., musicians playing fixed things and calling it improvising]. But what I do—you have noted that—from beginning to end, I try to make it fit. Anyone who will hear me will think these [improvisations] are all pre-fixed *bandiś*es. Am I right? So that finishing, even while composing [i.e., improvising], one should maintain. I think that is a very high state of improvisation, personally. And I have worked very hard. And it has been spontaneous with me. But I have thought about it. It is not like [I just] let myself go on. . . . I am thinking also, I am criticizing myself also, and finding out. . . . So, this is the thing where I find myself different from other artists. There are really great artists; they are wonderful at improvisation. *Sabhī hāĩ* [they all are], it is not that I am something unusual, but I have gone far ahead in this field. (Shankar 1995)

In these statements, two very different attitudes towards improvising in general and *tihāī*s in particular may be detected. For Shujaat Khan, it appears that *tihāī* construction is an intuitive process, using the broad outlines of mental imagery to gauge musical space. The mathematical demands of the musical process are of relatively little concern to Shujaat, whose use of rhythm could be characterized as directed more towards the phrasing of melody in a phased association with the *tāla* cycle than towards minute segments of individual beats *(mātrā)*. Shankar, on the other hand, delights in the subtle manipulation of rhythmic units at the level of microbeats. During the years that I have studied with him and attended or participated in his performances, I have observed a musical mind that rarely takes a rest from devising complex rhythmic exercises and intricately designed *tihāī*s. It is this penchant for calculated precision in rhythmic improvisations that demands a steady, metronome-like beat to provide the standard against which the calculations are made. The Imdādkhānī *gharānā* musicians, on the other hand, appear more concerned with rhythm at the macro level—the basic divisions *(vibhāg)* of the *tāla*. The following excerpts from an interview I conducted with one of India's premier tabla exponents, Pandit Swapan Chaudhuri, lends support to the views I have presented here:

> *SC:* Their approach [i.e., Ravi Shankar and Ali Akbar Khan] is so musical. I mean, both the melody as well as the rhythm combine so nicely that it is really very, very pleasant to everybody's ear. And second, we learn a lot during the performance. And it is sort of a challenge to attain those kinds of rhythmic patterns. And once you accept that challenge, then what happens, you try—maybe you will fail on the stage or maybe you will be successful, that doesn't matter; but that will be a learning [experience] for you,

so that you can think about that later on, and try to apply that some other time. Now with Raviji [Shankar], his whole approach is very rhythmic.

SS: And calculated!

SC: And calculated. . . . But the calculation is not mathematical so that he is counting every single beat. It is like a garland, but every time you make a garland it is a little different. So Raviji's approach is very different. Every time he plays, and every *tāla* whenever he plays, it is not the same pattern. It is a different pattern, and that is why it is so challenging, so excellent, for us, at least. Particularly for me, I definitely learned a lot from playing with him.

With Khansaheb [Ali Akbar], his approach is a little different. When he does the rhythmic changes or pattern, or *layakārī,* he is not that calculated. But. . . I think what he does, he just balances the *laya* from one beat to another beat. In between, these microbeats are there. So he balances; so sometimes you might see that the *tihāī* is not proportional, it's not even, like, okay—eleven, eleven, eleven [which would cover two cycles of sixteen]—you may not find that one, but it is very smooth, it is not like it is completely out of rhythm. But he takes chances, . . . and if he feels that— he can sense that I guess—that it is not going to work, then he changes it. He changes it in such a way that it does not hurt your ear. It's very smooth. And then it completes the whole cycle and comes to the *sam* very nicely. [With Ravi Shankar] It is very straight.

SS: And calculated. And if he misses, I feel he calculates the mistake and continues playing in a way that obscures the miscalculation, and the second time—it's on.

SC: Yeah. You see the thing is is that most of the musicians, when they play, . . . they are too much calculated [i.e, overly dependent upon memorized material]. So if they miss, they don't know how to manage and come back to *sam.* Any person, if he has a little bit of sense, can understand that he missed it. But, both with Khansaheb and Raviji, it is hard to find out where they missed it. They have such a different way, so many ways they change the whole thing. I mean the whole structure will be different.

SS: And in terms of Vilayat Khan's approach to rhythm, how would you say that requires a different kind of accompaniment?

SC: Vilayat Khansaheb's approach to rhythm is different. I think Vilayat Khansaheb's puts more importance to the k̲h̲ayāl style. Now everybody says this is *gayakī aṅg,* and ours is different. . . . I don't understand this. Everything is *gayakī.* The whole approach came from the *gayakī.* Now if you say that . . . we play in k̲h̲ayāl style, or k̲h̲ayāl *gayakī,* and you play in *dhrupad* style, I don't understand this. But what I think they want to mean is when you play in the k̲h̲ayāl style you have more freedom. Like certain *rāga*s you cannot sing very fast or you cannot do a lot of *tāns,* because if you do, you will miss those *śrutis* [microtonal ornamentation]. That is a strict regulation if you look at it in a theoretical way. But in k̲h̲ayāl style, a lot of musicians are singing those—say *Darbārī Kānaḍā, Śrī* or *Mārvā, Pūriyā, Śuddh Kalyāṇ*—but Vilayat Khansaheb's approach is more on that side, it is not rhythm oriented at all.

SS: So less scope for the accompanist also?

SC: Oh yeah. There is not that much scope, number one. And number two, there is not that much of a challenge. Yes, the challenge is that you get a chance, so you play your own way.

SS: You mean there is not as much interaction?

SC: Not much interaction, no.

SS: No sāth saṅgat [simultaneous accompaniment]?

SC: No, no. Not at all. Whereas playing with them [Ali Akbar Khan and Ravi Shankar], . . . every phrase is very challenging, because when they are doing this layakārī, you have to answer it; so it is more challenging. (Chaudhuri, 1992)

Conclusion

In a tradition as old and expansive as the śāstriyā saṅgīta (canonical music) of North India, it is not surprising that a variety of approaches to musical performance practice exists. Given the nature of the social milieu within which the tradition was transmitted, it is also not surprising that some degree of disjuncture exists between the way musicians talk about their music and what they actually do. In this chapter, I have characterized the concept of improvisation in North Indian music as a musical process that is intimately situated within the performance phase of the music-making process. In this sense, improvisation is clearly distinct from the process of creating fixed pieces of music.

In the Indian context, creating fixed musical units is an activity that takes place in the teaching and practice phases of the music-making process. There is a concept of composition that is very close to the Western sense of creating a free-standing musical piece. In the Indian case, the piece created (bandiś) is not necessarily free-standing—it will usually be expanded in performance by variation and interpolated with conventional types of improvisations—but it is relatively fixed in the sense that a basic version of the composition will be maintained for purposes of transmitting the tradition.

On the other hand, improvisation in North Indian music is a complex process involving precomposed fixed pieces; rehearsed patterns; spontaneous creation of new material based upon conventional models, including both paradigmatic and syntagmatic fields; spontaneous creation of new material through the launching of dynamic, generative "programs"; interactive creativity involving feedback between the soloist and accompanist and between the performers and audience; and self-reflexive awareness of one's own compositional activity and expressiveness during the act of musical creation. The resultant product is unique in that reproduction by any means other than mechanical recording is nearly impossible. Every performance is a new exploration of a particular musical experience that will lead both the performers and audience into uncharted musical territory. And once the musicians enter that territory, they must keep the conglomeration of music-making processes going until they are ready to leave it.

Notes

This article draws on research and study carried out over a considerable number of years and with the help of financial support from numerous sources. In particular, I wish to acknowledge the support from Junior (1981–82) and Senior (1991–92) Fellowships from the American Institute of Indian Studies (the latter carried with it extra funding from the National Endowment for Humanities) and a Summer Research Fellowship (1990) from the Dean's Office, College of Fine Arts, the University of Texas at Austin. Thanks are also due to Harold Powers, who read an earlier version of this paper and offered several constructive suggestions that have been incorporated here.

1. I follow Powers (1977) in the use of the terms syntagmatic and paradigmatic. Broadly speaking, syntagmatic aspects of Indian classical music making would include the linear rules of construction in piecing together a performance of a *rāga*. The paradigmatic aspect of a performance is primarily equivalent to *rāga*, conceptualized as a set of potential melodic phrases. Secondarily, *tāla* may also be viewed as paradigmatic in those sections of a performance in which it is present. Similar to the way in which melodic phrases act to confirm or mask the identity of *rāga*, various aspects of rhythm (phrasing, patterns of sound on accompanying drums, patterns of syncopation, etc.) can serve to confirm or mask the presence of a particular *tāla* in performance.

2. I was made acutely aware of the relative importance placed on syntagmatic and paradigmatic elements in Indian music when an earlier publication (Slawek 1987) received a lukewarm review by a native listener because of the minimal attention given to the implications of *rāga* in determining the nature of improvisation in instrumental music. Bharat Gupt wrote, "whether the book at all succeeds in giving an insight into the process of improvisation, let alone reveal its secret, is rather dubious. . . . But in the absence of *rāga* principles a description of *gat* structure remains only the outer shell without the inner spirit. It is in the relationship of the structure to the spirit that the process of improvisation lies" (1987, 52). I'm afraid that I must confess Mr. Gupt might voice the same concern for the present effort.

3. Titon's concept of "preform" (1978, 91) is of use in discussing differences between music that is composed prior to its performance and music that is composed, for the most part, in the act of performance. The preform is a model of what is to be rendered in performance, but is loosely put together and has spaces left unfilled to provide flexibility during the performance. A preform can relate to only a small part of a total performance, and can relate to only one component within the musical structure, such as text. Scholars who have theorized the creative process of improvisation have often alluded to models that serve as the basis of musical construction during performance. For example, I previously used the concept of template, a kind of mold from which a variety of final forms could emerge. There appears to be a distinction to be made between preform and template. Template suggests some rigidity of structure, and indeed, such rigidity can be found in Indian musical models that serve as a basis for improvisation, especially those of the syntagmatic variety. Preform, on the other hand, incorporates the notions of incompleteness and malleability within it. We might propose a continuum of model types as possible within improvisatory traditions, some leaning towards greater rigidity but still capable of producing unlimited variations in performance, and others leaning towards inchoate and changeable forms. Nettl presents similar ideas when he postulates the existence of "varying degrees of independence for the performer

in working from a model, that is, different degrees of compositional activity on the part of the performer" (1974, 7).

4. David Henderson has noted in conversations with me that evidence for such an aesthetic ideal can be found throughout various levels of Indian culture. "Please Sound Horn" is a common request seen painted on buses and trucks that is more than frequently obliged on the roads. Often, loudspeakers are jacked up beyond their capacity to support undistorted amplification. And I have witnessed countless public arguments of great vocal intensity during my years of residence in Banaras. I would venture that such an aesthetic is a natural consequence of the religious belief that sound is a form of God *(Nāda Brahmā hai)*. The more sound there is, the more divinity is present in the environment.

5. In Slawek 1990, I used audience feedback as a signal of musical communication to examine aspects of musical meaning that do not get attention when looking only at meanings produced by paradigmatic processes.

6. In perusing Paul Berliner's mammoth work on jazz improvisation, I am struck by more than a few similarities that emerge when comparing the sociomusical praxis of Hindustani musicians with jazz musicians. For example, Berliner writes, "Within the groove, improvisers experience a great sense of relaxation, which increases their powers of expression and imagination. They handle their instruments with athletic finesse, able to respond to every impulse" (1994, 389). Berliner also recognizes a similar relationship between fixed and flexible aspects of performance that I have characterized here as a dialectical process: "the spontaneous and arranged elements of jazz presentations continually cross-fertilize and revitalize one another" (383).

7. Wade discusses creativity (which she equates with improvisation) in the performance practice of Indian classical traditions using musical parameters such as dynamic contrast, timbral contrast, articulation, and intonation (1984, 43–46). Manipulation of these musical aspects certainly can and does contribute to an individual's musical style. What I focus on in the present study is not manipulation of preconceived parameters, but the actual nature of conceptualization as it relates to performance practice. While Wade makes it evident that there exist different approaches to realizing performable musical materials in Indian music, what I am trying to reveal here is that variant approaches are not exactly variations on a theme, but the outgrowth of different ways of understanding.

8. For the purpose of comparison with the South Indian approach to *rāga-ālāpanā* see Kassebaum 1987 and Viswanathan 1977.

9. The late Zia Mohiuddin Dagar would certainly have been included in this list were he still alive. There is presently such a limited market for the *rudra vīṇā* that it is dangerously close to extinction.

10. See Miner (1993, 165) for a thorough review, in English, of Roy Chaudhury's explanation of *ālāp* structure.

11. Ravi Shankar explained to me that within the Maihar *gharānā*, *ābhoga* precedes *sañcārī*. Most other explanations of *ālāp* structure reverse these terms. When asked by the author to corroborate Shankar's explanation of *ālāp* structure, Ustad Ali Akbar Khan listed the same terms as Shankar had, then indicated it was my responsibility to figure out from observing performance practice what the terms meant and where in the performance they occurred!

12. Miner gives a detailed overview of nineteenth-century interpretations of the terms associated with *ālāp* as presented in several manuals for the instrument published in the latter decades of the century and as described to her by elder musicians who have since passed away, such as Mushtaq Ali Khan (Miner 1993, 163–79). Her rigorous work demonstrates that the inconsistency of definition that exists today in North Indian terminology is nothing new. The degree of divergence in terminological usage appears to have been as great in the nineteenth century as it is today. The curiously cryptic nature of many of the explanations reported by Miner, many of which verge on the incomprehensible, combined with the barely rudimentary (and often ambiguous) notational practices found in the manuals (not to mention the probability of a high incidence of misprints in publishing) lead me to question how much of actual nineteenth-century performance practice we can glean from Miner's discussion. Early twentieth-century audio recordings appear to have much more in common with present performance practice than the representative examples drawn from the manuals by Miner. Are we really to believe that performance practice changed so much in the course of a few decades? The relative stability of North Indian instrumental music during the last fifty years is strong evidence against the likelihood of such radical change at the end of the nineteenth century.

13. *Ulṭā jhālā* ("inverted" *jhālā*) literally inverts the stroking pattern of regular *jhālā*. In *ultā jhālā,* groups of strokes are initiated by a drone stroke on the *cikārī,* followed by strokes on the melody wire.

14. North Indian instrumentalists utilize mnemonics as an aid in teaching and for providing a kind of aural notation of the music. This practice is more widely known as it is applied to the drumming traditions, as drummers often include the recitation of stroke syllables *(bols)* in their stage performances. Players of string instruments also use *bols* that specify stroking technique. On the sitar, the basic *bols* are an inward stroke of the index, called *"da,"* and an outward stroke, called *"ra."* In rapid alternation, these are paired as *"diri."* Strokes on the drone strings are recited as *"ra," "ya,"* or *"cik."* These *bols,* and slight alterations of them that indicate durational relationships, are applied to the sarod, too, but their manner of performance is reversed, as *"da"* is an outward stroke and *"ra"* is an inward stroke on that instrument.

15. Occasionally, tempo of the b.p.u. will be halved in order to accommodate increasing density of stroking, but the overall progression of the density referent remains upwards. For example, in Ali Akbar Khan's *jor,* the first four sections advance the b.p.u. to about 200 beats per minute. The last four sections continue the inexorable densification of stroking, but Khan drops the b.p.u. to a little more than half the 200 b.p.u. of the previous section in order to accommodate saturation density in the *"da–ra"* stroking without having to maintain a frenetic b.p.u. between improvisatory extemporizations.

16. This manner of foot tapping can maintain groupings of either two or four basic pulsation units. If one stroke is assigned to each foot movement, the sequence of movements counts out two basic pulsation units. If a melody stroke coupled with a drone stroke is linked to each movement, then four basic pulsation units would be contained in the sequence of foot movements.

17. See, in particular, the *vilambit gats* of the following recorded selections: "Raga Tilak Shyam" on *Ravi,* Capitol Records ST 10504; "Raga Hemant" on *Ravi Shankar, Sitar: Homage to Mahatma Gandhi and Baba Allauddin,"* Deutsche Grammophon 2532

356; and "Raga Kedar" on *The Doyen of Hindustani Music,* Oriental Records ORI/ AAMS CD 123.

18. Lipiczky relates an anecdote about the well-known tabla master of Banaras, Sharda Sahai. In a solo performance in 1973, Sahai displayed his command over *tihāī* construction by having audience members signal randomly and at will where in the *tāla* cycle he should start a *tihāī* that would cadence on the first beat of the *tāla* cycle. Sahai proceeded to give a demonstration not only of his command over *tāla* by succeeding in instantaneously introducing *tihāī*s of proper proportion on demand, but also of his artistic creativity by unifying all of the *tihāī*s with common thematic material (Lipiczky 1985, 159).

19. A textbook definition of *gat* would state that it is a precomposed item in the improvised performance. Some North Indian instrumentalists claim an ability to create *gats* at the moment of performance as one way of asserting their proficiency in improvising. Thus, while most *gats* one hears in performance have been worked out in advance or learned from a teacher, some may indeed be composed on the stage. Ravi Shankar is certainly capable of creating a gat on the spur of the moment. Beyond that, many of his improvisations sound so perfectly set that he has often been accused of playing only memorized music, not truly improvised music.

References

Berliner, Paul. 1994. *Thinking in Jazz: The Infinite Art of Improvisation.* Chicago: University of Chicago Press.

Chaudhuri, Swapan. 1992. Interview by the author. Bombay, India, 30 January.

Gupt, Bharat. 1987. Review of *Sitar Technique in Nibaddh Forms,* by S. Slawek. *Sangeet Natak* 84:52–54.

Kassebaum, Gayathri Rajapur. 1987. "Improvisation in Alapana Performance: A Comparative View of Raga Shankarabharana." *Yearbook for Traditional Music* 29:45–64.

Khan, Shujaat. 1995. Interview by the author. Austin, Tex., 6 May.

Kippen, James. 1988. *The Tabla of Lucknow.* Cambridge: Cambridge University Press.

Lipiczky, Thom. 1985. "Tihai Formulas and the Fusion of 'Composition' and 'Improvisation' in North Indian Music." *Musical Quarterly* 71, no. 2:157–171.

Miner, Allyn. 1993. *Sitar and Sarod in the 18th and 19th Centuries.* Wilhelmshaven: Florian Noetzel Verlag.

Nettl, Bruno. 1974. "Thoughts on Improvisation: A Comparative Approach." *The Musical Quarterly* 60:1–19.

Neuman, Daniel M. 1980. *The Life of Music in North India.* Detroit: Wayne State University Press.

Powers, Harold S. 1977. "The Structure of Musical Meaning: A View from Banaras (a Metamodal Model for Milton)." *Perspectives of New Music* 14, no. 2/15, no. 1: 308–334.

———. 1980. "India." (Sections I and II.) In *The New Grove Dictionary of Music and Musicians* edited by Stanley Sadie, vol. 9, 69–141. London: Macmillan.

Racy, Ali Jihad. 1991. "Creativity and Ambience: An Ecstatic Feedback Model from Arabic Music." *World of Music* 33, no. 3:7–27.

Roy Chaudhury, Vimalakant. 1975. *Bharatiya Sangeet Kosh* (Hindi translation). New Delhi: Bharatiya Jnanpith.

Shankar, Ravi. 1995. Interview by the author. Encinitas, Calif., 21 October.

Shringy, R. K., and Prem Lata Sharma, trans. 1989. *Sangitaratnikara of Sarngadeva,* vol. 2. New Delhi: Munshiram Manoharlal Publishers.

Slawek, Stephen M. 1987. *Sitar Technique in Nibaddh Forms.* Delhi: Motilal Banarsidass.

———. 1990. "*Kāku-bhed, Rāga-rasa,* Interpretive Moves, and Musical Intention: Parameters of Musical Meaning in North Indian Music." Paper read at the 37th Annual Conference of the Society for Ethnomusicology, 7–11 November, Oakland, Calif.

Tambiah, Stanley Jeyaraja. 1985. "A Performative Approach to Ritual." In *Culture, Thought, and Social Action: An Anthropological Perspective,* 123–66. Cambridge: Harvard University Press.

Titon, Jeff Todd. 1978. "Every Day I Have the Blues: Improvisation and Daily Life." *Southern Folklore Quarterly* 42:85–98.

Viswanathan, Tanjore. 1977. "The Analysis of Raga Alapana in South Indian Music." *Asian Music* 9:13–71.

Wade, Bonnie C. 1984. "Performance Practice in Indian Music," in *Performance Practice: Ethnomusicological Perspectives* edited by Gerard Béhague, 13–52, Westport, Conn. Greenwood Press.

Widdess, Richard. 1981. "Aspects of Form in North Indian Alap and Dhrupad." In *Music and Tradition: Essays on Asian and Other Musics Presented to Laurence Picken,* edited by D. R. Widdess and R. F. Wolpert, 143–81. Cambridge: Cambridge University Press.

CHAPTER FIFTEEN

Taqsim Nahawand Revisited: The Musicianship of Jihad Racy

BRUNO NETTL AND RONALD RIDDLE

This study is an attempt to gain insight into an aspect of the process of improvisation in Middle Eastern music by concentrating on the ways in which a single Arabic performer improvised in one *maqam,* using one form or genre, during one period of his life. In this respect, our study is somewhat similar to several mentioned in the introductory chapter of this work, particularly the studies carried out jointly with Bela Foltin, Carol M. Babiracki, and Dariush Shenassa by Nettl (1992), each of which shows the range of improvisatory techniques and of performance types used by Persian musicians when performing portions of three *dastgâhs* or modes. Among other studies are those of Katz (1968) which compares two generations of singers from a limited population group, performing one genre in an Arabic-Jewish musical tradition, Viswanathan (1977), which examines various performances of one Carnatic raga, and further studies of Persian music by Massoudieh (1968), Farhat (1990), and Gerson-Kiwi (1963).

The gathering of basic musical data was carried out in a style reminiscent of an experiment, as control of a mass of data was made possible by the elicitation of a large number of performances of a particular sort, from one performer, A. Jihad Racy, in a single context, during one short period of his life. Now a distinguished Arabic musician on the faculty of the University of California at Los Angeles and a noted scholar of ethnomusicology, Racy was born in a village in Lebanon and moved to Beirut at age eighteen. After undergraduate study (not in music) at American University of Beirut, Racy took up residence in the United States in 1968 to carry out graduate study in ethnomusicology. In Lebanon, he had studied traditional music with various musicians and independently and had become proficient on several instruments. He has continued his career as a performer of Arabic music in North America for over a quarter century and is highly regarded by the Middle Eastern community in North America and by musicians of Lebanon, Syria, and Egypt. Though Racy was unquestionably affected in his music by his experience throughout the world, the material upon which this study is based reflects a period in his life during which his musical contacts were principally Middle Eastern.

During 1971–72 it was possible to persuade Jihad Racy to perform and record 100 *taqsims* for the University of Illinois Archives of Ethnomusicology.

He was asked simply to perform and to record a *taqsim* of his choice every two or three days. It was hoped that while performing he could avoid feeling restricted by what he had recorded previously in the series. Before a recording session he was not to listen to the *taqsims* that he had already recorded. No audience was present, but during the months in which he made the recordings, he also gave many other performances in concerts and classes. We have here, then, a sample of material whose limits and limitations are clear, and which can be regarded as thoroughly representative of its universe, that is, the performance style of Jihad Racy, playing alone, in 1971–72. We cannot judge the degree to which these performances are representative of Racy's practice in concerts or informally with audiences, but we believe, on the basis of Racy's own evaluation and those of other Arabic musicians who have heard parts of this collection, that each *taqsim* would be at least acceptable as a proper Lebanese *taqsim* performance.

The degree to which Racy's performances are typical of Lebanese musicians in general, of musicians of his generation, of Arabic music at large, or, indeed, the degree to which they provide insight into the processes of Middle Eastern improvisation in general cannot be discussed here. Nor can the way in which his concept of *nahawand* fits into the Arabic conceptualization of that *maqam* be presently assessed. Further, we cannot attempt to show the relationship of Racy's performances of *nahawand* to that of other *maqams* in his repertory. All that we are attempting to do here is to make a case study of one musician's style of improvisation upon one model.

Among the hundred *taqsims* recorded by Racy, the sixteen that are cast in *nahawand* form the basis of this study. They were transcribed, analyzed, and compared, and a part of the analytical data, as well as conclusions drawn from it, is presented here. Fourteen of the *taqsims* of the basic corpus were performed on the *buzuq,* and two on the *nai.*

Taqsim

The *taqsim* is one of the major forms of the general tradition of Arabic music. According to Touma (1968, 18–19) it is an improvised representation of a *maqam* with an organization that is rigorous in the tonal parameters and free in the temporal ones, the latter including rhythm and length. A *taqsim* may be performed between or after metric, composed pieces; it may appear alone, and, most frequently, it is an introduction to a metric, usually vocal performance. The performances in these various musical contexts may differ, and the reader must bear in mind the fact that all of the *taqsims* performed for the present study were played alone, not in the context of other music. Moreover, there exists a metric genre of *taqsim, taqsim 'ala al-wahda,* but it is not considered at all in this study.

Touma (1968, 19) indicates that the organization of a *taqsim* is independent of the instrument upon which it is performed. While this is true, broadly speaking, there are obvious differences between the *buzuq* and *nai* performances of Racy, and hearing recordings by other musicians has persuaded us that the instrument used in a *taqsim* performance has, indeed, a considerable bearing upon the musical style. But perhaps these differences have a greater effect in the microcosm of individual performances than upon the overall organization.

We have attempted, through transcription and analysis, to find out the range of performances of *taqsim* in *maqam nahawand* as performed by one musician, indicating what all or most of the performances have in common and wherein they differ, and to identify the character of this particular concept of music in this musician's art. The analytical work proceeded in more or less conventional style, but concentrated upon the identification of structurally significant sections and their interrelationships, insofar as their motivic, tonal, and temporal aspects are concerned. It is obvious that there is literally an infinite number of things that can be said about any musical composition, no matter how simple, and we have no doubt omitted many considerations with which one might well also have dealt. In the first place, we do not deal with matters of cultural, social, and aesthetic context; but that omission should not be taken as a denigration of this kind of interest. We also do not study, in detail, matters of intonation. We have approached questions of rhythm only in a very general way. And we also did not address ourselves to the origins of specific melodic or motivic units, as, for example, the degree to which some of them were learned and memorized by Racy, others were variations of known motifs, and yet others were actually improvised by him. The extent to which the material is truly "improvised" is a question we do not attempt to assess. It may be of interest to point out that Racy himself, after seeing some of the analytical data, indicated surprise at the degree to which his performances followed certain patterns.

Touma (1968, 93–95) comments on the question of "composition versus improvisation." The dichotomy seems to him, and to us, in some respects spurious. Surely there is no improvisatory system that does not have some canon of rules and patterns, articulated or not, as its basis. On the other hand, Touma points out, and our study corroborates, the fact that in the performance practice of all but a few undistinguished performers, no two *taqsim* performances are identical.

The Instruments and the *Maqam*

It seems appropriate to comment briefly on the instruments used in the performances, especially taking account of comments made by Racy at various times while the recordings were being made. The *buzuq* is a Near Eastern type of lute especially common in Syria and Lebanon. Related to what medieval Islamic treatises on music have referred to as *tanbúr,* the modern *buzuq* bears close resemblance to the *saz* of Asia Minor and the *dotâr* of Central Asia. Typically plucked with a soft piece of animal horn, it has a wood sound box shaped somewhat like that of a mandolin. Its thin neck, which is about two feet long, has some twenty-seven nylon string frets tightly wrapped around it. Like the *'ūd,* the *buzuq* has a working range of about two octaves, but unlike this short-neck lute, the *buzuq* has steel strings, arranged typically in two or three courses. If two courses are used, one of them, comprising two strings, is tuned in unison to a pitch in the vicinity of middle C. The other course, comprised of two or three strings, is normally tuned either in unison or in octaves to a pitch a fourth below that of the other course. Both courses of strings are employed for performing melodies, but occasionally the higher course may be used as a drone. Some *buzuqs,* including the one used by Jihad Racy, have a third course of strings. The tuning is normally G-g, C-c, c-c. Yet, depending on the *maqam* to be used and the positions of the notes to be emphasized, the tuning may be varied, and the absolute pitch is not relevant.

The *nai* is an end-blown cane flute most common in North Africa and the Middle East. As it has no mouthpiece, it is considered difficult to play. It has a range of about two octaves and is furnished with six front holes and one thumb hole. The technique of playing the *nai* does not rely primarily on half-stopping or forked fingering since the holes on it are arranged, roughly speaking, in a chromatic order according to which, for example, going up a whole step would in most cases require the opening of two holes instead of one. The fundamental register on the *nai* produces very soft tones and is usually avoided in performance, and the production of the music relies substantially on over-blowing. Since certain notes are difficult to produce on the *nai,* a performer usually uses a set of at least five instruments of different lengths, which also enables him to play conveniently at different pitch levels.

The *maqam* of *nahawand* can be defined at various levels of musical conceptualization. Most accurately, but also with greatest difficulty, it would have to be defined in terms of all of the performances, improvisations, and compositions which are regarded as being cast within it. All of the musical events—from scale, ornamentation, and acceptable accidentals, to typical modulation patterns, norms of section lengths, relationships of all sorts among the sections, etc.—that are considered appropriate by those who contribute to the consensus about Arabic music must in the end be considered as contributing to that definition. At the opposite end of the continuum of definitions, in the simplest terms, *nahawand* is a weighted scale from which tones are selected for performance and composition. In these terms, the scale used by Racy, considering G as the tonic, is G A B♭ C D E♭ F G, with the lower tetrachord, G A B♭ C, the most characteristic configuration. Below the tonic, the F is usually altered to F♯, which functions as a leading tone to the tonic.

But the first, vastly more complex sort of definition, as it relates to the performance of one individual, is really in a sense the task of this entire paper. It should be noted, however, that other points along this definitional continuum have been struck, as noted already in an early study of *taqsim*s by Berner (1937, 68–69), who asserted that certain characteristic formulae of melody and rhythm typify this *maqam*. Similarly, Touma indicates the significance of central tones and their role in delineating sections of a *maqam* (Touma 1971, 43; Gerson-Kiwi 1970, 43). As a sample of the large body of continuing studies of the role of *maqam* as a basis for music making see essays by Elsner and Powers in Elsner 1989.

A number of other *maqam*s function as modulatory nodes. Their characteristic tetrachords or pentachords, or, where necessary, entire octave scales, according to Racy's tradition, are indicated in example 15.1. Their role in the performances is discussed below. Example 15.1 uses G as the tonic of each *maqam*, but in fact all *maqam*s appear at various pitch levels, both absolutely and in relationship to the tonic of the main *maqam*. Intonational details are not considered, and the intervals that are close to three-quarter tones are indicated by minus signs above the notes.

Length of the Performances and Their Sections
One of the most important ways of establishing what is characteristic of the performances as a group and how they vary from the norm is the study of the lengths of the performances and of their sections, and the interrelationships of the sections by length. Much of our data can best be presented in tabular form.

Table 15.1 indicates the length of each *taqsim*, the number of sections, and the length of each section. As may be seen, the lengths of the entire performances vary from about two minutes to slightly over eight minutes, with the majority (twelve) taking from just under five to just over seven minutes. The two performances on the *nai* are slightly shorter, on the average, than those on the *buzuq*.

The performances of *taqsim*s everywhere in the Middle East are always divided into easily perceived sections of varying length. In our terminology a "section" indicates material that is followed by a rest of one to five seconds, and that normally ends with a distinct closing formula. The sections themselves differ enormously in length, ranging from short bits of five, eight, or ten seconds to three, four, and in one exceptional case, over six minutes. The number of sections in the *taqsim*s also varies, but distinct patterning can be discerned. The smallest number is five, the largest twelve, and the majority (eleven of sixteen) are comprised of seven to eleven sections. There is some correlation between the length of a *taqsim* and its number of sections, but it is not precise and is obviously violated by several examples—for example, no. 43, a long performance with only seven sections, or no. 69, a relatively short one with ten—and by the relationship between nos. 1 and 91, a very short and a very long *taqsim*, each with five sections. It seems that Racy's tradition determines an approximate length of the *taqsim* and a range of section lengths and numbers, but that these two factors are not closely interrelated.

The lengths of the sections within a *taqsim* produce definite patterning. We may divide the sections somewhat arbitrarily into four groups, according to

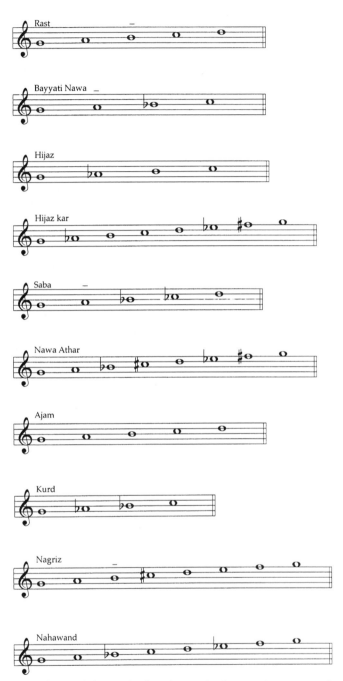

Example 15.1. Characteristic tetrachords and pentachords, or entire octave scales, in the secondary *maqam*s.

Table 15.1. Sixteen performances of *Taqsim Nahawand*

No. of Performance	Total Length (Min. and Sec.)	No. of Sections	Lengths of Sections
1	1:58	5	:20–:13–:28–:9–:50
8	6:15	10	:14–:22–:1:26–:9–:8–:13–:17–2:04–:15–1:19
13	5:40	7	:17–1:35–:15–:37–:6–:19–2:34
22 (Nai)	3:37	11	:8–:16–:5–:30–:20–:8–:47–:14–:8–:20–:37
25	5:33	11	:17–:18–:11–:19–:31–:7–:40–:20–:42–:59–1:21
32	6:43	6	:22–:18–:25–:6–1:1–3:32
39 (Nai)	5:03	10	:16–:51–:16–:42–28–:11–:12–:4–:28–1:35
43	7:10	7	:10–:20–:47–:13–:55–:6–4:37
44	6:07	12	:13–:19–:11–:4–:31–:24–:3–:44–2:28–:4–:3–1:25
51	8:20	7	:24–:46–:10–:5–2:48–:8–3:58
55	6:31	11	:27–:6–:32–:15–:40–:8–:11–:28–1:01–:8–2:39
56	6:12	11	:20–:18–:27–:10–:42–1:11–:6–:11–:35–:40–1:22
68	4:48	6	:10–:21–:8–:47–1:05–1:56
69	5:43	10	:28–:8–:40–:10–:40–:28–:37–:6–:57–1:31
85	7:10	8	:20–:6–:12–:17–:49–:12–2:20–2:58
91	8:10	5	:19–:11–:19–:51–6:25

Note: Numbers of the performances are those of Collection No. 92, University of Illinois Archives of Ethnomusicology.

length: minuscule (less than twenty seconds), short (twenty to thirty seconds), medium (thirty to sixty seconds) and long (a minute or more). This kind of classification reveals an interesting fact, namely, that the majority of sections in each group actually falls fairly near the center of the range of length, indicating that this grouping is not simply arbitrary but seems indeed to reflect musical functions. Using this classification, we find that of the total of 137 sections in the sixteen performances, seventy-four are minuscule, fifteen are short, twenty-six, medium, and twenty-two, long. The *taqsim*s themselves then can be classified as follows in accordance with sectional arrangement:

Type A   A number of minuscule or short sections followed by a long one: five performances, typically rather short ones (nos. 1, 32, 68, 85, and 91).

Type B   More or less regular alternation of short or minuscule sections, or of groups of such sections, with a medium or long one: four performances (nos. 13, 43, 51, and 69).

Type C   A series of short or minuscule sections followed by a medium or long section (or sometimes by two of these), after which a series of short sections appears, again followed by a long or medium one. This is the most common type and appears in seven performances. In nos. 22, 44, 56, and 25, the first medium or long section appears in the second half of the performance. In nos. 8, 39, and 55, it appears near the beginning.

These three types of *taqsim*s can be considered as representing three kinds of dramatic development. Type B is essentially without climax, while types A and C work, through the superimposition of short sections, towards climaxes that appear in the longer sections, which are distinguished not merely by their length but by greater range of melodic movement and the appearances of modulations to other *maqam*s. Type C provides an intermediate and a full climax, while type A has only the latter; and it is interesting to find that type A, thus, is usually but not predictably represented in shorter performances.

Finally, regarding the relationships of section lengths, it is worth noting that two long sections appear together, without intervening short sections, in only three of the performances. In each case, these pairs of long sections appear at the end. Two medium-length sections appear together only twice, each time before a final long section; and two short sections appear together only once. The basic structure is thus an alternation of one or more minuscule sections with a long, medium, or short one.

Minuscule phrases, on the other hand, appear in groups of two, three, or four on twenty occasions, and if one combines the minuscule and short phrases (i.e., everything under thirty seconds), one finds mainly groups of two and four, but also all numbers up to seven. Minuscule phrases appear alone in only twelve instances.

All of the sixteen *taqsim*s end with long (twelve) or medium (four) sections. Eighteen of the twenty-two long sections appear in the second halves of their performances, and this is also true of fifteen out of the twenty-six medium sections. This discussion of section length gives a picture of considerable variation within a rather well-defined system of patterns.

Arrangement of Sections by Pitch and Ambitus

According to the literature on Arabic music (e.g., Touma 1971, 41), the essence of musical forms associated with the *maqam* concept is their gradual ascent from low to high registers. To be sure, this type of arrangement, centering about focal points in the scale, is evident in the improvised and even the composed forms of South and West Asian music generally. A typical arrangement of a Carnatic *alapana* is to rise from material surrounding the tonic in the low register, stressing and embellishing increasingly higher tones until a climax is reached, perhaps an octave, tenth, or twelfth above the tonic, after which a quick descent closes the form. Likewise, the typical order of *gushu*s in Persian classical music is ascending (Farhat 1990; Nettl 1992). An examination of Racy's performances of *nahawand* illustrates the same principle. Patterning is easily identified, but a great deal of variation is again found.

The relationship of the sections in terms of tessitura is conveniently if mechanically expressed through identification of the highest note in each phrase. A more accurate view, on the other hand, is provided by a comparison of those tones in each section which appear to have greatest structural importance, or which, because of their frequency and the dependence of other tones upon them, could be regarded as temporary tonic notes dominating the individual sections. But this sort of comparison is also more subjective, and depends on a number of factors. Determination of this "tone of greatest structural importance" is a process which at least in certain cases may not be carried out identically by any two analysts. Furthermore, in some instances, a section is dominated in turn first by *nahawand* and then by another *maqam* to which the performer has temporarily modulated, or even by more than one such temporary diversion. Nevertheless, some insight may be gained by this examination.

Example 15.2 then, gives the sequence of highest tones and the sequence of tones of greatest structural importance for the sixteen performances of *nahawand*. Modulation is not taken into consideration, but the entire performance is treated as a unit. It will be noted immediately that the melodic movement is generally ascending, but that a zigzag arrangement is found, particularly in the order of highest notes. The endings of the performances tend to descend somewhat, as indicated by the comparison of tonic notes. It may also be noted that early and intermediate sections often show a coincidence of highest and tonic notes, while this is not true of the final sections; this fact may be tied to the typically greater length of the final sections.

A large number of different tones appears in the sequences of highest notes, while the notes of structural importance are more limited and are, in the majority, confined to the tonic (or its octave), the fifth, and the third. It will also be noted that in this respect the performances on the *nai* are different from those on the *buzuq,* for the former exhibit to a much smaller extent the ascending contour; the highest tones exhibit an undulating configuration and the tonic tones appear in a more or less arc-shaped order.

Despite the generally present tendency for the sequence of tonics to ascend, and the considerable degree of variation within this concept, it seems possible to divide the performances into types, the lines between which, to be sure, are indeed thin. Nos. 8, 22, and 39 exhibit an essentially arc-shaped contour, while nos. 1, 25, 32, and 85 exhibit ascent with zigzag motion. All of the rest have structurally important tones in ascending order (not counting repetitions of one note from one section to the next, and not counting the final section). The only exceptions are nos. 44 and 56, which are ascending, excluding the final and penultimate sections. An interesting point to be made is the approximate correlation between these types and those involving the relationship of section lengths, described above. The arc-shaped order is associated with type C, above, while all of the performances in type B have straight ascent. Type A is associated with the zigzag ascent group. Thus, while the two classifications do not really coincide, there is sufficient correlation to allow us to speculate on the existence of a typology of *taqsim* performances in Racy's playing.

Taqsim

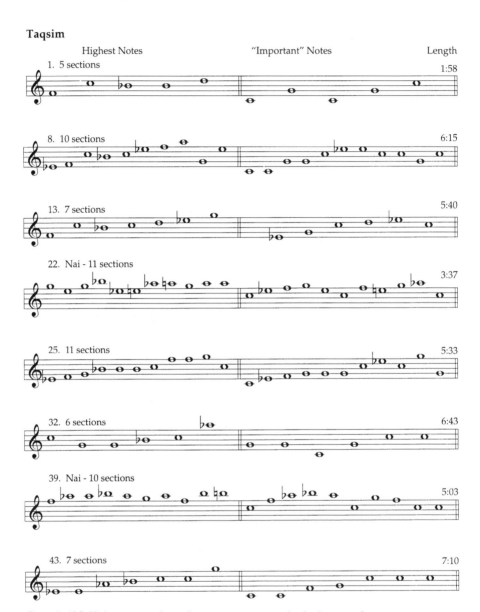

Example 15.2. Highest notes and most important notes per section in sixteen performances.

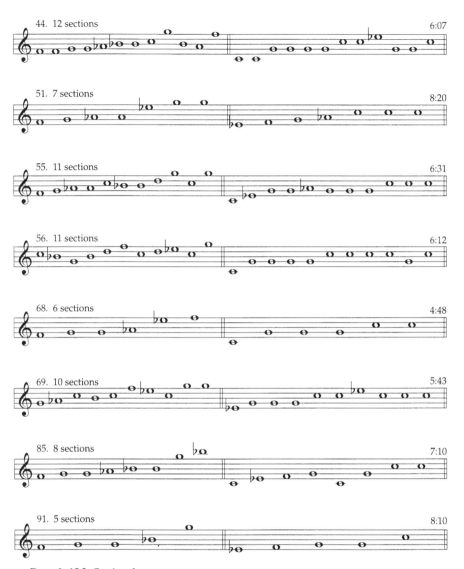

Example 15.2. *Continued*

Table 15.2 illustrates the way in which the higher tones are gradually introduced, from section to section, and the way in which the range of melodic material is expanded in two *taqsims* (nos. 55 and 68) which share the ascending form of section arrangement. This table shows that the introduction of new, higher tones is indeed consistent from section to section. Typically, a tone which is introduced in one section occurs in smaller numbers but is likely to

Table 15.2. Number of notes at each pitch level, per section in performances 55 and 68.

Section	C	C#	D	E♭	E	F	F#	G	A♭	A♭	A	B♭	B♭	B	Octave Higher C	C#	D	E♭	E	F	F#	G
Performance 55:																						
1	46		33	41		13																
2	2		2	3		4		1														
3	24		20	36		38		38	13													
4	7		6	10		11	1	20	4													
5	30		31	41		25		27	18			2			2							
6	5		2	1		1		5	2			1										
7	2					4		24	16						2							
8	18		16	26	1	25	9	19	8		5	13			12		3					
9	90		49	53		19		19		13	6	14		25	87		46	49		15	1	1
10	9							2	2			3			9							
11	90	9	71	201	1	81	2	182	45	40	9	75	22	15	46	2	18	21		11	1	6
Performance 68:																						
1	36		11	14		3																
2	22		21	31		24		6														
3	3		2	3		6		6														
4	28		21	31	1	41	1	43	20			2										
5	71		52	65		49	6	51	37		4	28			27		6	6				
6	142		71	58		72	6	92	8	17	28	19	22	19	82		23	17				

be found with greater frequency in the next section, which may, in turn, introduce one or two yet higher tones.

Modulation

One of the most important improvisatory techniques of *taqsim* performance involves the modulation to secondary *maqams,* sometimes known as *taqhir.* Racy's performances make ample use of this well-known phenomenon. It is our task to identify the *maqams* to which he modulates in *nahawand* performances, their order, and the distribution of their appearance. Racy stated that two basic types of modulation are used, that in which the secondary *maqam* is built on the same tonic as the main *maqam,* and that in which it is built on another tonic, most frequently the fourth or fifth above the tonic of the main *maqam.*

Example 15.1, which gives the main tetrachord or pentachord of each *maqam* to which Racy modulates, indicates a total of nine such *maqams.* Table 15.3 gives the order of the modulations (using abbreviations for the names of the *maqams* and the sections wherein modulation appears).

Only performance no. 1 lacks modulation, and in the others, from one to five secondary *maqams* appear. There is little correlation between length of performance and number of modulations. A quick look at tables 15.1 and 15.3 indicates that, as one might expect, modulations almost always appear in the longer sections.

Table 15.3 indicates, however, a distinct patterning of modulation usage. The two most commonly used *maqams* are *bayyati nawa* (which is used twelve times) and *rast* (ten times). Three others appear with some frequency: *hijaz* (six), *saba* (five), and *'ajam* (four). *Nawa athar, kurd, nagriz,* and *hijaz kar* appear only once each. It is interesting to find that in the collection performed by Racy, consisting, as stated above, of one hundred *taqsims* in nine different main *maqams,* only a few *maqams* appear that are not used in the *nahawand* performances: *bayyati* and *siga.*

The first modulation is to *rast* in eight of the *taqasim nahawand,* to *bayyati nawa* in six, and to *hijaz* in one. Those *maqams* which appear only once come at the end of a sequence of modulatory *maqams.* The order and frequency is similar, indeed, to practices found in the distribution of *gushehs* in Persian music, as indicated by the mentioned study of performances of the *dastgâh* of *chahârgâh* (Nettl and Foltin, in Nettl 1992, 41–75). In that repertory, the first *gusheh* after the main one, *darâmad,* is almost always *zâbol,* which also appears with greatest frequency, while those *gushehs* which appear rarely also are the ones that appear near the end of a performance. The conclusion regarding the improvisatory decision-making process seems obvious: a performer has in mind a typical sequence (but departs from it occasionally). At any point, however, he may decide to call a halt to the process, return to the main *maqam* (or *gusheh* in Persian music), and close the performance.

Table 15.3. Order of modulations and sections wherein they appear in *nahawand*

	Modulations in Order	In Sections	Length	No. of Sections
1	None		1:58	5
8	R H S B	8, 9, 10	6:15	10
13	B H	6, 7	5:40	7
22	R	8, 9, 10	3:37	11
25	R B NA	10, 11	5:33	11
32	B S A K	6	6:43	6
39	R A	6, 7, 8, 9, 10	5:03	10
43	B H A S Ng	6	7:10	7
44	H R B	9, 10, 11, 12	6:07	12
51	B	7	8:20	7
55	B S A	9, 10, 11	6:31	11
56	R H	9, 10, 11	6:12	11
68	R B	6	4:48	6
69	R B	8, 9, 10	5:43	10
85	R B S H R	7, 8	7:10	8
91	B R Hk	5	8:10	5

Note: A, *'ajam;* B, *bayati nawa;* H, *hijaz;* Hk, *hijaz kar;* K, *kurd;* NA, *nawa athar;* Ng, *nagriz;* R, *rast;* S, *saba.*

There is some association between the length of a section and the presence of modulations within it. That there is not much association between the total number of secondary *maqams* in a *taqsim* and its overall length may thus seem curious but is indeed a fact, as indicated in table 15.4. Those *taqsims* with four or five modulations are only insignificantly longer, with an average length of about six and a half minutes, than those with only one or two modulations, which average five minutes and thirty-five seconds.

All modulations appeared in the second halves of the performances, indicating the degree to which the main *maqam* must be established before secondary *maqams* may appear. It is difficult to establish a typology of performances on the basis of modulation patterning. Perhaps a few *taqsims* may be singled out for arrangements that depart most from the average: a group of performances in which one or two secondary *maqams* dominate three or four sections (nos. 22, 39, 56, and 69); and a group in which a single long, final section experiences modulation to three, four, or five secondary *maqams* (nos. 32, 43, and 91). While a sample of sufficient size for statistical conclusions is hardly extant here, it is worth mentioning that there is at least a modicum of correlation with the types according to phrase length arrangement given above. The first of the patterns given in this paragraph (nos. 22, 39, 56, and 69) agrees, with one exception, with type C of the length classification, and the second pattern (nos. 32, 43, and 91), with types A and B. The fact that the majority of performances do not fall into a similar typological arrangement but, rather, occupy intermediate positions along a continuum from the one extreme type to the other indi-

Table 15.4. Number of secondary *maqam*s related to length of *taqsim*s

No. of *Maqam*s	No. of *Taqsim*s	Range of Lengths	Approx. Average Length
0	1	1:58	2:00
1	2	3:37–8:20	6:00
2	5	4:48–6:12	5:25
3	3	6:07–8:10	7:00
4	3	5:33–6:43	6:10
5	2	7:10	7:10

Table 15.5. *Nahawand* as a secondary *maqam*

Main *Maqam*	No. of *Taqsim*s	No. Containing *Nahawand*
'Ajam	13	3 (22%)
Bayyati	15	2 (13%)
Bayyati nawa	8	3 (37%)
Hijaz	6	1 (17%)
Hijaz kar	12	5 (42%)
Kurd	6	3 (50%)
Nawa athar	1	1 (100%)
Rast	16	5 (31%)

cates that perhaps true types of performances are not to be found here. Moreover, there is only the barest correlation among the three typologies attempted in this paper—according to phrase length arrangement, distribution of modulations, and overall melodic contour—suggesting that Racy's performances of *taqsim nahawand* strike, in their configuration of parameters, at various perhaps equally spaced points of a continuum rather than representing types that can be easily distinguished. The only exception to this statement is the obviously considerable departure from the rest of the two *taqsims* performed on the *nai*.

Finally, regarding modulation, it may be of interest to examine the incidence of *maqam nahawand* as a secondary *maqam* among the eighty-four performances in Racy's corpus cast in a main *maqam* other than *nahawand*. Table 15.5 indicates the performances and the degree to which *nahawand* is present. As may readily be seen, the association of *nahawand* with *rast* and *bayyati nawa,* well established in the discussion of modulation from *nahawand* above, is established also in the counterpart. At the same time, it is interesting to see that *nahawand* also plays an important role in performances of *kurd, 'ajam, nawa athar,* and *hijaz kar,* while on the other hand, *kurd, nawa athar,* and *hijaz kar* do not play an important part in the *nahawand* performances of *saba* and *siga,* but these are the main *maqam*s in only seven performances of the corpus.

Melodic Devices

A study of improvisation techniques was undertaken from the point of view of melodic interrelationships among units shorter than the sections, which have been our main units of consideration thus far. The rather statistical approach followed in a consideration of the interrelationships of sections could not, however, be conveniently applied, and we are forced to rely on more generalizing commentary.

Melodic movement is an area in which the group of performances is relatively unified, and in which all of the sections of a *taqsim* are also essentially alike. The movement is almost always stepwise; intervals larger than the second are relatively rare except for the beginnings of sections. Such intervals are most commonly upward skips of perfect fourths or fifths, and they generally appear at the very beginnings of phrases and are emphasized by involving relatively long note values or notes repeated a number of times. Within this essentially scalewise melodic movement it is difficult to single out motifs that are recognizable and have significance different from their musical environment. Exceptions are the beginnings and endings of sections. But it is also possible to characterize the melodic movement somewhat more specifically.

The favorite short melodic figure seems to be one which moves from one note to an upper or lower neighbor and back, sometimes with ornamentation. There are rarely more than three notes moving in either direction, and when this does occur, more ornamentation than normal is usually present, each note being elaborately ornamented, resulting in a sequence composed of three or four tiny bits (as, for example, in no. 22, at the end of section 4 or the middle of section 6).

Repeated note figures are also pervasive and usually occur in two forms: repeated notes of longer than average value (written here as eighth or quarter notes), which usually appear on the tonic or the fifth degree of the *maqam;* and groups of three or four short repeated notes followed by two scalewise descending notes.

In general, the melodic material consists of short, scalewise or repeated-note figures oriented so as to emphasize the pitch that is stressed in their section. Melodies comprising motifs of extended length, that is, more than four or five notes, are not used. Stereotyped motifs are used to begin and end sections, but the improvisatory technique in general can be characterized less as melodic improvisation than as elaborate ornamentation upon or variation of very brief motivic-rhythmic units. An exception are two *taqsims* which begin with a precomposed melody, *dúlâb,* in a version that is characteristic of *maqam nahawand,* and that is used to begin nos. 32 and 56. *Dúlâb* (according to d'Erlanger 1959, 180–81) is a popular tune type in duple meter that is used to begin *taqsims,* but that may also be used in other musical contexts.

To the extent that one can identify significant "themes," they are concentrated at the beginnings and endings of sections. The special nature of cadential formulae has been noted as a characteristic of many musical styles. In the *ta-qasim nahawand* of Racy, most sections end with three notes in descending order. Interestingly, the *taqsims* performed on the *nai* differ from the rest, their sections ending more frequently with an ascending second.

Many sections tend to begin with one or two motifs, one consisting of an ascending fourth followed by repetitions of the higher note, and the other comprising three notes in descending order, like the closing formula just described. These two motifs account for the beginnings of about 40 percent of the sections. Some insight into the improvisation process can be gained from the observation that two consecutive sections, one short and the second long, will frequently begin with the same opening formula. The first of the pair of sections is in a sense preparatory to the second; or the musician can be thought of as beginning a train of musical thought, finding it unproductive, and beginning the section again, with the same formula followed by what is finally more satisfactory material. Whether this process is actually operative could not be ascertained. It is possible that at one time it was indeed functional, but that it later became a standard procedure of performance without actually performing this original function.

Melodic Sequence

One of the most obvious devices of melodic development is the sequence. While sequences, in the most specific form of this concept, actually occupy a small amount of the time in these performances, they provide nodes of structural organization. Moreover, the same principle which generates melodic sequence can be identified at larger, less specific levels of musical thought.

A number of different kinds of sequences can be identified in Racy's improvisations, and these are illustrated in example 15.3. It is possible to group them approximately by length, direction, degree of precision, interval, and by complexity. Most of the sequences are threefold, that is, a short figure is repeated twice at different pitch levels. But twofold sequences are found, and fourfold ones as well. The number of transpositions correlates somewhat with complexity and length, that is, longer sequences are found more frequently in twofold form than are shorter ones, and, indeed, the occasional fourfold ones are nothing more than ornamented scales. The vast majority of sequences descend, the ascending ones being groups of two notes which are also simply elaborations of scales. The vast majority of sequences employ the interval of the second for transposition; a very few examples use the third.

It is possible roughly to identify short, medium, and long sequences, the short type being by far the most common. Sequences in which the transposed portions are not precise repetitions of the original portion are here referred to as anomalous sequences. Portions of melody which exhibit elements of sequential treatment, that is, in which the same material, generally speaking, is treated at successively different pitch levels, may be referred to as sequential

a. Short sequence

b. Short sequence with characteristic ending figure

c. Sequence of medium length

d. Long anomalous sequence

e. Ascending sequence

f. Short anomalous sequence

Example 15.3. *a,* Short sequence; *b,* short sequence with characteristic ending figure; *c,* sequence of medium length; *d,* long anomalous sequence; *e,* ascending sequence; *f,* short anomalous sequence; *g,* truncated anomalous sequence; *h,* ornamented scalar sequence; *i,* sequential melodic line; *j,* sequence within sequence; *k,* sequence at the third.

melodic line. If all of these types of sequential materials are considered, we find that they occupy a rather large proportion of a *taqsim.* In performance no. 55, performed on the *buzuq,* lasting six and a half minutes, it is possible to identify forty-seven sequences of various sorts, twenty-one of them true or anomalous sequences, and twenty-six being sequential melodic lines. Sequential materials appear with greatest density in the last section, the longest, and they are quite rare in the short or "minuscule" sections, indicating that they have an important role in the more dramatic development typical of long sections and of the second halves of the performances, and also in the modulatory procedures typical of the long sections. In no. 68, lasting less than five minutes, there are twenty-seven sequences of various sorts, including seventeen of sequential melodic line.

Obviously, then, sequences and variants of the sequence concept are of great importance in Racy's improvisations. A rather large number of types of sequential treatments of motifs can be identified (as in ex. 15.3), and their presence

g. Truncated anomalous sequence

h. Ornamented scalar sequence

i. Sequential melodic line

j. Sequence within sequence

k. Sequence at the third

Example 15.3. *Continued*

in both the *buzuq* and the *nai* performances, as well as their density in the performances, also testifies to their significance. It is interesting, however, to find that sequences are not necessarily found with great frequency in all Arabic improvisations. For example, a number of *taqsim*s performed on the *'oud* in the 1930s examined by Nettl[1] indicate a large number of types of melodic movement, and sequences are, among these, much less common, though by no means absent. These recordings came from a Palestinian musician whose regional background, at least, is not very different from that of Racy, thus conceivably ruling out regional differences as the cause of the stylistic differences; generational, instrumental, and idiosyncratic styles might be relevant factors.

Some speculation about the role of sequences may be appropriate here, for they appear with great frequency not only in Arabic music but in all Middle Eastern music and, of course, elsewhere as well. We have been speaking of them in Racy's repertory as if they were to be viewed as treatments of motifs, with the shortest ones most often consisting of the more precise transposition, and with the longer ones subject to less exact reproductions at successive pitch levels. In other words, we have presented them as an important—perhaps the most important and certainly the most easily identified—method of motivic development. But it may be possible to consider them also as a function of another process in Arabic (and other Middle Eastern) music, that is, of its tendency to explore and develop successive pitch levels, each centering about one main pitch. Our analysis of relationship among the sections of the *taqasim nahawand* shows that each section has a main tone, or a tone of greatest structural importance, and that the relationship among the sections is in a sense defined by the relationship among these tones. It is possible to consider the sequences and the sequential melodic lines as functions of the same principle. We could state, therefore, that a basic structural principle of Racy's performances is the analogous exposition of successive, different pitch areas, and that this is done at different levels of musical thought—from the *taqsim*'s sections to the longer and not literally transposed sequential melodic lines, down to long but anomalous sequences, and further to short, literal sequences and ornamented scalar passages. This interpretation of the basic structural principles of the *taqsim*s can also be used to account for the relative lack, and lack of need for, specific and distinct motifs and melodies that function as thematic germs from which further material is developed, or which clearly alternate with nonthematic, episodic material.

Other Melodic Devices
Several other devices for melodic development and continuity, less prominent than sequences, may be mentioned. One is the use of scalar passages, sometimes ornamented and therefore related to sequences, but in other cases without ornamentation. Also interesting is the variation of short motifs. Again, this can be related to the sequential treatment, since the presentation of a motif in sequence may be considered a form of variation. While we have said that it is difficult, given the nonmetric rhythmic structure and the almost completely scalar melodic movement, to identify themes or motifs which could then be shown to be the subject of variation, occasionally there are identifiable bits of sufficient integrity and length to function in this role. The variation of a motif usually is accomplished by going over the same ground, as it were, with some reordering of tones. The kind of variation of a tune that involves duplication of tones, change in tempo, and thorough, systematic departure from the norm, such as is found, for example, in Javanese gamelan music, is not involved here.

One respect in which Racy's *nai* and *buzuq* performances differ is, of course, in the wider range available on the *buzuq*, and the special use of the lower strings for unusual effects. The techniques for which the lower strings are used must be considered among the improvisatory devices used by Racy.

The lower strings most frequently have a drone function, although it is an interrupted and, indeed, interrupting drone which consists of series of repeated notes interpolated in the melody performed on the higher strings. Occasionally, the two groups of strings change roles, the lower strings being used for melodic material and the higher ones for the drone. The drone appears most frequently on the tonic or the fifth of the scale of the main *maqam,* in about equal proportion. Other tones also appear. However, the lower string drones are much less common in the portions dominated by secondary *maqams* than in those that are distinctly in *nahawand.* When the drone tone is something other than the tonic or the fifth, it is usually an octave reinforcement of a prominent melodic tone of the moment.

The lower strings are also used for other purposes. They echo, anticipate, or complement rhythmic patterns of the higher strings. (See the very beginning of no. 68 for an example of some of these techniques.) They are sometimes even used to play the melody, accompanied by repeated tones in the upper strings, in which case the melodic material is quite contrastive to that which is typical of the style, often using large intervals—fourths and fifths. And occasionally, the lower strings play melodic material unaccompanied by the higher strings, in which case the usual style of Racy's melody, described above, is characteristic. The contrast between low and high strings is an important component of Racy's improvisatory style and is found more or less equally in all of the *taqsims* in *nahawand.* It thus interacts with other improvisational devices, with modulation which is more typical of later stages in a *taqsim,* and with sequence, which is also not typical of the beginnings of sections.

Ornamentation, Rhythm and Tempo

We now come to some areas of performance that are very difficult to discuss analytically and objectively. To the Western listener, Arabic music sounds extremely ornamented, but, of course, what constitutes an ornament in one culture may be part and parcel of the melodic material in another. An obvious approach would be to ask an Arabic performer to identify "ornamental tones" in juxtaposition to others, but this approach turned out to be unproductive in this study, despite the important role of ornamentation as an aspect of musical modernization and, in effect, inverse Westernization that Katz (1968) has made clear.

The presence or absence of ornamentation as a concept notwithstanding, it is possible to identify something functional in the music that may best be labeled ornamentation. Let us define ornamentation as the embellishment and the resulting emphasis of a tone. We note that longer tones (eighth and quarter notes) frequently have shorter neighbors or two-tone figures attached to them. At the other extreme, we have stated that the function of an entire section may be the establishment of a structurally important tone, or of the juxtaposition of alternating tonic levels, and that we could thus regard all of the other tone material of the section as basically ornamental to that main tone. Thus, again, as in the case of melodic sequence, a basic principle of performance can be seen to operate at the microcosmic as well as the macrocosmic levels of a performance.

Racy's *taqsims* cannot be readily divided into groups according to the provenance or position of ornamentation, for in this respect his performance practice is the same in all. It is possible to see that the microcosmic ornamentation increases in the course of a performance, showing a functional relationship to the use of the drone and to repeated note patterns that are unornamented and that are characteristic of the early sections and of the beginnings of later sections.

The rhythm of Racy's *taqsim*s has not been subjected to intensive study. The absence of meter (with the exception of the initial use of the *dúlâb* melody in two *taqsim*s) is part of the definition of this type of improvisation. But the absence is not complete. The grouping of tones and the use of the drone strings provide quasi-metrical organization at times, and it is further possible to identify portions of greater and lesser "metricity" within one section. A typical section is likely to alternate very rapidly between material in which there are elements of meter and those in which it is absent. Very characteristic is the kind of movement in which slow, fairly metrical material changes to quicker metrical and then quicker nonmetrical and, finally, slower nonmetrical improvisation, all within a few seconds.

It is possible to see change in degree of metrical organization from the beginning to the end of a *taqsim*. The early sections tend to be more metrical, and there is movement, within a section and in the over-all performance, towards more nonmetrical material. Both nonmetrical and relatively metrical material may be found at all stages of a performance. Relatively metrical material is associated with the use of drone strings and repeated note patterns. Thus, again, a procedure found in the microcosm of a section is also used in the overall structure.

Another aspect of rhythm worthy of mention is the arrangement of notes of equal length into groups. Groupings of from two to six notes of the same length are found to dominate rhythmic structure. Their frequency and their length decreases as the performance proceeds, something that may be a function of the gradual decreasing force of meter in the course of a *taqsim*. Many other aspects of rhythm could, of course, be examined. We are able to mention only one more: the use of stress, which is associated with volume. Alternating greater and lesser stress is a function of alternating directions of the plectrum. Beyond this, however, it is worth noting that long and repeated notes are stressed and that because of this, greater volume is found near the beginning of performances than near the end. Otherwise, while they are important components of performance, stress and volume do not seem to contribute greatly to the structure of Racy's *taqsim* performances.

Finally we should point out that the tempo of the *taqsims* remains generally constant from beginning to end of a given piece. However, fluctuation of tempo is characteristic, taking the form, for example, of prolongation of individual tones, slight accelerations and decelerations of tempo within phrases or larger sections, and pauses of varying duration. The tempo accelerates slightly when tones of relatively long duration are repeated several times. There is a tendency to slow the tempo slightly at cadential points of sections. Generally the concluding section—normally the longest section of the *taqsim*—is that in which the most tempo fluctuation occurs.

In their rhythmic character, the pieces for *nai* are most distinct. They reflect rhythmic characteristics that are inherent in flute performance, such as the capability of sustained tones and the necessity for breath pauses. The *nai* pieces tend thus to be less metrical in character than the performances on the *buzuq*. The use of fast, rhythmically pronounced repeated-note figures, so pervasive in the *buzuq* playing, is of course not found in the *nai* improvisations.

Conclusions

The results of this investigation, carried out 25 years ago but still tentative and not followed by parallel or explicitly contrastive studies, tend to confirm, with the use of a limited corpus, the generalizations in earlier publications regarding Middle Eastern improvisation. The thrust of our study has been to see whether it is possible to provide a picture of the range of performance and improvisatory practices in the experience of one musician improvising on the basis of one model, or performing what to him is basically the same material.

We find that the performances are relatively unified in terms of the use of melodic devices, ornamentation, and rhythm. In these respects, the musician does more or less the same thing in each *taqsim*, although he does not follow the same procedures in each section of a given *taqsim*. It is in matters of length, arrangement of sections, and modulation practice that he provides variety. Thus it is these aspects of the music which might be more properly labeled as improvised, while those revolving about melodic devices and rhythm, which are constant throughout our sample, might best be labeled as performance practice. Most significant perhaps is the identification of principles that are characteristic in the macrocosm and the microcosm of performances, and at points between these extremes. In certain parameters or elements of music, the performer carries out the same kind of musical thinking in bits of melody hardly more than a few seconds in length, in longer segments of melody, and even in sections and in entire *taqsims*. There is thus a high degree of structural integrity of these improvisations, suggesting again that improvisation, in those cultures in which it plays a major role, provides freedom only within a rigorous and tightly knit system of structural principles.

How did Jihad Racy react to the study when it was first carried out? "I didn't realize I was so predictable." It would certainly be desirable now to examine a number of Racy's more recent performances of *taqsim nahawand*. Only two have been available for study, but they suggest that in important ways, Racy's musicianship maintains consistency. In others, he has lightened his touch, introduced melodic fragments either from or reminiscent of Western popular music, and he has come to sound more lyrical. One ventures to say that the range of performance has broadened, and perhaps that he would consider himself as less predictable, but the recent performances of *taqsim nahawand* also have much in common with those performed for our project of 1971.

Notes

This study was originally carried out in 1971 and 1972 by Nettl and Riddle and published in the *Yearbook of the International Council for Traditional Music,* 1972 (5:11–50), with the inclusion of lengthy transcriptions of two *taqsims.* Nettl was responsible for the basic plan of research and for writing the draft, as well as for some of the analytical work. Riddle made the transcriptions and did much of the analysis. Aside from performing the music upon which this study is based, Racy (whose contributions are described in the body of the paper) provided an accounting of the modulation patterns and clarified other analytical points, and he approved the analyses and conclusions. Ronald Riddle unfortunately passed away in 1993, and the version of the study presented here has been revised and to an extent brought up to date, with some comments from Racy, but also considerably shortened by Nettl. The authors of the original gratefully acknowledged the help of the University of Illinois Research Board in making possible Racy's and Riddle's contributions to the project. Nettl's portion of the work was carried out while he was an Associate of the University of Illinois Center for Advanced Study. I (Nettl) am happy to restate here these expressions of gratitude. The numbering of the transcriptions and references to performances follows the numbering of Collection No. 92, University of Illinois Archives of Ethnomusicology.

1. In this unpublished study, carried out by Nettl in the middle 1950s, it was possible to divide a *taqsim* section into segments, each dominated by a specific type of melodic contour—scalar, undulating, closing formula, etc. It seemed most convenient to analyze the structure by plotting the distribution of the various types of melodic movement, and it was possible thereby to show structural patterns that establish a norm and limit departures. Although the impression they give the listener is quite different in certain details, such as melodic character, intervals, and contour, general rhythmic character, and closing and opening formulae, these *taqsims* are very much like those performed by Racy.

References

Berner, Alfred. 1937. *Studien zur arabischen Musik.* Leipzig: Kistner & Siegel.

d'Erlanger, Rodolphe. 1959. *La musique arabe.* Vol. 6. Paris: P. Geuthner.

Elsner, Jürgen, ed. 1989. *Maqam-Raga-Zeilenmelodik.* Materialien der 1. Arbeitstagung der Study Group "maqam" beim International Council for Traditional Music, 28. June–2 July 1988, Berlin. Berlin: DDR National Committee of the International Council for Traditional Music.

Farhat, Hormoz. 1990. *The Dastgah Concept in Persian Music.* Cambridge: Cambridge University Press.

Gerson-Kiwi, Edith. 1963. *The Persian Doctrine of Dastga-Composition.* Tel Aviv: Israel Music Institute.

———. 1970. "On the Technique of Arabic Taqsim Composition." In *Musik als Gestalt und Erlebnis.* Vienna: H. Böhlau.

Katz, Ruth. 1968. "The Singing of Baqqashot by Aleppo Jews." *Acta Musicologica* 40:65–85.

Massoudieh, Mohammad T. 1968. *Āwāz-Šur: Zur Melodiebildung in der persischen Kunstmusik.* Regensburg: Bosse.

Nettl, Bruno. 1992. *The Radif of Persian Music: Studies of Structure and Cultural Context.* Rev. ed. Champaign: Elephant and Cat.

Touma, Habib Hassan. 1968. *Der Maqam Bayati im arabischen Taqsim.* Berlin: H. Touma.

———. 1971. "The Maqam Phenomenon: an Improvisation Technique in the Music of the Middle East." *Ethnomusicology* 15:34–48.

CONTRIBUTORS

STEPHEN BLUM, professor of music at the City University of New York Graduate School, studied at Oberlin and the University of Illinois (Ph.D., 1972) and has also taught at the University of Illinois and York University. His publications deal with the music of Iran, Kurdish music, tonality, style analysis, and the disciplines of musicology and ethnomusicology. He is the editor of *Music-Cultures in Contact: Convergences and Collisions* (with Margaret Kartomi, 1994) and *Ethnomusicology and Modern Music History* (with Philip Bohlman and Daniel Neuman, 1991) and the author of major articles in *The Revised New Grove Dictionary of Music and Musicians.*

JODY CORMACK, archives assistant at Wesleyan University's World Music Archives, studied at Wesleyan (Ph.D., 1992), specializing in the classical music of South India. She received extensive training as a vocalist under T. Viswanathan and T. Balasaraswati.

SAU Y. CHAN, associate professor at the Chinese University of Hong Kong (where he has taught since 1987), studied music at that institution (B.A., 1981) and the University of Pittsburgh (Ph.D., 1986). He has done fieldwork in Singapore, southern China, and Hong Kong. His publications include *Improvisation in a Ritual Context: The Music of Cantonese Opera* (1991) and five other books (in Chinese) on Chinese opera.

VALERIE GOERTZEN, a faculty member at Earlham College, studied at Whittier College and the University of Illinois (Ph.D., 1987) and has also taught at Wesleyan University and the University of North Carolina at Greensboro. Specializing in nineteenth-century European art music, she is the author of articles on improvisation in that period and the editor of a forthcoming volume of the new Brahms *Gesamtausgabe.*

LAWRENCE GUSHEE, professor of music at the University of Illinois, studied at Yale (Ph.D., 1963) and has also taught at Yale and the University of Wisconsin-Madison. He has taught a great variety of courses, from ancient Greek music theory to avant-garde musical concepts; his principal research interests have been in medieval music and the early history of jazz. Among his publications is *The Musica disciplina of Aurelian of Réôme: a Critical Text and Commentary* (1975). He has also been known to improvise on the B-flat clarinet.

EVE HARWOOD, associate professor of music education at the University of Illinois at Urbana-Champaign, received her doctorate (1987) at that institution after study and a career of teaching in her native Canada. She teaches elementary music methods and administers the general music program for a K–8 laboratory school. Her research interests include children's musical folklore and music teacher preparation.

TULLIA MAGRINI, associate professor of the anthropology of music at the University of Bologna, studied at that institution and has been active in ethnomusicology since 1974. Her principal fieldwork has been in Italy and Greece, but she also made field trips to Bali and Madagascar. She was the founder (1996) of the multimedia Web journal *Music & Anthropology* and is the author of *Canti d'Amore di Sdegno* (1986) and *Il Maggio Dramatico* (1992) and editor of *Antropologia della Musica e Culture Mediterranee* (1993).

PETER MANUEL, professor at the John Jay College and the Graduate Center of the City University of New York, studied at the University of California, Los Angeles (Ph.D., 1983), and carried out fieldwork in India, the Spanish Caribbean, and among Indo-Caribbean societies. Among his books are *Popular Musics of the Non-Western World* (1988), *Cassette Culture: Popular Music and Technology in North India* (1993), and *Caribbean Currents: Caribbean Music from Rumba to Reggae* (with Ken Bilby and Michael Largey (1996).

INGRID MONSON, assistant professor of music at Washington University in St. Louis, studied at New York University (Ph.D., 1991) and is the author of *Saying Something: Jazz Improvisation and Interaction* (1996). Her main interests are jazz, musics of the African diaspora, and cultural theory. She has also published articles in *The World of Music, Critical Inquiry,* and *Journal of the American Musicological Society.*

BRUNO NETTL, professor emeritus of music and anthropology at the University of Illinois, studied at Indiana University (Ph.D., 1953) and has done fieldwork among the Blackfoot people in Montana, in Iran, and in India. Coming to the University of Illinois in 1964 from a position at Wayne State University, he has also taught at Harvard, Northwestern, and the Universities of Chicago, Louisville, and Washington. Among his books are *The Study of Ethnomusicology* (1983), *Blackfoot Musical Thought* (1989), and *Heartland Excursions* (1995).

JEFF PRESSING, head of the Cognitive Science Program at the University of Melbourne, studied at the California Institute of Technology, the University of California, San Diego (Ph.D. in physical chemistry, 1972), and at the University of Rochester and did fieldwork in Ghana and Nigeria. He taught for nearly twenty years in the music department at La Trobe University and has had an active international career as composer and as pianist/vocalist of contemporary music. His publications include *Synthesizer Performance and Real-Time Techniques* (1992) and *Compositions for Improvisors* (1994).

ALI JIHAD RACY, professor of ethnomusicology at the University of California, Los Angeles, studied at the American University of Beirut and the University of Illinois (Ph.D., 1977) and has written and lectured widely on music of the Near East and North Africa. A virtuoso performer on the *nay* and *bouzouq,* he has published a number of recordings of his performances, including traditional Arab music on *Taqasim: Improvisation in Arab Music* (1983), and his own composition, *Ancient Egypt* (1980).

RONALD RIDDLE studied at Yale and the University of Illinois (Ph.D., 1975) and until his death in 1993 was associate professor of humanities at New College of the University of South Florida. Specializing in the musical cultures of Asian-American communities, he is the author of articles on Asian musics in California and of a book, *Flying Dragons, Flowing Streams: Music in the Life of San Francisco's Chinese* (1983).

MELINDA RUSSELL, instructor in music at Carleton College, studied at the Universities of Minnesota and Illinois. Her principal interests are American and non-Western popular music and the ethnography of contemporary American musical life. She is the coeditor of *Community of Music: An Ethnographic Seminar in Champaign-Urbana* (1993).

STEPHEN SLAWEK, associate professor of music and Asian studies at the University of Texas in Austin (where he has taught since 1983), studied at the University of Pennsylvania, Benares Hindu University, the University of Hawaii, and the University of Illinois (Ph.D., 1986). He has done extensive fieldwork in India and published widely on Hindustani music and Hindu devotional music, including the books *Sitar Technique in Nibaddh Forms* (1987) and, with Robert Hardgrave, *Musical Instruments in Eighteenth Century India: The Solvyns Portraits* (1997).

CHRIS SMITH, lecturer in world music at the Indiana University School of Music, is a jazz guitarist and a Ph.D. candidate in musicology at Indiana. Active as a performer of a variety of music styles of Asia, Africa, and the New

World, as well as early Western art music, he has published on a number of contemporary and historical music topics and composed music for film and dance. He is host of a world music program for station WFIU in Bloomington, Indiana.

R. ANDERSON SUTTON, professor of music at the University of Wisconsin—Madison, studied at Wesleyan, the University of Hawaii, and the University of Michigan (Ph.D., 1982). He has conducted fieldwork in Java and in South Sulawesi, Indonesia. Among his publications are *Variation in Central Javanese Music* (1993) and *Traditions of Gamelan Music in Java* (1991), as well as numerous articles.

T. VISWANATHAN, professor of music at Wesleyan University, studied at the University of California, Los Angeles, and Wesleyan (Ph.D., 1972). One of the outstanding performers (flute and vocal music) in the realm of South Indian classical music and a member of one of India's most illustrious music and dance families, he is also a distinguished musicologist. He has received some of India's most prestigious music awards and a National Heritage Fellowship from the National Endowment for the Arts (U.S.A.). He has made numerous recordings, some with his late brother, the distinguished *mridangam* player T. Ranganathan.

INDEX

Page numbers in boldface indicate a musical example, table, or other figure.